# MEADE *of* GETTYSBURG

# MEADE
## *of*
# GETTYSBURG

*by Freeman Cleaves*

*Foreword by Herman Hattaway*

NORMAN AND LONDON
*University of Oklahoma Press*

By Freeman Cleaves

*Old Tippecanoe: William Henry Harrison and His Time* (New York, 1939)

*Rock of Chickamauga: The Life of General George H. Thomas* (Norman, 1948)

*Meade of Gettysburg* (Norman, 1960)

The publication of this volume has been aided by a grant from the Ford Foundation.

LIBRARY OF CONGRESS CATALOG CARD NUMBER: 60-7735
ISBN: 0-8061-2298-6

3   4   5   6   7   8   9   10   11   12

*To*
*Melvin J. Nichols*

# Contents

# Illustrations

## MAPS

# Foreword

## by Herman Hattaway

FREEMAN CLEAVES was born 13 October 1904 in Buxton, Maine. He died 21 July 1988. Educated at Bates College and the University of New Hampshire, and graduating from the latter in 1924, he subsequently did graduate work at Harvard. A long-time New Yorker, he made his living primarily as a newspaper reporter and financial writer. But history, especially biography, became his treasured avocation. Cleaves earned a niche in the scholarly world as a man who made a respectable attempt to rescue several noteworthy historical characters from relative obscurity. In 1939 he published a life of William Henry Harrison. But his great love was Civil War studies, and in 1948 the University of Oklahoma Press published his well-received biography of George H. Thomas, *Rock of Chickamauga*. In 1960, from this same house, came the first edition of the present and still-revered life of George G. Meade. Coming as it did, at the outset of the Civil War Centennial celebration, *Meade of Gettysburg* was welcomed by a legion of students and enthusiasts.

That Cleaves was Meade's first modern biographer is a strange reality in light of the general's crucial role in the struggle for the Union. Even more surprising, perhaps, Meade has remained untouched as a biographical subject in the thirty years since the initial appearance of Cleaves's book. Part of the explanation must lie in the fact that Meade, despite his stature among the Union generals, was nevertheless an indistinct figure, difficult to delineate in warm human dimensions.

A problem that vexed Cleaves—and would any other aspiring Meade biographer—was that it is nearly impossible to learn the details of Meade's daily experiences. The family chose to retain only the letters from his wartime years. Even so, some kernels have been gleaned from other people's letters. For example, Colonel Theodore Lyman, who late in 1863 joined the Army of the Potomac as an unpaid volunteer aide, recalled that several years before, Meade had placed a coastal vessel at his disposal, to enable the young Harvard graduate to search for new forms of oceanic life. The good turn probably earned Meade the wartime services of this intelligent and capable man. From similar sources we learn that Meade conducted himself with true singleness of purpose. One of his opponents, General Daniel Harvey Hill, remarked that "Meade . . . was always in deadly earnest," and he credited Meade with being "one of our most dreaded foes. . . . [H]e eschewed all trifling." Meade was particularly harsh with skulkers; once he personally struck with the flat of his sabre a man who was cowering behind a tree. An eyewitness confessed that at the time he thought Meade's action cruel and needless, but "I changed my mind when I became an officer." Meade's temper was short (hence his nickname, "the damned old goggle-eyed snapping turtle"), and after he became commander, "each corps was provided with a gallows and a shooting ground for Friday executions, an unpopular detail but routine." And he was determined that needful things be accomplished posthaste: once when red tape and a poorly functioning distribution system snarled the supply of necessary shoes for the mounts and draft animals of his command, from his own pocket he paid for the shoeing of some twelve hundred horses and mules. He rigidly forbade pillaging even though many of his men believed that plundering was their right.

Wounded in 1862, gravely ill during the spring campaign of 1865, and in innumerable perilous encounters, Meade was as hard on himself as he was on his men. A letter from his aide, Lieutenant Alexander Coxe, gives us a delightful detail about one of Meade's visits to Washington: Coxe overheard two gentlemen talking, and one asked, "What major general is that?" to which the other replied, "Meade." "Who is he?" said the first, "I never saw him before." "No, that is very likely, for he is one of our fighting generals, is always on the field, and does not spend his time in Washington hotels."

Meade was a quiet, reserved man, with but little flair in his manner. Once, during the Chancellorsville Campaign, Meade appeared before a large group of his men fording the Rapidan River and they began to cheer him. He doffed his forage cap and rode bareheaded through their lines making no other outward sign. He later reminisced that he never would forget that warm demonstration, but he was not one who sought to whip up personal feeling. He never waved his cap, until he did do so on the last day of the war. There are not many pithy quotes that anyone recalls uttered by Meade. Among the best is his incredulous response to an unwise deployment ordered by his then superior, Joe Hooker, in the Battle of Chancellorsville: "My God, if we can't hold the top of a hill, we certainly can't hold the bottom of it!"

It is the Gettysburg Campaign, above all else, for which we remember Meade. It was asking a great deal of anyone to step in to command, as he did, at so late a moment before the battle. And the machinery he took over was horribly flawed: not until the morning of 1 July 1863 did a topographical map of Pennsylvania reach army headquarters. The imperturbable Meade deserves much credit for directing the perilous battle to its spectacular conclusion. The war correspondent Whitelaw Reid saw Meade at headquarters on the morning of the most fateful day, 3 July: "quick and nervous in his movements but calm and . . . lit up with the glow of the occasion." "Victory! Waterloo Eclipsed!!" proclaimed the *Philadelphia Inquirer.* And so it was. Never again would the main Confederate army be so potent; never again could its commander take the initiative offensively. But Meade proved disappointing to President Lincoln, not a little with his unfortunate words concerning his desire "for greater efforts to drive from our soil every vestige of the presence of the invader," a great deal when he failed to pursue and destroy Lee's retreating army.

During the 1864 campaign, perhaps because generals such as Grant, Sherman, Sheridan, and Winfield Scott Hancock were such darlings of the reporters, the press essentially damned Meade with faint praise. One correspondent admitted that "Gen. Meade's name never appeared. . . . if it could be omitted." Quite bluntly, "Meade's work was withheld from public notice unless it could be presented unfavorably." Nor was Meade unconscious of this treatment. He "allowed that it soon would be proved that either he was not at Gettysburg at all or that his presence there had been a positive detriment." If these assertions are correct, if Meade was omitted from, and his work distorted in, so many passages that became principal sources for countless historians, we can understand why Meade is so often inadequately handled in scholarly writing. Small wonder, then, that for many Civil War students Meade remains an enigma.

United States Military Academy at West Point
9 September 1990

# *Acknowledgments*

MANY PERSONS HAVE contributed valuable assistance during the course of preparation of this work. The writer wishes especially to thank Melvin J. Nichols of Summit, N. J., for the loan of out-of-print books, of pictures, and of manuscript materials. Books also were lent by Thomas Robson Hay, Locust Valley, N. Y.; Mrs. James R. Y. Blakely, Jr., Stone Harbor, N. J.; Colonel Anthony O. Leach, Summit, N. J.; John Nanovic and Lewis Solomon, New York City; and Miss Charlotte Lawrence, North Yarmouth, Me. Joseph D. Bean of Millburn, N. J., furnished several back numbers of *The National Geographic Magazine* from his extensive collection. Gardner Osborne, director of the Federal Hall Memorial Associates, New York City, and Mrs. Muriel Slodden, onetime secretary of the Empire State Society, Sons of the American Revolution, were co-operative in making available a set of the *Official Records of the War of the Rebellion* which was then on S.A.R. library shelves. The Ira J. Lindsley Papers were lent by the Reverend James Elliott Lindsley, of Millburn, N. J.

A small company of librarians helped in many ways. R. Norris Williams II, director of the Historical Society of Pennsylvania, and J. H. Givens of the Manuscript Division provided access to the extensive Meade Papers. Robert W. Hill, director of the Manuscript Division, New York Public Library, called my attention to the Webb Papers at Yale University, where Miss Dorothy W. Bridgewater, assistant reference librarian, and Mrs. Zara Jones Powers saw that they were made available once permission had been obtained from family heirs, in this instance the late Vanderbilt Webb. Sylvester Vigilante, Louis H. Fox, and Wilmer R. Leech of the New York Historical Society were resourceful in providing aid. Permission to use the Meade family pictures was granted by Mrs. Richard Worsam Meade of Mount Kisco, N. Y.; and the writer was assisted at the Frick Art Reference Library by Mrs. Henry W. Howell. Mrs. Horace Hugh Francine of Ambler, Pa., granddaughter of General Meade, also kindly lent pictures and answered many questions. Elizabeth G. McPherson and Mr. Powell were helpful at the Manuscript Division of the Library of Congress, and E. G. Campbell, Miss Elizabeth Drury, and Wayne Andrews at the National Archives.

Histories of Connecticut regiments and other special materials were supplied by Mrs. John A. Forsythe, Jr., at the Fairfield Historical Society, Fairfield, Conn.; by Mrs. Grace A. Donaldson, the Pequot Library, Southport, Conn.; and by Guy de Lagerberg of Westport, Conn. George A. Lundell was of assistance at the War Library and Museum, Military Order of the Loyal Legion, Philadelphia, and Clinton R. Harrower in New York.

Among those who aided with suggestions and research were Thomas Robson Hay; the Reverend Harry J. Sievers, S. J.; John Carpenter, at the time a graduate student at Bowdoin College, Brunswick, Me.; Miss Catharine Driscoll of Boston; Robert J. Jurgen, Maywood, N. J.; Eugene Bozzo, Ridgewood, N. J.; and my wife, Gwendoline Chase Cleaves. A copy of the will of Richard Worsam Meade was made available through Joseph D. Burke, register of wills, City Hall, Philadelphia. Ross L. Muir of the Ruberoid Company, New York City, furnished data on one of Meade's Florida lighthouses, and Mrs. John E. Parker of West Orange, N. J., gave me some information concerning the family of Mariamne Meade Huger of Charleston, S. C., descendants of General Meade's sisters.

George Gordon Meade III of Ambler, Pa., and his mother, Mrs. George G. Meade, were invariably co-operative as well as hospitable. Colonel Leach, Thomas Robson Hay, and Edward Ryan of New York City spent many hours in reading the manuscript, and they made many useful suggestions. The detailed criticism of Wilson Follett of New York City was most helpful and is to be especially acknowledged.

*Freeman Cleaves*

Millburn, New Jersey
August 19, 1959

# MEADE *of* GETTYSBURG

# 1. "I Offer My Son, George Meade" (1816-1835)

A CHRISTENING at the church of Nuestra Señora del Rosario in Cádiz, Spain, brought together a group of richly clad residents who occupied several pews. The godmother at the ceremony, Christine Gordon Prendergast, bore in her arms the infant son of Richard Worsam Meade, Cádiz exporter and merchant, who had come to the church several times on such missions. Of nine children born to him thus far, seven had been cradled in Cádiz. Mrs. Prendergast's father, Jacob Gordon, also a merchant, accompanied his friend Meade, and two Spanish gentlemen were in attendance as sponsors. Dark-eyed *señoras* appeared in mantillas, laces, and heavy new silks.

The priest baptized the infant George Gordon Meade, born December 31, 1815, "legitimate son of Don Ricardo Worsam de Meade and of Doña Margarita Coates Butler de Meade."[1] The first George Meade, the boy's grandfather, had been a merchant and Revolutionary patriot of Philadelphia; the middle name came from Jacob Gordon, a Scotsman who left no further record. A man of two worlds, Richard Worsam Meade had been born in Philadelphia a Roman Catholic, his wife Margaret a Protestant, and she had remained in that faith. For two generations, Catholic Meades had been marrying Protestant wives.[2] But if religious convictions were strong, they were not, in those generations, obtrusive.

The party rode to a tall, whitewashed house where servants had prepared a collation. It was a home lavishly decorated with Italian marble and containing one of the finest art collections in Spain. From

[1] George Meade, *Life and Letters of George Gordon Meade*, I, 7 (hereafter cited as *Meade*); Archives of the Parish of Nuestra Señora del Rosario, Fourth Book of Baptismal Registry, 43 (copy in Meade family collection).

[2] "In the history of this family, for five generations, the eldest son, though a Catholic, has in every instance married a Protestant."—American Catholic Historical Society of Pennsylvania *Records*, Vol. III (1888–89), 208 n.

3

time to time, Richard Meade had seen fit to accept paintings to satisfy debts. Works by Titian, Correggio, Veronese, Rubens, Van Dyck, Velásquez, and Murillo hint of its richness; there were family portraits by the American artists Thomas Sully and Gilbert Stuart, and by the court painter Francisco de Goya y Lucientes of Spain.[3] Richard Meade also possessed a large Stuart portrait of George Washington, shown without his false teeth, which he would later present to the American embassy in Madrid.[4]

Only thirty-seven years old at this time, Meade had always lived well, although his future was clouded by financial stringencies arising from large, uncollectible debts owed him. In later years, recalling a happy life in Cádiz, Mrs. Meade would remind her son George that at the time of his birth her existence there had been one of affluence and luxury.[5] Thoughts at the christening feast may have turned to the three oldest children, Henrietta Constantia, Charlotte, and Elizabeth, who were then back in Philadelphia at school. But it was still a large family which filled the big house. The fourth child and oldest son, Richard Worsam Meade II, had been followed by Margaret, named for her mother, then by María del Carmen and Salvadora (the Spanish influence), by Catherine who died, and now by George.[6]

The family's roots were of Perth Amboy, New Jersey, Margaret Meade's former home, and of Philadelphia, where Meade ships occasionally called. Some years before, Mrs. Meade had returned there to escape the ravages of the Peninsular War and to place the three oldest girls in school. A vivacious lady interested in the theater and the arts, she was found at home by the painter, dramatist, and man-of-all-work William Dunlap, who had a theatrical troupe in Philadelphia for which he sought patronage. Dunlap, on April 2, 1811, wrote in his diary, "Mrs. Meade . . . seems much attach^d to Spain," and on another occasion he was entertained by a reading of one of Richard Meade's letters describing a Napoleonic battle fought just outside Cádiz.[7] Mrs. Meade,

[3] Copy of a Meade art sale catalog with executor's valuation of art works and other property, Frick Art Reference Library, New York City.

[4] *New York Times*, June 14, 1951: "Stuart portrait to hang in the rotunda of the Capitol if there is room for it. . . . At Madrid Embassy since 1818, gift of Richard W. Meade." See also John Hill Morgan and Mantle Fielding, *Life Portraits of Washington and Their Replicas*, 209.

[5] *Meade*, I, 45; Richard M. Bache, *Life of General George Gordon Meade*, 6.

[6] *Pennsylvania Magazine of History and Biography*, Vol. XXIV (1900), 243.

unfortunately, left no diary; but as the result of the theater manager's attentions, she and others of her circle, who had not been neglected, probably attended his play.

The war moving elsewhere, Mrs. Meade returned to Spain in the following spring, and after five years she again recrossed the Atlantic for the last time. This final return to Philadelphia, in June, 1816,[8] brought her son George to America at the age of one and one-half years, but Richard Meade was not permitted to leave with his family.

Since Richard Meade's quarrels, which had to do with money, were chiefly with the government of Spain, the situation was serious. In one respect he had been generous, having placed nearly his entire fortune at the disposal of the Spanish Loyalists and King Ferdinand VII. It had been altogether a gamble, for although the Loyalists with the help of Wellington had won the war, the royal treasury was bare, and Meade immediately needed funds to continue his business. Perhaps he pressed his claim a little too strongly. When the Treasurer General declared his personal honor involved, steps were taken to silence the King's principal creditor.

Meade was taken to the grim and massive Castillo de Santa Catalina, a harbor fort then used as a prison. In return for his freedom he paid a small fine but in the spring of 1816 was again jailed when exception was taken to the manner in which he, as executor, had handled the affairs of a private estate. Whatever his argument and rights may have been, it was, of course, more convenient to keep him behind bars and postpone discussion. While Meade had the freedom of the prison grounds and was permitted visits by his wife and children, little heed was paid his protests or those of the American minister at Madrid.[9] He had been in jail for almost a year when he sought to draw upon his last resource—the aid of powerful friends in Philadelphia.

One of these was Congressman John Sergeant, a giant of the law who was then legal adviser of the Bank of the United States. Sergeant was in a position to place the matter before Congress and the James Monroe administration, and the first of several pamphlets to detail

---

[7] *Diary of William Dunlap* (ed. by Dorothy C. Barck), II, 432, 450.

[8] Mrs. Meade left Spain in the American brig *Ariel* probably soon after June 13, 1847, date of Richard W. Meade's will. The Register of Wills, City Hall, Philadelphia, supplied a copy.

[9] *American State Papers, Foreign Affairs*, IV, 145 f.; *Daily National Intelligencer*, June 26, 1826.

Richard Meade's monetary claims and his unfortunate situation came probably from his hand. "The Case of Richard W. Meade . . . Imprisoned 2nd of May, 1816, by the Gov$^t$ of Spain and Still Detained (1817)" at least made interesting reading, and spirited petitions from Philadelphia citizens also were taken to Congress.

Others in high places, however, did not appear to be greatly concerned. November came, and a third son, Robert, was born to Margaret Meade, who was not then liberally supplied with funds. "In trembling anxiety," as the petition read, she herself signed a paper directed to President Monroe.[10] Something definite was done when Monroe referred the plea to Secretary of State John Quincy Adams, who wrote a demanding letter for the American minister at Madrid to lay before the King. But relations between the two nations were not entirely friendly, war-ravished Spain was still poor, and it was more expedient to hold Richard Meade in jail than to let him go.

The winter passed slowly for Mrs. Meade and her children—the oldest now sixteen—and for Richard Meade, who could see commerce other than his own plying the waters outside Cádiz. Elsewhere, on a remote and unknown frontier, events were shaping which in time would spring the prison gates. Commanding a volunteer army in pursuit of Indians, General Andrew Jackson marched into Spanish Florida and took prisoners. Would or would not the administration support him?

Although Jackson may never have heard of Richard W. Meade, his actions could not have been more timely in laying the groundwork for an amicable understanding between nations. First, however, belligerence awoke. The issue of fair dealing being raised, it was discovered that Spain had done a great injustice to the American citizen named Meade. On April 4, 1818, a special Senate committee plainly talked in terms of war: "Any United States citizen who demeans himself as becomes his character is entitled to the protection of his Government, and . . . whatever intentional injury may be done him should be retaliated against by the employment, if necessary, of the *whole force of this nation*."[11]

The House aroused itself. Prodded by Speaker Henry Clay, whose prize Merino sheep were from flocks imported in Meade ships, that body resolved that "the imprisonment of Richard W. Meade is an act

[10] *American State Papers, Foreign Affairs*, IV, 151.
[11] *Ibid.*, 145.

of cruel and unjustifiable oppression; that it is the right and duty of the Government . . . to afford to Mr. Meade its aid and protection, and that this House will support and maintain such measures as the President may hereafter adopt."[12]

Hurrah for General Jackson!

Weighing the dread prospect of another war, King Ferdinand threw open the doors of the Spanish bastille. On June 26, 1818, Secretary John Quincy Adams heralded liberation on two fronts: "After dinner there came to my house a Mr. Zamora, Spanish Consul, with a huge packet of dispatches . . . one communicating the release of R. W. Meade . . . another asking explanation of the article in the *National Intelligencer,* purporting that General Jackson had taken Pensacola by storm."[13] In view of events, the Meade case could not have been more timely or useful to the administration. At a cabinet meeting which was hurriedly called, War Secretary John C. Calhoun pointedly remarked that the result of the War of 1812 "had been to raise the tone of feeling in this nation . . . that the success of the menacing attitude assumed with Spain, in the case of R. W. Meade, had raised it still higher; that any concession by the Administration should tend to lower [it] . . . would give great dissatisfaction to the nation, and would be used as a weapon against the Administration."[14]

Assigned to the task of placing belligerent action in the best possible light, the able hand of John Quincy Adams made out a case for morality and justice on the part of the Florida invader.

There was the matter of a treaty to be made. Spain, to get back on its feet, would willingly cede remote Florida for a certain fixed sum—five million dollars was agreed upon—but it declined to ratify the document until definitely assured that the Meade claim was included. John Forsythe, the American minister, freely gave this assurance, since the United States, it was promised, would assume payment of all Spain's liabilities to American citizens. After months of haggling and hesitation, Spain ratified the treaty, although doubtless aware of a loophole. As far as Meade was concerned, the United States had only to adhere literally to the clause that confined payment to claims arising from

[12] *Ibid.,* 155.
[13] *Memoirs of John Quincy Adams* (ed. by Charles Francis Adams), IV, 104.
[14] *Ibid.,* 148.

"unlawful captures at sea and unlawful seizures in the ports of Spain and the Colonies," and thus side-step him as a claimant; for Meade had *voluntarily* turned over his wealth and his ships to the Kingdom of Spain.

In any event, the Meade claim was no longer the gadfly, and repayment was clearly up to the United States Congress. With the Florida question entirely solved, sundry items would have to pass severe scrutiny. Congress, which at one time had contended it would go to war for Richard W. Meade, authorized the distribution of only a limited amount to satisfy scores of insistent claimants. The $373,879.75 net amount requested by Meade would, in effect, have meant denial of payments to certain others.[15]

Would, indeed, anything at all be paid? Congress and the administration, which had used Meade as a pawn, showed signs of welshing on the Forsythe agreement. Secretary John Quincy Adams, for example, decided to take a personal dislike to Meade when the latter called upon him in Washington. Meade may have been tactless, but anyone who had been waiting ten years for his money might not be the embodiment of perfect diplomacy. Soon it became known throughout the capital that Adams stood definitely against any payment.[16] Lawyers possibly hired on a contingent basis got nowhere, and in 1824 an effort by friendly Whig senators to reopen the claim was blocked by Secretary Adams in a special report. Two technical points were considered. First, Meade had been unable to obtain his vouchers from Spain in time for them to be considered as proof of his claim. Again, only the committee originally set up to consider the claim had authority to satisfy it, and that body was no longer in existence.[17]

That the Meade claim transcended all other family business in importance was signified by removal of the family to Washington, but John Quincy Adams now occupied the White House. Another daughter, Mariamne, had been born in Philadelphia, meanwhile, and Henrietta, the oldest, had married Navy Commodore Alexander James Dallas, son of a former secretary of the treasury. In 1826, after a common-school education, Richard Worsam Meade II, "a bright,

[15] Richard S. Coxe, *Richard W. Meade*, 4–6.

[16] *Memoirs of John Quincy Adams*, V, 234, 272–73.

[17] From time to time the claim would be revived by Meade's sons and by later generations, with the same negative result. No one but the original committee was conceded to have any authority.

cheerful, enthusiastic spirit," joined the navy as an ensign.[18] George Gordon Meade spent three years at a Philadelphia elementary school, then entered a military academy at near-by Germantown which was modeled upon West Point.

The situation at Germantown gave George some incentive. The school attracted boys from some of the better-known Pennsylvania families, and the elder Meade was a member of its Board of Examiners. Witnessing his son's progress in arithmetic and algebra, he once remarked to his wife that the boy's mathematical head seemed to fit him for West Point,[19] but he did not live to direct his education further. On June 25, 1828, when he was only fifty years old, death came suddenly at his home in the Washington suburb of Georgetown.

By the terms of his will, art works, securities, and all else were left to the widow, whose "prudence and virtue" were cited.[20] But there was more property of all sorts than cash, and since money was lacking to keep George at school, he had to be summoned home. The family was still a large one for the widow to manage, even though Henrietta, who had married Commodore Dallas, was absent and Charlotte was wed that summer to Captain James Duncan Graham of the army. Another, Major Hartman Bache of the Engineer Corps, later came to marry María del Carmen; and Alfred Ingraham, a Philadelphia banker, sought the hand of Elizabeth. The Ingrahams afterward went south, first to a Kentucky plantation and then to Mississippi. Elizabeth was affectionately remembered, in spite of the hardy secessionist sympathies which she acquired. She has been described as her mother seems to have been—"a woman of remarkable energy, force of character, and sprightliness."[21] One would like to know more about her.

A small school presided over by Salmon Portland Chase, who divided his time between his pupils and law studies, was selected for George. As a breadwinner for a future treasury secretary and chief jus-

[18] *Army and Navy Journal* (April 23, 1870), 566.

[19] *Meade*, I, 45. Then in Mexico (January 20, 1846), Meade quoted from a letter received from his mother: "Although in my ignorance I was cruel enough to send you to West Point, an act for which I shall never forgive myself, and never cease to regret, I did not dream that you would enter the army, my dear George. It was the moral standing of the Institution, and the education which you could not escape if you remained there, also the intention of your lamented father, who said your mathematical head fitted you for it, that led me to commit the act."

[20] Will of Richard Worsam Meade.

[21] H. S. Fulkerson, *A Civilian's Recollection of the War between the States*, 156.

tice of the Supreme Court, the venture lasted but a few months. Becoming a success at the bar, Mr. Chase gave up his school.[22] George was placed in Mount Hope Institution in Baltimore, while his mother considered his future. Recalling her husband's remark about West Point, she consulted with Major Bache, who had stood high in his class. A future military career was never in prospect, but expenses at the Military Academy would be small. As a resident of the District of Columbia, Mrs. Meade on March 13, 1830, addressed her application to the Secretary of War: "I offer my son, George Meade, as a candidate for the appointment of Cadet in the Military Academy. . . . He was born in Cádiz, at which time his Father was U. S. Navy Agent, brought up from infancy in Pennsylvania, and is now a resident of the District of Columbia. . . . His character and qualifications will appear from the enclosed certificate of his Teachers at Germantown."[23]

Although tall for his age, George was not yet fifteen, but whatever the reason for his nonappointment, he remained through December at Baltimore. There completing his Latin, English composition, and elementary mathematics, he stood high on the rolls. Mrs. Meade sought a certificate from the headmaster. "The knowledge he has gained," it read, "is far greater than is usually acquired by young men of his age in a single year. He possesses an uncommon quickness of perception and is, therefore, capable of acquiring knowledge with great rapidity. His general deportment is worthy of high commendation."[24] Mrs. Meade again wrote to the Secretary of War and then waited five months. Early in July, 1831, the appointment was signed by President Andrew Jackson, who in the past had influenced the course of Florida's history and indirectly the Meade fortunes.

As long as the nation remained at peace, the idea that a youth should go to West Point merely for a general education was not uncommon. Since the Academy was turning out more officers than needed, many graduates resigned to become civil engineers, teachers, or clergymen. Some turned to the law or entered business. There is no record of what George Meade may have intended to make of his future career.

[22] Mary Merwin Phelps, *Kate Chase*, 4–5.

[23] To Secretary John H. Eaton, March 13, 1830, Meade letters in National Archives. The certificate set forth his ability as a student and cited him as a youth "of very great promise."

[24] F. Hall to Mrs. Margaret Meade, January 28, 1831, National Archives.

Had the elder Meade lived, he probably would have helped direct his son's course, but there was more incentive for young George to get to West Point than to do well there. Since the cadet attained his best marks in elementary science, French, rhetoric, and moral philosophy, military studies held little appeal. He borrowed few books from the library, and those were on general subjects. His military reading was thus postponed to the future, since it was later known to be wide. Because of his lack of attention to details of dress and equipment and apparent disinterest in drill, demerits began to pile up during his third year. They ultimately totaled 168 for the entire course, or only 32 short of expulsion. Dropping more than halfway down the conduct roll,[25] Cadet Meade doubtless experienced the penalties of extra marching and restriction of liberty.

He failed to live up to his early promise in mathematics, placing only twenty-first in this subject among the fifty-six graduates of his class. He was as far down as twenty-seventh in chemistry. That he stood twenty-second in civil and military engineering gave no clue to his successful later career. His final report also found him more than halfway down in artillery tactics, infantry tactics, drawing, and conduct. In general merit, giving weight to the French and the humanities in which he scored, he stood nineteenth. This, however, was only three places lower than he would have been but for the poor mark in conduct.[26] It was a wide miss of the rating necessary to gain entrance into the elite Engineer Corps, for which only the first two men were selected from the somewhat undistinguished Class of 1835.

No great names appear among his classmates, although he did rub elbows with Montgomery Blair, later Lincoln's postmaster general, and with Herman Haupt, who became military transportation chief in the East. Other than himself, the most famous soldier would be John C. Pemberton, a personal friend through the Mexican War, in later years an unhappy opponent of General Ulysses S. Grant at Vicksburg.

Only a few brief glimpses remain of Cadet Meade at West Point, where he did little to be remembered. One of his schoolmates recalled him as "dignified, courteous and gentlemanly but rather reserved"; another as a tall, slender, and graceful youth "with the air of the high-

---

[25] Isaac R. Pennypacker, *General Meade*, 13 (hereafter cited as Pennypacker, *Meade*).

[26] *Ibid.*, 13; U. S. Military Academy Records, 1817–37, West Point, N. Y.

est breeding."[27] In view of his background and training, this was as Richard and Margaret Meade's son would naturally be, but more might well have been expected.

Bound by signed articles to serve his country for one year, Meade on July 1, 1835, was named a brevet second lieutenant and assigned to Company C, Third Artillery. His appearance was more scholarly than rugged, but to earn money for an officer's outfit he toiled as an assistant surveyor on a right of way for the Long Island Railroad during his first three months' leave. He could not realize, of course, that this would serve as an introduction to a later engineering career. His tour of duty completed, he visited his mother and sisters in Washington, then joined his artillery company, which was in training at Governors Island in New York Harbor.[28]

[27] Herman Haupt, *Reminiscences*, 310; Bache, *Meade*, 557.
[28] *Meade*, I, 12.

## 2. To the Río Grande
## (1835-1836)

THE TINY NATIONAL military establishment was only dimly promising. A few scattered forts had to be manned, officers replaced as transfers were made, and there was a possible theater of war in Florida. The artillery regiment to which Meade was attached happened to be ordered there, but there seemed to be no pressing need for the services of the young artillery lieutenant, who chose to go by way of the West Indies by invitation of brother-in-law Commodore James Dallas. Consent was obtained from a neighborly War Office, and after spending a few days with his mother, Meade sailed from Hampton Roads on October 8, 1835, aboard the fleet flagship *Constellation*.[1]

Meade could sit at the Commodore's table with a family connection who was about to fill a consular post and enjoy a constant round of social affairs wherever Dallas dropped anchor. But since the fleet put in at several West Indies ports during a cruise of three months,[2] it was a roundabout journey and was not of any use in preparing a green soldier for an Indian war. Grim news met the *Constellation* as it put in at Key West about the middle of January. Some three weeks before, Major Francis L. Dade and a party of 108 officers and men had been waylaid while en route between two Florida forts. Only three had survived the massacre; two of the slain had been classmates of Meade's at West Point.[3]

Since help was needed at besieged Fort Brooke on Florida's west coast, Dallas engaged several small craft to take a battalion of marines, with naval officers and crews, to Tampa Bay.[4] Meade and other artillery officers were among the relief force which, arriving on January 22,

[1] *Army and Navy Chronicle* (October 8, 1835), 328; (October 15, 1835), 336.
[2] *Meade*, I, 13.
[3] These were Lieutenants Richard Henderson and John L. Keais
[4] Sandy Dallas to Captain George Meade, February 7, 1880, Meade Papers.

was hailed by a weary garrison as the Seminoles withdrew.[5] When boats bringing four companies of volunteers and supplies of food and arms arrived from New Orleans, most of the sailors returned to the fleet at anchor at the Key West coaling station.[6]

Had any correspondence between Meade and his mother been saved, there might have been some stories to tell, but no letters of the period have survived. One written in 1865 and cryptically signed "Medicine Chest" looked back over the years to recall an incident of March, 1836. Meade had been among a party sent to retrace the route on which Major Dade had been slain. "Your kindness on that occasion," wrote the unnamed admirer, "was illustrated by granting me permission to ride on a gun of your Battery, and subsequently I being ordered off . . . by a Lieut. of Marines you ordered me to again remount . . . thereby relieving me from great pain and fatigue in marching, I . . . being just discharged from the Hospital in Tampa."[7]

Meade, who also had been ill, was unable to finish the march. It had been too long a stride from an ordinary regiment to the Indian frontier. He sweat copiously from recurrent attacks of fever and unseasonable heat; early spring, 1836, was like summer in Philadelphia. To make some small use of his services as well as to shift him elsewhere, his colonel ordered him to escort a party of four hundred peaceful Seminoles to a new settlement west of the Mississippi River. Another invalid officer and an army surgeon were to assist in this task of unknown difficulties. About the middle of April the party left Tampa by schooner, then transferred at New Orleans to flatboats for the trip up the Mississippi and Arkansas rivers. On June 1, Meade reached the tiny settlement of Little Rock and picked up $300 for further expenses. The party continued into Indian Territory and, leaving the boats at a distant fort, marched overland to the assigned area. No incidents were reported, but glad to be rid of his saturnine charges, Meade made the down-river trip in good time and by June 28 was back at Fort Brooke.[8]

He was eased out by being ordered to Washington, where he was

[5] *Army and Navy Chronicle* (January 28 and February 25, 1836) gives details.

[6] Woodburne Potter, *The War in Florida*, 167.

[7] Letter from Troy, N. Y., dated March 25, 1865, Meade Papers.

[8] Meade Letterbook, "Appointments, Assignments and Reports," carries details on this western expedition. Application was made April 8, 1836, Meade Papers. The War Records Division, National Archives, has the order dated April 9. Meade turned his charges over to Lieutenant Thomas B. Van Horne, Third Infantry.—*Meade*, I, 14.

assigned to duty at the arsenal at Watertown, Massachusetts. On October 28, 1836, when his year of service was up, Meade escaped further dull routine by resigning.[9] Apparently he felt fit to return to Florida, this time as an assistant surveyor on a railroad project. Brother-in-law Major James Duncan Graham, the army officer in charge, was authorized to offer $1,000 a year plus the usual camp fare and traveling expenses. The railroad would connect the harbor town of Pensacola with the prosperous cotton market of Columbus, Georgia, and was expected to take at least two years to build.

Meade arrived at the top of a real estate boom in West Florida. Land speculators boasted that Pensacola would quickly grow to city size as the new railroad built up its commerce. When the panic of 1837 broke upon the country, the speculative bubble burst,[10] and Meade was left to reflect upon the hazards of a civilian career. Since he was now past his twenty-first birthday it may be assumed that steady work was important.

Only through the Topographical Bureau, a branch of the Engineer Corps, were two more jobs found, and there were intervals of idleness between them. Meade had the advantage of being in the South; he had only to cross the Gulf of Mexico to reach the Sabine River where he was sent that summer. For regular survey work in describing the Texas-Louisiana boundary line he was to be paid six dollars a day plus expenses.[11] Recruiting a boat crew, he measured depths over sand bars and along channels and plotted the Sabine's meandering course as far as shallow water upstream. He completed his task in only six weeks and, as the civilian in charge, made his report directly to War Secretary Joel Poinsett.[12]

There was no work on the important Atlantic Coast survey, to which he now applied, but in November he took a step upward through assignment to the Mississippi River Delta, where he took charge of a work brigade. Two such brigades under Captain Andrew Talcott of Connecticut were employed, and for about six months the crews

[9] *Army and Navy Chronicle* (November 3, 1836), 288. The July 21 *Chronicle* had noted appointment of Brevet Second Lieutenant George G. Meade as second lieutenant, as of December 21, 1835.

[10] Florida Historical Society *Quarterly*, Vol. IX, No. 4 (April, 1931), 224 f.

[11] Capt. W. H. Chase to Meade, April 19, 1837, Meade Assignment Book, Meade Papers.

[12] Meade to Secretary Joel Poinsett, undated, *ibid.*

sounded the depths and shoals and measured the march of the sand bars into the Gulf of Mexico. The meticulous task of finishing maps, organizing data, and drafting reports of the elaborate survey was not completed until the following winter.[13]

Now no more work could be found for nearly a year, although the regular army engineers seemed to be busy. It was not an easy time for a youth who hoped soon to marry. Meade had been courting the oldest daughter of Congressman John Sergeant, who had helped free Richard Worsam Meade from a Spanish jail. Sergeant had served for a time as John Quincy Adams' minister to Mexico, but as running mate of Henry Clay in the 1832 presidential race, he was deprived of historical fame when Andrew Jackson won re-election. Perhaps it is notable that he later refused a seat on the Supreme Court, a cabinet post, and the ministry to England.

For Sergeant, a widower, his daughter Margaretta (usually Margaret) was the hostess. No description of her face and figure exists, but it is known that her cultural interests were wide, that she read in three or four languages and played the piano with distinction. Her handsome sisters were married to men of affairs—one to Congressman Henry A. Wise of Virginia—but Margaret was attracted by the gallantries of the former West Pointer, a youth of good family but without large means or even fair prospects. John Sergeant would give the matter much thought before consenting to the match, but in the course of events he developed a fondness for Meade and seized upon occasions to praise his conduct.[14]

Anxious to prove himself, the suitor was rescued from miserable idleness by another assignment to Texas. In January, 1840, he sailed with Major Graham to trace an extension of the Texas-Louisiana boundary line from the Sabine to the Red River. The boundary question was all important for the independent state of Texas, which was then seeking a settlement with the United States. The work which Graham and his civilian assistant completed that winter provided the data later used in drawing up a formal treaty.

Nearly everywhere it was the nation's borders and coast lines that were being surveyed. That summer, Meade was vacationing with the Sergeants at Schooley's Mountain, a New Jersey resort for the gay and

---

[13] *Meade*, I, 14–15.
[14] *Ibid.*, 16–17, 204; Bache, *Meade*, 562–63; Pennypacker, *Meade*, 15.

fashionable, when he received a Topographical Bureau assignment to another geographical extreme.[15] A large-scale surveying task remained to be done on the northeastern boundary, which had been the subject of a perennial dispute among the United States, England, and Canada. Again employed under Major Graham, Meade helped organize the work during the fall months, then stored his equipment for the winter.

Since survey work among the winding rivers and deep woods of northern Maine would take years, promising steady work, Meade felt free to take the step for which both he and Margaret had been waiting. On his twenty-fifth birthday, December 31, 1840, the marriage was consecrated at the home of the bride "amid a brilliant assembly."[16] Army and navy uniforms were prominent at a party given by his mother in Georgetown in honor of the bride. Following the honeymoon, Meade applied himself to desk work at the Topographical Bureau and with the melting of snows returned to field work in Maine, where he soon found himself "sadly out of spirits at my separation."[17]

Much of his time was spent under the stars, which were used both as guides and as points of calculation for surveyors. He wrote a letter to Margaret's sister Sarah Sergeant Wise:

> We did not stop observing this morning till near 5 o'clock. We then went to bed and slept till 11—breakfasted, after which I filled some half a dozen sheets of letter paper with Astronomical calculations. We dined about 5 and after dinner I smoked a cigar while Schroeder played upon his guitar some of the airs of Margaret's piano pieces. This of course induced many lively imaginings of scenes of happiness now passed but which I hope soon to enjoy again. As soon as it was dark we commenced looking out for rockets and other signals which are made by the parties in advance placing stations on the line, and had it not proved a cloudy night the affair would have been closed by observing till 2 or 3 o'clock in the morning. The kind clouds have however given me a little time to yourself. ... Remember me to your husband.[18]

To avoid the snows, field duties ended early in November. Meade may have left early enough to witness, on the fourth of the month, the

[15] Col. J. J. Abert to Meade, August 18, 1840, Meade Assignment Book, Meade Papers.
[16] *Meade*, I, 17.
[17] Meade to (Mrs.) Sarah Wise, August 9, 1841, Virginia Historical Society.
[18] *Ibid.*

birth of a son, who was named John Sergeant after his eminent grand-sire. Although happily reunited with his family, the breadwinner be-gan to be concerned over a Congressional measure which would limit government surveys to the Topographical Engineers. Once the bill excluding civilians was passed, it became necessary, as Meade saw it, to obtain army reappointment. Margaret's brother-in-law, Congressman Wise, was happy to be of assistance, and on May 19, 1842, the appoint-ment was signed by President John Tyler.[19] Although Meade had lost nearly six years of seniority, he had fairly earned his rank of second lieutenant of Topographical Engineers.

The surveying work done, the Webster-Ashburton Treaty of 1842 settled the northeast boundary dispute. Meade was retained for several months to chart Maine's Aroostook River from its mouth to its source; then orders dated November 17, 1843, transferring him to Philadel-phia, were happily received. He now had two young sons, the second, born November 2, being named George after his paternal great-grand-father. The family soon moved from Washington, taking a house at 89 South Fourth Street, Philadelphia, and with Topographical head-quarters within easy walking distance, Meade rejoiced in an ideal arrangement come upon at last.[20] The officer in charge, brother-in-law Major Hartman Bache, was of the congenial sort—the "most thorough-bred gentleman," Meade once remarked, "I ever met."[21]

Their first large task was the design and construction of a light-house for the dangerous Brandywine Shoal in Delaware Bay. It was decided to do something new. Details of the screw-pile method of building were obtained from England, where the first lighthouse of this kind had been erected in the Thames estuary. The broad-bladed screws requisitioned were three feet in diameter. Fitted to the base of each iron pile—nine in all—they were bored into the mud to a depth of six feet.[22] Thus additional bearing surfaces were provided, as well as a means of forcing the piles downward. It was a rough outdoor life in all weathers, but Meade made light of the hardships as he absorbed himself in the technical details.

A coal collier, black with dirt, occasionally took Meade and others

---

[19] *Meade*, I, 17; B. H. Wise, *Life of Henry A. Wise*, 367.
[20] Meade's office was at Seventh and Spruce streets in downtown Philadelphia.
[21] *Meade*, I, 34.
[22] George R. Putnam, *Lighthouses and Lightships*, 63.

of the crew back and forth, and he was able to spend most evenings at home. His beloved family continued to grow. On February 26, 1845, his first daughter, who was named Margaret, was born. All things considered, he was ill prepared for news broken "as gently as possible" by Major Bache.[23] Texas had another disputed boundary—on the Mexican side—and armies were being assembled in the vicinity. Annexation of Texas to the Union, a measure which Mexico tried to oppose, was being debated in Congress. The quarrel seemed wholly remote, but still it meant that Meade would have to go. Orders received on August 12, 1845, read Aransas Bay, Texas, and in parting from clinging hands and tear-wet faces, the Lieutenant felt a "terrible agony."[24]

If one were not hurried, the journey would take some three weeks. Meade picked up some necessary articles at the Topographical Bureau in Washington, took a Baltimore and Ohio train to Cumberland, Maryland, changed to a stagecoach, and from Cincinnati proceeded by boat down the Ohio River. He stopped off at Louisville to visit his sister Elizabeth Ingraham, living near by, but much talk caused him to miss his boat when it went on. This meant only a night's delay. Arriving at St. Louis, he took passage on a heavily loaded craft which laid up each night on the Mississippi for fear of snags. Passage from New Orleans across the Gulf was engaged on a staunch brig carrying a cargo of hay. "I arrived here two days ago, well, hearty, and in good spirits, . . ." the seasoned traveler wrote from St. Joseph's Island near Corpus Christi on September 14.[25]

At United States Army headquarters at Corpus Christi, General Zachary Taylor shook hands with a lean, bespectacled six-footer with brown hair and beard, whose bearing suggested courtesy and diligence in duty. Meade found Taylor "a plain, sensible old gentleman," so writing home. With Captain T. J. Cram, the senior topographical officer, and Lieutenant Thomas J. Wood, his junior, he was attached to the General's modest staff.

Altogether the outlook seemed fair. The grizzled Taylor, who had fought his first battle on the Indian frontier thirty-three years before, scoffed at the idea of war. It was true that some hostile Mexicans were

[23] Bache, *Meade*, 558.

[24] *Meade*, I, 19. In this first letter of record to his wife (August 15, 1845), Meade urges her to keep up her spirits "and take care of your health and that of the children. No one can tell how my heart was rent at parting with you."

[25] Meade to wife, September 14, 1845; *ibid.*, 25.

about and that shots were occasionally heard, but headquarters appeared confident that the conflicting claims could be settled. "I find my position here most agreeable," Meade wrote Margaret.[26] The September weather was excellent, a fine breeze tempering the rays of the sun. From a convenient hard beach he could bathe in the sea. Above all, he was happy to be kept well occupied. The engineers were always the first to be employed in any large military undertaking, and, given his choice, he would belong to no other corps. For a look at the near-by country, five Mackinaw boats took Meade, Cram, and a guard of thirty soldiers up the Nueces River, and soon he was busy with maps. But in October the weather turned cold or uncomfortably changeable, and fever laid many low.

With both Cram and Wood in the hospital, Meade tried to keep on his feet. He led a surveying detail along an inner waterway running 120 miles to Point Isabel, but storms twice drenched him to the skin. Once back in camp, he took to his bed "yellow as an orange" with jaundice, as he described it. Working with papers placed on a lapboard, he managed to complete his maps and reports and to write several long letters home. The chilly fall weather did not improve, and several weeks of it gave the soldier another point of view: "You cannot imagine the total want of comfort which one is subjected to here," he wrote Margaret on December 9. "It has been storming and raining incessantly for the last three weeks, and when one is taking medicine it is no very agreeable accompaniment to be sleeping in wet tents. . . . The disease . . . made me very low-spirited and gloomy, and for some days, combined with the weather, rendered me quite miserable."[27]

Texas indeed was worse than Florida. To escape the bad climate and to get well, both Captain Cram and Lieutenant Wood had gone home. The chief surgeon thought Meade should do likewise. "It may take some time for you to get over this thing," he remarked, adding that General Taylor would willingly give him his leave. Meade confessed to wavering and almost giving way. "At night, when I thought of seeing you and my dear children," he wrote Margaret, ". . . I would be almost crazy, and determined . . . I would go and get my leave." But still believing that he could recover, he determined to stay. "I hope," he added gently, "you will not blame me for the course I have taken."[28]

26 *Ibid.*, 26–27, 29.
27 *Ibid.*, 37.

Unhappy idleness marked the convalescence. Action of any sort usually found the Lieutenant in fine spirits, but he would lapse into gloom whenever events dragged. He began to recall needlessly that much of his time and effort since graduation from West Point had been wasted and that advancement had been slow. Ten years had passed, and he was still a second lieutenant. "I tremble sometimes when I think what I might have been and remember what I am, when I reflect on what I might have accomplished if I had devoted all my time and energies to one object," he ruminated. "It is the better part now to . . . put the best face on it."

His army service was a sore point with his mother. In a repining letter, she bitterly regretted that she had been "so cruel" as to send him to West Point. Meade could not wholly sympathize with this view, but at night, on his cot, he recalled his last Christmas Eve, when he, his wife, his mother, and his sister Mariamne took a hansom cab and went shopping. "How thronged the streets were with crowds of happy faces," he reminded Margaret. "What hustle and commotion in each house when the bell was rung; what joyous and merry meetings! . . . Here nothing is seen or heard but the regular sound of the drum, sending the men to bed, and the shouts of drunken men in the little town adjoining our camp."

Yet inevitably, toward the end of his letter, he turned to happier thoughts:

I am most thankful to Almighty God for the blessings He has thus far showered upon us; you and my dear children, healthy, comfortable, and happily fixed; me, though separated from you, still in good health and in as good spirits as I could be under the circumstances. With ample means to support us, all our wants gratified, blessed with the loveliest children, at once a source of pride and the most perfect happiness, who that reflects on this picture but must say 'tis black ingratitude to complain![29]

Diplomatic exchanges between the United States and Mexico were slow and ineffectual. An envoy sent to Mexico City to offer twenty-five million dollars for a boundary line to be extended along the Río Grande instead of the Nueces River was not even received. General Taylor

[28] Meade called the opportunity to go home "a powerful temptation." *Ibid.*, 38–39.
[29] Meade to wife, December 25, 1845; *ibid.*, 41–42. He had now recovered from jaundice.

therefore was directed to take a position on or near the Río Grande, about 140 miles south.[30] Rain and mud kept the army immobilized for some weeks. Then on March 1, 1846, returning from a surveying expedition up a near-by waterway, Meade readily sensed excitement over the news that there would be action at last. The soldiers were delighted to leave, although it was an unhappy turn of events for the many shops and saloons of the town. Tales calculated to frighten General Taylor into remaining where he was were indifferently shrugged off.[31] On March 4 a wagon train escorted by one hundred men set out for the first depot forty miles beyond.

Dining at the General's mess table, Meade had hopes of accompanying him on the march. "I believe the old man has taken something of a fancy to me and I am considered as being in luck," he wrote Margaret. He would be with "a gallant, brave old man who knows not what fear is."[32] But it fell to him to plot the line of march for the army. Following closely behind the first detail, which later closed in behind, Meade rode with the Second Dragoons under Colonel David E. Twiggs, a snowy-haired veteran of the War of 1812 and of Florida. Major Samuel Ringgold's battery, guns polished and gleaming, came up smartly in the immediate rear, and one day behind marched General William J. Worth's First Infantry Brigade with which Taylor rode. Counting the Second and Third brigades, each with its own field artillery, and a supply train of 307 ox-drawn wagons, the little army of four thousand men made an impressive martial display for scouting Mexicans. As General Taylor suggested, however, the object of his forces "was not war."[33]

To the casual observer, there was no reason for it in the appearance of the land. Eying the scrubby, sparsely populated area, Meade could see no cause for nations to quarrel. The disputed stretch was but "the most miserable desert, without wood or water, that I ever saw . . . perfectly unfit for the habitation of man, except on the banks of a few little streams we crossed."[34] And potable water was so scarce that the thirsty marchers sometimes plodded through a whole day without finding any.

[30] Alfred Hoyt Bill, *Rehearsal for Conflict*, 66.
[31] Meade to wife, March 2, 1846, *Meade*, I, 50.
[32] Same to same, June 7, 1846, *ibid.*, 101.
[33] Same to same, April 23, 1846, *ibid.*, 70: ". . . nothing was to be taken by force."
[34] Same to same, April 7, 1846, *ibid.*, 56.

Army movements were closely watched all the way. Eight days out, Twiggs cautiously approached a patrolling party of armed Mexicans who rode away after a brief palaver; on March 20, as the advance gained the high banks of Colorado Creek, a sizable body of Mexicans seen in the distance threatened to fire. Twiggs at once halted and sent a courier back to Taylor, who hurried up with the First Brigade. A message from Mexico's General Pedro de Ampudia was brought under a flag. Any further advance would be considered an act of war. Taylor, however, had his orders. Meade watched the enemy closely as field guns were unlimbered and a road was cut from the high bluffs down to the water level. More forces—the Second Brigade—arrived, then the artillery moved on ahead, splashing through the creek which the soldiers found to be salty and undrinkable. The protesting Mexicans blew their bugles, closed ranks, and became lost in the distance.

Taylor camped where he was to await the Third Brigade and the wagon train. Well closed up, the army detoured toward Point Isabel on the coast, the base for supply ships then nearing port. Fresh supplies were unloaded and taken to the main body of troops, who then resumed the march, hailing the first glimpse of the Río Grande on the twenty-ninth. One of the first to reach the river bank with the advance guard, Meade narrowly escaped capture as Mexicans in ambush made off with two men.

The soldiers curiously eyed the dingy buildings in the little town of Matamoros on the opposite shore, where Mexicans could be seen working on defensive ramparts and emplacements for guns. The first thing accomplished on the Texas side was the raising of the Eighth Infantry regimental flag on the nearest-at-hand short pole. Meade then watched the homely details of the hoisting of the national colors. A deep hole was dug, a suitable pole thirty feet long obtained, and the dirty and dusty soldiers raised aloft Old Glory. Meade later sought to scotch the report that General Worth planted the flag with his own hands;[35] but wherever the honors of war might lie, that officer would make the best of them.

With Lieutenant J. E. Blake, the senior topographical officer recently arrived, Meade laid out the camp. At the apex of a triangle of tents extending back from the river, Taylor threw up a rugged bastioned fieldwork named Fort Texas, and lines were bulwarked with

[35] Meade's view was that of an antiromanticist. *Ibid.*, 100.

parapets and ditches. Meade and other former West Pointers then broached the subject of bridges. The army had no small boats, and it was then being debated in Congress whether a pontoon train should be sent. Meanwhile a bridge or two could be built and held in readiness; but, since Taylor felt that he would not be called upon to cross the river, he dismissed the idea.

Mexico, however, was in no mood to treat, and her prowling militia would strike down American officers and men at every chance. Meade always had a strong guard with him as he rode up and down the river, but soon there was the sad loss of Quartermaster Trueman Cross to report, ". . . father of the pretty Miss Cross who used to be in Washington . . . ," Mrs. Meade was reminded.[36] Colonel Cross, an able and popular officer, had been murdered while on a regular mission. It was learned that the assassin was riding about on the Colonel's horse and that General Ampudia possessed his gold watch, although denying any knowledge of the crime. Having lost others by capture and desertion, the army was seething. "This dastardly act, and the mean lie of the commanding-general on the other side, have inspired us all with a burning desire to avenge the Colonel's murder . . . ," Meade wrote home. Any sense of sympathy felt for the Mexicans was gone.[37]

Actual war drew closer when Lieutenant Theodoric H. Porter and ten scouts, whose muskets had been rendered useless by a sudden shower, were cut down. Meade prepared his wife for the worst: "Such acts as these, if continued, must bring on a general collision." Affairs were obviously at so serious a stage that Taylor called for five thousand volunteers to be sent by neighboring Texas, Louisiana, and Mississippi. Believing that war would be the quickest means of effecting a final settlement, Meade regretted that no bridges had yet been built and placed "in depot."[38]

[36] Two of his sons, Meade added, went to college with Mrs. Meade's brother. *Ibid.*, 62.

[37] Meade to wife, April 21, 1846, *ibid.*, 66.

[38] *Ibid.*, 75.

# 3. "Soldiering Is No Play"
## ( April-September, 1846 )

GENERAL TAYLOR'S FORCE of some 2,700 men had proved no deterrent to bloody forays along the American-claimed north bank of the river. Moreover, the rival army was beginning to demonstrate. On April 25, 1846, a new commander, General Mariano Arista, paraded some 7,000 troops, horse and foot, where they could be seen from just across the Río Grande. Speculation in the American camp turned to hot anger when it was learned that a scouting detail of sixty-four officers and men had been cut to pieces that same day, with but one survivor. "Hostilities may now be considered as commenced," Taylor wrote the War Office. Mexico, in fact, already had declared war, although the news had not yet arrived at Fort Texas.

Meade's letters home reflected headquarters opinion that a much larger force should have been sent to overawe the defiant Mexicans. "Ten thousand men would have effected this, and judicious economy would have suggested [it] . . . for a war will cost a hundred times as much," he wrote on the twenty-sixth.[1] Considering what might lie ahead, he hoped, he went on, to be able to tour Mexico's beautiful interior region leading to the city of Monterrey, where immense mountain peaks towered over a green valley.

Taylor was for bringing matters to a head where he stood. Should a reinforcement of several thousand volunteers show up, his regulars would be greatly outweighed in any battle to be fought and would receive no credit. But while the volunteer force was being organized, there were ways of inviting attack.

A courier rode in with word that five men had been slain at a United States post located about halfway to Point Isabel on the coast. Ordering up a force of 2,200, Taylor let it be known that he would march to the sea and pick up supplies. He took along two field batteries, leaving 500

---

[1] Meade to wife, May 3, 1846 (misdated May 2 in text), *Meade*, I, 74.

men under Major Jacob Brown and Captain Braxton Bragg's battery, plus some eighteen-pound guns recently brought.

Yet was Taylor actually in want of supplies? Meade wrote, after reaching Point Isabel, "Our object [was] to obtain provisions and other supplies, and to relieve this point, which General Taylor understood was threatened by the enemy." Meade later learned better, advancing the General a notch or two in his estimation as Taylor's strategy became apparent. *"We never were in want of supplies,* always having had an abundance," he insisted after being enlightened. "General Taylor, ... was anxious to try our strength before the volunteers should come."[2]

The General, however, did pick up supplies. The regulars had been disappointed in not meeting any of the enemy on the way out, and the more so because there were two hundred loaded wagons to protect on the return trip. These "acted as an anchor to us, preventing us from advancing on the field." The arena referred to, El Palo Alto, lay by a tree-girt pond where lurked some gaudily clad Mexican cavalry and infantry with the look of irregulars. They appeared to number 2,500 horsemen and some 6,000 men all told, against which Taylor could pit only about 2,000 infantrymen plus 200 mounted.[3] On this day, May 8, 1846, the first field battle would be fought by a United States army since Andrew Jackson's victory over the British on January 8, 1815.

As the army swung into position, the distant thud of an artillery battle could be heard from the direction of Fort Texas. Taylor must make haste in getting back. About 2:30 P.M., Mexican fieldpieces barked, and round brass shot began to roll through the American lines, although with little harm at seven hundred yards. Taylor's columns advanced farther and deployed, each battery protecting a flank, with two eighteen-pounders placed at the center. Meade rode here and there with orders, dodging enemy artillery fire.[4]

The wagon train in the rear was the prize. Enemy horsemen darted against the Third Infantry on the American right flank. Shells from two field guns broke the force of the drive as the Fifth Infantry swung over in support. Several volleys were poured in with effect. The Americans were yelling madly as enemy riders, their ranks broken, turned and sought cover.

---

[2] It was largely a matter of "our reputation," Meade explained. *Ibid.,* 93.

[3] *Ibid.,* 79.

[4] George A. McCall to Benjamin Gerhard, January 12, 1847, Mexican War Letterbook, Meade Papers.

Burning gun wads ignited the tall grass, concealing the field in smoke. The air clearing, a brass band led an assault on Taylor's left, but unexpectedly met some reinforced artillery. The band and infantry troops just behind it were punished, but the Mexicans declined to be badly beaten. Their infantry withdrawn, the troops settled down to an artillery duel until sunset, when Taylor slowly advanced and occupied the ground the enemy had held before vanishing into the brush.

The regulars had conducted themselves with credit, "never flinching," declared Meade, proud to be one. Casualties had been small, but he recorded a few dangerous moments in reporting the details to Margaret: "I was in the action during the whole time, at the side of General Taylor, and communicating his orders . . . . An officer of the General's staff had his horse shot under him, not two yards from me, and some five horses and men were killed at various times right close to me."[5] Perhaps they shuddered at home, but it had been a great day.

The enemy had retreated but returned to fight again on the ninth. Meade's own account of Resaca de la Palma showed a feeling for narrative, and no word was wasted:

> From the Palo Alto to the river there is a thicket called in this country Chapparal, which is almost impassable when you are off the road, and which consists of thick thorny bushes, that tear your clothes to pieces in trying to get through . . . . After passing this, till we came within two miles of the river, a heavy discharge of grape was fired into our advance, showing the enemy still disputed our march. The General ordered up his artillery, threw out his infantry on the right and left, and after several discharges from our batteries, charged their batteries . . . with our cavalry, and charged the bushes with the infantry; the result of which was that, after contesting the ground for some time, they gave way in all directions, and there was a total rout of the Grand Mexican Army that was going to eat us up. We captured seven pieces of artillery, all their pack-mules, several hundred in number, all their ammunition, several hundred stand of arms, and all their baggage. Took one general, two colonels, several captains and subalterns and some one hundred and fifty men, prisoners; and it is supposed it will take all day to-morrow to bring in their dead and wounded off the field, as the ground is said to be literally strewn . . . . We pursued them to the river, and had the gratification of seeing our flag waving in triumph over our little field-work,

[5] Meade's account of the battle is dated May 9, 1846. To wife, *Meade*, I, 80.

and all the officers in it safe, except its gallant commander, Major Brown, who died from a wound received from the bursting of a shell.

The affair of to-day lasted from one to four o'clock, and proved the superiority of our infantry, as that of yesterday did of our artillery. We have whipped them in the open plain, and we have done so in the bushes, and I now believe the war will soon be ended. . . . No troops could have behaved better than have ours both yesterday and to-day. Our loss to-day is four officers killed, many wounded; the number of men I cannot tell, as the returns have not yet come in; . . . I am writing to you from the field . . . to apprise you of my safety, and to ask your thanks may be returned to God for preserving me through all.[6]

The exhilarating victory had been total. Moreover, good use could be made of nearly everything taken, including General Arista's embossed official stationery, which had been found among his baggage. A portion fell to Meade as his only memento.[7] American losses—thirty-nine killed and seventy-one wounded—were greater than those at Palo Alto, where only nine had been killed and forty-four wounded; but the beauty of it all, declared Meade, was "that we had completed the whole thing, with our own force, without assistance, and when we were only expected to take possession of some point and defend it."[8] This fairly reflected the attitude of General Taylor.

The accidental death of the only other topographical officer, Lieutenant Blake, whose revolver was discharged as he dropped his gun belt, again left Meade the only officer of the corps with Taylor. On the tenth he helped to collect the dead and wounded and made a sketch of the field. Again on regular duty, he reconnoitered the banks of the Río Grande eight miles above and five miles below the main camp to select a crossing place.

Taylor would have to manage without that pride of the engineers, a military bridge. Strong swimmers reached the opposite shore by night and picked up boats which the Mexicans had neglected to destroy. Planking brought from Point Isabel was shaped into flatboats to accommodate artillery and wagons. On May 18, the army easily made the crossing at a point which Meade had designated three miles upstream,

[6] *Ibid.*, 80–81.

[7] George A. McCall, *Letters from the Frontiers*, 456; *Meade*, I, 102. Lieutenant Meade wrote a letter or two home on this stationery.

[8] Meade to wife, May 11, 1846, *Meade*, I, 82.

taking complete possession of Matamoros, which Arista had abandoned without firing a shot. Arista, Meade notified Margaret, was said to be "in full retreat for Monterey, some two hundred and fifty miles from here, at the foot of the mountains."[9] This in fact was where he himself wanted to go.

For most of the summer the army would remain at Matamoros, where Meade found no lack of work in inspecting enemy strongholds and the country beyond. Abandoned by all but "old hags, worse looking than Indians," the place was very disappointing, but, during trips outside, Meade found the fair sex more pleasing to the eye. Then he would test his facility with the Spanish language, asking for water, the name of the road, or trying some other time-honored gambit. He insisted to Margaret that he talked "purely . . . from a desire to acquire the language, which I find not difficult,"[10] but returning to the subject, he offhandedly remarked that a peasant lass would "hand you a cup of water in a graceful way that would put to blush many of our finely dressed ladies."[11]

Far away at home, Margaret Meade was doing her best with two lively boys—John Sergeant, now four years old, and George, two years younger. Little Margaret, who nearly one and one-half years old, also required much care. Mrs. Meade was, of course, subject to loneliness; and she could not take her daily problems to her husband. Since none of her letters were saved, the surviving correspondence between Margaret and the Lieutenant is entirely one-sided, and she remains a rather shadowy figure at home. But her response to his letter can be vividly imagined. Whatever may have been said in reply, this was the last to be heard of any pretty native girls.

The subject of newly arrived volunteers, of whom Meade could speak more freely, replaced his impromptu remarks on the fair sex. The volunteers' unsoldierly attitude, their improvised rules and excuses alarmed him. The ordinary routine of drawing water and cutting firewood was apparently not for them but for the regulars to perform. "They expect the regulars," exclaimed Meade in a mild state of shock, "to play waiters to them. No, soldiering is no play, and those who undertake it must make up their minds to hard times and hard

[9] To wife, May 19, 1846, *ibid.*, 85.
[10] This ingenuous note is sounded in a May 27 letter. *Ibid.*, 90.
[11] *Ibid.*, 107.

knocks."[12] Orders that no firing of guns was to be allowed in camp had no effect on men "ignorant of discipline and most restive under restraint . . . a most disorderly mass." For drunk or sober, the volunteer soldiers would collect along the north bank of the river and make a great noise with their muskets, wasting much army ammunition in the process. As the bullets came whizzing by or through the officers' tents in the town, Meade gravely voiced an observation much quoted by historians of the period: "I really consider spending a day in my tent, uninjured, equivalent to passing through a well-contested action."[13]

With hundreds of volunteers armed to the teeth arriving nearly every day, General Taylor could count on enough men, but he was lacking in wagons and supplies necessary for offensive warfare in the enemy country. It required nearly six weeks to receive a message from Washington, which appeared unaware or unappreciative of his difficulties, and thus more time slipped by. The longer the wait, the greater the difficulty in keeping the idle volunteers in check. Prompt and conscientious in duty on his own part, Meade filled more letters with justified complaints. The administration, he charged, should have anticipated Taylor's needs for subsistence and transportation. As for the "voluntarios," who always appeared to be drunk, they had killed five or six people in the streets for their own amusement, had robbed Mexican citizens, and had stolen the cattle and corn of poor farmers. Saloons and gambling houses, some moving down from Corpus Christi, were springing up here and there, and soldiers with time on their hands kept them well filled. "Their own officers have no command or control over them, and the General has given up in despair."[14]

Another senior topographical officer, Captain W. G. Williams (the third in succession over Meade), arrived in midsummer. The regular troops, by this time, were moving along to Camargo, about one hundred miles upstream, and as the boats were crowded and uncomfortable the "Topogs" seized the opportunity to accompany some infantry and an artillery battery going by land. This was actually a choice between two evils. After leaving Matamoros on August 5, the party marched through two days of rainy weather and then under a burning sun, but

[12] Meade to wife, May 28, 1846, *ibid.*, 94.

[13] *Ibid.*, 91.

[14] Matamoros was then invested with "grog-shops and gambling-houses." *Ibid.*, 110.

means were found to escape the rays of the sun. Reaching an undulating limestone outcrop which reflected much heat, the troops would wait until midnight before resuming the march and would finish before eight o'clock in the forenoon. Meade, however, was glad to be active.

By the middle of August, nearly the entire army was at Camargo. To the needy people of Camargo, ravaged by recent floods, the arrival of the Americans was a godsend. Women were paid to wash clothes, the men to gather forage for horses. Milk, eggs, freshly killed chickens, and scores of beef cattle and mules also were paid for in cash. Provisions of every kind went to the invaders, while the Mexican army was, of course, disregarded.

But the fact that Camargo happened to be at the head of navigation and so was a logical base did not help the situation in which the army now found itself. The floods had contaminated most drinking water, little breeze was stirring, and the town itself was hot, damp, and unhealthy. Ordinary sanitation rules were unknown among the natives and unpracticed by most volunteers. The regulars had to attend to the wants of the newcomers, who, as Meade testily observed, "had to be taken care of, as you would so many children."[15] Many regiments were reporting one-third of their number sick, some even a larger percentage, and so many funerals were held that everyone seemed depressed.

Meade's stay in the pestilential village was for only six days. Well satisfied to get away, he joined the advance under General Worth, who was setting out for Cerralvo at the foot of the Sierra Madre Mountains. For much of the way he rode with Lieutenant John C. Pemberton, a former schoolmate at West Point and now one of Worth's aides. Recently wed to a Virginia girl, Pemberton was hoping that the war would be cut short. Meade could quite agree, but he still wished to see more of Mexico. Cerralvo was found a delightful spot with cool mountain water running near by; lemon and orange trees shaded the town and yielded an abundance of fruit. At last the army was entering a healthier country. As other detachments from Camargo arrived, Meade listed 6,230 men and four batteries of light artillery available shortly before mid-September.

This force seemed sufficient to exercise authority. Mexican cavalry hovering in front proved only a nuisance, and occasional brushes with enemy bands left the invaders unscathed. Out reconnoitering, Meade

15 The "large number of sick is a dead weight upon us." *Ibid.*, 121.

rode with a task force of eighty men through an enemy picket line one midnight, "but the cowardly rascals were afraid to come after us, and not being strong enough ourselves to . . . attack them, we returned to camp unmolested."[16] Accompanying a larger force detailed to prepare a usable road, Meade left Cerralvo on September 12 and uneventfully reached Marin, only twenty-five miles from Monterrey. He was amused to report that, as the American detachments filtered in, villages dispossessed by raiding Mexican horsemen returned from the hills "loud in their denunciations of their own soldiers."

Taking the good with the bad, the war was not an unpleasant experience. The cool September weather, the grand mountain scenery, and the spice of mild danger compensated in some part for his enforced absence from his family. He would have liked to share some of this zest, writing Margaret from Marin: "I wish you were in this beautiful country, for here it is magnificent, the air balmy and pure, all the tropical fruits growing and we are just entering a level table-land, which leads to the mountains, twenty-five miles off, but so high we can see them towering away above the clouds, a most magnificent sight. Indeed, were I single, I should be tempted to spend my days in this lovely climate. On our march from Cerralvo I never had a covering over my head, nor anything but my old india-rubber cloak spread on the ground for a bed."[17]

So far, however, he had won no laurels which would have pleased Margaret. Although cited in General Taylor's report and recommended for higher rank, Meade still remained a second lieutenant when promotions based on the actions of May 8 and 9 were announced. Others, too, had been passed over, while some officers had been advanced two grades. But, inasmuch as staff work was seldom the road to fame and glory, Meade did not repine. "In truth, I have but little claim as far as the two battles are concerned," he commented. "I did my duty, and my duty simply [and] . . . knowing how these things are done, I was fully prepared for my not being noticed."[18] It was implied that some officers had been helped by administration friends in Washington, where Democrats were in the majority, whereas his antecedents were Whig.

The snow-tipped Sierras loomed larger hour by hour as the troops

[16] Meade to wife, September 3, 1846, *ibid.*, 127.
[17] "I . . . have no colds or rheumatism." To wife, September 17, 1846, *ibid.*, 131.
[18] *Ibid.*, 128.

happily marched on. Within the mountain shadows lay the white-stuccoed city of Monterrey, its cultivated valley skirting bold heights. On the right lay Loma de Independencia, the first of two craggy foot-hills fortified and manned. The road leading southwest ran between this and the one-thousand-foot ridge called Federación with its high fort, *El Soldado*. On September 19, Taylor moved up close enough for mounted Texas troops to exchange shots with some enemy horsemen who rode out from The Citadel, a stronghold on the north side of town. Puffs of smoke billowed out from the fort; men began to dodge cannon balls, one of them fanning Meade's knee. The dragoons were ordered to return out of range as camp was made at a tree-shaded resort known as Walnut Grove.

Topographical officers and the regular engineers began reconnoitering enemy positions, which were formidable. The Citadel or Black Fort, strongest of the outposts, lay just in front, while if the attack were made on the left, Forts Tenaria and Diablo would have to be stormed. On the other side, Independence Hill was guarded by a strong redoubt overlooking the heavy-walled Bishop's Palace, now an armed camp. El Soldado and an earthen redoubt supporting two guns topped near-by Federation Hill.

It could be seen that the forts of Monterrey were ringed with earthworks and that sandbags fringed the housetops for the protection of sharpshooters. Loopholes were being drilled in houses and walls, and evidence indicated that every principal street had been barricaded, some with tough masonry. Earthworks lined the bank of a small river which afforded natural protection along the farther side. "It is a perfect Gibraltar," one soldier remarked.[19] Inside the city with its 9,000 defenders, drums rolled, church bells rang, and bugles sounded their high-pitched staccato.

Riding in from his first survey of bastions among the mountains, Meade drew a field map to give General Taylor an idea of prospects. Aside from asking a few questions, Taylor said little; but he boldly planned to split his forces, attacking the two forts on his left and the fortified hills on his right. The latter assignment went to Worth, who was ordered to gain the Saltillo Road running between the two heights, and "if practicable" to carry them. The First Division and the volunteer brigades made ready to attack the other strongholds.

[19] W. S. Henry, *Campaign Sketches of the War with Mexico*, 219.

Worth's forces numbered about 2,000 resolute soldiers in trim condition following their long but leisurely march. At 2:00 P.M. on September 20, the Second Division (four regiments) plus 400 mounted Texans sent in advance and two artillery batteries moved out. Meade and another engineer officer piloted the troops on a detour through cornfields. Leaving his main force behind, Worth with his staff and 50 mounted Texans reconnoitered farther on. As Worth and Meade surveyed the lofty fieldworks, two guns spoke from Independence Hill, the balls rolling harmlessly by. The enemy perhaps had no explosive shell. Some Mexican infantry, which had worked their way around, opened fire from behind a fence, but the Texans smartly returned it, Meade related, "and we came quietly back to camp."[20]

Since fires were forbidden, the men went supperless, lying in the open beneath a cold rain. The mounted Texans and two infantry companies led the advance early next morning. After dodging more cannon balls, these troops met an enemy force estimated at 2,500 and routed them after a brief fifteen minutes of rifle and artillery fire. Worth moved out on the Saltillo Road and prepared to storm steep Federation Hill as his men scanned the height.

The elated army now faced the difficult task of fording the waist-deep Santa Catalina River and ascending the height. An interested spectator on horseback by General Worth's side, Meade watched the troops splash through the cold stream and inch slowly up Federation Hill as enemy bullets and artillery fire whipped over their heads. Taking shelter behind rocks and trees, they replied to such good effect that the disconcerted Mexicans suddenly took to their heels, and with a shout the invaders began waving their caps at the top of the hill.

El Soldado and the town itself had been flanked, but the news which came to Worth from the other attacking force was not good. Although Fort Tenaria was taken toward evening, American losses were so heavy that elated Mexicans were clanging the church bells. The honors, so far, lay with the Second Division, which was virtually unscathed. Worth had suffered only twenty-three casualties.

The greater task lay just ahead. Meade, who had studied Independencia's slopes, now had to help guide a storming party to the top, a matter of finding one's way in the dark. Again it was raining when at 2:30 A.M. on the twenty-second the word was passed: "Be careful of

[20] *Meade*, I, 133.

34

loose stones. Keep rifles from hitting rocks. Touch elbows with the next man."

Some of the soldiers were shivering violently from cold and excitement. At three o'clock precisely, a force of five hundred regulars and Texas volunteers began to move up, with Meade and Captain John Sanders of the Engineers pointing the way.[21] It was slow work on hands and knees or with bodies bent far forward, but by dawn the silent invaders had reached a point within one hundred yards of the crest. A few sharp volleys broke upon the morning air, and the troops rushed over the redoubt only to find that the artillery had been withdrawn. A twelve-pound howitzer, which, dismantled below, had been hauled up the slope by hand, directed bursts of shrapnel at the Bishop's Palace below. Enemy troops attempted a sortie "repulsed by one general discharge."[22] Replacing the Mexican standard, the Stars and Stripes was flung out amid cheers.

Guns removed from the Bishop's Palace and those taken on Federation Hill joined with the regular batteries in scattering defenders on crowded streets. The men on the heights foraged for food, attended the wounded, buried the dead of both sides, and prepared for an assault on the city early next day. Meanwhile General Taylor had rested his battered troops on the other side of the town, keeping only an artillery detail in action. When heavy firing was heard the next morning, the guns on the hills joined in the attack, driving the enemy to the great central plaza.[23]

The way was now open into the town. Worth took over the Plaza de la Purísima, a church and a cemetery, and placed a ten-inch mortar on the main plaza beyond. Soldiers broke into near-by houses and climbed to the roofs to pick off any enemy riflemen who showed their heads. Armed with crowbars and pickaxes, engineers burrowed from house to house, widening gaps with explosives. Troops on the American left likewise sliced through houses to by-pass the street barricades and shorten the distance to the main plaza. Meade saw the church roof crowned with two howitzers and a six-pounder ready for action next morning, the twenty-fourth, but operations were halted by a white flag as the enemy appealed for an armistice.

[21] *Life of General William Jenkins Worth*, 90.
[22] *Ibid.*, 93.
[23] Henry, *Campaign Sketches*, 210.

Taylor appeared a little magnanimous in arriving at terms; but he was far from his base, and his army had been badly hurt. The cost in men at Monterrey was about 450 killed and wounded, and of this number nearly 10 per cent were officers. The formal agreement provided for evacuation of the town within seven days and granted an armistice of eight weeks. The Mexicans, in withdrawing, were allowed to retain their arms.

The wisdom of these terms was hotly debated in camp, but Meade strongly approved. To Margaret he explained:

> They were still very strong in the town, having three thousand men and twenty pieces of artillery . . . . Then their strongest work, the citadel, . . . was untouched . . . . But our volunteer force, which had shared in the disastrous losses of the eastern side, were beginning to be disorganized . . . and they could not be longer depended on. The regulars were crippled almost to inefficiency, and in addition, the enemy were in hourly expectation of reinforcements. . . . if they had all been made prisoners of war, we could not keep them. . . . our old General was desirous of playing a liberal and generous part by them, and thought it impolitic to push them too hard.
>
> For my part . . . I was exceedingly rejoiced; many of our brave fellows slept in a nameless grave, for the bodies of some were never recovered; and any one who for four days and nights is in constant state of exposure to fire-arms of all descriptions will be very well satisfied to terminate so disagreeable an occupation.[24]

Written in General Worth's tent September 27, 1846, Meade's letter describing the battle would fill nine printed pages in his published letters, and it included a rough map. It was brought to a close at two o'clock in the morning with "a few private lines."

"I wish," Meade wrote tenderly, "to express to you my heartfelt gratitude that it has pleased God once more to pass me through untold dangers, and to allow me still to cling to the hope of once more being reunited to you. God knows what joy it brings to my heart to anticipate the happiness we shall have together, and the deep anxiety I have to behold again my blessed little children, whose images are as fresh in my heart as the day I left them."[25] He would have some stories to tell his two small boys when he got back.

[24] *Meade*, I, 138–39.    [25] *Ibid.*, 141.

# 4. The Long Way Home
## (October, 1846-March, 1847)

WITH TWO MESSMATES, Lieutenants John Pope and Jeremiah Scarritt, Meade made himself at home in a mansion decorated in luxurious French style—the former domestic establishment of General J. M. Ortega. The trio were surrounded by mahogany furniture, glass doors, fancy clocks, wax flowers, and tinted engravings. A cook, waiter, and hostler were engaged "so that we are quite comfortable . . . the envy of the army."[1] The scouting "Topogs" had been the first to find the place, and because of the valuable nature of their services they could not easily be ousted.

A few days after the battle, Meade again found himself the senior topographical officer in northern Mexico, and headquarters was beginning to jest that anyone sent to command him was sure to be killed or otherwise removed from active service. The first, Captain Cram, had gone home ill from Corpus Christi and had not returned. Lieutenant Blake, Cram's successor, had accidentally shot himself at Resaca de la Palma. Captain Williams, fatally wounded in the recent fighting, lingered awhile and then was buried in a convent garden. Replacements who began arriving included Captain Thomas B. Linnard, who was placed over Meade; but soon the newcomer fell ill, remaining inactive for some weeks.[2] Except for the period of Meade's own illness during the previous fall, topographical affairs were largely handled by the active young officer whose name was coupled in General Worth's report with the phrase "intelligent zeal and gallantry."[3]

[1] *Meade*, I, 147.

[2] *Ibid.*, 155.

[3] J. C. Pemberton to Adjutant General R. Jones, March 31, 1847, Mexican War Letterbook, Meade Papers. Lieutenant Pemberton explained that the reference to Meade "did not appear, so far as I am aware, in any of the public prints at the time of the publication of the Report; if the omission was originally at the Headquarters of the division, it was through my own inadvertence in copying." Meade himself commented

37

Dispatches from Washington disapproving the truce found him again defending General Taylor, who, as a Whig, was not of the war party. To Margaret and her Whig neighbors, Meade again explained that the terms had been arranged as a step toward peace. It had been General Taylor's hope "of inducing the Mexican Government, by not pressing too hard its army and granting it easy terms . . . to listen to the offers of our Government for negotiation." Ultimately, Taylor was left in the air.[4] The Polk administration not only disapproved the armistice, but gave the General no further orders than to remain where he was.

Still an eye had to be kept to enemy approaches to the south, where, it was rumored, the "Americanos" would be entirely cut up. As an interested sight-seer, Meade found it delightful to accompany General Worth to Saltillo, where he browsed about the town. Escorted by a mounted guard, he rode twenty-five miles farther to examine roads through mountain passes. The terrain neither held any serious obstacles for an invading army nor offered much protection for an enemy force which, he decided, could be easily turned. Returning with his penciled field books, he busied himself with drawings and maps for General Taylor and the War Office[5] and wrote more long letters home.

The administration had to make certain that not Taylor but others would take over the war. One of the preferred was General Robert Patterson, a Pennsylvania Democrat who, left behind at Camargo, had complained of being sidetracked. Orders, therefore, were sent directly to him—only a copy to Taylor—to proceed to the coastal town of Tampico. Since he was ordered to pick up some of Taylor's forces along the way,[6] it could easily be inferred that the theater of war was to be transferred to the coast.

Meade and his mates spoke in heated terms of the "outrage" of dividing up Taylor's army without reference to him,[7] but it was obvious that their leader was no hero in Washington. Taylor stubbornly set out toward Ciudad Victoria, which lay two-thirds of the distance to Tampico; but soon after he started, a courier brought the news that Santa

---

(November 27, 1846): "General Worth has been pleased to say of me more than I really deserved."—*Meade*, I, 166.

[4] *Meade*, I, 151.

[5] Lieutenant John Pope assisted in these drawings and sketches. Meade to Colonel J. J. Abert, October 20, 1846, File No. 1031, National Archives.

[6] Bill, *Rehearsal for Conflict*, 189; *Meade*, I, 189.

[7] *Meade*, I, 145.

Anna, a new Mexican leader, was threatening Saltillo. Taylor returned to his base with the regulars only, leaving the volunteers to go on, but the rumor would be found to be only another false report.

Meade unhappily saw it as a turn of the trail. With Engineer Linnard, mended in health and back in the saddle, he ultimately would have to join Patterson. He naturally hated to miss the battle which Taylor would await in his area, nor did he care to be separated from that beloved officer. "The old man was very kind to me on parting, and said he would recollect, if anything turned up in the way of peace, that I was the first to join him, and had been with him ever since,"[8] he rather sadly wrote Margaret. There was some small consolation in the fact that he expected to be the only Topographical Corps officer under Patterson.

Left to continue the march were about 2,000 volunteer infantry with some regular artillery, the entire force led by General John A. Quitman. Meade turned to mapping the wheel-rutted trail leading to Victoria. The sometimes difficult road ran through a broad, cultivated valley rich with fruit trees and sugar cane. Towering mountains were on both sides as the army plodded through Linares and Villagrán, where Meade sketched lofty Sugarloaf Mountain. A fragmentary note tells of his breakfasting there with General Quitman and Lieutenant George H. Thomas, a competent regular who commanded the artillery battery.[9]

The tale was heard that 7,000 Mexicans lay in front as the army neared Victoria, but the town was reached on December 29 without incident. Meade scouted the country roundabout to learn whether enemy guns would be able to approach on any other road. All, however, seemed poor, and the area remained undisturbed and quiet as the invaders took over the town. There was plenty of time for Meade to write more long letters home. His health, he could say, was perfect. He also assured Margaret, near the close of the year, "I . . . thought much of you and our dear children on Christmas Day; nor have I forgotten that to-morrow is our wedding day, and that I have been happy for six years."[10] It was a happy surprise, on January 4, 1847, when General Taylor unexpectedly came up with the regulars under Twiggs,

[8] *Ibid.*, 171.
[9] John F. H. Claiborne, *Life and Correspondence of John A. Quitman*, I, 285.
[10] *Meade*, I, 172.

with Patterson and his troops and, almost as important, with a large sack of mail for officers and men. The letter Meade received from home that day was dated November 14.

The force at Victoria, which now numbered almost 6,000 men, had little or nothing to do at that particular road junction. Since Polk had named General Winfield Scott to lead the planned expedition by sea, Taylor awaited orders from him. Ten days passed, but nothing was heard. The army would now move to Tampico. On January 15, Meade left with Twiggs's brigade in the van, but on the second day out he was disappointed to learn that his old commander had been turned back. Scott had ordered most of the regulars and half of the volunteers to join him at Tampico. Left to Taylor was a thin guard for the Monterrey-Saltillo line.

Meade left no doubt about where his own feelings lay, informing Margaret: "I must confess I regretted exceedingly parting with the old man. He has been most outrageously treated by the Administration, which hopes to play off General Scott against him, and by . . . leaving him in an exposed position, with one-third of the force which he had before . . . to break him down and destroy his popularity. I trust that it will signally fail."[11] The chance meeting at Victoria was the last that Meade would ever see of his favorite commander. He was glad, however, to be back with the regulars again; and he could see, of course, that the campaign to be led by General Scott would be the great effort of the war.

But no longer would he be the senior topographical officer. As he busied himself with reconnaissance work in and around Tampico, he found himself under Captain John McClellan, who, coming from Philadelphia, had brought along three pairs of extra spectacles from Margaret.[12] Meade had been down to his last pair. Although he did not use them for reading, they were essential for any far range. He took in all the sights in Tampico, which he described as delightful. It was quite a cosmopolitan town, having a large foreign influx of importers and merchants, excellent shops and fine cafés, he reported.

His initial duties completed, Meade sat in the cafés and debated Whig doctrine. Now Mexican newspapers were quoting Whig journals

[11] *Ibid.*, 175.

[12] *Ibid.*, 177. Meade spells the name "McClelland," presumably a slip of the pen, inasmuch as this officer was the brother of George B. McClellan of a Philadelphia family.

and Senator Daniel Webster's speeches opposing the conflict. These were but indications of its unpopularity at home. Mexican people were reported as saying, "Let us hold on and suffer, and in a short time the Government of the United States will be forced to respect Mexico and to withdraw all its exorbitant demands."[13] His answer to that was the employment of every available resource in bringing the war to a close. He exhorted his wife and whoever else might read his letters: "Let us show a bold and united front, forget *party* for an instant; now that we are in the war, prosecute it with all possible vigor, not in talk but in acts; treble our ships upon her coasts, and blockade . . . [Mexico] in reality, and not nominally, as is now done from want of vessels; threaten her [Mexico] from Saltillo and Vera Cruz with armies, each of twenty-five thousand men; let her see we are determined to carry everything before us."[14] This was the talk of a man of action; but it was recognized, too, that the sooner all this was done, the sooner everyone could get home.

But apparently there would be only one active front. General Scott, who bustled into Tampico on February 20, 1847, at the head of his fleet, seemed quite oblivious of everything but his own plans. When someone was bold enough to remind him of General Taylor's critical situation, he was heard to remark, "Men of straw, men of straw,"[15] which did nothing to endear him to the regulars who had come from an arena of actual fighting. Taylor would have to fend for himself. A defeat in the interior could hardly alter Scott's plans. Meade appealed to another high power: "God grant the old General may whip him [Santa Anna]!"[16]

As the fleet of two hundred sail leisurely set out for Veracruz, the regulars continued to discuss Taylor's chances with his army of about 4,000 men against a reported 15,000 with Santa Anna. By the time the fleet anchored, the battle had been fought, and its result noised about. To Scott's headquarters came Mexican newspapers brought from a British man-of-war anchored near by. Making due allowance for enemy claims, Meade judged the news from the field of Buena Vista to be good, if only for the reason that Santa Anna had been forced to retire. "Apprehension for General Taylor's safety is now removed," he joy-

13 *Ibid.,* 181.
14 *Ibid.,* 181.
15 *Ibid.,* 184.
16 *Ibid.,* 186.

fully wrote home. Later details which were received told of Santa Anna's retreat as far as Mexico City.

Now regretting more than ever that he had been separated from Old Zack, Meade sounded his praises: "His brilliant achievement at Buena Vista, exceeding any feat ever yet performed by our arms, or which ever will be," he rejoiced, "I should have gloried to have shared in."[17] The prospect was quite unattractive under General Scott, to Meade the antithesis of a true man "simple in all his tastes, adverse to everything like show, pomp or ceremony."[18] In later years, upon meeting General Ulysses S. Grant for the first time, Meade could pay him no finer compliment than to say that he reminded him of Old Zack.

Otherwise, a victory which had assured safety for the Río Grande boundary was treated with indifference as General Scott pompously busied himself with plans to seize Veracruz. A famous incident occurred as he reconnoitered the fortified harbor. March 6, getting aboard the little steamer *Petrita*, Scott and his officers eyed the hostile shore, where a massive castle fort guarded the city. It was a distinguished company on deck. Commodore David Conner, senior naval officer in Mexican waters, stood talking with Scott, Twiggs, Worth, and Patterson. Representing the Corps of Engineers were Colonel Joseph G. Totten, Captain Robert E. Lee, Lieutenants Pierre G. T. Beauregard and George B. McClellan. Also aboard with the other topographical officers, Lieutenant Meade may have been nearly shoulder to shoulder with Captain Lee on this occasion.

The *Petrita* approached too close to the fort. Hundreds of spectators on other ships watched anxiously as the land guns opened fire. All together, some twenty shots were flung at the unprotected *Petrita*, which, it was remarked, held "Caesar and his fortunes."[19] A single shot,

[17] *Ibid.*, 193.

[18] A lengthy account of Taylor's abilities and character has lain undisturbed for more than a century among the Meade papers. Apparently the paper was composed after Taylor's death in the White House, July 9, 1850. "I have often seen him blush & turn the conversation when allusion was made to his services," Meade related. "He had no pride of opinion, he ever listened with attention to the opinions of his humblest subaltern, and he had an extraordinary capacity for seizing what was good in the ideas of others and digesting them in his own mind. His judgement was very sound, and his good strong sense enabled him to see his way through difficulties that puzzled those having pretensions to much higher intellectual gifts. He was peculiarly fitted to be at the head of the Gov$^t$ in the crisis the country is now in, and his loss at this moment can not be too deeply deplored."

disabling the vessel, would have left it a floating target for the enemy guns. Luckily, the shells either fell short or splashed harmlessly near by.[20]

It was judged that the enemy would have resisted any landing. What part did Lieutenant Meade play? As Scott prepared for an assault on March 9, engineering duties were divided among the officers according to their rank and importance. The Engineers came first. Only a few lesser matters fell to the "Topogs," now headed by Major William Turnbull and Captains Joseph E. Johnston and John McClellan. "Colonel Totten," Meade observed in bad humor, ". . . wishes to make as much capital for his own corps, and give us as little, as possible."[21] Something of the kind has been a commonplace of every war, if not of every large engagement. As the invasion was launched on a beach below the town, Meade landed with Patterson's force and, all resistance failing, helped to make camp for the night; but while the Engineers labored on siege-gun emplacements next day, he was left standing by, "pretty much a spectator." Veracruz was easily taken without his help.

The one topographical officer taken from General Taylor's army, only to be left idle, Meade took his complaint to General Worth, who in turn mentioned the difficulty to Scott. When Major Turnbull was called to headquarters for an explanation, he had only to point out that Meade was unexpectedly with the army and that he had quite enough officers without him. Citing a lack of necessity for his services, Scott ordered Meade returned to headquarters in Washington.

Meade found himself somewhat less than overjoyed. He had hoped to be of some actual service; certainly he had not asked to go home. "What will you say to my return? and what will your dear father say?" he nervously inquired of Margaret. "I will frankly acknowledge that I had a most anxious time in making up my mind what to do. . . . it was my intention, from the first moment I left you, to perform my duty and remain so long as duty required."[22]

For Lieutenant Meade the honors of war would be scant. Yet he had efficiently performed his duties as first in the field. And as the first

[19] *Correspondence of Major General John Sedgwick* (ed. by H. D. Sedgwick), I, 67.

[20] Charles Winslow Elliott, *Winfield Scott*, 455; *Meade*, I, 187.

[21] *Meade*, I, 193.

[22] *Ibid.*, 194.

to stick with Taylor through thick and thin, he had demonstrated the practical usefulness of the Topographical Corps, a branch of the service hitherto untried in actual warfare. A belated but nonetheless heart-warming honor was a brevet rank received for services at Monterrey, of which he read in newspapers sent from home. On March 31, Meade said his farewells and took passage for New Orleans. He had served in Texas and Mexico for a little more than one and one-half years, but the war would be brought to an end in his absence.

# 5. The Sea and the Lakes
## (1847-1861)

MEADE REACHED WASHINGTON by way of the Mississippi and Ohio rivers, thence overland, in three weeks' time. Any doubt concerning where he now might be sent was resolved by an order to rejoin Major Bache, which happily meant a joyful reunion with his family.[1] He lingered in Washington to visit his aging mother and to settle the monetary affairs of the late Lieutenant Blake and Captain Williams of the Topographical Corps, then hurried away. For the benefit of friends and kinsfolk who flocked to his home, he recounted the great battles which General Taylor had fought. Listeners found his stories precisely truthful as well as entertaining. "He had the gift of clear statement . . . of ignoring the irrelevant, of treating his subject with sprightliness," it was observed.[2] From the citizens of Philadelphia he received the usual gold-mounted sword for "gallantry."

Since Major Bache had been absent on another mission for several months, little progress had been made on the Brandywine light to be erected in Delaware Bay. Again Meade went nearly every day to the site to fill his leather-bound notebooks with more details of soundings, meteorological studies, and measurements of the tides in every season. At other times, ice movements had been considered. The force of the winds, of high-breaking waves, ocean currents, and general exposure also were matters of importance in planning a durable structure. By early summer the exact site was selected and a platform erected from which the supporting screw piles could be driven.[3]

It was an ideal assignment for a man who appreciated the scientific

---

[1] Abert to Meade, April 20, 1847, Meade Assignment Book, Meade Papers.

[2] Bache, *Meade*, 559.

[3] Meade's notebooks detailing progress of the work and letters to the Topographical Bureau are in the National Archives. See also John D. Kurtz and Micah R. Brown, *Report on the Effects of the Sea-Water and Exposure upon the Iron-Pile Shafts of the Brandywine-Shoal Light-House* (Washington, D. C., 1874).

turn of the work. Save for only a few later months of duty at army out-posts, Meade would be occupied with waterways and lighthouses for the next dozen years and would come to regard that portion of his career as "of considerable importance."[4] Major Bache's duties also em-braced a survey of the Florida reefs and keys, where, the war concluded, a chain of lighthouses was to be erected to protect shipping. With the approach of fall weather, Meade was sent to examine the coast for him-self and to select sites for future building.

For some three centuries, dangerous hidden rocks off the coast had taken their toll of seafarers of all nations. Many sunken warships and merchant vessels could be seen lying in the clear waters, and millions of dollars' worth of salvage had fallen to wreckers. Meade observed that the rocky Florida keys, though rising only a little way above sea level, could support heavy lighthouses without any need of artificial founda-tions, as was the case in Delaware Bay. His notebooks filled with data taken down along both the east and west shores, he returned to Phila-delphia to assist in the planning of structures.

Another year had gone by when reports of Seminole outbreaks again appeared in the newspapers. The forced abandonment of white settlements bespoke the necessity of more army outposts. Meade found himself remembered for his work in Mexico. Early in October, 1849, he was ordered to Fort Brooke in Tampa Bay, where he reported to General Twiggs, a martinet, he recalled, when with Taylor's army. Twiggs coolly explained his duties—the location of military roads and lines of camps and forts to be extended across the peninsula. Asked his requirements, Meade responded, "Two men and a mule," which ap-parently satisfied Twiggs.[5]

Even this little command was used sparingly. Late one afternoon, Lieutenant John Gibbon, stationed at one of the camps, greeted a rider attended by a single orderly. "He was a gaunt, thin man with a hatchet face and a prominent aquiline nose," Gibbon recalled. "He introduced himself as Lieutenant Meade . . . just in from a reconnaissance on a hostile border. He was wet, tired, and hungry. It was my good fortune to be able to offer dry clothes, food, and a bed of blankets."[6] Satisfied

[4] Putnam, *Lighthouses and Lightships*, 107; *National Geographic Magazine*, Vol. XVII (January, 1906), 13; Vol. LXXX (December, 1941), 807 ff.; *Meade*, I, 200; II, 184.

[5] *Meade*, I, 201.

[6] John Gibbon, *Address on the Unveiling of a Statue of George Gordon Meade*, 3.

that his scout could do all things well, Twiggs enlarged his entourage with twelve mounted men, five mules, a wagon and driver, plus one non-commissioned officer for the long trips.[7]

During the winter, Meade traversed a rough wilderness extending from Tampa Bay to below Lake Okeechobee, and to forts on the east coast. When a dispute somehow arose over a location on Peace River, Twiggs rode to the site and crustily decided in favor of the engineer whose name, by way of emphasis, was attached to the fort.[8] Early in February, 1850, a softened Twiggs formally thanked him for the completion of "arduous duties" executed with "cheerfulness and intelligence,"[9] and Meade hurried home to greet a new son, born January 19 and named Spencer.

Brandywine light was now taking shape—an iron skeleton frame surrounded by massive icebreakers. A keeper's house was put up, a modern Fresnel lens installed, and in mid-1851 final completion was hailed. Materials for a light on the Florida coast had been put together in Philadelphia meanwhile, then dismantled and shipped to the site. Meade began his work on Carysfort Reef, not far from Key Largo. Of ill repute over the centuries, the reef had taken its name from a British frigate wrecked there in 1770, while not far away rested H. M. S. *Winchester*, sixty guns, lost in 1695 while en route from Jamaica to England.[10]

The new structure shadowed clear water filled with bright-hued staghorn and brain coral. Green parrot fish, sea gardens of rare beauty, sponges, and other curious natural forms flecked the warm ocean. On August 4, 1851, while still in Florida, Meade received a long-awaited first lieutenant's commission, a rank coupled with his name on the tablet fixed to the base of the completed lighthouse.

He returned to Philadelphia to plan other structures and to visit his mother, who was seriously ill. Some years before, sale of the Meade art collection had attracted wealthy buyers, the house in Georgetown had been sold, and the amounts realized easily paid for a home for the

[7] *Meade*, I, 201; entry of October 21, 1849, Meade's Florida Notebooks, Meade Papers.

[8] Pennypacker, *Meade*, 19; *Meade*, I, 202.

[9] Meade Assignment Book, order dated February 12, 1850, Meade Papers.

[10] *National Geographic Magazine*, Vol. XXIV (January, 1913), 25; Vol. LXXX (December, 1941), 807 ff.; and Putnam, *Lighthouses and Lightships*, 105–106, contain details.

elder Mrs. Meade near his own.[11] Richard Worsam Meade had also left forty-one shares of the Bank of Kentucky, an interest in a canal company, several thousand dollars in mortgages and bonds, and nearly $1,900—appraised value—in silver and wine.[12]

It proved to be the last illness for the former lady of Spain. Her death, on March 22, 1852, severed a close bond with her second son, maintained through the years "with . . . constancy."[13]

Lighthouse work all along the Atlantic Coast was becoming more active. In August, 1852, the Topographical Bureau set up the United States Lighthouse Board, and Meade was named a Seventh District engineer with duties continuing in Florida. Five more lighthouses were planned or in progress along that difficult coast. At isolated Sand Key, some miles below Key West, Meade erected a structure 121 feet high on a base 50 feet square and on July 20, 1853, let its light shine. Coastal work was exacting and arduous, but a man could take pride in its permanence. Some years later he would read about a hurricane which swept away all of Sand Key except the rugged screw-pile lighthouse, which stands to this day.[14]

Months of work on the keys were broken by a mission to the Crystal Palace Exposition in New York City, where Meade set up apparatus for a Fresnel lamp and explained its function to visitors. Plans and estimates for more lighthouses occupied him until fall, when he returned south to continue his chain of high structures around the Marquesas Keys and Key West. Learned dissertations on the effects of wind, wave, and atmospheric changes on iron-pile structures were exchanged with his superiors in Washington. After three more lighthouses below Florida's southern tip had been started, Meade sailed up the Gulf Coast to Sea Horse Key, below the mouth of the Suwanee River. On this site —one of the Cedar Keys, where tales of buried treasure and slave-running by smugglers were told—a tower of neat brick was erected and, fueled by whale oil, its Fresnel light raised to sweep the sky.[15]

[11] *Meade*, I, 204.

[12] Copy of a Meade art sale catalog, Frick Art Reference Library, New York City. The Bank of Kentucky shares may have represented a payment by Henry Clay, who imported Merino sheep in Meade ships.

[13] *Meade*, I, 204.

[14] Putnam, *Lighthouses and Lightships*, 108–109.

[15] *Meade*, I, 205–207; Hercules Powder Company, *The Explosives Engineer* (September, 1939), 258 f. C. A. Pound of Gainesville, Florida, leases the island from the government. Cedar Key Old Tower, so called, became inactive during the 1920's.

Few details of Meade's daily experiences survive, the family retaining only his war letters. Another source tells of his meeting a young naturalist from Boston, then at sea near Key West in the interest of science. Just graduated from Harvard, Theodore Lyman was casting his nets for oceanic life to add to the collection of the famed Professor Louis Agassiz. Meade placed his coastal vessel at Lyman's disposal and saw to it that he got a decent bill of fare. The two were to meet again under changed circumstances, for in late summer, 1863, Lyman would join the Army of the Potomac as an unpaid volunteer aide.[16]

Although still only an army lieutenant, Meade was performing highly advanced work. Promoted to superintendent of the Seventh Lighthouse District, he was assigned a wider range of duties as Major Bache of the Fourth District was transferred to the West Coast. The Fourth District, which took in Delaware and New Jersey, fell to Meade; while he continued to supervise the Florida work as well. One of his first assignments was the planning of a more powerful Barnegat Bay light, some distance north of Atlantic City; and, as the new structure was taking shape, the existing lighthouse was razed by a furious storm.[17] The structure built by Meade still towers 150 feet high as it casts its rays to the sea.

A fourth son, William, was born on March 18, 1855, and there were now three girls—Margaret, Sarah, and Henrietta—in the home circle. If assigned to any distant point again, Meade decided, he would take his family with him. In 1856, he was sent to Detroit to spend a few months on the extensive Great Lakes survey. Placed in full charge of the work the following spring and commissioned a captain, he moved his flock west by way of Buffalo and Lake Erie.[18]

Begun in a small way in 1841 and then interrupted by the war, the survey was still a long way from completion. The task of surveying the bottoms of immense inland seas and a coast line equal to that reaching from Maine to Texas had been undertaken with no idea of its great magnitude, nor had anyone foreseen the water transportation needs of a flourishing nation which was expanding her commerce. Already the traditional fur trade was giving way to more numerous cargoes of grain,

[16] *Meade's Headquarters, 1863–65: The Letters of Colonel Theodore Lyman* (ed. by George R. Agassiz). (Hereafter cited as *Meade's Headquarters*).

[17] Edward Rowe Snow, *Famous Lighthouses of America*, 133–34.

[18] *Meade*, II, 208, and family testimony.

and demand was increasing for other products transported in bulk. Michigan was becoming famous for her white pine, and already the first shiploads of iron had passed through the Sault Ste Marie Canal linking Lakes Huron and Superior. In Pittsburgh, the first slab of steel had been rolled for the Moline plow works of John Deere.

Yet in most of the Great Lakes area, shoals and rocks still had to be charted, ship channels marked, harbors dredged, and beacons and lighthouses built. Treacherous waterways which had never been natural passages would have to be converted to effective channels of trade. The great object of the work, Captain Meade summarized, was "the delineation of the shores and bottom of the lakes, bringing to light all hidden dangers; obtaining the evidence and capacity and depth of water in all the harbors and rivers and consequently the most practicable mode of improving them; furnishing the evidence of the wants of navigation in reference to lighthouses, beacons and buoys and the proper sites for same."[19]

Thus far, however, amounts appropriated for the work had been small. In his first report, Meade asked for only a modest sum for ship and shore surveying parties, but after becoming acquainted with lake captains and shipowners he began to enlarge his views. More liberal funds were asked for thereafter, but the requests were invariably reduced by Congress. The year of 1857 was one of financial panic which affected both public and private affairs. The failure of the Bank of Pennsylvania and the collapse of others seem to have involved some loss to the Meades personally. In future years, there would be no more references to "ample means to support us,"[20] but rather acknowledgment that Meade and his growing family were wholly dependent on an officer's pay.

Meade, however, would thoroughly enjoy his years on the lakes and his "quiet and happy days" spent in Detroit. He and his wife made friends easily in that expansive frontier town, and they went eagerly to public concerts, although Margaret was surprised at first to find her butcher among the audience. Young John Sergeant Meade was given a horse to ride and introduced to the outdoor life of a surveyor as a member of both shore and ship parties.

[19] Meade's Report of September 18, 1857, 35 Cong., 1 sess., *Senate Exec. Doc. No. 920*, 286.
[20] Meade to wife, December 25, 1845, *Meade*, I, 42.

As Meade took up his labors aboard the government steamer *Search,* he completed work already begun on Lake Huron's Saginaw Bay, then finished all of Huron. With more accurate instruments now available, he corrected sightings of latitude and longitude and drew new maps and charts. Dissatisfied with the older methods in surveying so broad a physical field, he improved upon the accepted means of determining longitude by means of transit of stars timed by electric observatory clocks located at two east-west stations. Hitherto only one clock had been used in recording the times of transit. The double-clock arrangement was "first suggested to me [by you],"[21] acknowledged Professor C. A. Young of Western Reserve College, who set up the extensive telegraph system.

Meade enlarged his staff by recruiting able young officers from West Point, and from an original $25,000 a year, costs grew rapidly as more personnel and equipment were pressed into service. Although Congress never allowed him as much as requested, western congressmen stressed the importance of the work in committee sessions and occasionally on the floor of the House and the Senate. In 1859, after gradually approaching that figure, Meade asked Congress for as much as $100,000, of which he was allowed three-fourths; but even larger amounts had to be sought in employing two surveying parties on ships and eight on shore duty.[22] As Meade entered the season of 1861, he was surveying harbors on Lake Superior and building lighthouses there and had parties, also, on the northeast end of Lake Michigan.

But although the survey was going well, everyone was aware of a great public crisis which diverted thoughts elsewhere. One by one the Southern States were seceding, and although, in his own words, Meade had sought "some glimpse of hope that the storm might pass away,"[23] he could only realize that the extremists of both the North and the South were hurrying on toward disaster. The news of the fall of Fort Sumter on April 14 further excited politicians and public, and local authority began to assert itself in Detroit. On April 18, a dark, rainy day, bands played, speeches were made, and a large crowd fringed by

[21] *Ibid.,* 211–12.

[22] George G. Meade, *Survey of the North and Northwest Lakes,* 19; Fred Landon, *Lake Huron,* 299–300; Pennypacker, *Meade,* 20. Meade's reports comprise portions of the reports of the Chief Topographical Engineer in 35, 36, and 37 Cong., *Senate Exec. Docs.*

[23] Meade to wife, October 29, 1862, Meade Papers.

militia regiments stood motionless and tense as a large American flag was raised above the post office. A resolution was read and adopted by the crowd that all civilian officials and military officers with their uniformed commands be assembled two days later for public renewal of the oath of allegiance.[24]

An issue had been raised amidst public excitement, but Meade kept his head and followed the book. That same evening he met with his staff to discuss what might be done. To headquarters came Lieutenants Orlando M. Poe, Charles A. Turnbull, and J. L. K. Smith of Northern antecedents, and two Southerners—Robert F. Beckham and William Proctor Smith. Meade openly urged that no army officer should take an oath at the bidding of local authority, and all but one of his staff (name not revealed) supported this view. An official paper was drawn up expressing the willingness of the signers to take or renew their oath whenever called upon by the War Office. Meade forwarded the paper to headquarters in Washington, and with the other signers he deliberately absented himself from the mass meeting held on the twentieth.[25]

As far as Meade was concerned, the overriding principle was soldierly responsibility. His own feeling, he wrote a friend, was that "duty required I should disregard all political questions and obey orders."[26] His position was clearly stated, although only as a private view: "I have ever held it to be my duty," he asserted, "to uphold and maintain the Constitution and resist the disruption of this Government. With this opinion, I hold the other side responsible for the existing condition of affairs."[27]

The family, of course, would be split. He had two married sisters living in the South—Elizabeth, now the mistress of a Mississippi plantation, and Mariamne, who had married a navy man from a prominent South Carolina family, Lieutenant Thomas B. Huger. Meade's wife's sister Sarah was wedded to Henry A. Wise, who, as Virginia's governor, had signed John Brown's death warrant. Thus two Meade girls and a sister-in-law were raising their families in the South. But Meade's roots were of the North, and, important to some, he was under an oath of allegiance. It was not a difficult decision to make.

[24] *Detroit Free Press,* April 19, 1861.
[25] *Ibid.,* April 21, 1861; *Meade,* I, 215.
[26] Meade to Joshua Barney, September 7, 1861, Meade Papers; *Meade,* I, 218.
[27] *Meade,* I, 218.

The absence of Meade and his command from the Detroit mass meeting was remarked upon and denounced. Senator Zachariah Chandler of Michigan, antislavery firebrand, learned of the episode and became harshly critical. Meade's position was further weakened when both Proctor Smith and Beckham resigned to join the Confederacy. Anxious to be assigned an active part in the war, Meade would find it difficult to leave his remote post and ere long would come to consider Chandler "my bitterest foe . . . [who] will show me no quarter."[28]

Although sensing public gossip and resenting it, Meade entertained some hope of soon getting away, nagging the Topographical Bureau into naming another officer to replace him. Notified that Captain J. N. Macomb would be sent, he moved his family back to Philadelphia, borrowing one thousand dollars to pay costs—an irrevocable step.[29] There followed only silence from Washington. Hearing nothing from Macomb, Meade hurried to the Capital to talk with Secretary of War Simon Cameron of his home state.

It was now June. Meade protested to Cameron against being retained in Detroit and asked for increased rank in one of the new regiments of volunteers. The War Secretary replied that he would be glad to do something, but Meade got no further work during the weeks following his return. Chafing in spirit, he felt no better upon learning that two topographical captains junior to him had been promoted to the rank of volunteer brigadier general. One was his old associate John Pope, who had been sinking artesian wells in Texas, the other William B. Franklin, graduated from West Point in 1843.

The Lighthouse Board's attitude was not helpful. Professor Joseph Henry, board member and secretary of the Smithsonian Institution, once visited Mrs. Meade while in Philadelphia to beg that she lend her influence to keep her husband where a brilliant future was promised. Science, he argued, would be the loser.[30] He probably received no encouragement from a lady whose views could be militant. She on her own part had been talking with influential friends.

Along in midsummer occurred the ignominious Union defeat at Bull Run. Meade felt mortified and angry: "This shameful disaster resulted entirely from our army not being efficiently *officered & or-*

[28] *Ibid.*, II, 187.
[29] Meade to wife, December 12, 1861, Meade Papers.
[30] *Meade*, I, 217.

*ganized,*" he stormed. "An army is like a complicated machine—all its parts . . . must know and do their work or you will inevitably have confusion & disaster."[31] He had just about decided to accept a colonelcy of a Michigan regiment offered to him by a friendly governor when word came that he would be asked to lead a company of Topographical Engineers under General George B. McClellan, now commanding in Washington. Nothing further, however, came of this idea, and another man was selected as McClellan's topographical aide.

But whereas Meade could do little in his own behalf while anchored somewhere out in Lake Superior, it may be expected that the daughter of John Sergeant made her voice heard. A note which passed from William M. Meredith, Pennsylvania's attorney general and a family friend, to Senator David Wilmot of the same state, clearly affirmed: "Captain Meade, who has for many years served with distinction in the Engineers, is desirous of being promoted. . . . If you give him the benefit of your influence to this end you will be aiding a gallant . . . & deserving officer in his legitimate professional aspirations. I should be much gratified at his success."[32]

Presumably Senator Wilmot took action. When word reached Captain Meade that a commission of volunteer brigadier general had been signed as of August 31, he lost no time in drafting his final report and with alacrity turned over his duties to Colonel James D. Graham, with whom he had begun his career.[33] It is true that political influence had been used, but so it was with many another appointment, including a new type of volunteer officer known as "political general," usually an influential person with perhaps some militia experience.

[31] Meade to unnamed correspondent, August 5, 1861, Meade Papers.

[32] Meredith to Wilmot, July 17, 1861, Meade Assignment Book, Meade Papers. Margaret Meade may have inspired this letter.

[33] Bache, *Meade,* 565; Meade to Barney, September 7, 1861, Meade Papers; *Meade,* I, 216, 263; and George B. McClellan, *McClellan's Own Story,* 140, contain details of the plans for Meade.

## 6. The Pennsylvania Reserves
## (September, 1861-July, 1862)

A MILD THREAT to a well-fortified capital, the Confederate army under General Joseph E. Johnston stood only a few miles south of the Potomac River. Hurrying to Washington, Meade was nervous lest fighting break out before he reached his command, but all was quiet save for the usual roisterers in the streets. Reporting to General George A. McCall, an army veteran who had come out of retirement on his Pennsylvania farm, he was allowed a little time to obtain an outfit.[1] Prices, however, were rising; and disregarding other items, he paid $150 for a horse which had been wounded in the nose at Manassas. This was "Old Baldy," who became notorious for a gait too fast for a walk and just short of a run, making it difficult for aides to keep the required distance behind.[2]

General McCall was then organizing the volunteer division known as the Pennsylvania Reserves. Since most of the troops were from the interior, Meade was a stranger to nearly all save a few regular officers who had served in Florida and Mexico. The Second Brigade saw a tall, scholarly looking man with a patrician, hawk-nosed face come to take charge. Meade introduced himself to the regimental officers and hurried off to meet General John F. Reynolds of the First Brigade, a fellow-Pennsylvanian and old friend. Businesslike and correct in conduct, a bachelor whose life was the army, Reynolds would often be seen with Meade discussing problems of discipline and drill. General Edward O. C. Ord, Third Brigade, was an efficient and likable officer who had served in California during the Mexican War and had been re-

---

[1] *Official Records of the War of the Rebellion* (hereafter cited as *O.R.*), Series I, LI, pt. 1, 470.

[2] *Meade*, I, 227 n; Morris Schaff, *Battle of the Wilderness*, 41–42. Old Baldy was originally owned by Colonel E. D. Baker, Seventy-first Cavalry Regiment, then by General David Hunter. The Military Order of the Loyal Legion of the United States, Philadelphia, has a complete description in its library and has the mounted head.

cently stationed in his native Maryland. General McCall was now past his prime, but Reynolds, Meade, and Ord would make a strong team.

Daily drills at Camp Tenallytown had hardly begun when General McClellan ordered a formal review for President Lincoln, members of his cabinet, and Governor Andrew G. Curtin of Pennsylvania, who made a patriotic speech and distributed the regimental flags.[3] A crowd of interested spectators waved flags and applauded. Looking on with other officers' wives, Margaret Meade had eyes for only one that day as she caught sight of an erect figure riding at the head of his little brigade. "Well do I remember your emotions when you first saw him," a friend recalled to her years later.[4] It had been a struggle to obtain the commission, but now here he was. Meade, who had never commanded more than a company before, got his three new regiments into line and eyed them critically. Within a few more days, the arrival of other troops filled out the division, with four regiments assigned to Reynolds, five to Meade, and four to Ord. Each brigade had its own volunteer artillery company, which practiced near by. The Fourth Pennsylvania Cavalry was also assigned to the Reserves, which at full strength numbered 10,465 men.

A regiment of daredevil mountaineers and backwoodsmen which originally fell to Meade was the Thirteenth Pennsylvania or First Rifles, otherwise known as the "Bucktails" from the squirrel or deer tails that dangled from their caps. They proved adept at illicit foraging, and possibly because they caused more than the usual difficulty in learning routine tasks, they were assigned to drillmasters coached by Reynolds and became part of his brigade, later returning to Meade. They would earn a reputation as fine marksmen with their breech-loading Sharps rifles,[5] but they were free with their ammunition in responding to false alarms at night. Special infantry details helped army engineers complete Fort Pennsylvania, a massive earthwork with two lunettes. No immediate action seemed in sight. General McClellan was building a chain of posts around the Capital while organizing an elaborate military camp.

The outdoor life was, as usual, quite agreeable to Meade. Speculating upon an unknown future, he acknowledged "a little sinking at the

[3] E. M. Woodward, *Our Campaigns*, 62–63.
[4] Jeannie McLaughlin to Mrs. Meade, July 8, 1863, Meade Papers.
[5] G. A. Townsend, *Rustics in Rebellion*, 15–16; Pennypacker, *Meade*, 22.

heart, when I reflect that perhaps I may fail at the grand scratch; but I try to console myself with the belief that I shall probably do as well as most of my neighbors."[6] He was not completely satisfied with General McCall, who had been Scott's assistant adjutant general in Mexico, and was a little skeptical about General McClellan, an army commander at thirty-five years of age. McClellan, he wrote Margaret, would have to be tried.[7]

So, of course, would the entire army, but the volunteer officers and troops, he observed, as in Mexico, were not soldiers in any sense of the word. There were too many fist fights in camp, for the war seemed nothing more than a large picnic. With the regulars who already had been under fire, it was a question of each man's knowing his duty at the moment that the lives of all were imperiled. Everyone was hopeful of action when, on September 30, the Pennsylvanians and other detachments started up the north side of the Potomac to intercept a reported enemy crossing. But when all the rumors had been run down, it became apparent that the Confederates had merely put on a show of activity in masking a withdrawal toward their main base at Bull Run. McClellan began talking of previous plans of his own for a surprise attack which, he said, had been spoiled by the enemy's sudden withdrawal.[8]

But at least he could now safely advance, and so on October 9, McCall's division clattered across Chain Bridge while the bands played "Dixie" and spontaneous cheers rolled along the line.[9] With other troops following, bivouac was made near Langley, Virginia, two miles west of the river, where the Pennsylvania Reserves took position on the army's right wing.

Meade enjoyed some activity in reconnoitering missions, but after being assigned to court-martial duty, he was limited to daily rides along the picket lines. Other than drilling and firing upon enemy cavalry which now and then dashed against some part of the Federal line, the troops had little to do. After nearly two months in camp, Meade indicated that more was expected. "Every one is beginning to be tired of inactivity, and to wonder when something will be done," he wrote Margaret as cold weather came on. "We are not positively informed

[6] *Meade*, I, 219–20.
[7] *Ibid.*, 232.
[8] *Ibid.*, 221.
[9] J. R. Sypher, *History of the Pennsylvania Reserves*, 123.

that we are in winter quarters, but the men are allowed to make themselves as comfortable as they can. I cannot say I am pleased with this."[10] Dr. Joseph Henry had visited camp, assuring his friend at a formal review that the Pennsylvania Reserves "looked and marched the best of all." But the most important piece of news that Meade could send home early in December was that he had acquired a handsome black stallion for which he had to pay $125 besides turning in a rheumatic mount originally purchased for Sergeant to ride.[11] "Blacky" now became his show horse, leaving the rigors of the march to Baldy of the long stride.

It was rather too late for any regular campaigning. Relieved of humdrum court-martial duty, Meade led a foraging expedition to nearby Dranesville to strip some farms of livestock and crops before the enemy could carry them off. Little enthusiasm was felt for a war on mere civilians, but his brigade nevertheless brought back fifty-seven loaded wagons, ten horses, some droves of cows, oxen, and hogs, plus five men who had resisted. "It made me sad to do such injury, and I really was ashamed of our cause,"[12] he confided to Margaret. He could write more lightheartedly concerning the society wedding of Captain Charles Griffin and Sallie Carroll, which he attended in Washington, on December 10.

> Of course there was an immense jam; of course the bride and groom looked splendid, as did the fourteen bridesmaids and groomsmen, the latter all handsome young officers in full uniform. . . . I saw McClellan and had the honor of making way for him to approach the bride. I saw Mrs. Lincoln, Lord Lyons [British minister], Governor [Treasury Secretary] Chase, Mr. [Secretary of State] Seward, and lots of other celebrities. All my old Washington friends greeted me with great cordiality, and any amount of rooms and plates at table were offered to me when I should come into town. . . . There was the usual amount of flirtations carried on by the old stagers, assisted by numerous younger fry. I had a very agreeable evening.[13]

His stay in the city with Aide Hamilton Kuhn was cut short by a telegram received early next morning. The enemy, it was reported,

---

[10] *Meade*, I, 231, 233.
[11] *Ibid.*, 232–33.
[12] *Ibid.*, 234.
[13] *Ibid.*, 235.

was threatening attack. After hurrying to the stable for his horse, Meade took but thirty minutes in getting back to camp, only to find it another false alarm. A Federal scouting party had mistaken another of its own for the enemy. Instead of a bold pursuit of the foe, a drill was held that same day for some wealthy Chester County neighbors of General McCall.[14]

The volunteers, however, would soon be tested in battle. "If they stand up to their work like men, and really fight with a determination to do or die, I think there is no doubt of our triumphant success,"[15] Meade argued in hoping for the best. An enemy brigade under Colonel J. E. B. Stuart had drawn closer, and pickets only four or five miles from camp seized two luckless Federals out foraging. To General Ord fell the duty of driving the pickets back and collecting more forage from around Dranesville. Early on the twentieth, Meade saw the men march off—four infantry regiments, a small mounted force, and an artillery crew with four guns. Troops who had witnessed no bloodshed other than that resulting from camp fist fights appeared excited and pleased over the fair prospect of battle.

The leaders were wary in guarding against surprise during the march, and upon arrival at Dranesville, Ord occupied the main roads and pointed two guns toward a southwest highway where some enemy horsemen were seen. After a dull hour or two spent in waiting, the advance was suddenly attacked, not from each side of the road as expected but entirely from a stretch of woods to the south, so that the troops had to be shifted. Men scattered and had to be brought together. An old artillery hand, Ord sighted the guns himself to demolish a Confederate battery which fortunately was aiming too high. Other enemy guns which did little damage had to be withdrawn to avoid capture.

One and one-half hours of fighting in underbrush and woods decided the issue soon after McCall and his staff appeared on the ground. Reynolds, whose brigade was held in support, galloped up ahead of it; and without waiting for orders, Meade started out, only to find the work done. Losses numbered but 6 killed and 61 wounded, the price of sixteen wagonloads "of excellent hay" and twenty-two of corn taken, and of the Reserves' first victory. Stuart would acknowledge 43 killed, 143 wounded, and 44 missing.

[14] Meade to wife, December 12, 1861, Meade Papers.
[15] *Meade*, I, 223.

Meeting together that evening, the brigade leaders discussed the performance and absorbed what lessons they could. The troops had been shaky and hesitant, Ord said, and time had been lost in getting them into action. "If they had charged when he first ordered them, he would have captured the whole battery and lots of prisoners," Meade reported to Margaret. "Had the artillery of the enemy been served as ours was . . . he could not have kept his command together five minutes."[16] This view is in contrast to reports and eyewitness accounts which made stalwarts of green troops in their first battle, and although they had drawn first blood and were ready to do more, their leaders felt less confident than the individual soldier. The fighting quality of the men in the ranks was still under appraisal; officers had cause to wonder what might happen when warfare became arduous.

Save for the usual false alarms, all was quiet after Dranesville. McClellan's coming down with typhoid fever put an end to hopes of a general advance before the onset of winter, but Meade resigned himself to spending Christmas in camp.[17] Gossip of sorts still flew about. That a homeopathic physician, a relative of Mrs. McClellan's, had been summoned to attend the army commander had made his next of kin very indignant. Homeopathy was thought to be some sort of disreputable cult. Meade learned from McCall, who had been in Washington, that McClellan's brother John had vowed he would never enter the General's house again.[18] McCall brought no other news save that affairs seemed to be in a dreadful state and that no one seemed to know what was to be done.[19] Meade therefore suggested a leave of absence for himself and in January managed to get home for ten days.

He found the children in good health and spirits—all except Sergeant, the oldest. Now in his twenty-first year, Sergeant had expected to prepare for the law and follow in the footsteps of his illustrious grandsire, but he now had a persistent cough and was threatened by tuberculosis. Laborious study, therefore, was out of the question. Meade was as much worried, however, over son George, who was in his first year at West Point and rapidly piling up demerits. The ques-

[16] *Ibid.*, 237–38; J. H. Stine, *History of the Army of the Potomac*, 30–41, presents more flattering details.

[17] *Meade*, I, 238–39; also MS letters of December 21–22, Meade Papers.

[18] Meade to wife, January 8, 1862, Meade Papers; *Meade*, I, 242.

[19] Same to same, January 9, 1862, Meade Papers.

tion was whether George could pass his mid-term examinations.[20] (Although George did pass, he managed through an after-hours night escapade to lift his score of demerits to the maximum of two hundred.) The third son, Spencer, now twelve years old, had been permitted to stay home from school to be with his father, but after Meade returned to camp, he was amused to learn that the boy still absented himself without benefit of an excuse. "Don't mind his being at times a little out of temper," he counseled his wife. "He gets that from both sides of the house."[21]

Cold rains turned the roads into mire. Throughout a tiresome winter Meade longed to see the day when something positive could be done; if only a few hard blows could be dealt in the spring, perhaps the war might be brought to a close. This was the sanguine view; there were others who foresaw a long war.

Meade's position was unchanged when in March, 1862, the Army of the Potomac was organized into four corps, and McCall's division was assigned to the First under General Irvin McDowell, West Point, 1838, who had commanded at Bull Run. General Ord received a division after being promoted to volunteer major general for the affair at Dranesville.[22] Another First Corps division was under General William B. Franklin, West Point, 1843; both he and Ord were younger than Meade. So was Reynolds, who was graduated in 1841; also General Truman Seymour, who replaced Ord as head of the Third Brigade, Pennsylvania Reserves. Franklin, however, had fought at Bull Run, which in effect had been a steppingstone for promotion.

Again the army was impelled to move just after the Confederates quit an advanced position. After several drying days which made the roads passable, the Pennsylvania Reserves on March 10 hopefully quit Camp Pierpont and approached Manassas, where the enemy had lain all winter. As McDowell's front division soon discovered, the camps at Centreville and along Bull Run Creek had been vacated only the previous day, and stores set on fire were still smoldering. For Meade's brigade, the campaign was over after a march of only fifteen miles to

[20] Meade to wife, January 16, 22, 24, February 9, 1862, *ibid.*

[21] Same to same, March 4, 1862, *ibid.*

[22] *Meade*, I, 265. Meade termed the promotion "just and deserved." Ord was succeeded as Third Brigade commander by General Charles Seymour, who was not as highly rated.

Hunter's Mills, where orders were to make camp but to be prepared to leave at a moment's notice.

This sounded encouraging. An idea that McClellan had been mulling over all winter was to take the army on boats down the Potomac River and the Virginia coast to the Rappahannock River, which he would enter to land at Urbana, about fifty miles northeast of Richmond. Whether or not with the aid of helpful information, General Joe Johnston had so read his mind before moving his own forces down to the Rappahannock. McClellan remained committed to the water route, but now he would have to make a farther end run and land on the York Peninsula, which bulged well out between the York and James rivers, and he would have a longer march toward Richmond. The main idea, however, was to get the Army of the Potomac moving.

Orders to march to the boats on the Potomac created a minor furor. As elated as any private thoroughly fed up with drill, Meade was confident that the army was "on the eve of decided and critical events."[23] Spirits remained high even through a pouring rain all the way to Alexandria, and now the Reserves had to wait while the other divisions embarked as fast as transports arrived. General McCall, apparently, was not a particular favorite of McClellan's. "Everyone, soldiers and all, are impatient to be off and at work," Meade wrote home on April 2, but it was not McClellan's fault—orders from Washington held McDowell's corps of 40,000 where it was to help cover the city.[24]

Some repair work on the Orange and Alexandria Railway fell to the corps, and after several days of routine labors Meade welcomed orders to accompany McCall as far as Falmouth on the Rappahannock River, a point less definitely in the rear. McClellan's command was being divided, and while Ord was held back, Franklin's division was permitted to join McClellan, who had been clamoring for reinforcements. But during a month-long siege of Confederate strongholds on the York Peninsula, McClellan displayed less dash than on the parade ground. These posts happened to be weakly manned, and yet it would take him until the end of May to close in upon Richmond.

Quite discontented to be out of it, Meade could do little but drill his men and participate in the usual dress parades before swarms of visitors. President Lincoln himself attended one such occasion, and in-

[23] *Ibid.,* 252.
[24] *Ibid.,* 255.

troducing himself, Meade took the liberty of complimenting him upon the rescinding of an early emancipation order issued by General David Hunter, who was operating along the Georgia coast. "I am trying to do my duty, but no one can imagine what influences are brought to bear on me," he heard the burdened President say.[25]

Since the field of action might shift at any time, news from McClellan's army was eagerly awaited at Falmouth. After Johnston's army failed to break his lines at Fair Oaks, fought May 31 near Richmond, reports that the enemy might threaten the camp subsided.[26] Twice wounded, Johnston was replaced by Robert E. Lee, who planned no more counteroffensives until he had strengthened Richmond's defenses. A Confederate army under General Thomas J. Jackson, who had worried Washington by harassing Federal detachments in the Shenandoah Valley, was called in. Federal authorities still retained McDowell with other forces for the protection of the capital but on June 9 permitted the Pennsylvania Reserves to go to McClellan.

A fleet of transports anchored in the Rappahannock several miles below Falmouth and Fredericksburg just opposite. Reynolds embarked, and most of Meade's brigade got aboard, but tempers flared when it was discovered that McCall and his staff had taken the only space available on the last boat. Left behind as the flotilla moved off, Meade had visions of remaining idle for days, but by early evening the arrival of several other vessels greatly relieved his feelings.[27] After steaming down the coast and up the York River and its tributary the Pamunkey, the fleet turned in at the White House, the army's main base. Hurrying from the shore with his staff, Meade overtook his command only a few miles away and led it to its assigned position on the army's extreme right—the north bank of the Chickahominy River.

Here on high ground the spires of Richmond could be easily seen. Confederate band music and the sound of bugle and drum drifted back to the bemused invaders. Meade issued the usual warning against unnecessary exposure, but as soon as he had gone elsewhere, an unsoldierly crowd gathered on a strip of open ground to witness an artillery duel.

[25] *Ibid.*, 267. Meade saw Lincoln at the headquarters of General McDowell, who was temporarily at Falmouth.

[26] *Ibid.*, 271.

[27] Meade to wife, June 11, 1862, Meade Papers; quoted in part in *Meade*, I, 272–73.

They made an obvious target for enemy gunners. Men scattered for safety, but none seemed to be getting badly hurt as Meade, very angry, rode up to see to it that they were sufficiently chastened. When orders were finally given to proceed to the selected campsite, Quartermaster Sam Ringwalt saw the men turn to "with the promptness and alacrity for which the brigade has been so distinguished."[28]

Meade still had to reflect on the uncertain qualities of the volunteer soldier who elected his own officers after the way of the militia system. Selected usually because of personal popularity or sometimes because they were known as "easy marks," these officers were likely to make common cause with the enlisted man against the regulars above them. This resulted in negative effort, as when the curious were permitted in Meade's absence to expose themselves to the enemy, or in the shirking of routine tasks. Believing themselves overdrilled as they started south, the men were not yet awakened to a sense of urgency. Now that they were on the actual front, it was their duty to be constantly on the alert, but extreme nervous tension was common. Nights were made sleepless at headquarters by false alarms of battle as well as by orders delivered at almost any hour. Meade and the other brigade leaders kept their men busy. Dirt flew as rifle pits were dug in front of each regiment. A strong picket line was thrown out with cavalry vigilant on the extreme right. On the afternoon of June 26, after an enemy line was seen slowly taking position, the thud of artillery opening actual battle came as a great relief.

While McClellan's forces lay precariously along both sides of the Chickahominy, the Pennsylvania Reserves were strongly posted behind Beaver Dam Creek, a stream joining the river from the north. McCall's left—Seymour's Third Brigade—was anchored at the junction of the two streams; Reynolds on the right extended across the creek and into thick woods beyond the village of Mechanicsville. Meade's strong Second Brigade was posted in reserve to support either flank as well as to prevent seizure of New Bridge just downstream from his position. Striking from the west, the enemy would follow the road past Mechanicsville, and it could be seen that its flank would be laid open along a curve. The immediate advantage of position therefore lay with McCall and others of General Fitz-John Porter's Fifth Corps, to which the Reserves were attached. One may be sure that the lay of the land

[28] *Philadelphia Press*, July 11, 1862; *Meade*, I, 277.

had been carefully scouted by Meade, whom McCall would cite that day for the "most valuable service" and advice.[29]

Because of their good position and the careful preparation made, Federal gunners and infantry in the center and on the left had only to maintain a steady fire as General A. P. Hill's division, after forcing Reynolds back, was checked in a bloody affray at Beaver Dam Creek. A direct assault by the enemy had to be given up, and Federal artillery evaded capture. An attempt to turn Seymour, whom Meade hastened to join toward the end of the day, resulted in serious loss to the Confederates. With pauses more than a half-hour long separating the attacks, musketry fire persisted until early evening; that of the artillery until well after sundown. Aside from the withdrawal by Reynolds to a more advantageous spot, the Pennsylvania Reserves had maintained their original position.

McClellan nevertheless had already decided to retire. Screening his movement with artillery fire during the morning of June 27, Porter retreated under orders to the next village east—Gaines's Mill. Here another stream coursed south to the Chickahominy, but little time was allowed for defensive works, although the men could take cover behind felled trees. First to reach his assigned position on the vital left flank as the army faced about, Meade promptly returned enemy fire upon detection of his movement. Until heavy dust clouds signaled the approach of superior forces, Reynolds also held firm.

Occupying an unprepared position in unfamiliar country, the isolated Fifth Corps began to break up—first the divisions in front, then the Pennsylvania Reserves. Entering the battle, Meade had the Third, Fourth, Seventh, Eleventh, and Thirteenth regiments; but the Fourth was temporarily lost when driven pell-mell across the river, and the Eleventh was captured almost to a man when an enemy familiar with all the back roads got in its rear.[30] Retaining his sharp sense of direction, Meade piloted the survivors to safety, but Reynolds was easily taken prisoner after losing himself in a swamp and spending the night there.[31] Casualties at Gaines's Mill were numbered in the thousands, whereas a mere three hundred had been lost along Beaver Dam Creek.

[29] *O.R.*, XI, pt. 2, 400.

[30] Meade to Benjamin Gerhard, July 11, 1862, Meade Papers; Pennypacker, *Meade*, 35.

[31] Edward J. Nichols, *Toward Gettysburg*, 97.

Now the full meaning of war could be realized by men who had to stand and fight unless they were disposed to straggle, often to concern themselves needlessly with the wounded.

That night the unhappy remnants of the Fifth Corps—the divisions of General George W. Morell, General George Sykes, and McCall—crossed over the river to accompany the rest of the army south to the James River. Assigned to the rear, McCall's men guarded a slow-moving artillery train strung out over seven miles. Halts were frequent as guides groped their way in the dark. Toward midnight on June 29, after resting a few hours, the Reserves were still trailing Porter's main column when Meade, who had been watching the stars, declared that they were on the wrong road. Halting his men, he began scouting the neighborhood and arousing inhabitants to ask questions. By missing a left turn from the curving New Market Road, he insisted, the corps was marching blindly southwestward toward the Confederate line.[32] It was supposed to be on the so-called Quaker Road, which could not be immediately found.

McCall relayed the word to Porter, who could not bring himself to agree until enemy pickets were struck. All that could be done now was to halt and face about for a countermarch, usually an awkward maneuver. A newspaper correspondent told of falling out of line about midnight to catch some sleep, only to discover early next morning that the regiment he had been with was now passing in the opposite direction.[33]

Only Morell and Sykes, however, were withdrawn. McCall was left on the same wrong road in the Federal rear. Apparently no one expected any fighting, and no preparations were made to meet an attack. Meade himself was aware of no immediate danger on the morning of June 30 as breakfast was served on the tailboard of his little farm cart.[34] It was the last day of the month, and the troops were mustered to receive their pay.

As was his habit since his introduction to war in Mexico, Meade got into the saddle to scout. Soldiers saw him riding everywhere to question pickets while examining the ground. The entire front, here and there boggy, was covered with woods and bothersome underbrush, and near-by farm clearings were small. The country road afforded no cover.

[32] Sypher, *The Pennsylvania Reserves*, 254.
[33] J. Cutler Andrews, *The North Reports the Civil War*, 211.
[34] R. Biddle Roberts MS in Meade Papers.

After examining a near-by ridge in company with Captain Alanson M. Randol of the artillery, Meade urged McCall to place men and guns there, but too few troops, finally, were sent.[35] Continuing to scout, he struck enemy pickets close to the rear. Only a small cavalry force stood between the unready Federal line and the foe. Farther on, it was seen, "the whole woods were full of rebels."[36]

After the two days of battle, McCall now had scarcely more than 6,000 availables, and because of almost constant marching these had been afforded little rest. Yet the position now occupied was of supreme importance at that moment. The Reserves were the only barrier to enemy penetration of the vital Quaker Road, the main highway to the James. No other Federal force was in direct contact. Farther back, General Joseph Hooker's division was resting behind some woods, and a division under General John Sedgwick was some distance in the left rear. It could hardly be expected that the enemy would neglect the chance of assailing the Federal rear. And if McCall would regain the Quaker Road, it would be to withdraw along Lee's advancing front.[37]

There would be no opportunity to withdraw except under fire. Toward midafternoon, the artillery of General James Longstreet opened the Battle of Glendale or Frayser's Farm. But the enemy lacked promptness in attack. When it did rush in, it found resistance "not as firm and determined as under other circumstances."[38] On McCall's right, Meade warned some German troops manning eight guns that he was bringing up his Third Regiment only to see it riddled by this same befuddled crew at short range. As the movement broke up, "drivers, cannoneers & all . . . ignominiously left the field," and six precious guns were lost.[39]

Meade was thrown on the defensive. Bad news came from Seymour, who was falling back on the left. General Hooker had to be summoned to repair the break in the line. In the center, Colonel Seneca G. Simmons, replacing Reynolds, was killed. McCall proved less than useful in this hardest fight so far. Either careless or confused while passing along his withdrawn front, he was made a Confederate captive.

[35] A. M. Randol to George Meade, February 2, 1881, Meade Papers.

[36] Roberts MS in Meade Papers.

[37] Douglas Southall Freeman, *R. E. Lee*, II, 199.

[38] Meade to Benjamin Gerhard, July 11, 1862, Meade Papers.

[39] Randol to George Meade, January 21, 1881, Meade Papers; *O.R.*, XI, pt. 2, 240, 265.

With sometimes long intervals between onslaughts, the heated hours wore on. Meade was seen exhorting his men wherever they were hard pressed, "encouraging & cheering them by word and example."[40] Several headlong enemy charges upon Randol's smoking battery were turned back. But casualties were mounting, gun carriages were being smashed or overturned in the tumult, and few horses survived. It was nearly sunset when Meade rallied two regiments around the nearly wrecked guns. Bullets whined among the headquarters group. Lieutenant Hamilton Kuhn fell dead from his horse, and Lieutenant William Watmough, Meade's second aide, left the battle wounded. After an interval of comparative quiet, another enemy charge seemed imminent when Captain Randol heard Meade say, "I am badly wounded in the arm and must leave the field. Fight your guns to the last, but save them if possible."[41]

Calling out instructions to officers and men as he passed by, Meade guided Old Baldy to the Federal rear. His wounds were more serious than he then thought, yet he was at least spared the mortification of defeat on the field. As the final charge hit the ragged Federal line, shouting Confederates swept over the guns in vicious hand-to-hand combat. Now almost leaderless, for Seymour was nowhere in sight, the defensive remnants were driven to shelter in the woods to their rear. Yet the enemy apparently had exhausted itself. As the gray-clads slowly retired from the field, the surviving Reserves crept back to retain their hold on the New Market Road, barely escaping disaster.

It was the forearm which gave pain, and the wound was plainly visible. A sting and ache felt lower down was thought to be the effect of a spent ball. But when Meade began to feel weakness and found blood dripping from a wet saddle, he yielded his command to Colonel Horatio G. Sickle, Third Regiment, and sought a field hospital.

Along the way he encountered the division surgeon, Dr. Isaac Stocker, who had a painful wound in the hand. The two rode on to a crowded hospital shed where limbs were being severed to be tossed out on the ground. The pain growing worse, Meade dismounted and lay down on the grass to await his turn when suddenly his little two-wheeled mess wagon came along the road and was hastily flagged down.[42] Deciding to make a run of it, Meade ordered his mess equip-

[40] Randol to George Meade, January 21, 1881, Meade Papers.
[41] *Ibid.; Meade*, I, 298.

MAJOR GENERAL GEORGE GORDON MEADE

"Not only a brave and skillful officer but a true man."—Abraham Lincoln. From a painting by Thomas Hicks, in the Union League Club, Philadelphia.

GEORGE GORDON MEADE ABOUT TWENTY YEARS OF AGE

One of his schoolmates recalled him as "dignified, courteous, and gentlemanly but rather reserved." From a portrait in the possession of Mrs. H. H. Francine.

ment and tent tossed out to make room for himself and Dr. Stocker. He handed an orderly his belt and the regulation saber which he had carried through the Mexican War, and lay down in the cart.[43]

There were vexatious delays as the cart was held up by the dense traffic of wagons and men en route to the James River. The jolting vehicle came to a final halt sometime after midnight at Haxall's Landing near the cool water. General Seth Williams, McClellan's adjutant general, brought Meade into his own tent to try to make him comfortable, but he continued to fret over his second wound—a shot in the back —and slept little. It was, he complained, an obvious disgrace, though Dr. Stocker theorized that a sharpshooter perched somewhere above had fired a ball as Meade was partially turned. Entering the upper right side, the bullet had passed out just above the hip.[44]

Meade insisted on writing a letter to forestall any false reports and to ease his wife's mind. "My wounds are not dangerous, though they require immediate and constant attendance. I am to leave in the first boat for Old Point [Comfort], and from thence home. Kuhn, I fear is killed . . . ."[45] Fighting had been resumed on the morning of July 1, and shells were bursting over near-by Malvern Hill as a hospital transport carried him and other wounded officers down the James River. Arriving at Fortress Monroe in Hampton Roads, he was transferred to the Baltimore boat, and at the city wharf as the craft entered, Margaret and his son Sergeant came aboard for a tearful reunion. The Philadelphia boat was then carefully eased along so that the stretcherborne patient could be passed over the side.

Home, at 2037 Pine Street, was reached on the Fourth of July. "General Meade . . . has been wounded but . . . is in good spirits," ran an item in the *Philadelphia Press* the next day. "He fought with great bravery and skill, and greatly added to his reputation as a soldier." Meade not only had proved himself a stalwart during the difficult campaign, but he would turn to defending the honor of the Pennsylvania

[42] *Meade*, I, 299.

[43] Description of Meade swords on view at The Military Order of the Loyal Legion of the United States, Philadelphia. Lost somewhere along the road, the sword was later picked up by a Confederate soldier and retained by a Virginia family until after Meade's death when a notice appeared in the newspapers in November, 1872. The sword was then returned to the Meade family.

[44] *Meade*, I, 299–300.

[45] *Ibid.* Meade's letter to his wife, dated July 1, 1862, was written at City Point.

Reserves, who, General Hooker would charge, had fled in panic when the move was made to help Seymour.[46] Feelings of respect between the regular officer and the volunteer soldier had become mutual.

[46] Meade commented, "There was a portion of the division that was overwhelmed and [which] fell back in good order . . . but there was no truth in the report that they ran or fled without cause."—*Meade*, I, 309.

# 7. Second Bull Run to Antietam
## (July-September, 1862)

NEIGHBORS ALONG Pine Street, Philadelphia, hurried to their windows when the General's Negro servant, John Marley, was seen riding one of his horses and leading another. The word spread that Marley, whose wife was the family cook, believed his master dead and so was returning with the horses and baggage for a family reunion.[1] The battle front was never to Marley's liking, but since everything now would have to be shipped back to Virginia, Meade was not at all pleased to see him.

The wounded forearm soon healed, but the bullet through the body kept Meade confined for a few weeks. Dr. Addinell Hewson, the family physician, opined that the ball would have been fatal had it not been deflected by a rib and forced out. Even so, it had missed the spine by barely an inch. The doctor advised an extension of leave to fifty days, which was granted. By early August, Meade began taking some horseback rides up and down the street.

The newspapers kept him informed of changes in military leadership. Considered a failure in carrying war into Virginia, McClellan was displaced as general in chief by Henry W. Halleck, one of the older army officers, who, although of little value in western campaigns where he had served, was believed capable of running the War Office in Washington. Meade's old friend John Pope, a success in the West, was to command in the field while McClellan took over the capital's defenses. It was quite a comedown for McClellan, who had been directing the war, but Meade was unable to sympathize. The former General in Chief, he believed, had "lost the greatest chance any man ever had . . . for want of nerve to run what he considered risks."[2] He also accepted with equanimity the displacement of McCall, whose work was now done. In an exchange of high-ranking prisoners, both he and Reynolds

[1] *Meade*, I, 301.
[2] *Ibid.*, 303, 345.

71

had been released, and the latter now had the division command.

A strong recommendation by Governor Curtin that Meade be promoted to volunteer major general preceded his return to the army,[3] but he would have to be content with the same rank and command of the First Brigade of the Pennsylvania Reserves. That division was now returned to the corps of McDowell, an unpopular as well as unlucky general, and was ordered back to the old campsite on the Rappahannock. This was distinctly bad news following the hard-fought campaign close to the enemy capital. "Our whole summer's work gone for nothing," grumbled a soldier, speaking for many.[4] Other troops from McClellan's army were to join General Pope at Manassas and beyond or man the defenses of Washington in the great withdrawal.

Meade could not wait until his time was up. Nine days before the expiration of his leave he made his farewells at the Delaware River wharf. It was a matter of duty, not inner desire. "I cannot tell you how miserable and sad I was and am at parting from you and the dear children," he wrote Margaret from Barnum's Hotel in Baltimore next day. "As the boat pushed off . . . I thought my heart would break."[5] Happy to rejoin Reynolds at Harrison's Landing, McClellan's last base on the James, he learned that he was to rejoin his command at Falmouth, for which the troops were then leaving by transport. Meade got there on August 17 and was gratified by cheers from each company in turn as he rode through the camp. "They all seemed right glad to see me, both officers and men, and I do believe they were sincere," he wrote Margaret.[6] He in turn left no doubt in their minds that he was glad to be back and that he had been pleased by their conduct in battle.

Assured by blind Federal strategy that Richmond was safe, General Lee decided to test the resources of John Pope, who, after bragging and uttering boasts, was moving his so-called Army of Virginia down the Orange and Alexandria Railway. The new Federal commander faced greater odds than he realized. Not only were there much better military minds than his own in his front, but difficulties arose from conflicts in Washington. Halleck wanted Pope to be heavily reinforced. McClellan, anticipating the worst under another's leadership, clung to all the men he could wangle to cover a likely Federal retreat.

[3] Meade Assignment Book, Meade Papers; William M. Meredith Papers, Historical Society of Pennsylvania.

[4] G. A. Hays, *Under the Red Patch*, 147.

[5] August 12, 1862, *Meade*, I, 302.

[6] *Ibid.*, 304.

Pope, however, would finally get enough men; his ultimate success was merely a question of skillful use of forces in Virginia's fields and woods, where the enemy seemed always at home. The campaign resulting in the Second Battle of Bull Run is a study in a choice of places to be at the proper time. Lee would make his choices successfully, but not Pope.

While the opposing armies drew closer together along the line of the Orange and Alexandria Railway, the Pennsylvania Reserves were summoned to join Pope. Eager for a fight or a showdown, "the sooner . . . the better,"[7] Meade set out during a hard rain on the night of August 22, but the advance soon lost its way, covering only four miles. On one of the hottest days experienced, the Reserves then marched twenty-three miles and soon after reached the main army which had been skirmishing with an enemy seeking to cross the upper Rappahannock and meanwhile confusing the Federals.

Pope would hardly be able to prevent the crossing. Until more reinforcements arrived, his army was outnumbered by Lee's forces. And while Pope had committed himself to a straight-out offensive, Meade scented danger in his isolated position. This army, he exclaimed, should be falling back toward Washington.[8] J. E. B. Stuart's cavalry and then General Thomas J. Jackson's command circled between Pope and the Federal capital, cutting his telegraph wires and looting his main supply base at Manassas, the unlucky Bull Run of the previous year.

Pope accordingly turned back, but Lee had seized the offensive. On August 27, a New Jersey brigade met disaster when, in a spirit of sacrifice, it dashed against a portion of Jackson's force at Bull Run bridge and was destroyed. On the Federal right, Hooker skirmished with General Richard S. Ewell's division; on the twenty-eighth, at Gainesville below Bull Run, Jackson brushed against Reynolds and Meade, and a bloodier clash flared up next day along the main highway at Groveton. There Meade kept his artillery active on a convenient height until ordered to retreat as the Federal center gave way. The withdrawal was to Bull Run. Meade himself would not have chosen this position, nor did he do so when in command in a similar situation fourteen months later.

August 30, 1862, which witnessed Second Bull Run, was but an-

[7] *Ibid.*, 305.
[8] Pennypacker, *Meade*, 51.

other bad day for Pope's army. Lee, the audacious, fairly caught it between Stonewall Jackson and Longstreet. Jackson was offered as the obvious bait while Longstreet, circling in through Thoroughfare Gap, got unexpectedly in position on the Confederate right. During a quiet forenoon, little action occurred. Pope then assaulted Jackson, but Longstreet suddenly pitched in to end the fighting on that side of the arena. His gray-clads then moved to and upon the battleground's best position, Bald Hill, on the Federal left where a single brigade of Pennsylvania Reserves was almost alone.

Seizure of the Warrenton Turnpike, the main highway to Washington, was threatened. It was saved by the mobility and fighting power of the Pennsylvania Reserves in an hour referred to by Meade as the most critical of the day. Just above Bald Hill stood Henry House Hill, a lesser height to which Reynolds boldly led his division. As an enemy wave sought to cut the road off, the hardy Pennsylvanians, flying in the teeth of peril, charged down the hill, scurried into an adjoining lane, and maintained a hot and continuous fire.[9] The pike was saved, if only for army retreat.

Meade saw little else worthy of more than casual mention. Old Baldy, he notified Margaret, was hit in the leg but not badly hurt. Assigned to covering Pope's withdrawal as the broken masses of troops crossed Stone Bridge over Bull Run, the Reserves passed over late at night in the rear of the army. The bridge was then razed and camp made a little farther on at Cub Run.[10]

Army morale, which had been low, sank even lower after the defeat. Only vainly obstructing enemy traffic, Pope had suffered heavy losses in killed and wounded and from disease during the campaign. Again encamped near the visible strength of capital defenses, the Reserves were plainly "back to where we left last March." Meade was in a black mood, declaring himself disgusted. The news that McClellan was to be returned to the command in the field did nothing to lift his spirits. All that officer's old friends, he remarked, would now become "as affectionate as ever."[11] He himself would be unable to join the cozy circle.

A week of inaction while the transfer of command was effected was

[9] Meade's Report, *O.R.*, XII, pt. 2, 398.
[10] *Ibid.*, I, 399; Sypher, *The Pennsylvania Reserves*, 347–48.
[11] Meade to wife, September 6, 1862, Meade Papers; *Meade*, I, 308.

thoroughly depressing. Early in September, McClellan took over six army corps, an extra infantry division, one of cavalry, and the Artillery Reserve. With McDowell as well as Pope retiring under a cloud, the Pennsylvania Reserves became a part of General Hooker's First Corps. A pleasant state of excitement returned as Lee began crossing the Potomac into Maryland and McClellan took up the pursuit. By September 13, the Federal army had reached Frederick, where Lee apparently turned west. Meade, however, was complaining that he had not been able to learn either the enemy strength or the position of the several corps. The outlook took a favorable turn when Reynolds was suddenly called to Harrisburg to enlist and train volunteers summoned to Pennsylvania's defense. Almost automatically Meade was named to the command of Hooker's Third Division—the Reserves. He had been awaiting a divisional command for months.

He would get along well enough with Hooker, a veteran of the Mexican War who in 1862 had won the nickname of "Fighting Joe" on the Peninsula. He invariably appeared cool and self-possessed to his troops. He was not only considered the army's handsomest general but appeared on the surface to be a thoroughly competent leader. Although never an intimate friend, Meade held a good opinion of him as long as he seemed to deserve it.

That Lee would not threaten Washington was decided when a copy of an enemy order fell into McClellan's hands. Enemy forces were to be divided: Jackson's division was to seize Harpers Ferry while Lee with his main force drew the Federal army toward that same direction. Three Federal columns turned westward on the fourteenth to engage enemy forces in isolated mountain passes. Lee would have to fight holding actions in the north-south Catoctin Range and on the thousand-foot South Mountain. Most of the army traversed scenic routes below the main road to fight at Crampton's and Fox's gaps. Hooker and Meade were at South Mountain on the army's extreme right.

Meade halted his men that morning on a hilly highway which, after leaving the Frederick Road, described an arc on the right and rejoined that thoroughfare at Turner's Gap about six miles north of Crampton's. As he and Hooker looked over the rocky and wooded terrain with some cultivated areas stretching out, it was agreed that two occupied ridges on the right of the mountain road should be taken.[12] There

[12] Meade's Report, *O.R.*, XIX, pt. 1, 267.

the Pennsylvania Reserves faced a rugged barrier occupied by part of General Daniel H. Hill's division.

Meade had witnessed a similar operation at Monterrey. Enemy artillery would serve little purpose in the woods and ravines, and his men could gradually work their way up behind natural shelter. The Third Division brigades led by General Seymour, Colonel A. L. Magilton, and Colonel Thomas F. Gallagher were no longer at top strength despite reinforcements, but spirits were still high. Opening the action with artillery at 7:00 A.M., Meade kept his guns at work against the first crest as soldiers from Pennsylvania's mountain country skirmished along the base and then slowly worked their way up from behind trees and boulders. Enemy snipers were picked off wherever exposed, but Union blood also was shed along the difficult slope, where occasional stone fences formed barriers. Upon gaining a position about 150 yards from the top and straightening their line, cheering Bucktails made a rush through bushes and swarmed over.[13]

The action on the right would take nearly all of one costly day, that which carried Fox's and Crampton's gaps only a few hours. Meade's artillery continued to blaze during a warm afternoon. Seymour's brigade skirmished in a thick cornfield and adjoining wood at the base of the second ridge until, toward the end of the day, they made their way up and were heard cheering at the top after a brief, climactic struggle.

Both ridges had been won but would have to be held. Meade sighted enemy troops moving over from the left; wary of being flanked in "almost the most rugged country I ever saw," he sent to Hooker for reinforcement. Hooker promptly obliged, but fresh forces from both sides found little to do as darkness set in. Turner's Gap, where the road rose six hundred feet, was made safe for passage to the main turnpike.

The veteran soldiers always remembered South Mountain. Officers, even when fatally wounded, had been heard urging them on. Prowess displayed along the Federal right was reflected in the remark of a Southerner taken prisoner: "Your men fight like devils."[14] General Daniel Hill, recalling South Mountain, would remark that "Meade ... was always in deadly earnest."[15] Satisfied that the troops trained by

[13] O. R. H. Thomson and William H. Rauch, *History of the Bucktails*, 205.

[14] A. F. Hill, *Our Boys*, 397.

[15] R. U. Johnson and C. C. Buel (eds.), *Battles and Leaders of the Civil War*, II, 574. General Hill credited Meade with being "one of our most dreaded foes . . . he eschewed all trifling."

Reynolds and himself were among the best in the army, Meade unstintedly praised his command in his battle report but paused near the end of his writing to consult a regimental commander. He sought to verify a claim made in behalf of Seymour, who had not fought well at Glendale or at Second Bull Run. "You know I do not like Seymour," Meade remarked to Captain D. Biddle Roberts. "They say his brigade took the mountain height first, and I want to know whether that is a fact."[16]

Pencil in hand, Meade outlined a map of the field for Roberts to follow. When the details were verified, he went the whole way. The conduct of the First Division, he had written, "was such as to uphold its well-earned reputation for steadiness and gallantry." As division commander, he now added, he was "greatly indebted to Brigadier-General Seymour for the skill with which he handled his brigade on the extreme right flank, securing . . . the great object of our movements."[17]

Unhurried in the pursuit, McClellan approached the village of Sharpsburg, lying west of the mountains, on the afternoon of September 16. Meade, described merely as "a dark-haired scholarly-looking gentleman in spectacles,"[18] rode with both Hooker and the army chief. Since Lee's forces were known to be somewhere near by, the conversation may have touched on the selection of ground. The fate of Harpers Ferry also may have been discussed. Lying below high bluffs and hills at the junction of two rivers, it never was and never would be defensible, and in fact had surrendered to the enemy early on the previous day.

Federal cavalry in advance trotted over a ridge and were silhouetted against the sky. A Confederate battery barked, and horsemen scattered for shelter. McClellan wheeled his horse about and rode toward the rear. Hooker remained for a little longer with Meade just behind Seymour's brigade, but as the shells flew nearer, he bade him a jovial good-bye and put his mount over a fence to ride out of range.

Still the army right, the First Corps was nearest the enemy. Meade hurried Seymour along while couriers brought up the brigades in the rear. Facing the Pennsylvania Reserves was General John B. Hood's division of Longstreet's corps. From a suitable height, Meade saw enemy fire coming from an immense cornfield and a wood east of the

[16] D. Biddle Roberts to George Meade, February 5, 1881, Meade Papers.
[17] *O.R.*, XIX, pt. 1, 265.
[18] A. D. Richardson, *The Secret Service*, 280.

highway, and an enemy battery supported by infantry was spotted among the high stalks. He ordered Federal twelve-pounders trained on the field, and after gaining an advantage from the superior height, he sent infantry in to seize a portion of the enemy position in both corn-field and wood. Little ground could be gained against the well-sheltered enemy.[19] Toward sunset the fighting spread along nearly a mile of front as General Abner Doubleday with Hooker's First Division and General James Ricketts with the Second came up on either side. As darkness fell, troops with other approaching units eyed with interest the dancing patterns of smoke and flame—the prelude to Antietam. The issue between McClellan and Lee would be finally decided the next day.

Opposing picket lines were so close and soldiers on watch so nervously alert that sporadic rifle fire robbed the men of sleep. But even before daylight on the seventeenth, Meade was heard calling out orders as he supervised troop movement. Artillery fire opened the day. Then Seymour, whose brigade had slept, again assailed the cornfield, supported on his left by Ricketts. As the musketry spread, Meade hurried his two other brigades into a sheltered ravine and carefully deployed them to ease the pressure on Seymour.

Hooker meanwhile found Ricketts closely pressed and in trouble. He at once called upon Meade to send a brigade, and although any withdrawal would leave a gap in the line, Meade had to send someone, and so took Magilton from the center, then rode to Dunbar Ransom's battery to see that his guns covered the gap.[20] As the brigade double-quicked to the edge of the wood, the General was seen sitting quietly on his horse, "calmly surveying the prospect through his spectacles while rebel bullets were scarring the ground at his feet and . . . singing about his ears."[21] The troops in motion were badly shaken by a volley from a Georgia regiment which sprang up among the cornstalks, but they could not stop to reply.

Ransom's battery and an enfilading fire from the First and Third brigades on either side held the gap long enough to permit the bor-rowed brigade, after it had eased the pressure on Ricketts, to return

[19] E. M. Woodward, *History of the Third Regiment of Pennsylvania Reserves*, 182–83; Stine, *The Army of the Potomac*, 191.
[20] Stine, *The Army of the Potomac*, 194; Meade's Report, *O.R.*, XIX, pt. 1, 269.
[21] Hill, *Our Boys*, 403.

and compel an enemy retreat. After another hour of fighting at close range, Seymour was compelled to shift ground. Although McClellan's forces quite outnumbered the enemy, on the right where troops were coming in from Harpers Ferry, numbers were equal or in favor of Lee. An untold number of casualties lay in the stalk-strewn cornfield and woods, where bullets thickened the air.

Individual scenes of that day of carnage were recalled by survivors. Among the Ninth Pennsylvania Regiment, three color bearers were killed or wounded before a fourth seized the flag and held it aloft until the unit was relieved. A brigadier general in full uniform—John Gibbon of Doubleday's First Brigade—served both as gunner and No. 3 man for several rounds among the cannoneers.

Men were cheering, laughing, or deadly quiet. To an Eighth Pennsylvania soldier, the "shock to the nerves was indefinable," as positions were shifted under close fire.[22] Not all could keep their heads in that fury of battle. "Get that man in rank," Meade called to a sergeant, pointing to a figure cowering behind a tree. When the sergeant could not get him to move, Meade dealt the skulker a blow with the flat of his saber and rode on. "I felt at the time the action was cruel and needless," an eyewitness recounted. "I changed my mind when I became an officer, with sword and pistol drawn to enforce discipline by keeping my men in place when going into the conflict."[23] Meade himself saw the straggling and shirking that day as "a serious and terrible evil," but one difficult to mend.[24] Participants believed the worst sight of all to be "the liberal supply of unwounded men helping wounded men to the rear."[25]

A spent grapeshot gave Meade a painful bruise on the thigh. The battle-scarred Baldy was hit in the neck and left for dead on the field as his master commandeered a cavalry horse.

Little could be seen of what the rest of the army was doing, but the action was disjointed as it was taken up by each corps in turn. On Hooker's left, General J. K. F. Mansfield's Twelfth Corps hurried to his assistance, and its gray-bearded leader—in uniform for forty years—was carried dying from the field. Next came the veteran E. V. Sumner

[22] Stine, *The Army of the Potomac*, 196; Augustus Buell, *The Cannoneer*, 34; Henry Steele Commager (ed.), *The Blue and the Gray*, I, 306.

[23] Commager (ed.), *The Blue and the Gray*, I, 306–307.

[24] *O.R.*, XIX, pt. 2, 348.

[25] F. W. Palfrey, *The Antietam and Fredericksburg Campaigns*, 82.

fighting Hill in the Confederate center, but the battle was late in start-ing farther on. It was still a punishing fight as the Twelfth Corps reached Hooker's division, now badly cut up. Riding a white horse, Hooker had just been warned of inviting danger when he received a severe wound in the foot. Ordering Meade to take over, he retired to receive medical care.[26]

Considering military propriety, Meade went to Ricketts, his senior in rank, encouraged his entering a protest, and actually turned the command over to him until two successive notes from McClellan set-tled the issue. By an order "given without regard to rank," Meade was definitely assigned to the First Corps command.[27]

Ammunition running low and his men nearly spent, Meade began to withdraw late in the forenoon to a ridge in the rear, re-formed his lines there, and replenished his supply of ammunition; but the corps was not called upon for further action that day.[28] The fight was taken up by General Alpheus S. Williams, succeeding Mansfield, then by General Sumner's Second Corps, but co-ordination was poor. Farther over, the Ninth Corps leader, General Ambrose Burnside, belatedly seized a bridge by which his men, who had been sent in piecemeal by divisions, could cross Antietam Creek instead of wading the stream. The time consumed was well employed by General A. P. Hill's di-vision, hurrying in from Harpers Ferry, and Burnside was stopped. Had McClellan's other two corps led by Franklin and Porter been thrown in, the thinned and exhausted enemy might have been routed, but first Sumner and then McClellan ordered the action halted. They had counted the cost while the battle was still going on, yet proportion-ate losses fell far short of those suffered by the opposing Army of Northern Virginia.[29]

[26] Andrews, *The North Reports the Civil War*, 278.

[27] *Meade*, I, 312–13. Originals of the McClellan notes timed at 1:25 and 3:10 P.M. are in Meade Papers.

[28] Meade's report, *O.R.*, XIX, pt. 1, 270.

[29] Military Historical Society of Massachusetts *Papers*, Vol. III, 69 (hereafter cited as MHSM *Papers*).

## 8. Leadership Weakens
## (September 18-December 13, 1862)

GENERAL LEE CLUNG to his position for another day. Actually the invasion was over. During the night of September 18, the Federal camp heard the clatter of enemy withdrawal across the Potomac. General Porter was sent in pursuit, but he was able to take only a few guns and prisoners before being turned back.

Meade felt no concern over McClellan's failure to pursue with his whole force. No Civil War commander, after any exhausting two-day battle, ever did pursue. The hard-won fight at Shiloh of the preceding April was a Federal precedent; on that occasion pursuit by the battered Unionists had not even been considered. Meade argued that the essential thing now was to get the army adequately supplied and then advance "with overwhelming numbers."[1] The long marches and the several battles fought in less than three weeks had left the army badly off for equipment of every kind.

Arriving for a visit, President Lincoln and his entourage rode over the near-by battlefields in company with a dozen generals, including Meade, whom McClellan praised openly for good work at South Mountain and Antietam.[2] Photographer Mathew B. Brady caught them all standing together, the President in his high silk hat towering over the six-foot Meade and Fitz-John Porter, among others, and the

---

[1] *Meade,* I, 311.

[2] *Ibid.,* 317. "General McClellan," Meade wrote, "pointed out to him [Lincoln] the various phases of the day, saying here it was that Meade did this and there Meade did that; which all was very gratifying to me." Meade would not have been gratified had he known of McClellan's letter of condolence to Hooker, dated September 20, 1862, in which occurs the following interesting passage: "Had you not been wounded when you were, I believe the result of the battle would have been the entire destruction of the Confederate army, for I know that with you at its head your corps would have kept on until it gained the main road."—Quoted in Stine, *The Army of the Potomac,* 194. This statement may be compared with stated reasons for Meade's withdrawal (lack of ammunition and exhaustion of troops).

short-statured "Little Mac." General Nathaniel P. Banks, commanding Washington's defenses, had come with Lincoln. Also prominent in the picture was General Reynolds, just back from Harrisburg and again in command of the First Corps. After only ten days in that coveted position, Meade was returned to the Third Division. It cannot be known what he said to his friend, but to Margaret he wrote, "Frankness compels me to say that I do wish Reynolds had stayed away."[3]

It was good, however, to report that Old Baldy, again wounded, had been found quietly grazing on the field the day after the battle. "Old Baldy is doing well and is good for lots of fights yet," the family was informed.[4]

Actual stragglers returned slowly. Because the First Corps, three days after the battle, appeared to number 12,000, whereas only 7,000 had responded to roll call on the night after the battle, Meade felt grave concern. After even more stragglers showed up, he made a special report to McClellan and gave vent privately to his feelings: "The difference of five thousand constituted the cowards, skulkers—men who leave the ground with the wounded and do not return for days, the stragglers on the march, and all such characters, which are to be found in every army but never in so great a ratio as in this volunteer force. . . . I believe all that saves us is the fact that they are no better off on the other side."[5] Lee's army of more than 50,000 had been weakened by about 25 per cent by much straggling and by fatalities and wounds.[6]

The first necessity, it had been pointed out, was to supply and equip McClellan's army, but Federal logistics were poor. Four weeks after Antietam, McClellan, who had been arguing with the War Office, probably heard Meade complain that, unable to obtain a shoe for either man or beast, he had paid for the shoeing of some 1,200 horses and mules out of his own pocket.[7] "It is the same thing with blankets, overcoats, etc., also with ammunition and forage," Meade charged. "Our artillery horses and train animals are literally starving . . . yet we can't get these things and I begin to believe it a part of a *policy* to *delay* us & thus charge McClellan with want of energy."[8]

[3] *Meade*, I, 315.
[4] *Ibid.*, 314.
[5] *Ibid.*, 318.
[6] Freeman, *R. E. Lee*, II, 411.
[7] Pennypacker, *Meade*, 92; *Meade*, I, 320.
[8] *Meade*, I, 320–21; MS letter of October 20, 1862, to Mrs. Meade, Meade Papers.

Some two hundred loaded freight cars were found on railroad sidings where they had lain for a week, but still more supplies were required. It would not be long before sarcastic shouts of "crackers and hardtack" would be directed by the soldiers at Meade, who indeed had vigorously protested.[9] But he had also laid down the law against pillaging, which the men believed to be their right.

The War Office offered the excuse that General Pope had suffered large and unexpected losses when his supply base was raided. McClellan then suffered in the same way when Stuart again rode around the Federal army to penetrate Pennsylvania. Public property, including some valuable stores, was burned at Chambersburg, and Stuart recrossed the Potomac without loss.[10]

While the Army of the Potomac stood idle near the village of Sharpsburg for more than a month, Meade worried also over the plight of his son George, who had failed to complete his second year at West Point. An excess of demerits coupled with an escapade by darkness had made him ineligible for final examinations. Since June 21, when he left the academy, George had remained more or less idle at home. He was still a minor, and so his mother had only to withhold her consent to his entering service until satisfied he had found the right place.

Meade had no room for an inexperienced man on his staff. Early in October he expressed regret that his wife did not accept, as he had suggested, an appointment for George in the veteran Third Pennsylvania Cavalry. This had been the first such volunteer regiment to take the field, and there were gaps to be filled.[11] "I think George has *waited* long enough," he again prompted Margaret. But since the somewhat high-toned Sixth Pennsylvania Cavalry, known as Rush's Lancers, needed more volunteers, a place was found where social standing, as well as other qualities, was a requirement.

The troop had taken its name from its nine-foot lances bearing scarlet, swallow-tailed pennants originally carried, but these implements had proved utterly useless in bushwhacking operations.[12] Happy to learn that George might yet become useful, Meade assured his wife in a jocular vein that he would have "a comparatively pleasant time"

[9] H. N. Warren, *Declaration of Independence and War History*, 125–26.

[10] *Meade*, I, 321.

[11] Meade to wife, October 5, 12, 1862, Meade Papers; F. H. Taylor, *Philadelphia In the Civil War*, 157–58.

[12] Taylor, *Philadelphia In the Civil War*, 162.

and be quite safe. "I will quote for your comfort," he added, "a part of a secesh lady's letter recently captured (i.e., the letter) in which she says: 'I want John . . . to go into the cavalry, because I see that very few of that arm of the service are either killed or wounded,' which is a fact; we have not lost over a dozen cavalry officers since the war began."[13] Nevertheless, the training was rigorous and duties often difficult once the Sixth Pennsylvania Cavalry was separated from a lazy life around headquarters and attached to an active command. Meade was pleased to see this done and to receive good reports of his son's progress under Federal cavalry leaders.

McClellan may have waited too long when, toward the end of October, the army took up the march. On the twenty-ninth, Meade's division crossed the Potomac on pontoons and camped at Leesburg; a few days later, after the army had paused at Warrenton, the startling news of McClellan's displacement was brought.

It was believed at Washington that McClellan was seldom prompt and that he had wasted much time, but there were also political implications in the move. The army leader had been friendly with backers of Horatio Seymour, an anti-administration candidate who on November 4 was elected governor of New York. This was interpreted as not only a Tammany Hall and Copperhead victory but also a rebuke to the Unionist candidate, General James Wadsworth, who campaigned only where bullets flew on the enemy front.

Lincoln waited no longer than he should have after receiving the news. Promptly on November 5 he signed an order relieving McClellan. Although there was reason enough to dismiss him, a question may be raised concerning the appointment of General Ambrose Burnside of Rhode Island to the command. Large of frame, good-natured, and breezy, Burnside, who had Abolitionist support, was acceptable chiefly on political grounds. His military record was good but hardly brilliant.[14] Fresh from West Point in 1847, he served briefly in the Mexican War, resigning then to enter business. He reappeared at First Bull Run as a brigade commander and was in line to receive a brigadier general's commission when honors were distributed in August, 1861. He won some prestige on a successful expedition to the North Carolina

[13] *Meade*, I, 325.
[14] Schaff, *Battle of the Wilderness*, 226; T. Harry Williams, *Lincoln and His Generals*, 180.

*Brady photograph*
*Courtesy Brown Brothers*

LINCOLN AT ANTIETAM, *Early October, 1862*

"I had the distinguished honor of accompanying Lincoln to the battle-field," Meade wrote his wife. Meade stands just behind the picturesque Lincoln, whom McClellan is facing. The heavily bearded Fitz-John Porter, Reynolds, and Humphreys are at Meade's left. General Nathaniel P. Banks (bareheaded) looks over McClellan's right shoulder.

GENERAL ROBERT E. LEE AT FREDERICKSBURG, *December 13, 1862*

"The day closed with the Federals listing some 12,650 casualties . . . Lee, however, had less than one-half the Federal loss." From a lithograph by Jones Brothers Publishing Company, 1900.

coast, where, against weak opposition, a chain of four outposts was captured. This success brought Burnside a volunteer major general's rank.

He experienced more of a test at Antietam, where he wasted several hours before delivering a blow. He had not shown good sense in stubbornly hammering away at a bridge in his front instead of deploying his men and wading the stream. Moreover, his standing among his fellows was not particularly high. General Burnside, one wrote in sorrow, is "a man of fine personal appearance, resonant general orders, windy proclamations, little military prestige, and, if possible, less sense. Such facts could not be concealed from men of such average intelligence and discernment as the army rank and file."[15] Had Lincoln gained a better personal acquaintance with Burnside, the chances are that he would not have been named. When notified, Burnside wept in distress, declaring himself unworthy,[16] and this in fact seemed to be the common opinion.

The President, however, had but a limited choice. General Sumner, a good fighter, tired quickly and was too old. Generals Porter and Franklin were known McClellan partisans, and the first-named was under a cloud for alleged disobedience to orders at Second Bull Run. Hooker, although anti-McClellan, was a junior in rank, and for this and other reasons was a second choice. The obviously competent Reynolds might have been considered had he not been absent at Glendale, Malvern Hill, South Mountain, and Antietam; but as a mere brigadier general of volunteers he was junior to all the other corps leaders. Meade had missed only Malvern Hill on July 1, but was still farther down the list.

Largely because the War Office had been tardy with supplies, Meade's ready sympathies had turned to McClellan, who in years past had been a Philadelphia neighbor, although he was not a personal friend as was Reynolds. On November 9, in company with Reynolds, Doubleday, and John Gibbon, the new Second Division commander, he visited army headquarters for a private farewell. Senior among the group, Reynolds expressed everyone's regrets as McClellan showed himself "very much affected, almost to tears."[17] Two days later, Meade witnessed "the sincere grief of the whole army," as he termed it, on the

[15] Buell, *The Cannoneer,* 45.
[16] *Meade,* I, 325.
[17] *Ibid.,* 326.

departure of Little Mac. He was, however, never wholeheartedly in his favor, as were Porter and Gibbon for example, and sentiment in his favor was modified with the passage of time. After a few weeks, Meade would agree with his wife that McClellan had his faults, although it would be difficult, he maintained, to ignore his capacity.[18] As more time passed, he outlined an indictment which struck closer home:

> We must encounter risks if we fight, and we cannot carry on war without fighting. . . . McClellan's vice . . . was always waiting to have everything just as he wanted before he would attack, and before he could get things arranged as he wanted them, the enemy pounced on him and thwarted all his plans. There is now no doubt that he allowed three distinct occasions to take Richmond slip through his hands for want of nerve to run what he considered risks. Such a general will never command success, though he may avoid disaster.[19]

To guide Burnside aright, General in Chief Halleck and Chief Quartermaster Montgomery C. Meigs visited Warrenton for war talks. Their joint recommendation was not brilliant. Meade was sharply critical when he learned they favored invasion down the Orange and Alexandria Railway, which was not only the longest route to the Confederate capital but also the farthest removed from coastal supply points. True logistics were being ignored. "The known capacity of the road is insufficient by one-third to carry the daily supplies required for this army," Meade argued. "The next line, and the one Burnside favors . . . is the one from Fredericksburg to Richmond. This is open to the same objection as the other except that it is [the shorter]."[20]

The war had been in progress for more than a year and a half, yet no one in authority seemed to have any idea what actually should be done. An "On-to-Richmond" campaign was going full blast in the newspapers as the army made a day's march to the old camp at Falmouth just opposite Fredericksburg. Discussing the bleak outlook with Reynolds, Meade began to doubt that there was any chance of arriving at Richmond that winter. "I predict, unless we have a cold spell, freezing the ground, that we will break down, lose all our animals, experi-

---

[18] *Ibid.*, 335.
[19] Meade to wife, January 2, 1863, *ibid.*, 345.
[20] Same to same, November 13, 1862, *ibid.*, 326.

ence great suffering from want of supplies, and if the enemy are at all energetic, meet with a check, if not disaster," he accurately forecast. Replying to what he termed "balderdash" in the public press, he outlined in a paragraph the essential strategy of the war—the course which ultimately would have to be followed.

All the present confusion, he told Margaret,

> comes from taking the wrong line of operations, the James River being the true and only practicable line of approach to Richmond. But I have always maintained that Richmond need not and should not be attacked at all; that the proper mode to reduce it is to take possession of the great lines of railroad leading to it from the South and Southwest, cut these and stop any supplies going there, and their army will be compelled to evacuate it and meet us on the ground we can select ourselves. The blind infatuation of the authorities at Washington, sustained, I regret to say, by Halleck, who as a soldier ought to know better, will not permit the proper course to be adopted, and we shall have to take the consequences.[21]

The same message to Lincoln would have brought no result. The great anchor was Washington, which felt imperiled unless it kept a large army somewhere near by. The military figures at the top—Generals Halleck and Burnside—were almost ridiculously incompetent, and either a defeat or a stalemate was indicated unless the habitually defensive attitude could be thrown off. But as long as the War Office held the reins (actually sixteen months longer), the Army of the Potomac would be so fettered as to be unable to perform its true mission.

The initial goal was now Fredericksburg, just across the Rappahannock (after that no one knew what), but instead of making all speed, Burnside declined to permit General Sumner, who was in the lead, to cross over. At that moment the initiative was lost. As the rest of the Federal army reached the north bank, General Lee, moving swiftly, occupied the town and began fortifying the heights in the rear. The opening of a supply route occupied Meade at Stafford Court House, just north of Falmouth, where he kept his men busy repairing the rail line and corduroying roads made almost impassable by wet weather. On November 22 his division moved farther up the railroad, but work was slowed by both snow and rain. The men found it difficult

---

[21] Same to same, November 22, 1862, *ibid.*, 330.

to build campfires, and even when they were started, so much dense smoke billowed out that few could get near enough to keep warm.[22]

Everyone began to feel a little better when steam trains began coming over the newly repaired railroad. Early in December, the men received a full supply of clothing, "liberal rations," and several weeks' back pay.[23] Meade was still hoping for favorable word regarding promotion, which on November 29 came to Reynolds, but notification of similar action in his case was simply delayed. Reynolds' promotion had been deserved, Meade bravely wrote Margaret while he still waited, but upon the arrival of his own volunteer major general's commission bearing the same date he could add, "I am truly glad, for your sake as well as my own."[24]

Otherwise, little would go right. Lee had seized all available boats, and so the army stood and waited for pontoons to span the river. Burnside probably could have built his own bridges, particularly since pontoon transport from Washington was delayed. When the floats were finally drawn up along the north bank, army engineers faced a punishing enemy fire. The town of Fredericksburg, in retaliation, was heavily shelled. Landing parties then made it a battle through barricaded streets and forced the withdrawal of enemy guns. Three pontoon bridges were then thrown over to connect with the town, and two were placed a mile downstream.

Some distance beyond and across a plain lay bristling Marye's Heights, which Burnside now proposed to storm, but without properly estimating his chances. There Lee's forces had been busily throwing up earthworks, and no time had been lacking for them to perfect their defenses. A naturally strong position was being made stormproof.

Army reorganization meanwhile brought the First Corps, Reynolds commanding, into the Left Grand Division under General Franklin, who would have more than half of Burnside's army of 125,000 at his disposal. The Sixth Corps under General William F. Smith, which had been practically untouched at Antietam, gave him a strong unit. Two Third Corps divisions and one of the Ninth plus Bayard's cavalry were temporarily assigned Franklin, who apparently was to carry the brunt of the battle across broken·and wooded country south of Fredericks-

[22] *History of the 121st Regiment of Pennsylvania Volunteers*, 27.
[23] Woodward, *Our Campaigns*, 227.
[24] *Meade*, I, 336.

BATTLE OF FREDERICKSBURG, DECEMBER 13, 1862

burg. Here a distant range of hills, somewhat lower than Marye's Heights, was to be penetrated.

Burnside planned to march the rest of the army through the town toward the heights—Hooker with the Fifth Corps and the rest of the Third in the Center Grand Division, and Sumner with the Second and two Ninth Corps divisions on the right. Starting around 4:00 P.M. on December 11, Smith's Sixth Corps was already over the river when an order was transmitted to bring back all but one brigade. The excuse given was that more work had to be done on the bridges upstream to make them safe for artillery.[25]

Any chance of catching Lee unawares was surely gone. The day of December 12 was largely consumed in the crossing. A confused outlook was reflected in orders to Franklin. Move up, "a division at least," he was told, "to seize if possible the heights near Captain Hamilton's . . . taking care to keep it well supported and its line of retreat open."[26] It was left to Franklin to decide what forces should be used in support and just how far they should go. In a detached movement of this kind, he would have to decide correctly.

Regimental bands were playing early on December 13 as Meade formed his line of less than 5,000 men opposite the woods and slopes downriver. On his right was Gibbon's division, on his left Doubleday, and Smith's Sixth Corps was near by. An open plain above the slopes was held by General D. H. Hill's division of Jackson's corps, but no enemy troops could be seen.

The morning fog was lifting. As Meade's well-drilled veterans moved up, the slanting rays of the sun glinted from polished rifle barrels of troops marching in fine precision. Regimental flags were whipped by the breeze; mounted officers rode stiffly with sabers drawn. "General Meade was possibly the best general in the Army . . . that day and he had some of the best soldiers," opined a Fifth Corps veteran.[27]

Enemy gunners drew first blood on Meade's left. The battery of Major John Pelham daringly remained in the Federal front until silenced by a maneuver as Meade began to shell the woods. For nearly an hour the infantry remained in position while Meade's guns blazed,

[25] *Battles and Leaders*, III, 131.

[26] *O.R.*, XXI, 448–49, contains the text of Burnside's order. See also John G. Nicolay and John Hay, *Abraham Lincoln*, VI, 203–204; Palfrey, *The Antietam and Fredericksburg Campaigns*, 177–79.

[27] J. R. Orwig, *History of the 131st Pennsylvania Infantry*, 108.

although enemy artillery withheld its fire. When the division was sent to take a wooded ridge just ahead, fourteen guns hidden there split the Federal line. Ranks were closed as the men kept on. (From his position atop the height, Stonewall Jackson admired the formation retained under such heavy fire.)[28] Then a second crashing volley brought Meade to a halt. Withdrawing his men beyond range, he began again with his own guns. As soon as enemy emplacements were cleaned out, up raced the infantry to gain distance.

Pounding over several hundred yards of cleared ground, Colonel William Sinclair's First Brigade gained a strip of woods and, passing through, was surprised to find it had penetrated the enemy line. A Confederate brigadier general was fatally wounded. Prisoners were taken among unready troops who had not even collected their arms. On both right and left, Meade struck at two other brigades, sending back some three hundred prisoners altogether, plus enemy colors. Himself under fire, he found his field hat ruined by two bullets and probably saved his own life by smashing the flat of his saber against the shoulder of a battle-crazed soldier. Ordered to move on, the man had merely pointed his gun at his commander. Meade must have hit hard—the sword blade was snapped off near the hilt.[29]

But now his ranks had been torn, and there were gaps among officers. General C. Feger Jackson, Third Brigade, had fallen early in the battle, and Sinclair of the First had been wounded. Instead of spurring on Doubleday and Gibbon, Reynolds seemed to be giving too much effort to the task of helping Meade keep the foremost division together. Meanwhile Doubleday had halted to give battle with artillery, his favorite weapon, while Gibbon on the right rear had lost contact during intermittent fighting along the jagged and uncertain line.

Three Confederate brigades raced up to support Hill; Federals still pushing on found a strong line drawn up to receive them. For about twenty minutes Meade alone clung to the heights, but he could not remain there without prompt reinforcement. Twice he sent riders to a supporting division for help, appealing to General David B. Birney, Third Corps, who had temporarily been placed under Reynolds.[30]

[28] Stine, *The Army of the Potomac*, 278.

[29] Pennypacker, *Meade*, 103; exhibit of Meade swords, Military Order of the Loyal Legion of the U.S., Philadelphia.

[30] *O.R.*, XXI, 362.

When, because the order had not been received from a higher authority, Birney did not move up, Meade galloped back and displayed his battlefield temper. "General," he exclaimed heatedly, "I assume the authority of ordering you to the relief of my men." Still more seems to have been said, although the words are not of record.[31]

Birney was thus persuaded to release two brigades, one in support of retreating batteries, but it was too late to help the infantry on the heights. As Meade and Reynolds rode about trying to rally the men, regiments and then entire brigades gave way under close enemy fire. Now it had become a matter of guiding the retreat, a most difficult maneuver under such conditions. Ragged withdrawal into the valley contrasted with the handsome advance. To Reynolds, Meade cried in exasperation, "Did they think my division could whip Lee's whole army?" And gesturing toward his thinned ranks, he exclaimed, "There is all that is left of my Reserves."[32]

He lost little time in going to Franklin to complain. It was obvious that staff work had been lax and that too little was known of what was happening up front. That Meade had been poorly supported "was then [made] known to me for the first time," Franklin later remarked.[33] All along the Federal line it had been a bad day as repeated assaults against Marye's Heights were thrown back with severe losses. Success on the left, however, had been within easy grasp. "I do not recollect of ever feeling so discouraged," said a soldier under Meade, "over the result of anything we ever undertook to do."[34]

Cooling off a trifle, Meade blamed Burnside for not being more specific in his orders to Franklin and not impressing him with the importance, as he himself saw it, of the attack on the left, where the bulk of army strength lay. "I . . . told Gen¹ Burnside . . . the first time I saw him after the battle that I did not think you were impressed," he notified Franklin,[35] but neither leader had shown much sense. Had he only been properly supported, Meade contended, the enemy line would have been badly broken, forcing abandonment of the fortified works on the right. With so much resource at his command, General Franklin

[31] Pennypacker, *Meade*, 102–103; Thomson and Rauch, *History of the Bucktails*, 235.

[32] Thomson and Rauch, *History of the Bucktails*, 236.

[33] Franklin to Meade, March 25, 1863, Meade Letterbook, Meade Papers.

[34] Warren, *Declaration of Independence and War History*, 26.

[35] Meade to Franklin, March 28, 1863, Meade Letterbook, Meade Papers.

should have seen to it. "A great captain," thought Meade, "would have . . . assumed responsibility."[36]

The day closed with the Federals listing some 12,650 casualties or about 200 more than at Antietam. Had the enemy suffered in like proportion, then December 11, 1862, rather than the second day at Antietam would have been the bloodiest day of the war. Lee, however, had less than one-half the Federal loss. Of Meade's little command of fewer than 5,000, about 1,400 were killed or wounded and some 400 were missing—altogether more than one man in three. This would be his most serious loss in proportion to the numbers engaged, and the effort had been a sheer waste.

[36] *Meade,* I, 362; Meade testimony, *Report of Joint Committee on the Conduct of the War,* I, 691.

# 9. "God Have Pity on Our Army!"
## (December 14, 1862-May 7, 1863)

MEADE MOURNED THE loss of an aide, Lieutenant Arthur Dehon, who fell early in the action while hurrying a message to the Third Brigade. At Frayser's Farm, Aide Hamilton Kuhn had been killed; now two young men had gone, each "so full of life and promising so much."[1] Meade had escaped not only the bullets that perforated his hat but also a ball that passed through the neck of a cavalry horse he was riding.[2] Although relieved because neither Baldy nor Blacky was hurt, he shared the general feeling of dejection as the beaten army recrossed the river on December 14, a cold and damp day. Enemy shot and shell sped the departure from the Rappahannock's south bank.

Newspaper accounts of the exploits of the Pennsylvania Reserves made them heroes in Philadelphia, but Meade could not rest until another tale was set right. During the artillery battle, a *New York Herald* correspondent, catching sight of some stragglers and wounded, reported that the Reserves had fled at the first fire. When the *Herald* reached camp, feeling among the troops ran so high that tar and feathers at the very least would have been applied, Meade acknowledged, had the correspondent again shown himself.[3] A *New York Tribune* man who called at headquarters for a list of the dead and wounded received an accurate account, which was printed, and the *Philadelphia Inquirer* sharply attacked the *Herald* for "enormous and malignant lying." The loyal *Inquirer* presumed it to be quite generally known that Meade's division had been the only one to capture an enemy position, "and if it had been properly reinforced it could have held it."[4]

Son George, whose cavalry regiment had been posted on the left,

[1] *Meade*, I, 365.
[2] *Ibid.*, 338.
[3] *Ibid.*, 339.
[4] *Philadelphia Inquirer*, December 25, 1862.

could inform his mother that everyone was speaking of the General in the highest terms. He heard one of Franklin's aides say, "Meade went in and by God he went in like a gentleman. There was not a braver or cooler man on the field."[5] Yes, Meade had been the lion, but between Franklin and Burnside there would be some explaining to do.

For the time being, Meade expected, the army would have to remain where it was. With winter at hand, it was no time to attempt a hard military campaign. He put in a request for leave to spend the holidays at home, but he decided not to press the matter when Burnside hinted that he would be given the Fifth Corps to command. Going to the War Office with complaints against Franklin and others but with praise for Meade, Burnside was able to obtain the consent of Secretary of War Edwin M. Stanton.

It was a rather odd turn of events. Dated December 23, 1862, the appointment to the Fifth Corps meant the displacing of General Dan Butterfield, a volunteer officer junior to Meade but one with enough political influence to have succeeded Fitz-John Porter as head of the Fifth. An American Express Company official in New York in civil life, Butterfield was receiving his full salary from the firm, so that army service represented no financial sacrifice, and he was known as a good host. After bringing forward a volunteer regiment, he had speedily risen from militia captain to major general of volunteers, thus overtaking several competent and highly regarded regulars, including his three division commanders.

Outstanding among the trio was General Andrew Atkinson Humphreys of Pennsylvania, who had been graduated from West Point the year Meade went in. Of unquestioned ability, Humphreys had been retarded in advancement by staff work as McClellan's chief engineer during the Peninsula Campaign, and he was associated, therefore, with the displaced army leader. Placed in command of a division, "he behaved with distinguished gallantry at Fredericksburg," in Meade's expressed opinion. After the battle, Meade went on to explain, Burnside had told Humphreys that both President Lincoln and Stanton had given assurance that he would be immediately promoted. "He now finds a long list sent to the Senate while his name is omitted, and he cannot hear that there is any record . . . to show he has ever been thought of," Meade commented sympathetically.[6]

[5] George Meade to mother, December 21, 1862, Meade Papers.
[6] *Meade*, I, 352.

The other division commanders were honest and reliable George Sykes, who had been graduated from West Point in 1842 along with Abner Doubleday, James Longstreet, and Daniel H. Hill, and the younger Charles Griffin, whose wedding Meade had attended in Washington. Griffin had done well in respect to rank thus far, advancing from captain to brigadier general, but some officers believed that prejudice existed against the Fifth Corps regulars because the unit had been a favorite with McClellan, who had praised it in general orders, and it had been commanded by Porter, who also was on the wrong side of the political fence. Promotions therefore were retarded "unless secured by political influence."[7] Hooker, to whose Center Grand Division the Fifth Corps belonged, had asked meanwhile that Butterfield be retained, but although the New Yorker was always his good friend, he was no favorite with Secretary Stanton or with most of the regulars. General Humphreys aside, the weight of demonstrated ability was obviously in Meade's favor. The shift in command was made without fanfare.

Butterfield himself felt rather let down. At a farewell dinner given on Christmas Day, he played host to Fifth Corps brigade and division commanders. Meade, who was taking over that day, was also present, and he lingered to smoke a cigar after the others had gone. In a position to sympathize, Meade remarked kindly that had he been displaced in the same way, he would have had reason to complain. This at once set off Butterfield, who began railing against Burnside. The army commander, he said, had assured him *"positively and distinctly"* that the Fifth Corps would be permanently his. That certainly aggravated the matter, Meade responded politely, but his true feeling was that Butterfield's misfortune had "resulted from the injustice that was done me when he was first assigned."[8]

Burnside may have been aiming a blow at Hooker in displacing the latter's friend Butterfield, for the two were never on good terms. But the upshot was that Meade had made his first real enemy in Butterfield, who would prove unrelenting.

The wounded spirits of the Pennsylvania Reserves did not easily mend. After the battle they were largely engrossed with refitting and with the selection of new officers as a few gaps were filled. Meade's

[7] Joshua L. Chamberlain, *The Passing of the Armies, xiii, xiv.*
[8] *Meade*, I, 342.

departure to assume his new command went almost unnoticed, but after several more days had passed, he received a letter from one with the rank of a private which pleased him. A staff teamster who had witnessed his day-to-day conduct while in command had a few personal words which he otherwise had no opportunity to convey. Private Levi Richards wrote:

> To relieve my mind of things that i wish to make known to you, i will take this opportunity. As i am a Private Soilder in the P. R. and as one soilder will express himself more readily than to an Officer i think i can tell you the feeling of this Division towards you. Since the battle for the Peninsula I have never heard but two men that had anything to say against you and one of them was an officer. They all as a Division loved you as a commander. They all appeared glad to hear of your Promotion but parted with you with Regret. . . . They all told the same tale and that was officers and men were used alike.
>
> And as for myself i consider you have used me as [would] a father . . . although strict yet no more so than i think it requires to make good soilders and i am satisfied if a man does his duty with you it is all that is required and as i have been with you for almost one year to my knowledge you have never given me a cross word or misused me in any way it was with regret that i left you and your staff. This is not written for any benefit that i wish to gain only that i wish you to know the feelings of the Reserves as far as i know and also the feelings of myself towards you.[9]

*"They all as a Division loved you as a commander."* Meade sent the letter home for Margaret to place among his cherished mementoes. On the next payday, the Reserves took up a collection to buy him a fine sword, sash, and belt, and "a grand jollification" was planned to be held at Willard's Hotel in Washington, but pressing events would cause the affair to be postponed several times.[10]

Most of the officers had received a few days' leave during the holidays. After nearly everyone was back, Meade hurried home for a visit limited to a single day, January 11, 1863, and then was summoned to appear before a military court in Washington which was trying Fitz-John Porter for failure at Second Bull Run. It was a case in which politics and the military record were so confused as to make a judicious

---

[9] Levi Richards to Meade, January 8, 1863, Meade Papers.
[10] *Philadelphia Inquirer*, April 4, 1863; *Meade*, I, 361, 363.

finding difficult. Marching from below Washington, Porter, on August 29, 1862, was ordered to come up on the Federal left and support McDowell. Meade testified that the Pennsylvania Reserves had looked to him for relief that day and that there had been room for him on their flank had he moved promptly. Porter, a McClellan supporter, was in bad odor with the War Office and with powerful Abolitionist forces. The trial, therefore, became something of a witch hunt. Though it was Meade's belief that Porter's failure stemmed from "want of judgement & capacity added to an indifference whether success or disaster followed,"[11] he was cashiered on the ground of disloyalty. Not forgetting that Porter had marched blindly into enemy pickets and endangered the army on the night of June 29, 1862, Meade considered him simply a bad general. Long after the war Porter was cleared on the ground that Longstreet had come up to stand in his way, but had he displayed enterprise and a willingness to fight, his corps surely would have been serviceable.

Reaching camp during early morning on January 13, Meade was complimented by General Burnside at dinner that evening as being possibly the only officer who had not overstayed his leave.[12] He heard Burnside make certain vague remarks which apparently hinted at another offensive, and on the surface a move appeared feasible, since the weather had been cold but pleasant and the roads were frozen hard. Even Meade began to believe that to march in any direction was better than remaining idle in camp, and he was hopeful of success provided the attack was made "in heavy force, well supported."[13] In riding out

[11] Meade to Mrs. Meade, January 26, 1863, Meade Papers. Porter "certainly should have attacked on the 29th," Meade wrote. "He was twice ordered by Pope to do so, and once directed by McDowell. He shows no good reason for not doing so, and acknowledges he *fell back* instead of advancing—with my knowledge of the circumstances for we [the Reserves] were on the left that day, and were anxiously looking for him & the relief which his attack would bring, I can not shut my eyes to the fact that he was guilty of disobedience of orders in the presence of the enemy, and that he deserves the sentence." Through skillful defense, Porter in 1879 was exonerated.

[12] *Meade*, I, 346–47. His aide, Lieutenant Alexander Coxe, Meade wrote Margaret in giving further detail concerning his Washington visit, "was greatly delighted with the number of inquiries as to who I was, and the very general knowledge of my name, but not of my person. He overheard two gentlemen talking, one of whom said, 'What major general is that,' to which the other replied, 'Meade.' 'Who is he,' said the first, 'I never saw him before.' 'No, that is very likely, for he is one of our fighting generals, is always on the field, and does not spend his time in Washington hotels.' "

[13] *Ibid.*, 347.

to examine suitable fording places along the upper Rappahannock, he caught sight of a Federal pontoon train moving up the river. His expectation was correct—Burnside apparently planned a flank attack on the enemy left.

Actual preparations took nearly a week. On January 20, a bright, clear day, the army started up the north bank of the Rappahannock. The outlook had been fair, but toward evening the sky clouded; then a drizzle set in, turning into a wind-driven wintry rain. Next day the continuing storm turned the roads into quagmire one to three feet deep which engulfed wagons, artillery, horses, mules, and sometimes an unfortunate soldier. Men, though not all the mules, were dragged out, but it had become impossible to move. Meade saw an end to the winter campaign then and there.[14]

Burnside, however, had no sense of timing and never knew when to stop. The vain effort was pursued on January 22 as more rain fell. Under such sodden conditions, cheerful campfires were unavailable to the shivering troops. Many became sickly and all went hungry as provision trains became engulfed in the rear. Since it was obvious that any farther advance was impossible, Meade forehandedly ordered his troops to cut heavy logs and corduroy the road back.[15] No objections were raised, and early on the twenty-third, Burnside belatedly issued the recall.

Confederate troops seen on the opposite bank were shouting derisive remarks at the sight of clay-covered wagons, mules, and men. It took two laborious days to struggle back to the old camp near Falmouth. Meade had raised no objections to the march, which had begun under auspicious conditions, but as he had predicted in November, the army, by taking the wrong line of operations, had experienced great suffering and met with disaster. Again the outlook was drear. "I never knew so much discontent in the army before," avowed a survivor of the Mud March, which had taken not a few lives.[16] Meade still could sympathize with the army leader from whom he had received his corps command. "I told him warmly . . . how sorry I felt, and that I almost rather had lost a limb than the storm should have occurred," he wrote Margaret.[17]

[14] *Ibid.*, 348.
[15] Bruce Catton, *Glory Road*, 104–105.
[16] D. G. Crotty, *Four Years Campaigning in the Army of the Potomac*, 80.
[17] *Meade*, I, 348–49.

Burnside showed his gratitude by elevating him to the command of the Center Grand Division. This gave Meade the Fifth Corps of Sykes and the Third of General Daniel Sickles.

Any small success might have saved Burnside, but his only hope now was that the resignation he sent in would be accepted. Lincoln had no choice except to select another. Together with Secretary Stanton and General in Chief Halleck, he again went down the list. Of the two senior commanders of Grand Divisions at Fredericksburg, Franklin had been forced into the role of scapegoat for the defeat and the aging Sumner had seen his last campaign. Next came General Hooker, who had an impressive physique, a good fighting record, and a magnetic influence among men. A favorite of Treasury Secretary Salmon P. Chase, he was acceptable to the Abolitionist forces, as indeed was General Burnside, who despite failure was still politically strong. Hooker had not hesitated to criticize both Burnside and Franklin. No one who really knew Hooker ever expected him to have a good word for anyone standing above him.[18]

Stanton and Halleck raised certain objections to Hooker, as the report was phrased, but they doubtless had in mind his convivial habits.[19] Hooker was seldom fortunate in his boon companions. One of the closest was General Sickles, a volunteer officer selected from the political ranks. A Tammany lawyer and Democratic member of Congress, Sickles had figured in a lurid Washington scandal, slaying his wife's lover. A plea of temporary insanity was entered, and with Edwin M. Stanton among the defense counsel, he escaped the legal penalty and continued in Congress. The war gave him a chance to restore his name; in 1861 he made a place for himself by raising some volunteer troops.

Choice food and drink were dispensed at Sickles's headquarters, and flouncy lady visitors were not unknown. At a New Year's Day party, related an onlooker, "the collation . . . was abundant and choice, the champagne and whiskey ran in streams."[20] After Dan Butterfield had been made chief of staff, it was remarked that the two Dans and Hooker were running "a combination of barroom and brothel," that headquarters "was a place to which no self-respecting man liked to go

[18] "Hooker was not subordinate to his superiors."—Ulysses S. Grant, *Personal Memoirs*, II, 539.

[19] *Battles and Leaders*, III, 239.

[20] Régis de Trobriand, *Four Years with the Army of the Potomac*, 398.

and no decent woman would go."[21] Meade upheld Hooker as a good soldier, although conceding that the influence of such men as Butterfield and Sickles might be harmful in time.[22]

In making his choice, Lincoln would make no move that would tend to split his own political forces if he could help it, nor would he gamble on anyone thought to be as independent as McClellan. One report has it that he asked Halleck to talk with Reynolds, who already had a mark against him for being a McClellan adherent, as it appeared. Reynolds may have eliminated himself by indicating that he would have to be permitted freedom of action. While there is some doubt that any such conversation took place at the time, this was still Reynolds' view.[23]

Looking farther afield, President Lincoln inquired about others, including Meade, who was favored over Hooker by both Stanton and Halleck but who had little backing elsewhere. Hooker was not only the favorite of Treasury Secretary Chase but was supported by the powerful Joint House-Senate Committee on the Conduct of the War. But it was with lingering doubts and misgivings that Lincoln signed Hooker's appointment on January 26.

Since Hooker, too, had been saying that he would not accept unless "perfectly untrammeled,"[24] Lincoln permitted him to by-pass the War Office and communicate directly with him. It was realized that Hooker and Halleck had never been on good terms. "What I now ask of you is military success,"[25] the President wrote his new leader, who appeared supremely confident that he would deliver it.

Meade commented fluently on personalities and events. Burnside, he said, lacked knowledge and judgment, and he believed that Hooker would be at least an improvement. Yet no Army of the Potomac leader should ever be envied. He could not see that Hooker or anyone else named to the post would last very long. One of Hooker's first moves was to eliminate the Grand Divisions, and after Meade returned to the Fifth Corps, he declared that he looked no farther than his present command, "as it is one of the best, including as it does the regulars."[26]

---

[21] Charles Francis Adams, *Autobiography* (Boston and New York, 1916), 161.

[22] *Meade*, I, 351.

[23] *Battles and Leaders*, III, 240; Nichols, *Toward Gettysburg*, 222.

[24] *Meade*, I, 351.

[25] Lincoln to Hooker, January 26, 1863; *Complete Works of Abraham Lincoln* (ed. by Nicolay and Hay), VIII, 206–207.

[26] *Meade*, I, 352.

Sykes's division had two United States infantry brigades, and there was a regular army regiment in Griffin's. Meade would be content with the Fifth Corps.

Hooker's energy was never in question as he set to work to rebuild a dispirited army. With Dan Butterfield, an able business executive, lending his aid as chief of staff, more contractors were hired, and soon ample supplies were coming through promptly on improved roads. The cavalry arm was built up as a strong fighting unit under General George Stoneman, and badges worn on the cap for each army corps were adopted—a popular plan. The infantry began to look up to Fighting Joe as their leader. There was no question but that the jaunty soldier impressed the troops as a man who knew what he was doing. As March waned, the healthy military body flexed its toughened muscles in the bracing spring air. With their new corps flags and emblems and with spirits high, the men paraded magnificently as President Lincoln, appearing grave and careworn, reviewed the army early in April.

"Look out for Fighting Joe's army and for the grand reaction in our favor," Meade notified his wife. "Joe says we are to do great things when we start." Meade shared his leader's good cheer and appeared influenced in his favor. Questioning the charge of drunkenness brought against Hooker, he pronounced him "very sanguine of success"[27] and avoided speculation on possible failure.

Lincoln, however, seemed aware of cause for concern. Hooker, like McClellan, was at his best on the paradeground. He had the same "easy confidence and nonchalance," resembled Pope in being too sure of himself, and talked more loudly than anyone else of taking Richmond. Noah Brooks, a newspaper correspondent close to the President, remarked that Hooker "seemed to regard the whole business of command as if it were a large sort of picnic."[28] For some of his associates at least that was actually it.

By late April, the army was quite ready for its spring offensive. It was apparent that the enemy would not move first. Lee had sent Longstreet with two divisions to support the coastal defenses of southern Virginia and North Carolina. This left him with Jackson's corps of four divisions plus two of Longstreet's command, or possibly 60,000 avail-

[27] *Ibid.*, 365–66.
[28] Noah Brooks, *Washington in Lincoln's Time*, 52; A. M. Stewart, *Camp, March, and Battle-Field*, 307, describes the army on parade.

ables, including cavalry and artillery against a massive 135,000 under Fighting Joe. It was known that Hooker had mapped out a grand movement, but he confided his plans to only a few. As Meade finally grasped the details, the initial phases at least were to be the same as the campaign attempted by Burnside. Most of the army was "to make a forced march, cross the Rappahannock so high as to preclude opposition, cross the Rapidan [a southern branch] at the lower fords, drive away the defenders . . . at the crossings . . . nearest to Fredericksburg, and when one of these was opened, the rest of the army was to join the advanced corps, be concentrated, and push the enemy away from Fredericksburg."[29] In other words, Hooker would march up the river and, once across it and its lower tributary, would then turn back to unite with the corps of Sedgwick and Reynolds as they advanced in turn below the river. The combined movement was confidently expected to sweep away enemy defenses both south and west of Fredericksburg.

Thus the campaign envisioned field battles of some kind, but there was no plan to be resorted to in the event that it failed. The war was still in an elementary phase of military maneuver. One or two small details may be criticized. Hooker's first move was to send most of his cavalry on a roundabout route to raid the enemy's main supply depot and cut his rail line, a tactic which he counted on to distract General Lee. That leader, however, held back nearly all his cavalry while General Stoneman and the Federal horse did only scattered damage and remained too long out of touch with the main force.[30] Again, Hooker restricted his gifted artillery chief, General Henry J. Hunt, to administrative duties at headquarters. With Hunt confined to purely routine tasks, his field abilities were lost to the army, and the artillery would not be so well served as in earlier battles.[31]

Orders were distributed during the last week end in April. At 2:00 A.M. on the morning of Monday, the twenty-seventh, Meade arose and hurriedly dressed. Getting astride Old Baldy, he led the Fifth Corps in advance, followed by the Eleventh and Twelfth later that day. The Third under Sickles and the Second under General Darius N. Couch completed that army wing detached from Falmouth. Two days out,

[29] *Meade*, I, 370.

[30] Freeman, *Lee's Lieutenants*, II, 639.

[31] *Battles and Leaders*, III, 259. The transfer of the artillery command to headquarters "resulted in . . . mismanagement and confusion at Chancellorsville."—General Henry J. Hunt.

Meade's troops quickly crossed the Rappahannock on pontoons, which were then left behind. The Rapidan was found swollen from the spring rains and the current was dangerously strong, but Ely's Ford a few miles up from the juncture had to be waded.

The men piled their extra ammunition, haversacks, knapsacks, and cartridge boxes on top of their heads, pressed the load down with the rifle grasped in both hands, then strode through the chilly waters waist-deep or even deeper. To rescue those overborne in the treacherous footing, cavalry riders on the bigger and stronger horses took positions downstream.

The men were in a cheerful mood despite hardships. As General Meade appeared at the ford, they rose to their feet and began cheering. Scarcely checking the speed of his horse, he stood almost erect in the stirrups, doffed his forage cap, and passed through the lines bareheaded, but made no other outward sign. Although he later remarked that he would never forget that warm demonstration, he would not wave his cap in response or seek to whip up personal feeling. Not until the last day of the war would he wave his cap.

Once across the Rapidan, Meade stood on the far bank and watched the infantry splash through. It could be seen that soldiers in wet clothing would be cold as they tried to sleep that night; a brigade commander standing near by broached the subject of campfires. Rejoining that it was supposed to be a secret movement, Meade glanced at the men, then softly remarked, "Well, we must have no big fires." His long nose sniffed the air as if to test the temperature. "I don't see," he mused as if to himself, "how we are to avoid them."[32] So orders were given to make the fires low, but nothing was said when they were built up to radiate enough warmth for the men to dry their clothes and sleep well. By early morning everyone was "ready and eager for any movement."[33]

Noisy enthusiasm greeted a report that the enemy had quit his position behind Fredericksburg. A courier hurried to Humphreys, leading Meade's Third Division, which was farthest back. "Push forward with all speed," Humphreys was urged.[34] Griffin's division was the first to

[32] Anecdotes of the river crossing related in the *Philadelphia Press*, November 12, 1872.

[33] *Antietam to Appomattox: The History of the Corn Exchange Regiment* (118th Pennsylvania Volunteers), 169.

[34] *O.R.*, LI, pt. 1, 1017.

arrive at a wilderness clearing occupied by a large white mansion. This alone with its several outbuildings was known as Chancellorsville.

As Griffin came up at 11:00 A.M. on April 30 an enemy brigade on patrol fired a parting volley and fell back on the Fredericksburg Turnpike. Four Secessionist ladies sitting on the upper porch freely offered advice, urging the troops to keep moving.[35] This Meade was quite anxious to do. The wooded and brush-strewn country extending for miles back of the Rapidan—the great Wilderness—was surely no place to fight a battle. To carry out Hooker's involved plan, he must complete the end run by turning toward the nearest river crossings on the left, eliminating opposition and pushing hard toward Fredericksburg. His task was to send out patrols, determine where the enemy might be, and then drive ahead, taking care to occupy suitable high ground along the turnpike.

By early afternoon Sykes's division was well up and Humphreys' was not far behind it. The other two corps then on the way were certainly within striking distance. If the troops kept on moving and lost no time, the way was open to roll up Lee's flank. Reynolds and Sedgwick would be pushing from the other direction.

Meade sent two cavalry patrols to scout the roads leading to the river while Griffin took an infantry brigade along the turnpike. Within the hour Sykes and Humphreys came up, and about midafternoon, Slocum, with the Twelfth Corps. The army appeared poised for a decisive stroke. Meade could scarcely contain himself: "This is splendid, Slocum," he called out, "Hurrah for Old Joe."[36] Obviously anxious that the march be pursued, he urged that Slocum take one road and he the other.

A self-contained and unemotional officer never known to exceed his orders, Slocum announced that he had other instructions. He had been told, he informed Meade, to assume command of the three leading corps and make no advance until the columns were concentrated. Meade began to ask why they should wait. "We ought to get into the open country beyond."[37] Slocum could only refer him to Hooker's orders timed at 2:15 P.M. that day. There was to be no advance beyond Chan-

---

[35] John Bigelow, *The Campaign of Chancellorsville*, 216.

[36] Bache, *Meade*, 260.

[37] MHSM *Papers*, Vol. III, 228; James Biddle to Alexander A. Webb, December 10, 1885, Webb Papers, Yale University.

cellorsville until General Howard, Eleventh Corps, Sickles with the Third, and Couch's Second Corps also were up.

It seemed as if Hooker was interfering too much. The delay might be long. Meade felt deeply chagrined; now he had no choice but to recall Griffin. Penetrating the wooded country east of Chancellorsville, Griffin had encountered some enemy pickets and what appeared to be a superior force. Just ahead, however, lay high ground which he was anxious to occupy. Unaware that Hooker's military machine had ground to a halt, he sent back for reinforcements to take the ridge and hold it. Up came an aide with a detachment from Meade bearing positive orders not to bring on an engagement but to withdraw. Ordinarily bellicose and a hard-talking critic of whatever resembled dead wood at the top, Griffin swore mightily, but to no avail. Major James C. Biddle, the aide who brought Meade's orders, recalled Griffin's attitude of disgust: "Call that a position!"[38]

Between five and six o'clock, General Hooker arrived to broadcast a general order complimenting the three corps in advance on a "succession of splendid achievements." The army was not yet in position and the real work was still ahead, but Hooker was saying, "Our enemy must either ingloriously fly or come out from behind his intrenchments and give us battle on our own ground where certain destruction awaits him."[39] Soldiers cheered and tossed their hats in the air as the order was read, but there were a few who watched the noisy demonstration in silence. They still could recall General John Pope, whose windy pronouncements far exceeded the work actually done. The talk among Meade's own veterans was that "someone had again blundered."[40]

Hooker's flourishes merely gave Lee time to hurry troops over to occupy the high ground denied Meade and Griffin. Dictating other inspirational messages, Hooker counterattacked: "The rebel army is now the legitimate property of the Army of the Potomac. . . . God Almighty could not prevent [my] destroying the rebel army." The more talk, the more uneasiness spread.[41] Corps and division commanders began to wear an anxious look. General Couch, a clear thinker, held that no sane general could talk so.[42] The army was concentrating on

[38] MHSM *Papers*, Vol. III, 157, 229.
[39] *O.R.*, XXV, pt. 1, 171.
[40] *Antietam to Appomattox*, 236–37.
[41] Bigelow, *Chancellorsville*, 236–37.
[42] *Dictionary of American Biography* (New York, 1928–36), IV, 463.

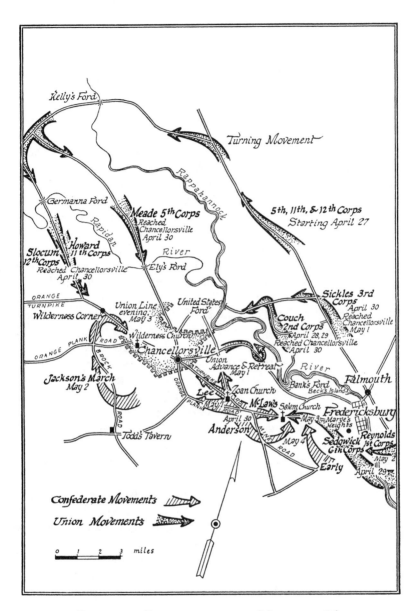

Kelly's Ford

Turning Movement

Rappahannock

Germanna Ford

Rapidan

Meade 5th Corps
Reached
Chancellorsville
April 30

5th, 11th, & 12th Corps
Starting April 27

Howard
11th Corps

Slocum
12th Corps
Reached Chancellorsville
April 30

River

Ely's Ford

ORANGE
TURNPIKE

Wilderness Corner

ORANGE PLANK ROAD

B ROCK ROAD

Union Line
evening,
May 3

Wilderness Church

Chancellorsville

United States
Ford

Sickles 3rd
Corps
April 30
Reached
Chancellorsville
May 1

Couch
2nd Corps
April 28, 29
Reached Chancellorsville
April 30

Jackson's March
May 2

ROAD

Todd's Tavern

Union
Advance & Retreat
May 1

Lee
May 1

Zoan Church

McLaws

Anderson

ORANGE PLANK ROAD

MINE ROAD

River

Bank's Ford
Beck's Island

Falmouth

Salem Church
May 3

Marye's
Heights

Fredericksburg

May 4

April 30

Sedgwick
6th Corps
May 3

Reynolds
1st Corps

Early

May 2

April 29

Confederate Movements

Union Movements

0    1    2    3    miles

BATTLE OF CHANCELLORSVILLE, MAY 1–3, 1863

unfavorable ground, and time was running in favor of the opposition.

Friday, May 1, was a fine, bright day. Soft breezes flicked the regimental banners and national colors. Appearing wholly confident as usual, Hooker talked with his corp leaders in terms of victory. General Howard was coming up, and Sickles was crossing the Rappahannock. Quite tardily, Hooker began to look about him. He asked that Meade send Sykes down the Fredericksburg Road—to the same area where Griffin had been. Meade himself took the divisions of Humphreys and Griffin to reconnoiter enemy-held Banks Ford. This Rappahannock crossing, the one nearest Fredericksburg, would have to be opened for the supply train and for the corps of Reynolds, who had been summoned.

Riding close to the ford, Meade saw that it could be easily taken. Bridges could then be thrown across for the supply wagons. But before anything could be done, again came the recall.[43] Meade unwillingly returned to Hooker to learn that Sykes, after hard fighting, had gained some of the high ground in front, but finding himself outnumbered by Jackson's troops, had requested aid. Although Sykes intended to hold on until reinforced, Hooker asked that he be ordered back.

Meade was more than disappointed—he was dismayed. Gazing toward the heights twice lost, he exclaimed to some officers near him, "My God, if we can't hold the top of a hill, we certainly can't hold the bottom of it!"[44] General Humphreys saw the army drawn too closely in, as if wholly on the defensive.[45] Hooker's passiveness seemed to invite attack. Next day, while a dangling defense line was being assumed, Hooker was heard to remark that the enemy would have to fight him on his own ground. So much was true.

Both Reynolds and the wagon train would have to cross the Rappahannock higher up than Banks Ford. As lines generally facing east were formed on May 2, Meade extended his troops to the river to protect them; then came Couch, Second Corps, past the Chancellorsville clearing. Slocum, Twelfth, was next; then Sickles, who connected with General Howard, the youngest of the corps leaders. Howard's Eleventh Corps, probably the poorest trained, had been relegated to the far right. The first essential was to keep the entire line unbroken, but when

[43] MHSM *Papers*, Vol. III, 195.
[44] Francis A. Walker, *History of the Second Army Corps*, 224.
[45] *Complete Works of Abraham Lincoln*, VII, 97.

Sickles persuaded Hooker to allow him to go after an enemy column apparently heading south, a gap of more than a mile was left between the Third Corps and Howard. Sickles took some prisoners in a preliminary skirmish, moved on into some enemy trains, then called for reinforcements, which Hooker sent from both Slocum and Howard.

Meade had nothing to do with the movement, but he would have to pick up the pieces when the attenuated army right collapsed. The unskilled Sickles was no man to send into the woods or to seek out any useful information. Actually, the passage of enemy troops past his front was the march of Stonewall Jackson's corps towards the vulnerable Federal right. A little after 5:00 P.M., a shower of bullets and canister struck the extended flank. As thousands of exultant gray-clads poured in, surprised troops turned and ran. Refugees from the lethal storm dashed pell-mell through the rest of the army, some not halting until they had penetrated the enemy line on the other side, there at last to be taken prisoners.[46]

Meade, whose trained ear told him at once what had happened, ordered a line thrown along the nearest road, where he sought to hold the retreating troops. Sykes was sent on the double to defend the Ely's Ford road, a second line of defense which the army would have to retain to keep from being cut off.[47] As many guns as could be quickly brought up were placed in a position which could not be forced. "This was done," related one of Meade's aides, "in an incredibly short period of time. . . . About sixty guns were collected, and with the Fifth Corps in line they [the enemy] would have received a warm reception."[48] Some remnants of Howard's troops were shepherded to the Fifth Corps rear; others were commingled with almost every other corps. Slocum and Couch also had a task in attempting to block the retreat.

Hooker was in no state of mind to recall instructions. "In your next fight, put in all your men,"[49] Lincoln had told him, but he would use only about one-third of his army. On Sunday morning, May 3, the Federal line was reversed as Stonewall Jackson's men resumed the fight without their leader, who had fallen from bullets from his own men the evening before. Jeb Stuart, in command, assaulted Couch in the

[46] Walker, *History of the Second Corps,* 229.
[47] Pennypacker, *Meade,* 120.
[48] MHSM *Papers,* Vol. III, 229.
[49] *Battles and Leaders,* III, 155.

Federal center. Meade was anxious that the Fifth Corps should aid in a counterattack, but he had no orders to do so. Still he could respond to a call for help from Couch. When a rescuing brigade sliced through the enemy front line and got into the rear, seizing prisoners and guns, Colonel Alexander S. Webb of Meade's staff saw that Stuart had no reserve.[50] The enemy line, he reported, could be easily swept aside.

Reynolds had arrived sleepless but eager to fight, and his troops were now pouring in. Yet nothing could be done without orders, so taking Colonel Webb and another aide, Meade went to find Hooker. The Commander in Chief at that moment was lying in pain on his cot. Meade learned that a fragment of a porch pillar at the Chancellor House, riven by a solid shot, had struck him a partially disabling blow on his head and right side. Entering the tent, Meade thought he appeared rational, though fighting inner despair.[51]

Earlier, Hooker had promised an attack in force, but the fight was entirely gone out of him.[52] Meade, standing there begging, urged that he and Reynolds be permitted to assault the enemy left, which was known to be weak. Together they could roll up Jeb Stuart's line. Clutching Webb by the arm, Meade said that this man could reveal the enemy's real situation. His argument impressed Webb, who later wrote, "I have never known anyone so vehemently to advise an attack on the field of battle";[53] but it left Hooker cold. Raising himself up, Hooker found fault with Meade's action in reinforcing Couch and forbade the detachment of any more troops.

Meade took his leave in a truculent mood. "I tried all I could . . . to be permitted to take my corps into action and have a general battle with the whole army engaged," he wrote Margaret, "but I was *overruled* and censured. . . . Hooker never did allow himself to be influenced by me or my advice."[54]

Contrary to Meade's own impression, one of Hooker's aides considered his leader irrational. "The blow the General received seems to have knocked all the sense out of him," it was said. "For the remainder

[50] MHSM *Papers*, Vol. III, 226; J. C. Gray and J. C. Ropes, *War Letters, 1862–65*, 115.

[51] *Meade*, I, 380.

[52] Bigelow, *Chancellorsville*, 362.

[53] MSHM *Papers*, Vol. III, 222, 230–31.

[54] *Meade*, I, 372, 380.

of the day he was wandering."[55] In any event, Hooker acted to protect the army rather than to utilize its strength. Couch, the senior corps leader, was temporarily placed in charge but was told to fall back to a position indicated on a sketch that Hooker showed him. Meade eyed Couch inquiringly as the latter emerged from the tent but received no encouragement. Orders as given would have to stand.[56]

With Meade and Reynolds held motionless, the fighting that day was entirely defensive as the troops made more use of spades and axes than of their guns. General Sedgwick did his part by taking Marye's Heights back of Fredericksburg that same morning, then moving west toward Hooker and fighting again at Salem Heights, but no attempt was made to relieve the orphaned Sixth Corps. Instead, on the night of May 3, Lee withdrew troops from Chancellorsville to block Sedgwick. The drive toward Hooker and the heavy losses suffered had gone for nothing. Sedgwick, imperiled, fought through a hot, weary day on May 4, and when ordered by Hooker to make his way back as best he could, he managed to reach Banks Ford just above to recross the Rappahannock that night. Fredericksburg could now be, and was, re-occupied by the enemy. Along Hooker's front, sharpshooters on both sides were active and the artillery sometimes was heard, but results were inconsequential.

Hooker would have to talk his way out of it. With no trace of aggressiveness left, he summoned his generals to a late evening council of war. As his argument ran, the Capital had to be protected and the army made safe. Ostensibly it was left to the corps leaders to decide whether to remain or retreat, as Hooker and Chief of Staff Butterfield left them alone to talk.

They left a group with mixed opinions and logic. Meade, the most outspoken, argued in favor of an attack at daybreak. If the army did retreat, he added, perhaps it could not carry off its guns. Reynolds muttered something in agreement, then dozed off. General Howard, his corps shattered, still wanted to fight. But Sickles considered victory doubtful. Defeat, he argued, "would endanger Washington."[57] This clearly echoed Hooker's view. Couch was doubtful of success, although only because Hooker had reassumed the command. With Meade and

[55] Bigelow, *Chancellorsville*, 363 n.
[56] *Battles and Leaders*, III, 169.
[57] Emerson G. Taylor, *Gouverneur Kemble Warren*, 110.

Reynolds squarely behind him, he would have been satisfied to fight if he himself could have selected the point of attack.

Hooker returned, and opinions were polled. Both Howard and Meade voted to fight. The army, said Meade, would not be able to withdraw. Reynolds, awakened, urged staunchly, "We ought not fall back."[58] Couch's vote went the other way because he felt that no positive effort could be made under Hooker.[59] The vote stood three to two as Sickles argued for withdrawal. Hooker, however, had already made up his mind. To the surprise of nearly everyone, he said he would assume the responsibility for ordering the army to recross the Rappahannock in retreat.

Almost at once the council broke up. Officers stared into the darkness or at one another. "What was the use of calling us together at this time of night when he intended to retreat anyhow?"[60] Reynolds protested as soon as he got outside. General Slocum now arrived, and although it was obviously too late for his vote, he went on record as opposing withdrawal. Hooker approached Meade to remark that he had seen quite enough of the Federal command, that he was ready to turn the troops over to him, and that he almost wished he had never been born.[61] It still could not be known whether he was in his right mind.

Early on the morning of May 5 the wagon trains were ordered to return to Falmouth. The wounded were removed from the field hospitals and started on their way to Washington. Ambulances were sent into the woods to pick up the remaining sick and disabled, but many had been captured or were now beyond help. The dead on the battlefield of Sunday, May 3, were left as they lay.

Nothing was said of retreat. Early in the afternoon, Hooker turned his back on his troops and recrossed the river. Much already had been endured in the vain effort, but the grim test of the army's physical strength had only begun. The May day grew dark. A steady rain began falling, and soon it descended in torrents, filling the rifle pits as the disheartened men bailed. Roads were deluged and the corduroys torn up. Came the order to retreat, which surprised nearly everyone.

There was still a remote chance. "We all prayed that the bridges

[58] John Gibbon, *Personal Recollections of the Civil War*, 120.
[59] Walker, *History of the Second Corps*, 251.
[60] *Battles and Leaders*, III, 171.
[61] *Meade*, I, 373.

might be washed away,"[62] Colonel Webb wrote his father, Lincoln's minister to Brazil. The river rose rapidly, overflowing the ends of the pontoons placed upriver at United States Ford. But the way was made safe by taking up the upper pontoon to lengthen out the others. Pine boughs were spread out to muffle the noise of crossing. Early that evening, the artillery and wagons began plowing their way through the mud as mules, horses, and men strained to turn the slippery wheels. Drunken officers were berating the troops; more than once an abusive martinet rolled helplessly from his saddle to be reluctantly rescued from the yielding mire.

The May night grew chilly. Rain swept against men's faces and bodies as another mud march got under way. Frequently the ranks had to be halted, sometimes for hours, and many soldiers slept standing up with rifles used as supports. First to arrive at Chancellorsville, the Fifth Corps, covering the retreat, would be the last to leave. To Meade's great relief, the enemy pushed up only a few lines of skirmishers, which were held off by pickets and artillery placed along the river bank.[63] It was thought that Lee, to no one's regret, had committed a blunder by not attacking vigorously, but enemy intentions to cross above and attack the Federal flank were frustrated by high water.

Waiting anxiously in the rear, Meade received his first inkling that Hooker had crossed in advance when an engineer officer, explaining that a pontoon had been damaged, said he had been unable to locate the army commander. Meade sent a staff officer to examine the bridge, notified Couch that Hooker had fled, and, as soon as he could, conferred with both Couch and Reynolds. It was agreed to fight it out if necessary, but soon after midnight the bridge was repaired and the crossing resumed at that point.[64] Other pontoons, meanwhile, had been utilized, even though the water was now running swiftly through a twenty-foot gap between bridge and bank, "where only the sagacious horse could smell the distance and leap the chasms."[65]

In the morning, the mud was over wagon axles and up to men's waists. But safe on the north side of the river, the troops bound cables around the heavy pontoons and hauled them by hand up the slopes.

[62] Webb to James Watson Webb, May 12, 1863, Webb Papers.

[63] *Antietam to Appomattox*, 200–205; Robert G. Carter, *Four Brothers in Blue*, 259–61.

[64] MHSM *Papers*, Vol. III, 230; *Battles and Leaders*, III, 171.

[65] Chamberlain, *The Passing of the Armies*, 335.

Again the march was resumed as soldiers deserted by the hundreds to forage far and wide for provisions. Spirits sagged to their lowest as the tired and beaten army came within sight of its old winter quarters around Falmouth. Meade seemingly spoke for everyone when he said he was "fatigued and exhausted with a ten-days' campaign, pained and humiliated at its unsatisfactory result."[66] Hooker, he added, had dug in "quicker than McClellan," while losses had exceeded 15,000 men, "greater than in any battle or series of battles."[67]

Feeling the disgrace quite as strongly, Colonel Webb would argue that Meade had been foremost in trying to avert it. Meade, Webb wrote his father, had "shown the true soldier," and twice had asked to do the right thing. But because of "a want of backbone," nothing was done. The end of the rope had been reached. *"God have pity on our army! We have not decent officers enough, & political Generals will not fight for our holy cause."*[68] And as a veteran artilleryman recalled the mood of himself and his comrades, "the sole misgiving was about the Commander-in-Chief."[69] General Hooker, who had once been so popular, was no longer well received in the camps—"there was something in the air of the men which said: 'We have no further use for you.' "[70]

[66] *Meade*, I, 370.
[67] *Ibid.*, 372, 375.
[68] To James Watson Webb, May 12, 1863, Webb Papers.
[69] Buell, *The Cannoneer*, 61.
[70] Gibbon, *Personal Recollections*, 424–25.

## 10. *"Command . . . Is Not to Be Desired"*
## *(May 7-June 28, 1863)*

BLAME FOR THE greatest military failure thus far hung cloudlike over army headquarters. Cheerfulness returning, Hooker did not seem wholly aware of failure, although in making his excuses to President Lincoln, he wrote that he had found no way to engage in a general battle with any real prospect of success. Therefore he had decided that he should find a better place to fight. He would say nothing definite when Lincoln asked for details. He knew in his own mind, he replied, what he would do if the President wished him to renew the campaign. Lincoln would have to be satisfied with that.

Hooker again wrote to say that army strength would soon be reduced by 23,000 expiring enlistments and that he was impatient to move, possibly by "tomorrow." Lincoln replied warily that he might go ahead if he thought his plan promised success, but he saw fit to add that some of the corps and division commanders were "not giving you their entire confidence."[1] This was a shock. Now action must be taken to counteract any idea that he should be replaced as head of the army.

Most of the talk in officers' tents revolved around Meade, who as the result of Fredericksburg, where he had fought, and of Chancellorsville, where he had not been allowed to, was the first choice for replacement. Inspector General Webb had been strongly urging a brother stationed at Washington to spread the word that Meade was "head and shoulders above all in the field" and that the attacks which he had urged "would have gained the day." Everyone should know that Meade had advised Hooker not to fall back. Webb strengthened his appeal by declaring that three corps commanders senior to Meade had agreed that they would willingly serve under his leadership.[2] These

[1] *O.R.*, XXV, pt. 2, 438, 473–74; Williams, *Lincoln and His Generals*, 244–45.
[2] The original of this undated message is in the Webb Papers; copy in Meade Papers; slightly altered version in MHSM *Papers*, Vol. III, 222.

were Generals Couch, Sedgwick, and Slocum, none of whom ever sought the command for himself.

Just who may have seen this letter is not known, but quite a number of people in Washington must have heard from Governor Curtin of Pennsylvania, a forceful persuader. Curtin, who naturally wished to see a Pennsylvania general in command, either Reynolds or Meade, had made his own inquiries in camp. He first talked with Reynolds, but only his visit to Meade is recorded. Appearing angry and "very much depressed" in Meade's tent, he spoke out bitterly against Hooker. His host sought to put him in better humor, but what Meade said to the Governor was probably much the same as he revealed in a letter to Margaret. "All I can say," he wrote, "is that Hooker has disappointed the army and myself in failing to show the nerve and *coup d'oeil* at the critical moment. . . . I was clearly in favor of tempting the hazard of the die and letting Washington take care of itself. I am sorry for Hooker because I like him and my relations have always been agreeable with him but I cannot shut my eyes to the fact that he has on this occasion missed a brilliant opportunity of making himself."[3]

Governor Curtin went to Washington to tell whomever he met that Hooker had lost the confidence of the army and that both Reynolds and Meade had lost confidence in him. Hooker also dashed off to the capital to try to discover just what was behind the sting in his letter from Lincoln. When Curtin's words got back to him via another army officer, it seemed to him that Meade was to blame. As the tale went round and round, he appeared at Meade's tent to ask him to explain. No ground could be given at this point. Meade reminded Hooker that he already knew that they had differed in judgment. You have "no right to complain of my expressing my views to others," the army commander was told. Apparently Hooker did not seek a quarrel, and Meade did not appear to be coveting the command. Agreement was reached on the basis that Meade had a right to a private airing of views.[4]

Soon Hooker was back. Although he had banned critical newspapers from camp, an item printed in the widely read *New York Herald* was likely to arouse talk. Four corps commanders, the *Herald* correctly reported, had opposed the retreat from Chancellorsville. The position taken by both Reynolds and Meade, Hooker now argued, was that

[3] *Meade,* I, 374.
[4] *Ibid.,* 376.

retreat was impractical or impossible and therefore they had not favored an advance. He, however, had known that he could withdraw, so he determined to do so. Meade retorted that the decision to retreat had already been made prior to the council of war. Hooker did not appear to take offense, but declined to give ground.[5] At this point he could not unless he wished to resign.

Direct solicitation was made by Slocum and Couch. The delegations of important visitors which could be expected after any major battle had begun to stream in, and Lincoln had arrived with General Halleck. It was thought that the President might listen to dissenting views. Meade therefore was asked by Couch to join "in a representation," and Slocum also sought his support in "action to have Hooker removed." Meade declined both requests. "I told these gentlemen I would not join in any movement against Hooker but that if the President chose to call on me officially for my opinions, I would give them."[6] This did not stop Couch, who went to Lincoln to say that he did not wish to serve any longer under Hooker. He mentioned only Meade for the post.[7]

Summoned to headquarters to see Lincoln and Halleck, Meade was politely received. During a two-hour visit, including lunch, "all sorts of things" were discussed, but little was said regarding Chancellorsville, nor were any opinions asked. Lincoln appeared almost indifferent. The result of the battle, Meade quoted him as saying, "was in his judgement most unfortunate ... he did not blame any one—he believed every one had done all in his power; and that the disaster was one that could not be helped."[8] Lincoln was tired of changing generals after every battle, but if his summons to Meade was for the purpose of gaining a better acquaintance, he probably had not wasted his time.

Lincoln's attitude was not unlike that of members of the Committee on the Conduct of the War, who were friendly with Hooker. They also came to talk with the army commander, but again no questions were asked of anyone who had criticized him. After Fredericksburg, the committee had blamed Franklin, but it was unable to find anyone to make a scapegoat after Chancellorsville, and no positive action was taken. Despite huge Federal losses—11,550 killed and wounded, with

[5] *Ibid.*, 377–78.
[6] *Ibid.*, 379.
[7] *Ibid.*, 373.
[8] *Ibid.*, 372.

5,700 missing—and the disorderly retreat, Hooker's backers could easily consider it an indecisive affair.

The momentum of the campaign against Hooker was not even checked. General Sedgwick, when sounded out, avowed, "Why Meade is the proper one to command this army."[9] Couch, who was not in very good physical shape and unwilling to participate in another campaign under Hooker, obtained a brief leave and went to the White House. If Hooker were not replaced, he told Lincoln, he would much prefer to serve elsewhere, although he would continue with the Army of the Potomac with Meade in command. Lincoln tested his caller by suggesting that he accept the leadership, but Couch preferred to obtain a transfer to the newly organized Department of the Susquehanna with headquarters at Harrisburg.[10]

Meade heard from his sister Margaret, who did some copying at the War Office, that everyone in Washington was saying he would get the command. Mrs. Meade backed off in alarm when she heard the news, warning her husband, "Do not accept—it would only be your ruin." Meade quite agreed. "I am of your opinion," he replied, "that the command of this army is not to be desired or sought for and that it is more likely to destroy one's reputation than to add to it."[11] He was met one morning in camp by one George W. Smalley, a former lawyer who had turned to journalism to give expression to his antislavery views. Apparently Smalley had been asked by a number of army officers to approach him on the subject of a change in command, but as he did so, Meade responded, "I don't know as I ought to listen to you." He continued to listen, nevertheless, "his face impassive—a model of military discretion."[12] Smalley received no further comment or reply, but in a letter to his wife, Margaret, Meade said it was possible that he was overappreciated. In a single day, he reported, one of the camp sutlers had sold four hundred prints of his photograph to soldiers and visitors.[13]

One positive action was taken—a rebuttal of Hooker's idea that

[9] *Ibid.*, II, 6.

[10] *Ibid.*, I, 373; *Battles and Leaders*, III, 241; Walker, *History of the Second Corps*, 254.

[11] Meade to Mrs. Meade, May 10 and 20, 1863, Meade Papers.

[12] George W. Smalley, *Anglo-American Memories* (New York and London, 1911), 158–59.

[13] Meade to wife, May 17 and 30, 1863, Meade Papers.

Meade was indirectly responsible for the decision to retreat from Chancellorsville. A form letter went out from Meade's headquarters to each corps commander. Reynolds, the first to reply, asserted, "Your opinion was decided and emphatic for an advance at daylight."[14] General Howard recalled that Meade had considered it wise to attack and had prophesied that retreat would be disastrous.[15] Sickles, who saw to it that the *New York Herald* reprinted his letter, apparently agreed, only to add that Meade had changed his mind in the light of his commander's "clear conviction" of the necessity of returning to the Rappahannock's north bank.[16] Possibly other replies were received, but Meade made no use of any, since no real investigation was made. Hooker, however, was then in Washington discounting unfavorable views. General Griffin, there on sick leave, sent a warning to Meade that the commander was apparently unfriendly.[17] Out of this came a rumor that the Fifth Corps might be given to another, but Meade could reflect that if that removed him, then others who thought as he did would have to be penalized. There was hardly another corps commander at Chancellorsville, he asserted, "who was not more obnoxious [to Hooker] than myself."[18]

Rumor also had it that Reynolds would receive the command. But going straight to the White House, he advised the President that he neither wanted the command nor would accept it unless given free rein. Not so much his taciturn self with Lincoln, Reynolds talked rather freely concerning Hooker. Appearing unmoved, Lincoln, however, said he was not disposed to throw away a gun because it missed fire, but "would pick the lock and try it again."[19] Nevertheless, Reynolds had scored. By taking the initiative and going to Lincoln, he would avoid the possibility of any peremptory order assigning him to an unsought and unwanted command.

One month after Chancellorsville, therefore, the army had definite

[14] *Meade*, I, 382; original in Meade Papers.

[15] Howard to Meade, May 26, 1863, Meade Papers. Howard hedged a little: "After Gen¹ Hooker returned to the tent just before we broke up & gave his decided opinion that he would withdraw, I think you made no further objection," he stated.

[16] Sickles to Meade, May 26, 1863, Meade Papers and James Gordon Bennett Papers. Sickles or his amanuensis kept in close touch with the *New York Herald*.

[17] Griffin to Meade, May 25, 1863, Meade Papers.

[18] Meade to wife, June 2, 1865, Meade Papers.

[19] *Meade*, I, 385; H. G. Pearson, *James S. Wadsworth of Geneseo*, 201 n.; Nichols, *Toward Gettysburg*, 220–21. Reynolds saw Lincoln on the evening of June 2, 1863.

word that Hooker would be retained after all. Despite the strained relations between him and most of his corps leaders, only one officer, General Couch, was transferred. Meade decided, however, that under the circumstances he would not ask for a leave to attend the presentation of swords ceremony in Washington planned for himself and Reynolds by the Pennsylvania Reserves. He clung to the belief that Hooker might yet do well, as there was still "a good deal of merit in him."[20] And as long as Hooker was retained in the post, then he might be left undisturbed in his own.

Reinforced by the two divisions under Longstreet, who had returned, Lee's army was now more formidable than in April, while Hooker's was less strong. Although several new regiments were arriving, men whose terms of service had expired were too wearied and disgusted to consider enlistment again. When nearly a division in all evaporated from Meade's command, General Humphreys was transferred to a Third Corps division to replace General Hiram Berry, killed at Chancellorsville. The loss of Humphreys, esteemed by Meade as "a most valuable officer," was regretted.[21]

Now at full strength, numbering nearly 75,000 men, Lee's army needed supplies, and it was logical to seek them where they were more plentiful. Mapping an invasion north, Lee put General Richard S. Ewell, successor to Jackson, over the Second Corps and organized a Third Corps under A. P. Hill. On June 3, the Army of Northern Virginia began moving up the Rappahannock. When Lee's intentions became clear, the Federals again marched toward the Potomac.

Meade was confident that the enemy, now on the aggressive, could be found and fought at an advantage. Even if Hooker's army were forced into a defensive battle, "we will give them better than they can send."[22] Except that he expected that Hooker would have the advantage if Lee again crossed into Maryland or penetrated Pennsylvania, it is a little difficult to account for his optimism. Some officers and many men in the ranks were more skeptical. One veteran wrote of "a sullen resolve to whip the fight if each man had to do it all himself."[23] Leadership was doubted.

[20] *Meade*, I, 382.
[21] *Ibid.*, 378.
[22] Thomas Biddle to Colonel George Meade, July 18, 1874, Meade Papers; *Meade*, I, 383.
[23] Buell, *The Cannoneer*, 61.

In the clear June weather the march through green valleys was enjoyable. Both armies garnered much fresh produce, either through purchase by commissaries or by other means. The country itself was all lovely landscapes, Meade wrote while in the Bull Run Mountains. He relished a fine view from the James Monroe estate, Oak Hill near Leesburg, whose absent owner was Major John W. Fairfax of Longstreet's staff. Riding near by, Meade received a hospitable note from Mrs. Fairfax, to whom he went to apologize for the "intrusion." The lady replied that she did not so consider it. Meade heard her say she was always glad to see the officers of his army, knowing they took an interest in the place from its having been the former residence of a President.[24] It was a tactful approach in wartime. However the mistress of the house may have felt about the invasion, her first concern was her home.

Public alarm spread as Lee's army crossed the Potomac and moved still farther north. There were uneasy feelings concerning Hooker, who had been criticized in the press. Word came to Meade that many were still thinking of him as the first choice for the army command. Even his wife was turning to this view, but, Meade argued, was this not idle talk? Ever since the ouster of McClellan, politics had played a part in the choices. He therefore did not believe that he stood a chance. "I have no friends, political or others, who press or advance my claims or pretensions, and there are so many others who are pressed by influential politicians that it is folly to think I stand any chance upon mere merit alone. Besides ... I know there are plenty of others equally competent with myself."[25]

A sign that the President had ceased to support Hooker might be read in his instructions dated June 16 that he take orders from General in Chief Halleck, who personally was unfriendly, but Meade may not have known of the change. Lincoln at the same time had urged Hooker to cut Lee's communications, but instead of acting upon the idea, the army leader began (as Lincoln saw it) to act like McClellan—to balk at orders and beg for reinforcements.[26] Some infantry and all the cavalry near Washington were sent, but this did not seem quite enough. Hooker faced a familiar specter—the idea that he was outnumbered.

[24] Meade to wife, June 25, 1863, *Meade*, I, 389.
[25] *Ibid.*, 388–89.
[26] *O.R.*, XXVII, pt. 1, 47; Gideon Welles, *Diary*, I, 348.

Although he still had the advantage, he made an issue of being allowed to take over 11,000 men at Harpers Ferry, which guarded the junction of the Potomac and Shenandoah rivers. The garrison was under General William H. French, an old friend of Halleck's who only recently had been sent there, and was a separate command. Neither Lincoln nor Halleck wished to give the post up, and when Hooker visited Washington on June 23, his request was refused. Hooker reacted by beginning to drink more than he should—he would now have to cross the Potomac and fight.

On June 25-27, Hooker made his crossing not far west of Washington and approached the Catoctin and South Mountain ranges. As McClellan had marched to Antietam, he occupied the passes and ground east of each. His position was now intrinsically strong, and in line with orders, he had Washington and Baltimore covered. But at the same time his assigned goal was Lee's army. In moving north, Hooker would have both to attack and to defend.

He divulged no plans to his subordinate commanders. Meade confessed to ignorance which was shared by others whom he had seen; no one yet knew what might be expected. Meade appeared less friendly as military affairs approached a crisis: "This is what Joe Hooker thinks profound sagacity—keeping his corps commanders, who are to execute his plans, in total ignorance of them."[27] Lee was then nearing high tide. Longstreet and Hill were close to Pennsylvania's border, and Ewell had penetrated dangerously into that state.

Still obsessed with Harpers Ferry, Hooker rode over on June 27 to discover some way to abandon it. His chief engineer, General Gouverneur K. Warren, agreed that the garrison should be transferred to the field. But this could hardly be done in view of a telegram from Halleck to French, which was informally worded, "Pay no attention to Hooker's orders." It was as if French and the Harpers Ferry situation were being used to get rid of Hooker. General French at least was available for this purpose. Shown Halleck's blunt message, Hooker despondently asked to be relieved, and as matters then stood, he had only to ask.[28]

Late on that same day, Meade completed a hard march from Vir-

[27] *Meade*, I, 389.
[28] Walter Hebert, *Fighting Joe Hooker*, 245; O.R., XXVII, pt. 1, 60.

ginia soil to the vicinity of Frederick and saw his men properly bivouacked along a creek south of the town.[29] His great anxiety was for
information of any kind, and although it was a Saturday night, he hurried off to find Hooker, whom he had not seen for two weeks. Unable
to locate the army commander, he returned to his tent in an irritable
mood. No one whom he had seen seemed to know anything of military
plans or even of the precise location of the enemy. It was known that
at least part of Lee's army was in Pennsylvania, which was bad news.
Meade threw off a wrinkled and mud-stained uniform and worried
himself to sleep.

Leaders in Washington as well as military men in the field seemed
to be agreed that another battle should not be risked under Hooker.
Musing that night over Hooker's request to be relieved, Secretary
Stanton sent for the President. According to one account, Lincoln appeared at the War Office looking rather gloomy and not disposed to
make conversation. After a few perfunctory remarks the Secretary took
up the matter at hand. He did not feel, he said, that Hooker would be
equal to the present emergency, but he could find no fault with the
record and ability of General Meade. Lincoln on his part felt that
Meade would fight well in Pennsylvania "on his own dunghill,"[30] and
thus it was decided to act.

Since whatever was done had to be done quickly, the cabinet would
not be consulted that night. Halleck was called in, and the several necessary orders made out and signed. A steam locomotive was made ready,
and the papers, together with cash for expenses, were entrusted to
Colonel James A. Hardie of the War Office staff. A racing locomotive
brought Hardie into Frederick sometime after midnight. Now the task
was to find Meade. No provost marshal had been appointed for the
town, discipline was slack, and merrymaking soldiers who filled the
streets on that week end had been sampling Maryland whiskey.

After looking about for some time, Hardie managed to hire a driver
and buggy for no modest fee. The route to Meade's headquarters had
to be guessed at, and roads were made difficult by roistering soldiers
and army wagons en route to their bivouac. Hardie was clad in civilian
garb and thus was unable to wield any authority over the troops, but he

[29] *Antietam to Appomattox*, 231.
[30] G. C. Gorham, *Life and Public Services of Edwin M. Stanton*, II, 99.

did manage to obtain help from army officers in finding his way. It was nearly three o'clock on the morning of June 28 when he arrived among Fifth Corps tents.[31]

No one around headquarters could imagine what had brought him at such an hour. Staff members began to feel that something was wrong. After some wrangling, Hardie was permitted to enter Meade's tent without first making his mission known. Bending over the sleeping officer, Hardie aroused him, mentioned his name, and said he came from the War Office. When Meade sleepily inquired his errand, the visitor remarked with ill-timed humor that he had come to give him trouble. All Meade could think of at the moment was that Hooker had ordered his arrest on some charge. His conscience was clear, Hardie was told; he was prepared for whatever might come.[32]

Hardie lit a candle and came to the point. Meade was given a brief order from Lincoln assigning him to the high command, and a detailed message from Halleck outlining his course. The army was to cover Washington and Baltimore; Harpers Ferry and its garrison would come under Meade's own jurisdiction, etc. It was acknowledged that the transfer was being made at a critical time. "Considering the circumstances," Halleck had written, "no one ever received a more important command."[33]

Yet Meade would have none of it. He agitatedly asked why Reynolds had not been named, and then stressed the point that he knew nothing of the army's position or of Hooker's plans. He wished to wire Halleck immediately to ask to be excused. All these objections had been anticipated, Hardie responded. He had his own orders to escort the new army commander to Hooker's tent and there witness the transfer of authority. Meade again began to argue, but realizing that the order was mandatory and that he actually had no choice, he could only say as he threw on his soiled uniform, "Well, I've been tried and condemned without a hearing, and I suppose I shall have to go to execution."[34]

Meade called for his son George, a staff member and captain since June 3. While coffee was prepared and a horse was saddled for Hardie, he went to the tent of Chief Engineer Warren and awakened him to

[31] *Battles and Leaders*, III, 242.
[32] *Meade*, II, 1–2, 12.
[33] *O.R.*, XXVII, pt. 1, 61.
[34] *Battles and Leaders*, III, 243 n.

say that he wanted him as his own chief of staff. The two men talked briefly in the dark. Warren did not wish to accept, suggesting that Butterfield be retained because of his better acquaintance with army affairs.[35] After a light breakfast with Hardie and George, the trio started on a ride of several miles to army headquarters on the other side of town. Very little was said along the way. Meade asked a few brief questions but appeared largely absorbed in his own thoughts. He could reflect that only success in the present crisis would enable him to retain the position into which he had been plunged.[36]

Word that someone of importance from the War Office was in camp had already reached Hooker, who appeared in full uniform. Colonel Hardie lost little time in breaking the news that his resignation had been accepted and that he had now been replaced. Hooker soberly broke open orders relieving him of his present command and transferring him to Baltimore, a minor military post, though possibly of importance if threatened during the present invasion.

Chief of Staff Butterfield was summoned. During a long and trying conference the position of the several corps was outlined as Hooker contended that Lee, who had no bridge equipment, would not attempt to cross the Susquehanna River and threaten Harrisburg, but would turn southeast and follow the right bank to cut off Baltimore and Washington. Meade could not agree that the enemy would not try to cross at low water. In point of fact, Lee had issued orders so to move.[37]

There was a flare-up when Meade expressed surprise at the scattered condition of the Federal army. One of his first ideas was to bring it together and hold a review as a means of getting acquainted with his command.[38] However, as Butterfield pointed out, a review was hardly practical at that time. The columns, it was agreed, would continue the march. Hooker, however, would outline no plans of his own, and Meade could not see that he had any.[39]

Harpers Ferry was discussed. Meade favored leaving that garrison intact to provide military access to or from the Cumberland Valley above. Again Butterfield and Hooker dissented. The post lacked pro-

[35] Taylor, *Warren*, 119.

[36] Meade to General Hancock, December 11, 1863, Meade Papers.

[37] Comte de Paris, *The Battle of Gettysburg* (Philadelphia, 1886), 73; *O.R.*, XXVII, pt. 2, 316.

[38] *Battles and Leaders*, III, 243.

[39] *Meade*, II, 355.

visions, it was argued, and a small enemy force could cut off communications and prevent it from being supplied. It was partly this testimony that influenced Meade in his later decision to abandon the post, as in effect he had been empowered to do when it was placed under him.[40]

The talk concluded, Meade stepped from the tent and announced to his son, "Well, George, I am in command of the Army of the Potomac."[41] His son had received only an inkling but did not appear surprised. After asking that the rest of his staff come to join him there, bringing his personal effects, Meade entered a tent used as an office and penciled a brief message to Halleck:

> The order placing me in command of this army is received. As a soldier I obey it and to the utmost of my ability will execute it. Totally unexpected as it has been, and, in ignorance of the exact condition of the troops and position of the enemy, I can only now say that it appears to me I must move toward the Susquehanna, keeping Washington and Baltimore well covered. . . . If the enemy is checked in his attempt to cross . . . or if he turns toward Baltimore, [I intend] to give him battle. I would say that I trust every available man that can be spared will be sent me, as from all accounts the enemy is in strong force. So soon as I can post myself up I will communicate more in detail.[42]

It was a plain and clear statement which drove at the heart of the matter. To those waiting in Washington for some word from the immediate front it meant that the new commander would cheerfully co-operate in a subordinate role. Lincoln took the letter, which he read at the War Office, and placed it among his own papers. At the White House he was heard to remark as if to himself, "I tell you I think a great deal of that fine fellow Meade."[43] He knew his new man as an energetic, courageous, sympathetic, and dutiful officer whose well-disciplined troops were among the best in the army.

[40] Meade to Butterfield, February 4, 1864, O.R., XXVII, pt. 1, 21; original in Meade Papers; also Butterfield's reply in Meade, II, 362.

[41] Meade, II, 2.

[42] Ibid., 4–5.

[43] Carl Sandburg, Abraham Lincoln (one-volume edition), 409.

## 11. *"Met on a Great Battlefield"*
## *(June 28–July 2, 1863)*

THE ALARM HAD SPREAD from the Cumberland Valley towns to Philadelphia, where Mayor Alexander Henry summoned all able-bodied
men to arms. "CITIZENS OF PENNSYLVANIA!!! THE REB-
ELS ARE UPON US!" newspaper headlines blared.[1] Policemen
carried enlistment blanks from house to house and into the factories,
shops, and stores.[2] A few hundred volunteers had been sent to General
Couch at Harrisburg, but in Philadelphia also it had come to be a matter of home and fireside defense.

Margaret Meade unfolded the morning *Philadelphia Inquirer* and
pored over an editorial hailing the new army chief. "Gallant officer . . .
so well known . . . our cordial gratification," she read.[3] A note from
son George said he supposed she already had the great news, and finally
the letter arrived for which she had been waiting. His appointment,
the General explained, was but an act of God and was accepted as such.
Since apparently it had to be, he was resigned to it but considered it no
cause of rejoicing. "Dearest, you know how reluctant we both have been
to see me placed in this position, and as it appears to be God's will for
some good purpose—at any rate, as a soldier I had nothing to do but
accept. . . . I am moving at once against Lee. . . . Pray earnestly, pray
for the success of my country (for it is my success besides). . . . Oh,
what I would give for one hour by your side to talk to you, to see my
dear children and be quiet!"[4]

The Federal Army leader was not the only one in travail. At this
very time another of the Meade family was caught up by invasion.
Down in Mississippi, where General Grant was clutching at Vicksburg,

[1] *Philadelphia Inquirer*, June 29, 1863.
[2] Taylor, *Philadelphia in the Civil War*, 244.
[3] *Philadelphia Inquirer*, June 29, 1863.
[4] *Meade*, II, 11–12; MS letter of June 29, 1863.

sister Charlotte Meade Ingraham, her husband's plantation invaded, prayed that Lee might be "swarming and pillaging Pennsylvania." Charlotte never was known to ask any favor on her brother's account. Instead, "if New York could only be fired," she wrote, "I think I would feel better."[5] Her son Frank had been lost at Chancellorsville, and son Edward had been killed the previous spring. "The name of this branch," Charlotte bitterly reminded her daughter Apolline (already a widow), "dies with your father—no son!"[6]

General Lee reflected on the news brought by spies that the Federal Army had crossed the Potomac and that the command had passed into the hands of a man known to be in deadly earnest. He at once decided to abandon his plan to take Harrisburg. He would check Ewell's advance and move east of Pennsylvania's mountains to draw Meade after him. The first essential, with Meade in command, was to safeguard his extended line of communications. Of the new Federal Army head he was once heard to say, "General Meade will commit no blunder in my front and if I make one he will make haste to take advantage of it."[7]

News of the shift in command was well received where Meade was best known, but elsewhere there were other favorites, particularly Sedgwick or Reynolds. The promotion was accepted by most of the troops "without protest but without enthusiasm." "What has Meade ever done?" one soldier asked, but many responses were warm. In letters and in campfire talk, Meade was declared "a rattling fighter," "a clear-headed honest soldier," "brave and judicious . . . and a good man." Of those officers well acquainted with Meade, stated one of them, all thought highly of him. A Pennsylvania soldier believed that the news was generally greeted "with favor and ready acquiescence." The army, remarked another, was willing to take Meade on trial. Word of his popularity with the Pennsylvania Reserves was spread.[8]

[5] Sarah A. Dorsey, *Recollections of Henry Watkins Allen*, 417.

[6] *Ibid.*, 420.

[7] Freeman, *R. E. Lee*, III, 64.

[8] A. E. Ford, *Story of the 15th Massachusetts Regiment*, 260; A. W. Bartlett, *History of the 12th New Hampshire Regiment*, 130; Buell, *The Cannoneer*, 61; Frank A. Haskell, *The Battle of Gettysburg*, 6; E. W. Emerson, *Life and Letters of Charles Russell Lowell*, 271; R. L. Stewart, *History of the 140th Pennsylvania Regiment*, 88–89; Samuel Toombs, *New Jersey Troops in the Gettysburg Campaign*, 129; Nichols, *Toward Gettysburg*, 191–92.

On trial and facing disgrace if he failed, Meade well realized that success had to be certain. If he blundered in his effort to force Lee out of the state, then Pennsylvania and its inhabitants would be systematically plundered. On the morning of June 28, a newspaperman saw Meade standing alone and lost in thought as if "weighed down with the sense of the responsibility resting on him."[9] To ease the burden of care which Meade acknowledged he felt, he called upon dependable sources for help.

He was confident that he could rely on his soldiers. An appeal went out to them that same morning: "The country looks to this army to relieve it from the devastation and disgrace of foreign invasion. Whatever fatigues and sacrifices we may be called upon to undergo . . . let each man determine to do his duty. . . . I rely upon the hearty support of my companions in arms to assist me."[10] The foremost of these, General Reynolds, First Corps, was to Meade "a lieutenant important to me in his services . . . a friend and brother."[11] Summoned to headquarters, Reynolds came meticulously clad; hurrying outside to meet him, Meade grasped his arm and took him into his tent.

An aide working unobserved behind a desk heard Meade say that he had never dreamed of receiving the command and that it was not by his own free will that he had accepted. He assured Reynolds that he counted on him for the support which he would have given his friend had the latter been placed in the same situation. Reynolds was satisfied that the command had fallen in the right hands, and he also appeared relieved that another had been chosen. "Had it come to me in the same way," he told Meade, "I would have been obliged to have taken it, but I am glad it did not."

The two leaders agreed that Lee would have to be either lured out of Pennsylvania or attacked in some suitable position above the Maryland line. With the bulk of the army interposed between the enemy's known position and Baltimore, Reynolds would remain on the Federal left and head northward. Should Lee march in an easterly direction and through the mountains, the First Corps might be the first to fight.

Meade pointed on a map to Emmitsburg, just below the Pennsylvania line. Eleven miles farther on lay the town of Gettysburg, focal

[9] C. C. Coffin, *The Boys of '61*, 261.
[10] *Meade*, II, 5.
[11] *Ibid.*, 315.

point of several main roads. Meade knew nothing about that locality, but Lee might come through there. With the First Cavalry Division preceding Reynolds wherever he went, he was to select a suitable battle position, should any be found. It was understood between the two men that the rest of the army would then be brought up to fight, but if no advantageous position was discovered, Reynolds was to fall back to the first supporting corps.[12] Thus no one could say where the fighting might start.

Meade adverted to Harpers Ferry, where provisions were said to be low. It was agreed that since the course of the march was being changed, then the post should be abandoned and the public property there sent down the Potomac to Washington. As far as the command under General French could be made use of, Meade decided that 3,000 men would be detached to escort the boats, while General French and the remaining force would guard the railroad in and around Frederick and occupy South Mountain Pass. It was Meade's broad decision to abandon the thrust at Lee's communications which Hooker appeared to be attempting and to act more defensively by occupying the broad valley between the enemy and Baltimore. General Howard, Eleventh Corps, who like Reynolds was then west of Frederick, was ordered to draw his troops in and follow closely behind the advance on the left.

Still searching for a chief of staff, Meade talked with General Humphreys, who now had a Third Corps division, but this admirable soldier declined to accept as matters then stood.[13] General Seth Williams, genial and trusted adjutant general, was approached with the same result.[14] Meade therefore had to resign himself to Dan Butterfield, whose relationship lacked any personal friendliness.

The lively sound of band music and of the drum echoed from the wooded hills as seven army corps, the flanking cavalry under General Alfred Pleasonton, the artillery reserve, and the engineers and bridge trains picked up and marched. The morning of June 29 was warm and humid, and soon the heat increased. Before midday, the troops were

[12] C. F. Benjamin to Col. George Meade, August 7 and 17, 1887. Benjamin says that Gettysburg was mentioned, but when questioned regarding a similar statement that he had made, he admitted that he had inserted the word "Gettysburg" in his account of the conversation. Actually the point is of little consequence, but see Nichols, *Toward Gettysburg*, 222–23.
[13] *O.R.*, LI, pt. 1, 1064; *Meade*, II, 352 n.
[14] *Battles and Leaders*, III, 413.

marching in their underwear, with handkerchiefs tied about heads and necks; many were barefoot and some in their stocking feet. As the sun climbed high, scores were felled by sunstroke, and straggling almost got out of hand. The marches ordered on the first day were so long (because of poor maps in some instances) that it took until the morning of June 30 for some of the troops to reach their assigned stations.

Starting from below Frederick, the Second Corps of General Winfield S. Hancock fell short of its goal because of a late start—a headquarters clerk had failed to call the staff's attention to the delivery of orders early that morning. Hancock did not get under way until 7:00 A.M. Trudging over roads which at first were dusty and then muddy from showers, the corps halted at Uniontown at 2:00 A.M. the next day, but the village of Frizzelburg, which he was supposed to have reached, was farther along than the maps showed.[15] Ordered to reach Union, General Sykes, again commanding the Fifth Corps, was in turn held up by Hancock. On the army left, the Twelfth Corps was blocked by wagon trains, which, General Slocum argued, "do not . . . belong on this road."[16] The trains, which were Sickles', were too widely dispersed. Meade sent Sickles a sharp note asking him to look into this situation, and again the next day that picnicking officer had to be reminded that his progress was too slow.[17]

Late on the twenty-ninth, Meade found time to write a note home. He still did not know much of what was ahead but could report progress.

> We are marching as fast as we can to relieve Harrisburg but have to keep a sharp lookout that the rebels don't turn around and get at Washington and Baltimore in our rear. They have a cavalry force in our rear, destroying railroads, etc., with the view of getting me to turn back, but I shall not do it. I am going straight at them and will settle this thing one way or the other. The men are in good spirits . . . and with God's blessing I hope to be successful.[18]

So many orders and instructions were issued on June 30 that Chief of Staff Butterfield began to fall behind in his work, although quite

[15] *Meade*, II, 12.
[16] *O.R.*, XXVII, pt. 3, 398.
[17] *Ibid.*, 399, 420.
[18] *Meade*, II, 13–14.

inexcusably, it was thought. Since Meade was still groping, most of his ideas were tentative, and instructions issued in that vein were soon outdated. Would Lee advance toward him or simply occupy gaps in the mountains and wait? Would Reynolds find a suitable position to fight across the Pennsylvania line? During the forenoon Meade wrote his most trusted lieutenant, who, preceded by General John Buford's cavalry division, was moving directly toward Gettysburg, that he might fall back if he found Emmitsburg the better position. The services of General Humphreys, an experienced topographical officer, were offered, and Warren finally was sent.[19] Buford, who reached Gettysburg promptly, reported back at 10:30 A.M. that the enemy was advancing and that infantry and artillery pickets were within four miles of the town. At Hanover, thirteen miles east of Gettysburg, General Judson Kilpatrick's cavalry division drove a body of enemy horse in a northerly direction where infantry were known to be.

Lee obviously occupied a very wide front in Pennsylvania. His army early that day had been spread out from York to Chambersburg and as far north as Carlisle. Meade lightened his center and strengthened the flanks. Leadership of the three army corps on the left was assigned Reynolds, Sickles moving by the left flank and then forward toward him. Howard was between the two, although the closer to Reynolds, as both the First and Eleventh Corps moved over the Pennsylvania line. Meade's right, which protected the cities, was strengthened by Sykes, who had a good day's march northeast from Liberty to Union Mills. The Sixth Corps also plodded some twenty miles as it moved within two miles of Manchester on the extreme right; by nightfall Sedgwick was about abreast of Sykes, who camped just west of him. Slocum inched past the state line to Littlestown, southeast of Gettysburg, and Hancock was held about where he was near Uniontown, in reserve.

Meade moved his headquarters from Middleburg to Taneytown and digested more information. Since battle somewhere seemed imminent, corps commanders were told to be ready "at a moment's notice . . . to march against the enemy." Supply the troops and study the roads, it was ordered, and keep all wagons except ammunition trains parked in the rear. Let the officers tell the troops, "The enemy are on our soil; the whole country now looks anxiously to this army to deliver

[19] O.R., XXVII, pt. 3, 460–61.

it from . . . the foe. . . . Honor, firesides, and domestic altars are involved." Instant death was ordered for any soldier who failed in his duty.[20]

Attack or defend? Meade had to be prepared for either and to make sure that he won. He already had told Reynolds that his position "was given more with a view to an advance on Gettysburg than a defensive point," which might well be selected elsewhere. Chief Engineer Warren and General Hunt of the Artillery were surveying the area extending from Hancock's left roughly northeast to Manchester. Parr's Ridge and winding Pipe Creek were the main defense barriers along this "true place," as it was characterized by Hunt.[21] The line lay squarely between the enemy's known position and Baltimore.

More than immediate physical advantages were seen. If the enemy could be lured within striking distance and defeated, pursuit could be made across a broad valley rather than through mountain passes, which Lee could defend if the battle were fought in Pennsylvania. "All the elements of the problem," avowed General Hunt, "were in favor of the Pipe Creek line."[22] Many years later that very terrain would be frequently utilized in military studies of actual tactical problems.

By the evening of June 30, four army corps were already beyond and three were behind Pipe Creek, but Meade adopted the plan as a provisional move. It would therefore alter the pattern of marching orders for July 1, which were as follows: First and Eleventh Corps to Gettysburg; Third Corps to Emmitsburg; Fifth to Hanover; Twelfth to Two Taverns on the Gettysburg road; Sixth to Manchester, only a short march; Second to Taneytown. Directions for withdrawals were given, but the plan was essentially flexible. "The time for falling back can only be developed by circumstances," Meade broadcast in a circular. "The commanders of the corps are requested to communicate at once the nature of their present positions and their ability to hold them in case of any sudden attack at any point."[23]

He remarked to Hancock, who was with him at Taneytown, that he would fight in front if practicable, and if not there, "then to the rear or to the right or the left."[24] He could not yet tell what Lee might be

[20] *Meade*, II, 15–16.
[21] MHSM *Papers*, Vol. III, 239.
[22] *Battles and Leaders*, III, 291; Gibbon, *Address on the Unveiling of a Statue*, 14.
[23] O.R., XXVII, pt. 3, 458–59; *Meade*, II, 385–86.
[24] *Meade*, II, 35, 379.

doing, nor did he know the ground where Reynolds was probing. Not until the morning of July 1 did a topographical map of Pennsylvania reach army headquarters.[25]

The Pipe Creek circular went out that same morning, but it was obsolete even before being placed in couriers' hands. General Butterfield had been slow in getting it out, and events elsewhere were moving much faster. The good news had arrived that the enemy was apparently retiring from the Susquehanna, and as Meade awaited further word from the army tentacles farthest north, a courier from Buford hastily dismounted. The cavalryman warned in a penciled note that the enemy was advancing upon Gettysburg from two directions. A. P. Hill's men, coming from the west, were driving in his pickets and skirmishers, he reported, but Reynolds with his leading division was within three miles of the town.[26]

Meade made no hasty move. A battle probably would be fought that day, but Reynolds, who had Warren with him, would decide the ground. The size and strength of the enemy force was all important. Major James Biddle of headquarters was sent to Sedgwick, who led the largest corps and was farthest away from Gettysburg. Get ready, Sedgwick was asked, to move "in such direction as may be required at a moment's notice." Biddle was invited to lunch with the General. "Has Meade retained Butterfield?" Sedgwick inquired. He looked a little solemn when Biddle answered, "Yes." He said that he knew Butterfield well and that Meade would live to regret it.[27]

Meade's present difficulties with Butterfield were not major, but the latter was getting behind with his work. A message sent to General Halleck, dated 12:00 noon, July 1, described events as Meade had known them much earlier. It said nothing of the news from Buford, which must have reached headquarters at least an hour before. A. P. Hill, the message stated, "was massed behind the mountains at Cashtown." In view of the enemy's withdrawal from the Susquehanna River, it added, the army could concentrate between Middleburg and Manchester along the Pipe Creek line.[28]

But at 11:20 A.M. Captain Stephen M. Weld had arrived on a

[25] D. B. Steinman, *The Builders of the Bridge*, 258.

[26] *O.R.*, XXVII, pt. 1, 70–71.

[27] James Biddle to Webb, December 10, 1885, Webb Papers; *Meade*, II, 31.

[28] *O.R.*, XXVII, pt. 1, 70–71. The timing on messages and letters handled by Butterfield cannot be trusted.

spent horse after racing fourteen rugged miles from Gettysburg in one hour and twenty minutes—good time. Weld happened to be the youngest man on Reynolds's staff, and if also the lightest in weight, he may have been selected on the basis of poundage for the horse. The oral message he brought was of first importance—Reynolds had told him to kill his mount if necessary.[29]

Meade asked that the message be repeated. "The enemy are advancing in strong force," Reynolds had said tersely. ". . . I fear they will get to the heights beyond the town before I can. I will fight them inch by inch, and if driven into the town, I will barricade the streets and hold them back as long as possible."[30] Weld heard Meade say emphatically, "Good! That is just like Reynolds, he will hold on to the bitter end."[31] Meade's thoughts were racing. His first concern was the danger to Gettysburg and the army's left flank, but almost in the same breath he carped at Butterfield's tardiness, saying it caused orders to be seriously delayed. In a message wired to Harrisburg by way of Washington, he had asked General Couch to threaten Ewell, who had been at Carlisle, from the rear. This could never be done. Ewell on July 1 was coming down to Gettysburg, thirty-six miles south of Pennsylvania's capital.

The note to Sedgwick was the only written message sent, but other corps leaders were kept informed. Meade was satisfied that Reynolds would hold on until Howard and Slocum also got there. Then the worst news was received.

It was about one o'clock when Major William Riddle, arriving from Gettysburg, painfully revealed that Reynolds had been killed. Riddle saw sorrow and shock reflected in Meade's drawn face. As the word spread, men exclaimed in astonishment, "Reynolds dead? Reynolds!" A bulwark had been snatched away almost before the battle had begun. "It was hard to believe and harder to bear."[32]

Asking for details, Meade learned that Reynolds had just placed his First Brigade into position to support Buford, then fighting dismounted, when he was struck in the neck by a ball. An orderly, Sergeant Charles Veil, gently bore him away to a sheltering clump of trees,

[29] Stephen M. Weld, *War Diary and Letters*, 230; *Meade*, II, 36.

[30] *Meade*, II, 36; Weld, *War Diary*, 230.

[31] *Meade*, II, 36, 222, 230, 232.

[32] A. B. Underwood, *Three Years' Service in the 33rd Massachusetts*, 115.

where he lived no longer than fifteen minutes. The body was then taken to a near-by dwelling as Riddle raced to Howard and then to Meade. On the road from Gettysburg he met Captain Weld, whom he informed.[33] It was a sad rider who returned to the field, where the Federal position was worsening.

Under the dauntless leadership of General James Wadsworth, Reynolds's First Division had entered the fight, but greater enemy forces were arriving from both north and west. Both Hill's Corps and Ewell's would be fighting west of and through the town. To replace Reynolds, Meade picked General Hancock, an unfaltering Pennsylvanian then in his fortieth year. "Authority was in his open face," it was said of this officer who was dependable not only on the march but wherever bullets flew.[34] Placing a map in his hand, Meade directed him to assume the command on the field at Gettysburg and there carefully examine the Federal position. If it was found unfit, he was to seek out and report the nearest place where the army should concentrate. If that position happened to be good, then all the troops would be ordered up.

Hancock set out with Major W. G. Mitchell, his chief of staff, and two aides, riding in an ambulance with their horses led behind. For a while he studied the topographical map, but as the noise of guns began to be heard, he halted the ambulance, had the horses brought around, then mounted to make better time. When an ambulance was seen approaching, the riders stood aside. "General Reynolds," the escort called out. A pall of silence hung over the riders until the battle scene was reached.[35]

Until a battleground was definitely selected, Meade would remain at Taneytown, where riders were constantly leaving and those arriving usually obtained fresh horses. He was chafing over the scarcity of news

[33] Testimony of Captain William H. Willcox, A. D. C., in *Philadelphia Inquirer*, July 5, 1863; of Captain Stephen M. Weld in *War Diary*, 230; and of Major Joseph G. Rosengarten, A. D. C., in *Philadelphia Weekly Times, Annals of the War*, 63–64. Willcox says Reynolds was shot at 9:30 A.M., but Weld timed his own departure from the field with Reynolds' message at ten o'clock. General Wadsworth, who was near by, said it was nearly 10:30 A.M. *O.R.*, XXVII, pt. 1, 266. "General Reynolds attacked the enemy about 10:45 A.M. . . . and was killed at 11 and a quarter A.M."—Howard to Meade, *ibid.*, 696. Howard didn't know. Nichols, *Toward Gettysburg*, 205, 253–54, analyzes events.

[34] MHSM *Papers*, X, 53; Schaff, *Battle of the Wilderness*, 42.

[35] Francis A. Walker, *General Hancock*, 109.

when, about 3:30 P.M., he heard from General Howard, who had reached Gettysburg sometime after the noon hour. But other than reporting his arrival with his Corps and that he had ordered General Sickles up, Howard had nothing to say.[36] Meade must have closely questioned the bearer of this message. It was known that losses were severe and that the action was spreading. Superior enemy forces had been pushing the First Corps back. Probably more than one hour later came a note from General Buford addressed to his superior, General Pleasonton, who was then at headquarters. "In my opinion," said Buford after giving early details of the fight, "there seems to be no directing person. We need help now." The enemy, he continued, occupied a "semi-circle on the height, from north to west." This was exasperatingly brief. Buford believed that enemy corps—Hill and Ewell—approaching from two directions had joined forces.[37]

Meade saw General Gibbon, temporarily placed over Hancock's Corps, move past headquarters. Six batteries of the Artillery Reserve came rumbling along. He ordered Sedgwick and his large command to Taneytown to form the army reserve, but Meade especially wanted to obtain his opinion concerning General John Newton, a division commander with the Sixth Corps whom he planned to name as head of the First. General Sykes, who had reached his previously assigned goal of Hanover, was told to prepare for additional marching that night. Nothing further could be done until headquarters heard from Hancock.

It was not until about six o'clock that the first message came. Hancock, reported Major Mitchell, said he would hold the ground until dark to allow time for Meade to make his own decision. It was added that the position seemed good for defense, although it might be easily turned.[38] "It seems to me," Meade responded, "that we have so concentrated that a battle at Gettysburg is now forced on us, and that if we can get up our people and attack with our whole force tomorrow we ought to defeat the force the enemy has."[39]

This message crossed another from Hancock timed 5:25 P.M.: "The battle is quiet now," he said. "I think we will be all right until night . . . when . . . it can be told better what had best be done. I think we can

[36] *O.R.*, XXVII, pt. 3, 457–58. The message was timed at 2:00 P.M.

[37] *Ibid.*, pt. 1, 924–25.

[38] *Battles and Leaders*, III, 287; *Meade*, II, 38; Walker, *History of the Second Corps*, 267.

[39] *O.R.*, XXVII, pt. 3, 466.

retire; if not, we can fight here, as the ground appears not unfavorable with good troops."[40] This was good enough for Meade, who knew that Warren was with Hancock. Everyone, including Sedgwick, would now move forward. Meade was most anxious to get the Sixth Corps on the ground next day, believing that otherwise he might be outnumbered.[41] Sedgwick already had put some distance behind him in heading toward Taneytown, but now he had to face his command about and get on the road to Gettysburg. He would have the longest march, covering about thirty-four miles during that night and part of the next day. Sykes resumed his march from Hanover after a four-hour rest. Slocum with the Twelfth Corps reached the field by early evening after Hancock and Howard had withdrawn to the hills just south of Gettysburg. As ranking officer, Slocum would assume the command on that field.

Aides and orderlies hurriedly packed up at headquarters. Meade was hunting for some lost spectacles when Hancock and Warren surprised him by returning shortly before ten o'clock. Hancock told how the First Corps had been forced back, following Howard through the stricken town of Gettysburg. Losses had been high, although not solely from wounds and fatalities. Many soldiers had fled north for safety.

Although Howard, upon arriving, believed himself in command, it was Hancock who rallied the army along Cemetery Ridge, a north-south elevation flanked by convenient hills. A late note from Howard reported his loss as "about 3,000 killed, wounded, and missing." He, too, believed the position suitable for battle "unless you fear its being turned."[42] A little after ten o'clock Meade started out with Hunt and Warren and Captain W. H. Paine of Warren's staff, who served as guide.

The moon was not yet up, and the road was badly congested by the Artillery Reserve and by Second Corps troops and wagons. Nevertheless, the little cavalcade reached Gibbon's headquarters, eight or nine miles distant, in fifty-seven minutes by Captain Meade's watch.[43] The entire army, Meade told Gibbon, would collect at Gettysburg and fight there if the enemy attacked. Let the Second Corps resume its march "at the earliest daylight," when Hancock would be along.[44] After per-

[40] *Battles and Leaders*, III, 292.
[41] O.R., XXVII, pt. 3, 467.
[42] *Ibid.*, 1067.
[43] George Meade II, *With Meade at Gettysburg*, 69.
[44] Haskell, *Battle of Gettysburg*, 19.

Adapted from *Battles and Leaders*

BATTLE OF GETTYSBURG, EVENING, JULY 1, 1863

The map shows Newton on field. Newton himself arrived on the second day, when Meade placed him over the First Corps. The lines are beginning to form.

haps twenty minutes of discussion, Meade resumed the road. About three miles south of Gettysburg, Big and Little Round Top were sighted, the extreme left of the Federal army. These formidable rock piles loomed high in the darkness; Big Round Top was the more heavily wooded, and trees filled the little valley between. The road ran along the top of Cemetery Ridge, where a rising moon revealed sleeping troops. Shadowy guns lay beside haystacks, ammunition was piled near by, and rows of army wagons were parked in groups. Meade absorbed what he could of the near-by terrain.

Shortly before midnight, the party entered the rear of the little graveyard on Cemetery Hill just south of the town.[45] Riding past broken tombstones and monuments, Meade dismounted at the gatekeeper's lodge. An orderly went to awaken General Howard. Slocum then arrived from a farmhouse on Powers Hill some distance back, and Sickles from his encampment behind Cemetery Ridge.

After an exchange of greetings, Meade turned to the junior corps commander. "Well, Howard," he said, "what do you think, is this the place to fight the battle?" "I am confident we can hold this position, General Meade." Other opinions, as polled, agreed that it was quite suitable for defense. "I am glad to hear you say so, gentlemen," Meade responded. "I have already ordered the other corps to concentrate here and it is too late to change."[46] He indicated where the late arrivals on the ground were to take position, ordering Sickles to place his left flank on Little Round Top, then bade his chieftains good night.[47]

[45] Meade, *With Meade at Gettysburg*, 95; *Meade*, II, 62; George Meade to Alexander S. Webb, December 2, 1885, Webb Papers.

[46] Loyal Legion of the United States, Illinois Commandery, *Military Essays and Recollections*, Vol. IV; O. O. Howard, *Autobiography*, I, 423; *Meade*, II, 62.

[47] George Meade to Webb, December 2, 1885, Webb Papers.

# 12. "Now Sickles' Blunder Is Repaired"

FEDERAL CAMPFIRES still flickered behind Cemetery Ridge as Meade took his son George and another staff officer to examine the ground.[1] Under a bright moon the disorder of battle was revealed—the dead horses, broken artillery wheels, shattered caissons, and bits of infantry equipment—but there were a few rows of whole guns pointed down the valley. To the north and west, along Seminary Ridge opposite, Lee's campfires signaled the enemy encampment; somewhere within that distant glow General Reynolds had fallen. Meade must have reflected upon his own loss and the army's at that hour. With the exception of Hancock and Sedgwick, he had no other highly esteemed corps commander.[2]

His little entourage had come up the Taneytown Road atop Cemetery Ridge. Other highways radiating into Gettysburg narrowed the front, but because an irregular pattern of hills lay just below the town, the battle would be continued there. Meade strolled down Cemetery Hill as far as the Baltimore Pike, which angled in from the southeast. This was the main route to the supply base at Westminster, Maryland, and should the Federal right give way, the enemy could get astride this road. But its front was protected by Cemetery Hill and wooded Culp's, where the extremity of the Federal line bent to the right. Part of the battered First Corps guarded Culp's, while the Eleventh clung

[1] *Meade*, II, 62; George Meade to Webb, December 2, 1885, Webb Papers.

[2] Pennypacker, *Meade*, 143. Isaac Pennypacker had little esteem for several of the corps leaders, "one of whom," he wrote, "prided himself upon serving through the war without friction by never assuming a serious responsibility if he could avoid it; another of whom, of undoubted courage, was not a trained soldier, and whose military methods often seemed to savor of the practices adopted to produce political effects; while a third was lacking in moral stamina, a fourth in vigor, and a fifth, an unassuming and excellent subordinate, was probably outweighted with the command of a corps." These officers as described appear to be Slocum, Sickles, Pleasonton of the cavalry, Sykes, and Howard.

to Cemetery and Little Cemetery Hill. Some First Corps troops also were anchored on the lesser height, the thin line trailing off to the left.

The third main road south of Gettysburg, the Emmitsburg Pike, which the Federals held, formed with the Baltimore Pike an inverted "V" bisected by Cemetery Ridge. Scattered hills and slopes that had been carved out by great glaciers made it a topographical patchwork. Whoever put this terrain to best use would win the coming battle.

Meade already knew the main outlines of the ground and where each command lay. His thoughts turned to the Baltimore Pike, for the defense of which he had assigned Slocum's fresh corps to Culp's Hill. Most of these troops were then sleeping some distance in the rear, but since the importance of Little Round Top had early been recognized, two regiments of General John W. Geary's division had been posted there, the others occupying part of Cemetery Ridge. Rising two hundred feet above near-by terrain, Little Round Top was practically bare about its summit, permitting the use of artillery. In the morning, when Geary's division left for Culp's Hill, Sickles was to move in from his bivouac behind Cemetery Ridge. When the Second Corps came up, he was to fill the gap between Sickles on the left and Howard, replacing both Twelfth and First Corps troops.

Meade's son does not reveal whether the General slept that night. It is stated only vaguely that the General returned to the cemetery and "addressed himself to the task of making preparations."[3] Even before daylight he was riding over the ground with Howard, Hunt, and Captain Paine of Warren's staff. He saw that heavy barricades of timber slashings and piled cordwood were strengthened about Culp's and Cemetery Hill, then surveyed the Ridge and its contours as far down as Little Round Top. Headquarters were set up in the Widow Leister house, conveniently near the front line. This little frame building, to the left rear of Howard's position, contained only one sizable room on the ground floor and little space above, but Meade would be almost up to the line of battle, and little time would be wasted in the transmittal of orders.

Horses were tied to a white picket fence running along the front. On a field map drawn by Captain Paine, Meade marked the positions for each army corps and distributed tracings. Morning coffee was being brewed as Chief of Staff Butterfield and Adjutant Seth Williams ar-

[3] *Meade*, II, 62.

rived. Riders were sent to hurry along Gibbon and Sykes. Word came that Humphreys' Third Corps division had been delayed by a straying enemy brigade which had temporarily blocked a back road. Meade could depend on Humphreys, but he was disturbed to learn that Sickles had left his artillery ammunition many miles to the rear. The resourceful Hunt, who was then placing his guns, dispelled Meade's concern by pointing out that he always had an ammunition reserve on hand to cover just such deficiencies.[4] About eight o'clock, Sykes brought up two Fifth Corps divisions (the third coming up at noonday), which were placed in reserve on the right.

Meade talked with General John Newton, arrived from the Sixth Corps after an all-night ride. Newton had seen fighting from Gaines's Mill through Chancellorsville, and although he was not regarded as daring or brilliant, Meade preferred him to Abner Doubleday, temporarily leading the First Corps, whom he considered slow and pedantic. When Newton observed that Doubleday outranked him, Meade rejoined that he had been authorized to make any desired changes.[5] As he stood talking with Newton, a rifle ball whizzed between them. It was thought to be only a chance shot until a *New York Herald* man who was near by uttered a sharp warning, "Look, General," pointing to a church belfry where enemy marksmen were perched. So warned, Newton and Meade withdrew to safer ground.[6]

An aide with Newton saw Meade looking pale and careworn, with great dark lines under his eyes. Of toughened frame and well stored with nervous energy, he still appeared fit for the day's work. General Warren remembered him on that day as "quick, bold, cheerful, and hopeful, and he so impressed others."[7] General Butterfield, long after the war, would recall Meade's "self-possession and absolute coolness— strong and pronounced."[8] He received no cheers from his busy troops as he rode a second time along the Ridge that morning, but officers and men were responding nevertheless with buoyant spirit and lively energy. It was definitely sensed that Gettysburg would be the big battle,

[4] *Battles and Leaders,* III, 297–98.

[5] Loyal Legion, Illinois Commandery, *Military Essays and Recollections,* Vol. I, 169.

[6] Andrews, *The North Reports the Civil War,* 421–22.

[7] Taylor, *Warren,* 123.

[8] Julia L. Butterfield, *Biographical Memoir of General Butterfield,* 128.

and the troops, digging in, somehow had a feeling that another day had come.

Meade, however, did not overlook marching orders for use in the event of forced retreat. In General Hunt's words, "Prudence dictated that arrangements should be made in advance."[9] The choice of roads to be taken by the several corps was left to Butterfield, who went upstairs to work quietly with drawings and maps. Otherwise, Meade's initial plan called for "a strong and decisive attack"[10] to prevent Lee from working around the Federal right and seizing the Baltimore Road. After being sent to reconnoiter, Warren and Slocum advised against it, finding the ground in front too rough and too much exposed to enemy guns. The position was considered only good for defense. Meade went no farther. From one end of the line to the other it was understood that the army would strengthen its fortified works and await enemy attack.[11]

Hancock, followed by the Artillery Reserve, came up smartly, and gunners began filling their limber chests. Crisp orders echoed from the slopes as troops marched to their assigned places. The portion of the First Corps that had slept on the Ridge was returned to the right as Hancock extended his men close to Sickles on his left and to Howard on the Gettysburg side. General John W. Geary's Twelfth Corps division marched to Culp's Hill from its temporary position on the extreme left of the line, but before withdrawing, Geary sent an aide to remind Sickles of the importance of continuing to hold Little Round Top. Geary maintained that he was explicit; in his stated opinion "possession by the enemy would give him an opportunity of enfilading our entire left wing and center with a fire which could not fail to dislodge us."[12]

Sickles, who was of a mind to fight the battle in his own way, paid no attention. After waiting uselessly for a reply to two notes, Geary marched off to join the rest of his corps on Culp's Hill. Save for some Signal Corps officers at work on the height, Little Round Top was left unoccupied. Nor did Big Round Top have any troops, although the

[9] *Battles and Leaders,* III, 297, 300.
[10] *O.R.,* XXVII, pt. 3, 480. The attack was to be made as soon as the Sixth Corps was up.
[11] "The additional risks of an offensive battle were out of all proportion to the prospective gains."—General Henry J. Hunt in *Battles and Leaders,* III, 303.
[12] *O.R.,* XXVII, pt. 1, 825.

area beyond assigned infantry positions was shielded by cavalry, as Meade was given to suppose. Any real difficulty with Sickles, however, was hardly foreseen. Summoned to headquarters, Captain Meade heard his father ask "in his cheery and familiar way" that he ride over to see if Sickles was yet in position.[13]

Soon George returned to report that Sickles was not in position and that no one at Third Corps headquarters seemed to know where he belonged. Speaking now in "his sharp, decisive way," Meade told his son to hurry back and tell Sickles to carry out the orders already given.[14] George found Sickles mounting his horse. His troops, he said, were then finding their places. Moving forward, Sickles connected on his right with Hancock, but made no move to get astride Little Round Top. About eleven o'clock he returned George's call, remarking to Meade that he did not like his position. He complained that the Ridge dipped slightly just before meeting Little Round Top. There was higher ground, however, farther to the front. Meade asked General Hunt to ride back with Sickles and examine any area which he might take up "within assigned limits."[15]

Within the hour, bursts of fire were heard from Sickles' position. General Hunt, soon coming up, informed Meade that he had advised Sickles that the higher ground in front was obviously too far out for the Third Corps to occupy without creating gaps which would have to be filled. Since Sickles appeared unconvinced, Hunt had suggested moving up skirmishers to see if the woods in that area were occupied. One hundred green-clad U. S. sharpshooters armed with breechloaders and supported by the Third Maine then stole forward to engage in a bloody exchange with the surprised men of Longstreet.

Since this enemy column was in marching order and heading at almost right angles from the direction of the attack, it was unprepared and vulnerable. So concentrated was the Federal fire that the small force was mistaken for two regiments. The skirmish lasted only twenty minutes, but the slaughter, said a prisoner, "beat all I had ever seen."[16] And in bruising the enemy so badly, the reconnoitering force had delayed the advance of the enemy left by about forty minutes.

---

[13] George Meade to Webb, December 7, 1885, Webb Papers.
[14] *Ibid.*
[15] *Battles and Leaders,* III, 301.
[16] Robert V. Bruce, *Lincoln and the Tools of War,* 256–57.

Without remaining to see the end of the skirmish, Hunt had decided that the enemy was both well covered by trees and too close to the ridge in Sickles' front for the Third Corps to occupy it. He suggested that Sickles talk further with headquarters, and he now advised Meade to examine the position for himself. His mission accomplished, Hunt rode off to Cemetery Hill, where guns were blazing in a random exchange typical of that Gettysburg day.[17]

Hindsight suggests that Meade erred in not riding off to see that Sickles assumed his true position and stayed there, but he was then intent on watching his vulnerable right. As yet there was no concerted attack there. Toward noon, unexpected and disturbing news came from the cavalry. General Buford's division, which had been sent to the far left, beyond the Round Tops, to warn of enemy moves, had been permitted to leave the field to rest and refit without being replaced. General Pleasonton was sharply reminded, "The general expected, when Buford's force was sent to Westminster, that a force should be sent to replace it."[18] General David Gregg's Second Division, which had been guarding the Baltimore road, was ordered to cover the position, but it still would not be able to arrive there until close to 2:00 P.M.

Thus General Hood, on Longstreet's right, found the Federal left unguarded and apparently neglected. Scouts creeping past Devil's Den, a wooded, boulder-strewn pocket, and toward the Round Tops found them unoccupied. Hood asked three times that he be permitted to attack the position, but Lee's orders to Longstreet had specified an attack "up the Emmitsburg road,"[19] or in effect toward Sickles' position. Hood, however, remained in a position to threaten the heights.

The day was dragging on with but little fighting. Along the right of the line, which had been the point of most concern, the defenders had made themselves so secure on the heights that Ewell and the Confederate Second Corps hesitated from caution. Hill's Third Corps remained in position as the enemy center while Longstreet moved over, consuming some hours in getting into position beyond him. Aside from replacing Buford, Meade's only move was to draw Sykes back to a

---

[17] *Battles and Leaders*, III, 302–303; *O.R.*, XXVII, pt. 3, 482; *Meade*, II, 75.

[18] *O.R.*, XXVII, pt. 3, 490. M. D. Hardin in *History of the 12th Pennsylvania Regiment*, 150, pointed out that Meade did not believe he would be attacked on the left. "He thought his cavalry would certainly give him ample notice of any threatened attack on that front so that he would have time to prepare for it."

[19] Freeman, *Lee's Lieutenants*, III, 120.

position behind Hancock, where he could also support Sickles if required.[20] This would allow room for Sedgwick's larger corps on the Federal right. Meade let it be known that as soon as Sedgwick came in sight, the corps commanders would meet at headquarters to discuss what the enemy might do.

Just before three o'clock the head of Sedgwick's column was sighted far down the Baltimore Pike, banners aloft and infantrymen drooping. Many had moved along quite asleep on their feet until awakened by hitting against some obstruction.[21] The dazed plodders were trying to keep their eyes open after an all-night march without a halt long enough to brew coffee. By day, the heat and dust had been fearful. Meade notified General Halleck on the hour: "The Sixth Corps is just coming in, very much worn out. I have . . . awaited the attack of the enemy, I having a strong position for defensive. . . . He has been moving on both my flanks apparently. Expecting a battle, I have ordered all my trains to the rear."[22] He advised Halleck that, if not attacked, he would then take the offensive; but if a flanking movement uncovered his position, he was prepared to fall back to stronger ground.

Meade was quite unaware of a gap in his line. In spite of Hunt's warning and his instructions, Sickles had advanced in full battle array to occupy the ridge in his front. Just as he had nonchalantly broken off contact with Howard at Chancellorsville, Sickles, in moving up, now left a gap between himself and the Second Corps. When Humphreys, the Third Corps right, found himself in a marshy hollow, he was again ordered forward, thus widening the gap. The Third Corps maneuver was handsomely executed, but Hancock was never advised; and as he watched it, he was heard to growl, "Those troops will be coming back very soon."[23] Hancock faced the fact that his own left, as well as the Third Corps flank, was quite unprotected.

At army headquarters, where Sickles and Hancock were awaited, Meade saw one of Warren's aides ride hurriedly up. He went first to Warren, who took him to Meade. Sickles, he related, had advanced about three-quarters of a mile in front of Cemetery Ridge. Obviously disturbed, Meade called to Sykes to move as fast as possible to fill the

[20] *O.R.*, XXVII, pt. 1, 592.

[21] George W. Bicknell, *History of the Fifth Maine Regiment*, 242.

[22] *O.R.*, XXVII, pt. 1, 27. This message was received in Washington at 10:20 A.M. the next day.

[23] Walker, *General Hancock*, 125.

breach and "hold it at all hazards."[24] As Sickles belatedly arrived, Meade signaled for him to remain mounted. Cannon smoke was seen on the left, and gesturing toward it, Meade asked the Third Corps leader to return to his own front, where he would soon join him. Summoning General Warren, Meade galloped on Old Baldy toward the firing line.

The dozen or more staff riders following after kept too closely bunched in plain sight of the enemy, but no shells happened to fall in their direction. Halfway along, one of Meade's aides turned aside to spur on General Sykes. Sickles also was hastening a rider to ask help of Sykes, but the army regular contended that it was impossible to give it. "*The key of the battlefield* was intrusted to my keeping," Sykes coolly argued, "and I could not and would not jeopardize it by a division of my forces."[25]

Second Corps gunners were seen leaning on their pieces as interested spectators. Dark masses were maneuvering on higher ground to their left and in front. As the cavalcade reached Hancock's uncovered left, an anxious Warren remarked, "Here is where our line should be." Meade waved him on toward undefended Little Round Top.[26]

Sickles was encountered in the rear of a peach orchard near the Emmitsburg road. "General, I am afraid you are too far out," Meade rasped. Sickles tried to explain that he had been seeking more elevated ground and that his new position was somewhat higher than that which he had left. "*General Sickles*," came the retort, "this is in some respects higher ground than that to the rear, but there is still higher in front of you, and if you keep on advancing you will find constantly higher ground all the way to the mountains." Sickles did not attempt to argue. Meade heard him quietly offer to withdraw.

The colloquy was interrupted by an artillery burst. A cannon ball passed over and struck the ground just beyond as Old Baldy began prancing. It was obviously too late to withdraw. "I wish to God you could," Meade shouted above the uproar, "but those people will not permit it. If you need more artillery, call up the Reserve."[27] He at-

[24] *O.R.*, XXVII, pt. 1, 592; Paul A. Oliver to George Meade, May 16, 1882, Meade Papers.

[25] *O.R.*, XXVII, pt. 1, 592.

[26] Taylor, *Warren*, 122.

[27] Various accounts of this encounter appear in Pennypacker, *Meade*, 169; Earl Schenck Miers and Richard A. Brown (eds.), *Gettysburg*, 133–34; and in *Meade*, II,

CONFEDERATE CHARGE ON CEMETERY HILL AT GETTYSBURG,
*Thursday night, July 2, 1863*

"Had the Confederate attack been started earlier and firmly supported, there would have been trouble." From a sketch by Edwin Forbes.

COUNCIL OF WAR AT GETTYSBURG

Army of the Potomac leaders meet at the Widow Leister house, late evening, July 2, 1863. "The session had an air of a routine municipal council meeting as the calm and mild-mannered officers detailed their losses and conditions along their front." Left to right: Generals Warren, Sykes, Newton, Meade, Butterfield (seated, taking notes), Getty, Howard (empty sleeve), Pleasonton (in foreground, but said to be absent), A. S. Williams, Slocum, Hancock (gesturing), Gibbon, Birney, and Sedgwick. From a drawing by James Edward Kelly, in the Melvin J. Nichols Collection, Summit, N.J.

tempted to add a promise of infantry support, but Old Baldy showed fright, rearing and plunging. Meade managed to guide him toward safer ground, then let him run as he would for a short distance.

With a half-dozen aides streaming behind, Old Baldy piloted the group out of artillery range. Anxiously looking back, Meade threw support to a threatened battery and then was met by a rider from Warren, who urgently declared that Little Round Top had been found naked. Warren had seen enemy troops clearly outflanking the height. A Federal division "at least" was required.[28] Meade at once ordered up the nearest Third Corps division, that of Humphreys, who promptly moved in good order, but as another rider came with word that Fifth Corps troops were flocking to Little Round Top, he countermanded the stroke and turned Humphreys back to a place where he was sorely needed.

Warren, meanwhile, had saved the left from the disaster invited by Sickles. As the head of the Fifth Corps came racing up, he gathered up the foremost brigade—General Strong Vincent's— which, gaining the height, rolled some boulders together and poured fire on some of Hood's men who were then breasting the slope. In the face of desperate volleys, the enemy was too few in numbers. The next two brigades from Sykes's First Division were thrown into a defensive line behind Sickles' left, but Warren took over the leading regiment of the Second Division and motioned to brigade leader Stephen H. Weed to follow.

Again it was just in time as a reinforced enemy made a second or third thrust. But no time was allowed to fix bayonets or load weapons. Yelling troops rushed down the slope, and the attacking force wavered. Temporarily secure in possession, Weed's men began hand-hauling six guns to the top to turn them on the valley below.[29]

At the extreme left of the Federal line, troops of the Twentieth Maine fought it out from an outlying spur as a storming party entered the gorge between Big and Little Round Top. By quickly facing part of his command at right angles to the regular north-south line, Colonel

---

29. The following is at least characteristic of Meade's language: "And hardly had Sickles replied: 'Very well, sir, I'll withdraw them,' when down crashed such a fire from Longstreet's massed artillery as could only presage a serious attack in force. 'I only wish you could sir,' rapped out the angry Meade, 'but you see those people don't intend to let you.' "—Taylor, *Warren*, 125.

28. *Warren*, 123.

29. *Battles and Leaders*, III, 307–308; Catton, *Glory Road*, 315–16.

Joshua Chamberlain concentrated firepower from small arms where it was most needed. The game was one of shooting behind cover such as a strategically placed stone wall. Enemy troops threading the gap were not only surprised but disheartened. Some were forced directly back, while others found safety on wooded Big Top. The barrenness of much of Little Round Top, however, made it fearful for exposure. Colonel Strong Vincent was mortally wounded by a sharpshooter's ball, then Colonel Patrick H. O'Rorke, 140th New York, and General Weed.

There was competition for men and arms along the storm-swept Federal line. Sickles persisted in seeking help from the Fifth Corps, and after he got a message through to someone who did take heed, an angry Sykes discovered some of Weed's troops vacating Little Round Top. Back they went, Sykes reported tersely, "at the double-quick step."[30] At some undefined moment, the voice of General Meade was heard: "Bring up the Pennsylvania Reserves."[31] This Third Division of Sykes's, General Samuel W. Crawford commanding, scurried Little Round Top in active defense of home soil. Five Pennsylvania regiments charged down the slope, then raced across Plum Run and a marshy area in front. In an area some distance to the right of Devil's Den, the Second Pennsylvania planted its colors thirty feet beyond a stone wall.

With little natural defense in the Peach Orchard, the Third Corps was more than decimated by Longstreet's blazing front. The stricken regiments, a First Infantry regular bore witness,

yielded the ground inch by inch, foot by foot, the corps now a rabble. . . . We fell back to an open piece of ground flanked on both sides by heavy timber, closely pressed by the enemy. Not knowing what the bushes contained, they hesitated, and their hesitation saved the day. . . . A Sergeant of the battery which belongs to our brigade dashed along the line like an infuriated tiger and cried, "Boys, you said you'd stick to us . . . is this the way the brigade is going to leave the field? There's the guns [pointing to the rebel masses] if you're men, come on!" and with that he wheeled around, struck his spurs deep into his horse, and dashed into the enemy's disorganized ranks, his sword flashing like a meteor as his brawny arm laid about with mad recklessness. Then with one impulse the whole line yelled "Charge," and "Hi—hi—hi—i—i—i" —away we dashed after

[30] O.R., XXVII, pt. 1, 592; Meade, II, 332.
[31] Stine, The Army of the Potomac, 508.

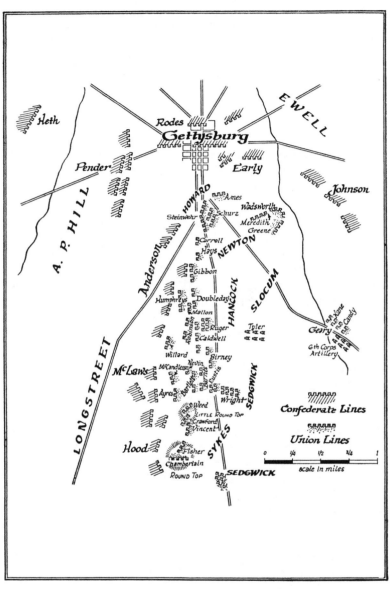

Adapted from *Battles and Leaders*

BATTLE OF GETTYSBURG, JULY 2, 1863

Division Commander Crawford is placed on Little Round Top to indicate the position of his Pennsylvania Reserves during part of the battle. There were many troop movements.

him. . . . It was irresistible and glorious—oh we went through their shattered columns like a thunderbolt, and in the thrilling excitement of the
desperate rush we seemed to be borne on wings. We were standing beside
the guns, mad with success, before we were scarce aware we had started
to do it. The 12th Corps just arrived on the spot in time to save us from
annihilation as the enemy were coming down on us again.[32]

For almost two hours Meade had been frantically maneuvering.
Wherever he turned, he discovered some weakness despite his efforts
to be fully prepared. After reining in Old Baldy, he had watched
anxiously along the Third Corps right until he saw it would be unable
to stand. He called upon Hancock to ease the pressure on Sykes, who
was forming behind Sickles' retreat while extending his left to Little
Round Top. The struggle on the left then brought Meade to Sykes as
the Pennsylvania Reserves were sent up the slope. Hancock flung shell
and canister at the masses in front, but the gap on his left still remained
open. Back to Hancock again, Meade sent riders to Newton and Slocum
to beg for all the reinforcement they could spare. Howard was called
upon to aid Hancock, and borrowing from all parts of the field, Meade
even called up two dusty brigades from Sedgwick.

His leg torn by shrapnel, Sickles was carried to the rear for immediate amputation. Meade summoned Hancock to take over the
stricken Third Corps, leaving the Second to Gibbon.

Awaiting attack by Ewell on the Federal right, Slocum made the
best bargain he could, although retaining none too many men. He
parted with two brigades under Geary, who started down the Baltimore
Pike only to lose his way and fail to get into the action. Responding to
a second call, Slocum sent off a division and more under General
Alpheus S. Williams, and Newton set out with two of his own. Part of
the Third Corps was still fighting, but these troops would have to be
relieved, and, in addition, there was a gap to be filled.

Meade and four aides alone occupied the gap as enemy standards
began moving toward them. Because most of his escort had dashed off
to corral fugitives in retreat, he had only his immediate staff with him.[33]
The last-ditch force of five men seemed rather small for the work
immediately at hand, but the General's aides saw him stand apparently
unmoved. It was for them to follow their leader. As Meade suddenly

[32] Undated Gettysburg letter, Felix Brannigan Papers.
[33] Paul A. Oliver to George Meade, May 16, 1882, Meade Papers.

straightened himself in his stirrups, the four aides nervously did likewise, and as he drew his sword from its scabbard, four more blades
rattled and then flashed in the sun. The meager handful stood poised
against an enemy regiment now only about six hundred yards distant.
Would the General, someone was wondering, lead a desperate charge?
Glancing aside from the enemy, aides were looking about anxiously for
help when, with great relief, the cry was heard, "There they come,
General."

Down the Taneytown Road were racing two First Corps divisions
"amidst the wildest excitement and shouting," and just behind came the
troops led by Pop Williams. The First Corps divisions of Doubleday
and General John C. Robinson made a right wheel in close formation.
As they were about to go in, General Newton, a cool sort, "rode up to
General Meade for orders . . . pulled out a flask and offered it. A shell
dropped in front and covered General Meade with dirt but it did not
seem to interfere in any way with the [libation]. . . . The men advanced
with a cheer, preceded by a line of skirmishers. General Meade galloped through, and removing his hat, said, 'Come on gentlemen,' thus
leading the charge with his staff." Continued Lieutenant Paul A.
Oliver, an aide from Slocum, "This act of pluck and daring helped
inspire the men with confidence."[34]

First Corps troops were in full motion when someone rode up to
report that A. P. Hill's corps stood massed in front. This was entirely
in error; the enemy line was unsupported. Knowing only what he was
told, Meade tried to bring the troops to a halt, but everyone was still
running.[35] It required hardly more than a volley to check the enemy
advance. Twelfth Corps troops meanwhile dashed over to save Sickles'
remnants from annihilation. Four guns previously lost were retaken,
and two Confederate pieces also were brought in.

It was nearly dark when the relieving troops formed a permanent
line along Sickles' original position, and the last of his regiments was
escorted to the rear. "Now Sickles' blunder is repaired," exulted a Second Corps officer who had witnessed his early advance. "Now, Rebel
chief, hurl forward your howling lines and columns."[36] The hours had
been tense. Hearing someone remark that affairs had looked quite desperate for a time, Meade heartily responded with a ring in his voice:

[34] *Ibid.*
[35] W. H. Locke, *The Story of the Regiment*, 244.
[36] Haskell, *Gettysburg*, 52.

"Yes, but it is all right now! It is all right now!"[37] He had escaped a bad wound by inches when a bullet pierced his saddle flap and lodged somewhere within Old Baldy's stout frame. Although retaining the bullet, the war horse would return for another campaign.[38]

Meade's urgent calls for more troops had thinned Slocum's line along Culp's Hill, where the lower breastworks bordered close on the Baltimore Pike. With the enemy probing the position and threatening attack, Slocum had wished to retain a full division at least. "But Meade was obstinate," said a Twelfth Corps partisan.[39] After nearly everyone had hurried off to the left, only General George S. Greene's brigade of 1,350 men remained to occupy the barricades on the hill. Other works guarding a low-lying spur had to be left vacant.

Ewell's opening cannonade was outmatched by Federal guns. Tardily for enemy success, about five o'clock, General Edward Johnson sent three Confederate brigades against Culp's as Jubal Early's division assaulted Howard. Because troops had been drawn from Howard to aid Greene, as well as to the left, Hancock hurried over a brigade in return for help previously sent him.

The reinforcement reached Howard in time to save Cemetery Hill, although had the attack been started earlier and firmly supported, there would have been trouble. Greene manfully clung to his fortified height until well after dark, when the firing died down, and then his men rested. The slaughter in the Confederate ranks had been heavy. Yet, as elsewhere, the scales had tipped back and forth so that "the least disaster would have sufficed to force us from the field," in the opinion of Captain Jesse H. Jones, Sixtieth New York.[40]

As darkness fell, the Twentieth Maine began forcing enemy troops from Big Round Top and, supported by other regiments which were sent over, securely anchored the Federal line. A detachment from the Fifth Maine sallied out to retake a battery and brought it in by hand.[41] The long day ended with an earth-shaking artillery duel. As the last echoes died away under a starless sky, Meade summoned his corps commanders to meet in a council of war at the Widow Leister house.

[37] *Meade*, II, 89.
[38] *Ibid.*, 89; Meade to Captain Sam Ringwalt, September 24, 1864, Meade family collection.
[39] C. E. Slocum, *Life and Services of Major General Henry W. Slocum*, 105–106.
[40] *Battles and Leaders*, III, 316.
[41] Hardin, *The 12th Pennsylvania*, 152; Bicknell, *History of the Fifth Maine*, 244.

# 13. *"We Had a Great Fight"*
## *(July 2-3, 1863)*

A CANDLE HELD UPRIGHT on a small pine table by its own wax cast its feeble light about the room and its other poor furnishings—a large bed in one corner and a few cane-bottomed chairs. An orderly refilled a wooden pail with water to be drunk from a battered tin cup lying near by. Several cigar-smoking officers casually entered the room, and after the first arrivals had divided up the chairs, the latecomers had to stand.

General Warren, who had been struck a glancing blow in the neck by a piece of shell and who seemed utterly worn out, sought the bed, where he soon slept.[1] Chief of Staff Butterfield sat at the table, and Meade had a chair, although he remained standing most of the time. The army leader was clad in the familiar dark blue flannel blouse with two-star shoulder straps, light blue pantaloons, field cap, and high-top boots (known in Philadelphia as troop boots), and he wore an officer's leather belt and the regulation sword.[2] Lieutenant Frank Haskell, aide to General Gibbon, marked the scene from where he waited just outside the Widow Leister house:

> Meade is a tall spare man with full beard quite thickly sprinkled with gray, Romanish face, very large nose, fibres all of the long and sinewy kind. Sedgwick is quite a heavy man, short, thick-set and muscular with dark, calm, straight-looking eyes. Slocum is small, rather spare, movements quick and angular. Howard is the youngest of them all, a very pleasant, well-dressed little gentleman. Hancock is the tallest and in many respects the best looking, dignified, gentlemanly and commanding. Sykes is a small, rather thin man with the general air of one who is weary and a little ill-natured. Newton is well-sized, shapely, muscular, with blunt, round features, walks very erect, curbs in his chin. Gibbon is com-

[1] *Battles and Leaders,* III, 313.

[2] George Meade to J. E. Kelly, October 22, 1879, Melvin G. Nichols Collection.

pactly made with ruddy complexion, full jaws and chin, with an air of calm firmness in his manner.[3]

Came also General Birney, now leading the Third Corps, "good soldier, energetic";[4] and full-bearded Alpheus S. Williams, who had led the troops sent to the left from the Twelfth. The session had an air of a routine municipal council meeting as the calm and mild-mannered officers detailed their losses and conditions along their front.

Straggling from the First and Eleventh Corps had been serious on July 1, and in addition to their dead and wounded, the Third and Fifth had suffered heavily the next day. Taking down the returns from each corps as now given, Butterfield reckoned that 58,000 fit for duty remained in the lines exclusive of artillery and cavalry. Meade opened a general discussion by asking views on whether the army should remain or withdraw.

Newton, an experienced engineer, could argue soundly that Gettysburg was a poor position and that Lee could easily turn it if he chose. Slocum was for staying and fighting it out. Birney said that he had not yet made up his mind—all he could think of was that his command had been badly cut up and scattered. Others generally favored retaining the position now held. Meade put the next question: Should the army attack or await attack, and when should an offensive be attempted?

Sedgwick was doubtful of the wisdom of attacking early, and nearly everyone believed that they should wait at least another day. Hancock dissented only slightly: "Can't wait long," and Howard suggested a time limit of 4:00 P.M., July 3. Since the feeling of everyone, including Birney and Newton, was clearly no retreat, Meade was satisfied that everyone favored holding his ground and would fight heartily to do so. John Gibbon, who left a record of that interesting session, considered him "perfectly in accord" with the sense of the meeting. "Such then is the decision,"[5] Meade said quietly, although adding in agreement with Newton that he thought Gettysburg no place to fight a battle. He would decide later whether to launch a general offensive.

A dispatch sent General Halleck while the council was still in ses-

[3] Haskell, *Gettysburg*, 67–70.

[4] *Meade*, II, 235.

[5] *Ibid.*, 96, 415–19; *Battles and Leaders*, III, 313–14; Gibbon, *Personal Recollections*, 144–45.

156

sion summed up the day: "The enemy attacked me about 4 P.M. . . . and, after one of the severest contests of the war, was repulsed at all points. We have suffered considerably in killed and wounded . . . have taken a large number of prisoners. I shall remain in my present position to-morrow, but am not prepared to say, until better advised of the condition of the army, whether my operations will be of an offensive or defensive character."[6]

The meeting concluded, Meade spoke pleasantly to Gibbon, a good fighter although a great admirer of McClellan. Assuring the younger officer that he was glad that he had attended the council, Meade added significantly, "If Lee attacks tomorrow, it will be in *your front*. He has made attacks on both our flanks and failed, and if he concludes to try it again it will be on our center."[7] Yet it was clearly Lee's best strategy, if he could not turn either the Federal right or left, to remain in position and let the other side carry the fight.

Meade may have slept for a few hours, but within a short time a courier from Slocum reported that the enemy had gained a footing on the vacated lower spur of Culp's Hill. Slocum should attack at day-break to regain the lost ground, Meade ordered. The troops which had been borrowed were being returned from the Federal left. General Hunt would be sent to help place more guns.

The morning of July 3 dawned bright under a clear sky. Early in the saddle, Meade rode with Hunt and Warren from Culp's Hill to Little Round Top. An offensive had not been deemed feasible on the right, and there was too much open country in front of the Federal center. Lee, on Seminary Ridge, had the advantage of woods. Meade decided, as he advised Hancock, that he would make no general attack, although, should Lee be repulsed, the Fifth and Sixth Corps would then be advanced against the Confederate right.[8]

Slocum, who was banging away at the intruder, was reinforced by a Sixth Corps brigade while Geary, returning, had to fight his way in. Hunt's artillery blazed, and concentrated rifle fire punished the enemy

[6] *O.R.*, XXVII, pt. 1, 73–74; *Meade*, II, 96, 419. The latter source, which is reliable, gives the time of the dispatch as 11:00 P.M., or about one hour before the council adjourned. In the *Official Records*, the time is stated as 8:00 P.M., obviously an error inasmuch as Meade then had no data and the outcome had not been fully determined on General Howard's front.

[7] Gibbon, *Personal Recollections*, 145; *Meade*, II, 97.

[8] *Meade*, II, 104.

front. Within an hour Johnson's division fell back through a bordering forest broken and splintered by shrapnel and ball. The day had begun with a victory; five hundred prisoners had been taken, and the field-works close to the Baltimore Pike had returned to Federal hands.

Meade had remained on the far right during most of the fighting on that side of the line, but returning to headquarters as time allowed, he got off several messages by telegraph or courier. He early advised Sedgwick: "The enemy intends to try and pierce our center. Any available portion of your force should be massed in a central position so it can be thrown in support as desired."[9] General French, who had been halted by Meade's order at Frederick, was advised of alternatives: "Should the enemy be beaten, reoccupy Harpers Ferry and harass his retreat; should we be forced to withdraw, hasten to Washington to protect the city." General Couch at Harrisburg was asked to join forces with the main army: "Should Lee withdraw we must co-operate to destroy him."[10] A note to Mrs. Meade bore assurance that all was going well: "We had a great fight yesterday . . . today at it again . . . army in fine spirits and every one determined to do or die. George and myself well."[11] Having discovered that many troops not actively engaged had left off their arms and equipment, Meade directed his corps commanders to keep everyone fully prepared to move at a moment's notice and likewise ordered that all stragglers and other absentees be brought up.

Correspondent Whitelaw Reid of the *Cincinnati Gazette* saw Meade at headquarters that morning "quick and nervous in his movements but calm and . . . lit up with the glow of the occasion. He looked more the General, less the Student."[12] But General Gibbon thought he looked haggard at midforenoon and was shocked to learn that he had not eaten. He suggested and then insisted that Meade take breakfast with him at division headquarters. "I pointed out," Gibbon related, "that we were close at hand in plain sight, and that he would be absent but a few minutes . . . and besides he must keep up his physical strength."[13]

Food was no longer plentiful near the battlefield area, but a farmyard hen of uncertain age had been caught to yield a savory stew. Some

[9] *O.R.*, LI, pt. 1, 1068.
[10] *Ibid.*, XXVII, pt. 3, 501–502; *Meade*, II, 104.
[11] *Meade*, II, 103.
[12] Quoted in Andrews, *The North Reports the Civil War*, 424.
[13] Gibbon, *Personal Recollections*, 146.

butter had been found, also a battered loaf of bread which could be divided. Potatoes, sugar, and coffee were available in quantity from stores. The generals and their aides sat about on camp stools or on the ground and ate well. Newton and Pleasonton, sniffing the air, rode up and dismounted. They, too, were served, and after cigars were lighted, Meade lingered comfortably and discussed the day's prospects. He issued a few orders from where he sat and did not ride off until about 12:30 P.M.[14]

From the way both sides were arranging their guns, an artillery battle appeared imminent. A mass of enemy batteries could be seen already in place or going into position to be pointed in a great arc toward the Federal center. General Hunt accepted Meade's theory that the main attack would come there and so brought up more pieces. Yet the narrow Federal position could not accommodate more than some eighty guns, or fewer in line than Lee had. Nor was ammunition in plentiful supply. Meade agreeing, Hunt planned to conserve it for the enemy assault that would follow the prolonged barrage. His orders were transmitted all along the Federal line: "Withhold fire for 15 or 20 minutes after the cannonade commences; concentrate accurately on batteries which seem the most destructive; return the fire slowly."[15] When an enemy signal gun was heard at 1:07 P.M., the tireless Hunt had just completed his task, having reached Little Round Top.

A following enemy signal was slightly delayed. After the second gun was heard, there was perhaps a half-minute of silence, then the explosions multiplied and grew so thunderous that they generated a great wave of sound heard 140 miles away.[16] When the order to fire came from Hunt, Federal artillerists standing near their guns could sense the sudden flash and jolt, though individual explosions were lost in the general uproar.

Men hugged depressions in the ground or sought cover behind rocks and trees, but Confederate marksmanship was generally poor, most shots carrying high. Many shell fuses were cut too long, resulting in numerous overshots which brought destruction to the Federal rear. Wagons, ambulances, livestock, and army stragglers were riddled, and to see the shirkers shot up was to the fighting troops in the line the

[14] Haskell, *Gettysburg*, 90–93.
[15] *Battles and Leaders*, III, 372.
[16] Jacob Hoke, *The Great Invasion*, 363 n., 508.

most comical sight of the day. Caissons violently erupted, cascading fragments of woodwork, wheels, and shell. Meade's headquarters seemed to be directly in range as shells exploded among the helpless and frantic horses tied to the white picket fence. Several of the poor creatures were killed and many others wounded. At one blow the steps of the house disintegrated, followed by the supports of the porch. Cannon balls crashed through both the garret and the main room of the house. Carried away were two legs of the table at which Lieutenant Roebling and General Seth Williams were sitting as they studied a battle map, both escaping death by inches. Meade was fanned by a shell as he stood in the open doorway.[17]

Officers and staff scrambled out and sprawled on the ground in the rear as Meade began striding back and forth in his preoccupied way. Seeing his staff huddled together he was reminded, he said, of the man who drove the ox team which brought ammunition to Palo Alto in the Mexican War. When General Taylor chided him for hiding from enemy shells behind a mere up-tipped cart, declaring him no safer there than anywhere else, the simpleton rejoined, "It kind o' feels so." The joke fell flat as a spherical shot ripped through the house, exploded near the rim of the circle, and wounded a visiting staff officer.[18]

Since no dispatch rider could easily reach headquarters under fire so hot, Meade moved to a barn near the Baltimore road, where a shell fragment caught General Butterfield in the neck. Butterfield retiring, headquarters went to Slocum's headquarters on Powers' Hill, almost directly behind Hancock but nearly a mile away. Meade was occupied in shifting some troops in reserve when a complaining citizen showed up. He complained that his house was being used as a hospital, that soldiers' bodies had been buried in his garden, and that the grounds were littered with amputated limbs. His stated opinion that he probably had a claim upon the government was crushed by Meade's stinging reply, "Why, you craven fool, until this battle is decided, you do not know, neither do I, if you will have a government to apply to. . . . If I hear any more from you, I will give you a gun and send you to the front line to defend your rights."[19]

[17] These scenes are variously described in Howard, *Autobiography*, I, 437; S. P. Bates, *Battle of Gettysburg*, 155; Steinman, *The Builders of the Bridge*, 259; Coffin, *The Boys of '61*, 294; Hoke, *The Great Invasion*, 365–66; and elsewhere.

[18] Paul A. Oliver to George Meade, May 16, 1882, Meade Papers; *Meade*, II, 107; *Meade's Headquarters*, 13. The wounded officer was Colonel Joseph Dickinson.

The handling of Gettysburg troops was so flexible on July 2 and 3 that brigades and divisions at different times occupied two or three parts of the field. On this afternoon, Meade not only reinforced his center but saw to it that the flanks were well secured against any enemy turning movement. The Sixth Corps brigade—General Alexander Shaler's—which had fought at Culp's Hill, was marched to the left and rear of Hancock. The brigade made a run for it, yet a few men went down in moving through the barrage of enemy shots skimming over the Ridge. Meade shifted other Sixth Corps troops as temporary reserves to be thrown in at the right moment, and most of the battered Third Corps was now in reserve.[20] The Sixth had ceased to act as a unit; the Fifth and First also were somewhat broken up. General Sykes, who held Big and Little Round Top with part of his command, had to be reassured that no troops would be withdrawn from the position he now occupied, no matter where the main line was attacked.[21]

The minutes were wearing away slowly. All sense of time was lost as minds were numbed by the artillery thunder and sharply exploding shells. Smoke which filled the valley between the opposing lines aided the enemy, who also had the advantage of covering woods; some Federal batteries on more open ground were being badly cut up by shell fragments and flying shot.[22] After one hour of fearful stress except at the far ends of the line, General Warren signaled from Little Round Top that more smoke would only provide cover for an infantry attack, and since the enemy appeared to be but little hurt, he suggested that the firing be stopped.

General Hunt meanwhile had been looking into his limber chests, only to find ammunition running low. He tried to notify Meade, but, unable to find him, decided to silence the guns himself. The idea coincided with Meade's thoughts, for riders from Powers' Hill were then seeking Hunt with the same order. As the word to cease fire was passed along the line, tired gunners threw themselves on the ground beside their pieces. Hunt pieced damaged batteries together and ordered the Artillery Reserve to replace the worst hit. Guns loaded with canister were run well forward to sweep a wide area if and when needed. But

[19] John W. Storrs, *The 20th Connecticut Regiment*, 104–105.
[20] *O.R.*, XXVII, pt. 1, 663, 681; *Meade*, II, 107.
[21] *O.R.*, XXVII, pt. 3, 500.
[22] Hoke, *The Great Invasion*, 371; Buell, *The Cannoneer*, 93.

rather than permit his men to be scourged without replying, Hancock opened again with his guns when he might well have saved his small ammunition supply for the worst of the fight.[23]

Soon all guns on both sides were silent, and everyone on Cemetery Ridge watched to see what might be occurring in front. From the lower part of the Ridge the troops could see for a little way under the smoke, and under a mild west wind the hovering cloud began to break up. When it became certain that enemy masses in front were revealed, men were seen gesturing and a loud shout arose, "Here they come!"[24] Broad lines of uniformed men were advancing in perfect alignment with battle flags flying and with confidence and vigor in their stride.

Union gunners sprang to their feet to resume fire as the order was given. Infantrymen lying on the far slope of Cemetery Ridge picked themselves up and got back into line. Messengers went pounding to Meade, who rushed about for a quick look at his defenses. Though damage had been heavy in some places, the Ridge could still be held.

There was never a very clear view of the three infantry divisions of Longstreet and A. P. Hill which were swarming through woods, orchards, and farmland. Until toward the last, the advance never moved hurriedly—after sweeping over a post-and-rail fence, the line was halted to dress up the formation. Union guns were blazing again, the range about half a mile. Shells clipped the enemy right as the advance sheered off from the hottest fire by making a half-left wheel.

Part of General Gibbon's front was covered by a small clump of oak trees and a rail fence which turned back at a right angle for a short distance, then turned again to meet a stone wall. Two enemy brigades were diagonally approaching the trees from the left, and a stronger force appeared directly in front. Other enemy invaders threatened Howard and Newton on the Federal right. It was a strong assault— fifty-seven regiments or about 15,000 men. Would this be enough?

Gaps were opened by the exploding shells; figures carrying battle flags went down. "Give them canister, pour it into them," a Federal officer was shouting.[25] Two enemy brigades halted to deliver the first volley just as Union rifles were raised in reply. The small-arms fire

[23] *Battles and Leaders*, III, 386–87.
[24] Coffin, *The Boys of '61*, 294.
[25] *Ibid.*, 295.

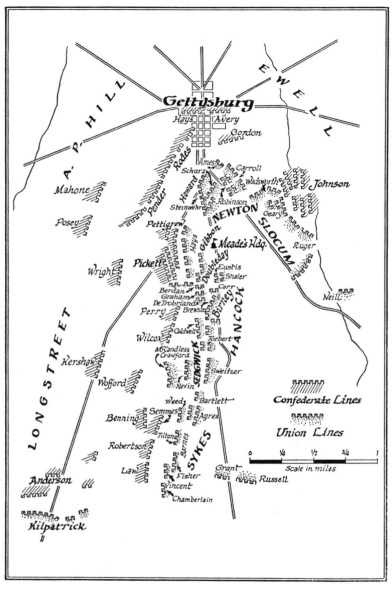

BATTLE OF GETTYSBURG, JULY 3, 1863

The map shows brigade leaders Weed and Vincent still on field. These officers were killed on July 2, their commands being assumed by others.

raised a clatter heard by anxious Union prisoners and wounded inside the town. A high-keyed Confederate yell rose over the uproar.

Toward the Federal right, where the enemy line was unaccountably thin, two flanking brigades were seen advancing quite unsupported. Gunners timed their blow exactly; as the smoke drifted up from the concerted discharge, the shattering effect of canister was disclosed. Not a man reached that part of the Ridge. Toward the center the enemy was deeper, and although the ranks were buckled in front, there was no relaxation of the coiled spring. General Alexander Hays, whose Second Corps division stood next to Howard, witnessed a march "as steady as if impelled by machinery, unbroken by our artillery."[26] Dust and smoke seemed heaviest along Gibbon's front, where battle flags converged upon the fences and bullet-flecked trees. General Alexander S. Webb and his Second Brigade found themselves squarely in the path of the Confederate rush, which was quickened by the musketry of some First Corps troops half-hidden in the tall grass along the left front. Thus the oncoming brigades were crowded together to form a blunt wedge in their slanting drive.

Second Corps artillery, already badly cut up, had spent its ammunition. As the defending Federals reloaded small arms, they unconsciously drifted back a step or two, giving the appearance of retreat. Hancock was gratified to see Lieutenant Frank J. Haskell "at a critical moment . . . when the contending forces were but 50 or 60 yards apart, believing that an example was necessary and ready to sacrifice his life if necessary, ride between the lines with the view of giving encouragement to ours and leading it forward, he being at that moment the only officer in a similar position."[27] But Haskell was struck and his horse hit in several places. General Gibbon, also wounded, was carried from the field. Hancock was struck by what was believed to be only a tenpenny nail ("The enemy must be short of ammunition,"[28] he thought), but a ball which may have flicked the nail from a fence would be found lodged deep in his thigh.

With the passage of some furious moments which almost deprived men of thought, it could be seen that the drive could not be contained beyond the defending front line. As Webb's brigade gave way, organization was lost. A hundred or more enemy troops began pouring over

[26] O.R., XXVII, pt. 1, 454.
[27] Ibid., 376.
[28] Ibid., 366.

GENERAL ELON J. FARNSWORTH'S CHARGE ON THE FEDERAL LEFT
AT GETTYSBURG, *July 3, 1863*

"The order was too hastily given, and the ill-fated charge from the left of Round Top was made with too small a force."

PICKETT'S CHARGE AT GETTYSBURG, *July 3, 1863*

"Out of the 5,500 men which Pickett took into action, 1,499 surrendered, 224 were killed, and 1,140 were reported wounded. Pickett lost twelve out of fifteen battle flags."—Pennypacker, *Meade*. From a pencil drawing by Alfred R. Waud, 1863.

the fence. Webb, his head bleeding, was waving a broken rifle in an effort to rally his men. He was looking about for help, but Doubleday on the left was too far off "and too slow,"[29] and although Meade was bringing up reserves from the other side of the Ridge, they might not arrive in time. Haskell and other alert officers still on their feet borrowed from the First and Third Brigades, sending a few regiments to pitch in; otherwise, Webb remarked, "the enemy probably would have succeeded in piercing our lines."[30]

Nevertheless, the Federal line had been pierced, as Webb should have realized, though senses were blunted and reality was full of strangeness. Rapid fire seemed slow, and reinforcements coming on the run appeared to be dragging their feet. Oncoming troops found gentle slopes as difficult as steep hills. No support was in view for the dauntless few who had scrambled over the fence. On Webb's left, where General John C. Caldwell's division of four brigades stood, the enemy halted, delivered its fire, wavered when it was returned, and then fled. When those in the first wave began looking about them for reinforcements, the defenders knew they had won. Gray-clads still on their feet rushed toward sheltering trees and woods to their rear, and some lay down to be picked up by the Federals seen all about them. These and others were swept together as prisoners and escorted up the slope of the Ridge.

But some Federal troops were still in retreat at the same time that prisoners were being gathered in. Officers and men coming suddenly on the scene had no means of discovering at once who were the victors. Hancock's own Chief of Staff, bringing up a battery on the run, mistook the situation for a successful enemy assault and gave orders to retire.[31] Troops coming up from the other side of the Ridge had to sort out their impressions during the strange jumble.

The field was still noisy and turbulent as Meade rode past a swarm of prisoners toward the Second Corps. Lieutenant Haskell looked into his deeply lined face, "earnest and full of care," and heard a quick, sharp voice: "How is it going here?"

"I believe, General," Haskell replied, "the enemy's attack is repulsed."

[29] Haskell, *Gettysburg*, 122.
[30] *O.R.*, XXVII, pt. 1, 428.
[31] Haskell, *Gettysburg*, 139–40.

Meade could hardly believe it. "What! Is the assault already repulsed?"

"It is, sir."

Again scanning the mad scene before him—the milling prisoners, the dead, the crying wounded of both sides, the captured battle flags, and the ragged enemy lines ebbing from the smoke-filled front—Meade muttered, half to himself, "Thank God," and eyed the shifting panorama for some moments in silence.[32]

It was now about four o'clock. Meade knew that both Hancock and Gibbon had been carried off. Who, he asked Haskell, was the ranking Second Corps officer? Haskell replied General Caldwell, First Division, but to save time, Meade gave his orders directly to the wounded Lieutenant before him. The lines were to be re-formed and the men held in their places to beat off any renewal of the assault. "If the enemy does attack, charge him in the flank and sweep him from the field, do you understand?"[33] Haskell saluted and turned away, but he well realized that too many officers were missing and that the Federal center was too exhausted for anything more than defensive action.

Satisfied that the worst at least was over, Meade rode off to inspect his right. Son George, his only escort, was trailing behind him when a piece of shell tore through the back of his saddle and fatally wounded his horse, the second lost to him on that busy day. Unaware of the incident, Meade continued directly on his way, and George was left to foot it alone.[34] It was a relief to find Howard's forces in very good shape with no new attack expected on that front. Howard had acquitted himself much better than at Chancellorsville. A message was flashed to the far right: "We have repulsed them on every part of the line."[35]

First and Eleventh Corps officers began to crowd around Meade and offer their congratulations. He shook a few hands, bowed, and saluted, then rode at a gallop toward the other end of the line. Catch-

[32] *Ibid.*, 136–37; Gibbon, *Personal Recollections*, 182. The interesting battlefield letter quoted by Gibbon appears to be from the pen of Haskell.

[33] Haskell, *Gettysburg*, 138.

[34] *Meade*, II, 125, 134. George Meade to Webb, November 11, 1883, Webb Papers. Colonel Meade, as he was then, relates that he ran into Webb, also afoot, his hat off, his sword drawn. Webb was seeking some officer to help restore a partially wrecked battery, and he left George to his own devices when a wounded artillery lieutenant happened along.

[35] *O.R.*, XXVII, pt. 3, 501.

ing sight of their commander, soldiers mounted the breastworks, cheering and waving their caps. From the other side of the valley a British military observer with Longstreet heard spontaneous cheering, "loud and continuous," and saw an officer followed by perhaps thirty officers riding along the opposite ridge.[36] Although an entourage of this size invited artillery fire, the enemy did nothing to halt its progress.

As Meade had instructed Hancock earlier that day, he planned to strike the enemy right with troops from the Fifth and Sixth Corps following the battle. The only enemy action seen from the crest of Little Round Top was an enemy battery in the wheat field, but a conference was cut short by sharpshooters' bullets, one whizzing under Warren's arm and past Meade's shoulder. His orders given, Meade, in a jovial mood, descended the slope with Warren.[37]

A Federal cavalry brigade was then moving on the far flank of the enemy line, but the force sent in was too weak and had moved too soon for concerted action. Complaint would be made that the troops from the Round Tops failed to get started in time. "Why the infantry, when they heard fighting in [E. M.] Law's rear, or when, afterward, we delivered to their skirmish line our prisoners, did not advance and drive his brigade into the valley . . . has never been explained," argued a cavalry officer.[38]

It had been overlooked that the passing of orders to the dispersed infantry brigades would take more time than word given directly to a single cavalry unit. Infantry ranks were somewhat disordered, the troops had been occupying defensive positions, and those holding Big

[36] This happened to be "your humble servant," Meade wrote his wife upon reading Colonel James Arthur Lyon Fremantle's eyewitness report in the September, 1863 (Vol. XCIV), issue of *Blackwood's Magazine*. See *Meade*, II, 153, and *The Fremantle Diary* (ed. by Walter Lord), 216.

[37] *Philadelphia Press*, November 12, 1872.

[38] *Battles and Leaders*, III, 396. In his Gettysburg report, Meade credited the cavalry with good service in assaulting the enemy line and occupying its attention, but no relation between cavalry and infantry action was defined. The enemy's powerful artillery and infantry blows and the Spartan resistance of that day left gallant cavalry action almost unnoticed, but Meade was very well served by his mounted arm, which in no other battle had fought so effectively. East of the town and north of the Hanover Road, Jeb Stuart had been held back by General David Gregg's Second Cavalry Division, which prevented him from reaching the Federal rear as had been planned. On the extreme left, along the Emmitsburg Road, General Wesley Merritt and the Cavalry Reserve skirmished with enemy infantry and possibly averted encirclement.

Round Top never did get in line.[39] Some time after 5:00 P.M., two of Sykes's brigades and one from the Sixth Corps advanced toward the wheat field. Pennsylvania Reserves under Colonel William McCandless cleaned out the woods on the right, then faced about, that officer related, to charge the enemy on the left, "routing him, capturing nearly 200 prisoners, also a stand of colors."[40] The ground lost by Sickles on the second day was again in Union hands.

The new position flanked boulder-strewn Devil's Den, which sheltered Confederate sharpshooters. This, too, was taken after a short fight, but some of the hidden riflemen who had joined their dead comrades would not be recovered for days. The hour was now late, the troops hungry and tired after their long day. On July 3, 1863, the Federals had faced the worst artillery blows yet delivered and had repelled a determined enemy charge on their center and right. No major counterstroke was believed possible under these circumstances. It was commonly felt, General Warren observed, "that we had quite saved the country for the time and that we had done enough; that we might jeopardize all that we had done by trying to do too much."[41] An artillerist claimed that an organized counterattack was no subject for discussion "among the hungry, exhausted, battered, and mangled men whose strong arms and stout hearts had won the fight."[42] Such discussion would be confined chiefly to others.

The separate cavalry and infantry actions on the Federal left had closed the day. Toward evening, swallows in search of food flew low over the ground—a harbinger of rain—and songbirds seemed to be hunting their shattered nests.

It remained for Captain George Meade to forward an account of battle to Philadelphia. Scribbled on a torn piece of paper, his battle report personalized the day's great events: "Papa is all safe, a splendid victory, Baldy shot [on July 2], I am safe, two horses shot, hole in coat, all our friends are safe so far."[43] Meade again moved his field headquarters, although not to the Widow Leister house, which was now a crowded hospital, but to a little grove near by. He sent a reassur-

[39] A. M. Williams, *Disaster, Struggle, Triumph*, 197; Hoke, *The Great Invasion*, 438, 440.
[40] *O.R.*, XXVII, pt. 1, 654, 671.
[41] Quoted in Hoke, *The Great Invasion*, 440–41.
[42] Buell, *The Cannoneer*, 116–17.
[43] George Meade to his mother, July 3, 1863, Meade Papers.

ing message to General Halleck to mention the artillery duel, the repulse of enemy infantry under the command of General George Pickett, the bagging of 3,000 prisoners, many enemy casualties, and a "considerable loss" for the Federals.[44]

It had been an exhausting day for General Lee, who was unaccustomed to defeat. Sometime after one o'clock in the morning, feeling fatigued and depressed, he dismounted at his headquarters tent, and after confessing it "a sad, sad day," sought repose on his cot.[45] On the Federal side, a newspaperman found Meade sitting on a large flat boulder "stooping and weary, his slouched hat laid aside so that the breeze might fan his brow."[46] The boulder that night became Meade's couch, son George and other aides sleeping near by. A torrential thunderstorm interrupted their rest, and by the sharp flashes of lightning George caught a glimpse of the rain-drenched army leader sitting bolt upright, a picture of sorry discomfort.[47]

[44] *O.R.*, XXVII, pt. 1, 74.
[45] *Battles and Leaders*, III, 421.
[46] Coffin, *The Boys of '61*, 299.
[47] Pennypacker, *Meade*, 201.

# 14. Lee Steals a March
## (July 4-14, 1863)

THOSE AT HOME could only wait. In every city, crowds flocked outside the newspaper offices to read the battlefield bulletins posted in windows. Extra editions went quickly whenever they appeared on Saturday, July 4. At the Union League Club in Philadelphia, word of victory at Gettysburg came over its wartime telegraph wire. Now the price of gold would fall, and securities would rise in value.

After dinner that day, as soon as everyone could be collected, Mayor Alexander Henry, the Philadelphia City Council, and some Union League members paraded with a brass band to the Meade residence at 2037 Pine Street, a distance of nearly three-quarters of a mile. It was rather late when they arrived, but after being serenaded, Mrs. Meade appeared in the doorway to hear the Mayor make some complimentary remarks and to receive the cheers of the crowd. It was pleasant to be so honored for the sake of her husband, and she graciously acknowledged the courtesy in a few words, then retired amid "deafening applause for herself and . . . the victor of Gettysburg."[1]

No newspapers were published on Sunday, July 5. The Union League Club again was crowded as members and guests scanned the telegraph messages tacked on the bulletin board. Doctrinaires pontificated on Waterloo, a battle within the memory of many. Gettysburg, too, was a pounding match fought in the style of Wellington and Napoleon. The long week end over, the *Philadelphia Inquirer* went to press:

VICTORY!

WATERLOO ECLIPSED!!

Battlefield dispatches took up most of the front pages, the *New York Tribune* printing fourteen columns written by one man alone.[2]

[1] *Philadelphia Inquirer*, July 6, 1863.

Down around Wall Street, a sellers' market for the newsboys, everyone seemed "very jolly."[3] Some people even thought the war was over, an idea which stimulated trading at the New York Stock Exchange. Summing up events, diarist and eminent citizen George Templeton Strong wrote that Gettysburg probably would be ranked as one of the great decisive battles of history. The immediate results, indeed, were "priceless," since Philadelphia, Baltimore, and Washington had been saved, the Confederate army routed, and "the charm of Robert Lee's invincibility broken." Strong set down the opinion that the Federal Army at last had a general who could handle it.[4]

The national capital, which had been under a long nervous strain, reacted wildly during the night of July 3 and all the next day with church bells, firecrackers, and rockets. Although the victory was not actually announced until midafternoon on July 4, whispers had generated excitement. A joint celebration for Independence Day and Gettysburg was held on the grounds south of the White House. "I *never* knew such excitement in Washington as when the news arrived that he had whipped Lee," Miss Margaret Meade wrote 2037 Pine Street. "Several persons have called to know if I could give them a good picture of him." Brady the photographer, Margaret ran on, "is crazy to have a good likeness of you as well as of the Gen¹."[5]

Believing that Lee could be beaten again, President Lincoln could not consider Meade's work yet done, and his message to the nation was somewhat restrained. The latest word from the Army of the Potomac, he said cautiously, was such as to cover it with the highest honor and to promise further success, but he forwarded no thanks or praise to Meade as to Grant after Vicksburg, a July 4 triumph which incited more bell ringing and artillery salutes later that day. Meade received the compliments of Secretary of War Stanton, while to Grant went the President's "grateful acknowledgment for the almost inestimable service you have done the country."[6] Vicksburg, Mississippi, was definitely in Union hands, while Lee still lingered near by in Pennsylvania.

The White House excepted, praise was coming in from all sides. General Couch, who had to deal with some rather hopeless recruits as

[2] Royal Cortissoz, *Life of Whitelaw Reid*, I, 94.
[3] *Diary of George Templeton Strong* (ed. by Allan Nevins), III, 320.
[4] *Ibid.*
[5] Miss Margaret Meade to Mrs. George G. Meade, July 10, 1863, Meade Papers.
[6] Lincoln to Grant, July 13, 1863, *Complete Works of Abraham Lincoln*, IX, 26.

well as with a few hundred Federal refugees from the first day's battle, was tremendously relieved. "The glorious success of the Army of the Potomac has electrified all," he telegraphed Meade. "I did not believe it [the enemy] could be whipped when fought in a body. . . . My dear general, I congratulate you & your whole army."[7]

Warm messages came from two former army commanders—George B. McClellan and John Pope. "You have done all that could be done," wrote McClellan, "and the Army of the Potomac has supported you nobly." Pope congratulated his onetime messmate "with my whole heart on the glorious victory . . . which entitles you to any reward the Government has the power to bestow."[8] Meade saw that these letters were preserved but averted his face from public acclaim. That which to others might have served as a stimulus was written down as "exaggerated laudation."[9] He would thank God, he assured Margaret, if he could be relieved from his unsought command and permitted to live in peace and quiet at home.[10]

Independence Day dawned fair at Gettysburg after the rain, but clouds soon gathered and lingering smoke from spasmodic picket firing settled down heavily. Woods and the opposite ridge effectively concealed enemy activities. Meade kept his cavalry out on both flanks to scout enemy movements, but the question of a concerted counter-assault did not arise. To send men blindly across the death valley was out of the question, particularly with many wounded soldiers all around. Not only had this been proved tactically unsound, but Meade's assigned task was defensive. "You will manoeuvre and fight in such a manner as to cover the Capital and also Baltimore," his original orders had stated. For the time being it was necessary to remain where the enemy could not dislodge or get around him.

The immediate and most pressing task was to supply and refit a battered army which obviously needed rest after several days of marching and fighting. The field was roughly strewn with dead and wounded, the bodies of horses, arms of all description, blasted chunks of metal, wagon wheels, pieces of clothing, shoes, cartridge belts, mess gear, and other items to be salvaged or scrapped. Ordnance officers gathered up

[7] *O.R.*, XXVII, pt. 3, 515, 549.

[8] General Pope's letter of July 10, 1863, and McClellan's of the eleventh are in the Meade Papers.

[9] *Meade*, II, 234.

[10] MS letter of July 5, 1863, Meade Papers.

the cartridge boxes of the dead and wounded and carefully sorted weapons. Barefoot soldiers, some weak from hunger, scouted the field for shoes and scarce rations.

Harried surgeons turned to the less seriously wounded first to save as many as they could. There were few houses to shelter these thousands; each corps was assigned a patch of woods to use as a hospital. Salvage and burial crews toiled throughout the day. Most of the stiff and swollen Union dead were buried in pits, with separate graves for identified officers, but as the task grew tedious and time short, dirt was simply shoveled over the bodies. Unburied Confederates were left to the last, some bodies in remote places not being picked up until several days later.

The driving power of the army had been seriously reduced by losses in veteran troops and officers, including Reynolds and Hancock. No division commanders had been killed, but two had been wounded—General Francis C. Barlow, Eleventh Corps, who was taken prisoner on the first day, and General Gibbon. Seven brigade commanders had been killed and several wounded. Returns from farther down the line revealed the loss of some 300 Union officers—a bad blow. Total losses were reckoned at more than 23,000, with nearly as many, it was believed, for the enemy. After he had seen the returns from each corps, Meade believed that he should have about 57,000 availables left, not including the cavalry units.[11] Because of the heavy loss in horses, the War Office was urged to send 3,500 fresh mounts as soon as possible.[12]

Before abandoning his stronghold on Cemetery Ridge, Meade advised General Halleck, he would try to discover Lee's actual intentions. General Barlow, abandoned with other Federal wounded as the enemy evacuated Gettysburg, got word back that Lee would only pretend to retreat and would waylay him, but Meade had to await more definite information. In a general order to the army, he saw more fighting ahead: "Our task is not yet accomplished and the commanding general looks ... for greater efforts to drive from our soil every vestige of the presence of the invader."[13]

Viewing little more than murky weather and smoke, Meade laid aside his field glasses. From their station on Little Round Top, Signal

[11] *Battles and Leaders*, III, 440; *O.R.*, XXVII, pt. 1, 173.
[12] *O.R.*, XXVII, pt. 3, 524.
[13] *Ibid.*, 519; *Meade*, II, 122–23.

Corps officers flashed word that wagon trains carrying enemy wounded were filing down the Fairfield Road.

Except on the left, Meade would not move toward Seminary Ridge "in consequence of the bad example he [Lee] had set me, in ruining himself attacking a strong position."[14] So, on the left, Fifth Corps pickets were advanced during the afternoon until gunfire revealed the enemy's presence some distance behind its position of the evening of July 3. But just as a brigade formed in line of battle, rain descended heavily. Men jammed their bayonets into the ground to keep the water from running down the gun barrels, and battle was postponed.[15] On the far right, in Gettysburg itself, Federals lounging in a public square were "a joyful sight" to civilians who had not felt safe for a week.[16]

General Lee proposed an exchange of prisoners, but inasmuch as those which he had would only add to his burden, Meade properly declined. Federal corps commanders voted five to three that evening to retain their fortified position until it became certain that Lee was retreating.[17] In the latter event, pursuit could be made by either of two routes. The direct route meant chasing the enemy through mountain passes where delaying actions could be fought, and while Lee would be marching directly back on his own supply line to his river crossing at Williamsport, Maryland, Meade's direction would be away from his supplies at Westminster. As an alternate, Meade could march by the left flank into Maryland, where trains from his supply base could overtake the army as it swung west. Meade planned to be prepared to go either way.

Good news came from General French, who had been ordered to destroy enemy communications. Mounted troops from his division had cut loose some boats and pontoons and burned a bridge platform at Williamsport. This success was expected at least to delay Lee's retreat across the river when attempted, and it was reported, moreover, that the water was high.[18]

Rain fell that night on a Confederate army trying to escape over heavily mired roads. Only a few miles were covered, and from the

---

[14] *O.R.*, XXVII, pt. 3, 539.

[15] *Antietam to Appomattox*, 262.

[16] Miers and Brown, *Gettysburg*, 268–69.

[17] General Couch wired that the passes were "unquestionably fortified."—*O.R.*, XXVII, pt. 3, 515.

[18] *Ibid.*, 524; Hoke, *The Great Invasion*, 471; *Battles and Leaders*, III, 432.

scanty information at hand, Meade could not tell whether Lee was retreating or simply seeking a new position. Provisional orders were prepared for a march into Maryland, but no troops were to move far until General Sedgwick, assigned the direct pursuit along the Fairfield Road, felt out the situation in the mountains. "Time is of great importance," Meade urged. "I can't give orders without explicit information from you."[19] But Sedgwick could not get started until early afternoon, July 5, and in the morning a heavy fog prevented him from testing enemy defenses in the rugged terrain near Fairfield Pass.

Other troops already in motion were supposedly prepared to turn in either direction, but the plan was spoiled by the uncontrollable Butterfield, who issued the provisional orders, sending the Third and Fifth Corps toward Middletown, Maryland.[20] This, it was decided, would be his last blunder with the Army of the Potomac, and for the time being staff duties were divided between Pleasonton and Warren.

Since the Fifth Corps was now beyond easy recall, Meade ordered two aides to detain the First and Third, which were on the same road. On edge with impatience, having sent couriers to Sedgwick throughout the day, he finally got word that enemy rear-guard action in the mountain passes, as had been witnessed, would only delay the army and waste time. The decision now could be made to move directly into Maryland. A part of Sedgwick's command strengthened by cavalry remained temporarily in place to guard Fairfield Pass from the near side while General Couch was ordered to hurry an infantry regiment from Harrisburg to protect the field hospitals and the entire battlefield area, which curious sight-seers now threatened.[21]

A full day's time had been lost in investigating which route to take, but by the late afternoon of July 6 nearly the entire Federal army was plodding through rain and mud along routes leading to South Mountain. It was hard going. "As soon as possible I will cross South Mountain and proceed in search of the enemy," Meade informed Halleck.[22] He still counted on meeting Lee somewhere north of the swollen Potomac, and hopes were high that he would. Men were considering what might happen now that Vicksburg had surrendered to Grant. Presi-

[19] *O.R.*, XXVII, pt. 3, 535.

[20] *Ibid.*, 470; *Meade*, II, 123.

[21] *O.R.*, XXVII, pt. 3, 580. The first battlefield excursion train from Harrisburg arrived promptly on Sunday, July 5.

[22] *Ibid.*, XXVII, pt. 3, 80–81.

dent Lincoln was anxious that the war be ended entirely. "Now if General Meade can complete his work, so gloriously prosecuted thus far, by the literal or substantial destruction of Lee's army, the rebellion will be over," he wrote General Halleck.[23] Captain George Meade had much the same idea: "Papa will end the war."[24]

General Herman Haupt, rail transportation chief, suggested that part of the army be moved on pontoons across the Potomac to cut Lee's supply line and prevent any building of bridges. Meade may have recalled criticism hurled at McClellan for dividing his forces on each side of the Chickahominy in late June, 1862. In any event, he was unwilling to flout military rules in dealing with Lee, Longstreet, and Hill. Haupt was confident that if his plan were adopted, "Lee . . . would have sent in a flag of truce and capitulated."[25] On the contrary, as experience showed, Lee would have maneuvered or fought.

General Couch spoke over the telegraph wires concerning Williamsport: "It has many strong points for defense."[26] He believed that Lee would not cross "as the Potomac is not fordable," yet to attempt to destroy an enemy posted behind strong works might invite another Fredericksburg. Meade was pondering what the next few days might bring as he received word from Halleck that he had been named a brigadier general of the regular army as of July 3, "date of your brilliant victory at Gettysburg."[27]

On the seventh, another rainy day, the army tried to make distance by forced marches through mud. Although the troops were hungry and soaked to the skin, spirits were buoyed up by hope and by the excitement of the chase. But dirt-clogged boots became water-soaked and heavy as they waded through rushing streams born of mere rivulets. Bad roads and dripping skies prevented several divisions from reaching their appointed destinations that night, and artillery progress over difficult hills was poor. Wagon trains en route from Westminster were delayed, and until they should arrive, the troops were ill equipped for much fighting.

Headquarters rode through to the front of the army and detoured

[23] *Meade*, II, 307.
[24] George Meade to his mother, July 8, 1863, Meade Papers.
[25] Haupt, *Reminiscences*, 229.
[26] *O.R.*, XXVII, pt. 3, 588.
[27] Halleck to Meade, July 7, 1863 (misdated 1862), Meade Papers; *Meade*, II, 307.

south to pick up General French at Frederick. Entering the town, Meade was showered with oratorical praises, floral wreaths, and bouquets as loyal citizens applauded. Meade saluted cordially, but as soon as possible he went to a hotel to enjoy the luxury of a hot bath. He donned fresh clothing for the first time in ten days. After telegraphing Margaret to send him two pairs of spectacles, he forwarded certain homely details: "From the time I took command till today [July 7] I . . . have not had a regular night's rest, and many nights not a wink of sleep, and for several days did not even wash my face and hands, no regular food, and all the time in a great state of mental anxiety. Indeed, I think I have lived as much in this time as in the last thirty years."[28]

Meade looked to General Humphreys for needed assistance as chief of staff. An iron-nerved and confident figure who went into battle as if about to take a morning stroll, Humphreys had fought well at Fredericksburg, Antietam, and Gettysburg, but more than a good field record was essential for promotion in a bitterly competitive atmosphere tinged with the war's ideology.[29] Humphreys had seen thirty-two years' service and was highly regarded, yet he had found himself under the command of such men as Butterfield, Fifth Corps, and Sickles, Third. His present superior, the less-experienced Birney, happened to be the son of a onetime Abolitionist candidate for president. Birney had been promoted to volunteer major general after Chancellorsville.

On grounds of seniority, Meade gave the Third Corps to Halleck's friend General French and relegated Birney, who was hardly pleased, to the First Division, his former command. Humphreys, leading the Second, was still behind him. Meade, however, could offer Humphreys promotion to major general if he would join him at headquarters. Mulling it over for a day or two, Humphreys gradually came around to the idea that if he couldn't obtain any better field command than the one he now had, then he should accept. On July 8, he rode ahead to overtake Meade and was warmly welcomed in his new post. Meade knew that he could count on this methodical and precise officer.

Wagon trains from Westminster coming in sight were hurried on to Middletown and Boonsboro, where the troops were heartened by

[28] *Meade,* II, 132; MS letters of July 7–8, 1863, Meade Papers. On July 12, Meade told a London newspaper correspondent that his health was remarkably good and that he could bear almost any amount of physical fatigue. Pennypacker, *Meade,* 3.

[29] H. H. Humphreys, *Andrew Atkinson Humphreys,* 201–202; *Meade,* I, 352; MHSM *Papers,* Vol. X, 86.

new uniforms, shoes, knapsacks, cartridge belts, and other gear. They appreciated the fact that refitting had been prompt in a campaign which had "made carpet-rags of almost every uniform."[30] Guns and ammunition also were supplied; enemy soldiers had already received theirs. On July 6, a trainload of supplies had been ferried across the Potomac in time to help repel Federal cavalry which broke into and for a time threatened seizure of Lee's huge wagon train making its way toward Williamsport. The flatboats used as ferries were made useful on return trips by carrying prisoners and any Confederate wounded who were able to care for themselves.

The fact that Lee was ferrying troops and supplies back and forth created something of an uproar at Washington. Federal scouts, to get word to both Meade and Halleck, wired General Couch at Harrisburg that enemy trains were crossing the river. Contrasting interpretations of the news were soon on the wires. Halleck telegraphed to Meade in a regretful tone that the enemy seemed to be crossing; Meade declared it was only the wagon train.[31] Believing that Lee's force was already partly across, President Lincoln, through Halleck, sought to apply the spur. "The opportunity to attack his [Lee's] divided forces should not be lost," Halleck obediently telegraphed. "The President is urgent and anxious that your Army should move against him by forced marches."[32]

Forced marches? Up to now there had been nothing but forced marches both before and after Gettysburg. General Grant, during his eight months' campaign against Vicksburg, would stuff War Office messages into his pocket and there leave them, but Meade always read every word. Already on that same day he had carefully outlined his situation and pledged that he would do all he could, but his message had not been received when Halleck sent his. In no very good humor, Meade went over the situation again: "My Army is and has been making forced marches short of rations and barefooted. . . . Our Corps marched yesterday and last night over 30 miles. I take occasion to repeat that I will use my utmost efforts to push forward this Army."[33]

[30] Buell, *The Cannoneer*, 122.

[31] *Meade*, II, 308–309.

[32] *Ibid.*, 308.

[33] *Ibid.*, 309. Meade's first dispatch of that day was timed at 2:00 P.M. After receiving Halleck's telegram of 12:20 P.M., he sent his reply at three o'clock.

Halleck tried to be conciliatory, writing: "Do not understand me as expressing any dissatisfaction. On the contrary your Army has done most nobly. I only wish to give you opinions formed from information received here. . . . My only fear now is that the enemy may escape by crossing the river."[34]

No one with the army believed that the enemy would cross over. After routing a cavalry force at Boonsboro, General Buford kept going to the Potomac, which, he reported, was five feet higher than when he last saw it and was still rising.[35] Writing Halleck next day, July 9, Meade contended that Lee would now have to prepare to receive his attack. The decisive battle of the war, a contest of "momentous consequences," would be fought within a few days. All the information he had received, Meade added, indicated that the enemy was preparing to fight. A self-styled deserter from Stuart's command had stated that a pontoon bridge had been thrown across the river for the purpose of bringing over supplies, while the talk among the men was that "they mean to try it again." Accepting these views as reliable, Halleck pushed on reinforcements from Washington.[36]

Refitted and provisioned, the army continued to plod over wretched roads in crossing South Mountain, which took its toll of artillery horses, immobilizing guns. Once over, Federal skirmishers on July 11 made contact with enemy infantry thrown well out below Hagerstown and Antietam Creek. The army moved more cautiously as it pushed slowly ahead; that evening the forward columns threw up breastworks as a normal precaution. Meade's associates could sense his concern over lack of information, that military essential. He had questioned the deserter from Stuart's command who said that Lee would fight, and he could read an item in the Hagerstown paper quoting Lee as telling his troops that they were about to meet their old enemy again.[37] But was it actually a deserter, and what did Lee really intend? "I have to grope my way in the dark," Meade wrote Margaret on July 12.[38] Early that day, Fifth and Sixth Corps troops drove enemy forces through a

---

[34] *Ibid.*, 309.

[35] *O.R.*, XXVII, pt. 1, 925.

[36] *Meade*, II, 310.

[37] *Philadelphia Inquirer*, July 17, 1863, quoting an item in a Hagerstown paper of July 11 which apparently circulated within the Federal lines. This ruse has gone unnoticed by Lee's biographers.

[38] Meade to wife, July 12, 1863, Meade Papers.

village below Hagerstown and occupied the heights beyond.[39] Meade made Hagerstown, taken after a skirmish, his headquarters and rode out to see what he could make of an enemy line extending south from a point about two miles west.

The cavalry probing where it could, a defiant enemy was found strongly lodged on both flanks. From Lee's right resting on the Potomac, the fortified line took advantage of every ridge and hill as it ran northward and curved west to the wooded banks of a creek. Earthworks cut across all roads within the area, and good use was made of stone fences. The position was effectively covered by guns on the heights. An enemy sortie was considered quite possible. Pushing close up on the Federal left, General Slocum reported his position untenable in the face of two ranges of fortified hills in his front, one commanding the other. The enemy, he complained, could pass around his left flank.[40] Meade permitted him to withdraw a short distance and sent cavalry over.

To test enemy resistance, picked divisions from the Second, Fifth, and Sixth Corps closed upon an occupied wheat field that afternoon, a Sunday, and pickets were thrown out. The enemy lines were carefully scanned by Meade, Humphreys, and Warren, but much was hidden from view. Clouded skies appeared threatening as Meade turned and gave his orders. Brigades filed up by companies to support the pickets, and all was ready when along came a regimental chaplain, wearing a solemn air. Couldn't the battle be as well fought on the next day as on the Sabbath? inquired Father William O'Neill of the 119th Pennsylvania. Those familiar with Meade's temper on battle days expected to hear him make a cutting rebuke, but he happened to be facing a man of the cloth.

Meade answered calmly that he was like the man with a contract to make a box; four sides and the bottom were finished and the lid ready to be put on. This final step could be achieved only through the action now planned. Standing unmoved, the chaplain responded, "As God's agent and disciple I solemnly protest. . . . I will show you that the Almighty will not permit you to desecrate his sacred day. . . . Look at the heavens; see the threatening storm approaching." This argument

[39] George H. Gordon, *A War Diary of Events*, 143; A. A. Humphreys, *From Gettysburg to the Rapidan*, 4–5; Sypher, *The Pennsylvania Reserves*, 483.
[40] *O.R.*, XXVII, pt. 3, 646.

was unanswerable. Thunder and lightning played about, and "copious showers" soon fell. Officers sought shelter, while the men in the ranks had to stand as they were until the projected movement was abandoned about suppertime.[41]

It was Meade's wish to drive ahead next day without further preliminaries, "for the reason that delay will strengthen the enemy and will not increase my force."[42] Enlistments about to expire would be equal to new troops. Meeting that night with corps leaders, he declared himself in favor of an outright assault if it were so voted. To attack fortified heights without first reconnoitering appeared a little rash, and although General Hunt then favored the move, upon reflection he would refer to it as Meade's only error in judgment during the campaign.[43] Sedgwick suggested moving two corps around the enemy left and attacking both front and rear, but felt that some preliminary scouting was necessary, for when it came to a vote only Wadsworth of the First Corps and Howard of the Eleventh supported Meade's proposal of immediate assault. The decision, then, was to take a closer look at undoubtedly strong enemy works.[44]

Because of the bad weather, an order from Halleck, received on the thirteenth, would have made little difference had it come earlier: "You are strong enough to attack and defeat the enemy before he can effect a crossing. Act upon your own judgement and make your generals execute your orders. Call no council of war. . . . Do not let the enemy escape."[45] In the army it was still taken for granted that Lee would be unable to cross the swollen Potomac. "We are watching intently for your prey," General Hays, Second Corps, wrote a friend. "We are very sanguine but cautious. Yesterday it rained torrents and today gives

[41] *Antietam to Appomattox*, 282.

[42] *O.R.*, XXVII, pt. 1, 9.

[43] Hunt to Webb, January 19, 1888, MHSM *Papers*, Vol. III, 239, quoted in part in *Battles and Leaders*, III, 412. This and Howard's letter to Lincoln (*O.R.*, XXVII, pt. 1, 700) comprise the outstanding defense of Meade at Gettysburg.

[44] *Meade*, II, 363; Haskell, *Gettysburg*, 148; Gordon, *A War Diary*, 160; Sedgwick, *Correspondence*, II, 34–35. Colonel Martin T. McMahon, Sedgwick's chief of staff, wrote in *Battles and Leaders*, IV, 82: "General Sedgwick proposed . . . to take the 6th and 11th corps from our right, and, moving by night through and beyond Hagerstown, to occupy by daylight a position upon the enemy's flank and rear." Rain and fog would have seriously interfered with such a movement.

[45] *O.R.*, XXVII, pt. 1, 92.

promise of more, which will keep up the Potomac."[46] A newspaperman who called at headquarters was assured by Adjutant Seth Williams that it would be impossible for Lee to escape. "He has no pontoons, we have him in a tight place." The rain, fog, and mist which hung over the hills permitted no clear view of the situation. Entered Meade dripping from the rain after inspecting his lines. "We shall pitch in," he said confidently.[47]

A Federal sympathizer who taught at the College of St. James behind the Confederate lines could see everything plainly. Between the two ranges of hills which Meade confronted lay a marsh and open fields, an obvious trap for any attacking force. Confederate sharpshooters swarmed over the top floors of the college buildings and climbed trees. An officer was heard to remark, "If he attacks us here, we will pay him back for Gettysburg." But it was generally felt on the opposite side that Meade probably knew better.[48] In view of the bad weather and the high water in the Potomac, his orders to probe the enemy lines had been permitted to stand.

High water aside, the rain and mist would serve the enemy well. Toward evening on this thirteenth of July, General Howard on the Federal right thought he could distinguish a column in motion just opposite him. "I fear Lee is getting away," he remarked in disquiet, and sent an aide to inform Meade.[49] But it was a little too late in the day for anyone to change his mind concerning enemy intentions.

Resuming the movement previously tried on Sunday, four Federal divisions cautiously crept forward early on the fourteenth. General Williams, Twelfth Corps, marched at 6:00 A.M. and pushed up a regiment of skirmishers from each brigade. It came as a surprise that there was nothing in front. Williams turned left and proceeded downriver toward Falling Waters. The bad news came while he was still on the way—the enemy, a cavalry aide said, had nearly all crossed. Hurrying skirmishers could only engage the rear of the retreating columns, bagging between two and three hundred prisoners.[50]

General Horatio G. Wright, Sixth Corps, had a similar tale: "At daylight on the 14th I received intelligence from the picket line that

[46] G. T. Fleming, *Life and Letters of Alexander Hays*, 411.
[47] Coffin, *The Boys of '61*, 303.
[48] Sypher, *The Pennsylvania Reserves*, 485.
[49] Coffin, *The Boys of '61*, 303.
[50] *O.R.*, XXVII, pt. 1, 771–72.

the enemy had retreated during the night, and at once ordered the skirmishers forward, proceeding with them some two miles beyond the enemy's entrenchments when I ordered the advance of the division to Williamsport where it was found the enemy's force had crossed . . . some hours before and that further pursuit was impracticable owing to the depth of the river which was rapidly rising and then too deep for fording."[51]

Lee, then, had not intended to fight. Enemy preparations for the crossing would later be told. At Falling Waters, where the work was concealed by a steep bank and a wide bend in the river, warehouse timbers had been converted into a passable bridge laid on pontoons, some of which had been recovered following General French's cavalry raid. The bridge was then covered with branches to deaden sound. Rickety as it was, it supported guns, the artillery train, and the corps of Longstreet and Hill. Ewell's Second Corps actually forded the river at Williamsport, the tallest men of each company standing in midstream and passing shorter-statured men on. All through that night the enemy troops had manfully toiled in the mud and the rain until nearly everyone was safe. Only the rear guard under General Harry Heth was left to fight for their lives as Federal horsemen and infantry cut off the hindmost.

[51] *Ibid.*, 667.

# 15. Lee Twice Turns Back
## (July 14-October 18, 1863)

A SUDDEN CHANGE in point of view was expressed by some who had considered Lee trapped. Those who had plodded over the long road to Williamsport had done so, as they thought, for a purpose. The men in the ranks really wanted to fight, and, in view of their labors and sacrifice, they believed Lee's escape tragic.

In the ranks and in certain high places, many felt that a timely attack would have resulted in the capture of the entire Confederate Army and that the war could have been ended within sixty days.[1] At Meade's headquarters, where confidence yielded to chagrin on the morning of July 14, newspaperman Noah Brooks met Vice President Hannibal Hamlin, who "raised his hands and turned away his face with a gesture of despair." General Wadsworth, who had voted to fight, was seen almost in tears.[2]

Meade could only realize that he and his generals had miscalculated and that the administration had been right in its fears that Lee would escape. Lincoln in fact had been dissatisfied all along with his effort. The wording of Meade's July 4 order to the troops—that he would look to them "for greater efforts to drive from our soil every vestige of the presence of the invader"—had disappointed the President, who had looked for nothing less than complete victory. Now he was dismayed to learn that a council of war had been called on July 12 and that, seemingly as a result, nothing was done.

Although the council of war in no way affected events, it looked as

[1] John D. Vautier, *The 88th Pennsylvania Volunteer Regiment*, 158; Charles E. Davis, Jr., *Three Years in the Army*, 255; Charles Francis Adams, Jr., *Studies Military and Diplomatic*, 311; James H. Wilson, *Life of Charles A. Dana*, 249.

[2] Brooks, *Washington in Lincoln's Time*, 95. Captain George Meade referred slightingly to Vice President Hamlin in a letter to his mother dated July 23: "What they sent him for, God only knows, he does not look as if he had two ideas in his old beastly head."—Meade Papers. Apparently Hamlin was not particularly welcome at headquarters.

if Lincoln would never forgive his new general. "I do not believe you appreciate the magnitude of the misfortune involved in Lee's escape," he wrote moodily in a letter intended for Meade. "He was within your easy grasp, and to have closed upon him would, in connection with our other late successes, have ended the war. As it is, the war will be prolonged indefinitely."[3] It was a bad day for the President, but good sense prevailing, he laid the letter aside. The national leader was in need of strong counsel which might logically reveal where and how the war could be won. Certain obsolete ideas would have to be overcome before Lee would be finally beaten. Yes, great as Lincoln was in politics and statecraft, he still needed guidance—and in due course would obtain it—concerning what should be done with his army.

Lincoln, however, could hardly visualize what others now saw directly before them—in effect, a second Fredericksburg. As soon as the men got a good look at the massive enemy works, it began to be sensed that Lee's crossing was good riddance. After riding out with Meade to obtain a clear view of the natural and man-made defenses, General Humphreys gave the opinion that an assault would have resulted only in disaster.[4] Sedgwick was of the same mind. Lee's position was so strong, he remarked, that the army "could not with safety attack."[5] Even Howard, who had voted to fight, considered it "by no means certain that the repulse of Gettysburg might not have been turned against us."[6]

Supported also in these views by Warren and Hunt, Meade was satisfied that Lee's flight had served the true purpose.[7] An attack against

[3] *Complete Works of Abraham Lincoln*, IX, 28–30, contains the full text of this long letter.

[4] Humphreys, *From Gettysburg to the Rapidan*, 7.

[5] Sedgwick, *Correspondence*, II, 134–35.

[6] Howard to Lincoln, July 18, 1863, *O.R.*, XXVII, pt. 1, 700; *Battles and Leaders*, III, 289.

[7] Meade, testified General Hunt after long reflection, "was right in his orders as to Pipe Creek . . . right in pushing up to Gettysburg after the battle commenced—right in remaining there—right in making his battle a purely defensive one—right therefore in taking the line he did—right in not attempting a counter-attack at any stage of the battle—right as to his pursuit of Lee. Rarely has more skill, vigor, or wisdom been shown in any such circumstances." This message was addressed to Alexander S. Webb, January 19, 1888, as part of an effort by Meade's friends to counteract some current propaganda of glory-seeking Dan Sickles. See Webb Papers; reprinted in MHSM *Papers*, Vol. III, 239 and in part in *Battles and Leaders*, III, 412.

Further comment may be found in Haskell, *Battle of Gettysburg*, 145–53; Taylor, fortified heights as at Fredericksburg was by its very nature as well as by precedent ill advised. Indeed, General Longstreet and other enemy officers had been eager to fight.[8] An aide to Lee observed that his chief "would not have been sorry if Meade had attacked . . . but he did not stop specially to invite it but because the river was high."[9]

Although Lincoln withheld the letter in which he had unburdened his mind, he still did not hesitate to make his views known. A telegram of that day from Halleck pointed out that the President was greatly dissatisfied over the enemy's "escape" and that he required an active and energetic pursuit. In view of enemy defeat and flight through two states and feeling a unanimity of officer opinion behind him, Meade could hardly accept reproof. "Having performed my duty conscientiously and to be the best of my ability," his reply ran, "the censure of the President conveyed in your dispatch . . . is in my judgment so undeserved that I feel compelled most respectfully to ask to be immediately relieved from the command of this army."

Halleck answered fairly promptly but softened his words. Instead of "dissatisfaction," the "disappointment" of the President was cited. And no actual censure was intended, only "a stimulus to an active pursuit."[10] But "stimulus" hardly helped matters; Meade resented the prick of the spur. Everything considered, he wrote Margaret, he would esteem it the greatest of personal favors if Lincoln named someone else to the command. His own temperament was not "sufficiently phlegmatic," he explained, for leadership of an army commanded by these authorities in Washington. He deplored the lack of energetic subordinates. Very serious now was the loss of Reynolds and Hancock: "Their places are not to be supplied."[11]

---

*Warren*, 122; *Meade's Headquarters*, 272; Henry Kyd Douglas, *I Rode with Stonewall*, 252; Hardin, *The 12th Pennsylvania*, 157; Thomas L. Livermore, *Days and Events, 1860–1866*, 271–72; G. J. Fiebeger, *Campaign and Battle of Gettysburg*, 106, 147; Alexander McClure, *Colonel Alexander K. McClure's Recollections of Half a Century* (Salem, Mass., 1902), 351, and *Lincoln and Men of War-Times*, 360; William Swinton, *Campaigns of the Army of the Potomac*, 370; Coffin, *The Boys of '61*, 305; Pennypacker, *Meade*, 206, 212–13; Weld, *War Diary*, 242; *Philadelphia Inquirer*, July 15, 1863.

[8] *Annals of the War*, 443; *Battles and Leaders*, III, 367.

[9] Charles Marshall, *An Aide-de-Camp of Lee* (ed. by Frederick Maurice), 249.

[10] Meade-Halleck correspondence, *O.R.*, XXVII, pt. 1, 92–94; original Meade letter in National Archives.

[11] MS letters of July 14 and 18, 1863, Meade Papers; see also *Meade*, II, 136.

Again the bugles sounded and the drums rolled. Early on July 15, Meade turned the columns southeast for the river crossing. The troops were singing "Carry Me Back to Old Virginny" as they plodded over pontoons laid down at Harpers Ferry and at Berlin (later Brunswick), Maryland. Still guarding the capital, his primary duty, Meade kept well east of Lee's route, but was unable to determine whether his opponent was actually retreating or seeking to renew the advance. The sniping grew hot in Meade's rear. His ear to the ground, General Hooker sought permission to rejoin the Army of the Potomac. Many critical letters, some of them anonymous, were received at headquarters. "You will fail," said one, "as McClellan has failed." "Your course," said another, "will prove that engineer officers in conducting campaigns are failures."[12]

It seemed to be a bad time for former army engineers. Lee, too, was tarred with the same brush. For twenty-three years he had served with the Engineer Corps but in 1855 had been transferred to the Second Cavalry, then doing duty in Texas. Meade had gone directly from surveying and scientific work to a command of the line, but it was actually, now, one former engineer against another. Although less criticized than Meade, Lee, too, would ask to resign, citing military failure. Confederate President Jefferson Davis would not allow it. Lee would have to remain, and Meade also.

General Dan Sickles was telling tall tales to newspapermen and others who sought him out at his hospital in Washington. Disturbed over the newspaper articles that began to appear, General Howard addressed a letter directly to Lincoln. Since Howard was not of Meade's circle, his testimony was disinterested. To write such a letter was a little irregular, but in the last analysis it was but a simple act of loyalty. Victory at Gettysburg, Howard told Lincoln,

> was due mainly to the energetic operations of our . . . commanding general prior to the engagement, and to the manner in which he handled the troops on the field. The reserves have never before during this war been thrown in just at the right moment. In many cases when points were just being carried by the enemy, a regiment or brigade appeared to stop his progress and hurl him back. Moreover, I have never seen a more hearty co-operation on the part of general officers as since General Meade

[12] Gordon, *A War Diary*, 160–61.

took the command. . . . He was in favor of an immediate attack at Williamsport, but with the evident difficulties in our way, the uncertainty of a success, and the strong conviction of our best military minds against the risk, I must say that I think the general acted wisely. . . . We have, if I may be allowed to say it, a commanding general in whom all the officers with whom I have contact express complete confidence.[13]

This placed Meade a few notches above other army commanders. Lincoln, who had "grieved silently but deeply"[14] over what he considered failure to end the war, responded with an open heart. It had been his conviction, he replied, once Lee had crossed the Potomac to invade the North, that the enemy could be destroyed, but above all he was "profoundly grateful for what was done without criticism for what was not done." General Meade, he concluded, "has my confidence as a brave and skillful officer and a true man."[15]

This much at least was heartening to Meade when Howard showed him the letter. Another voice was heard in Washington when Adjutant Seth Williams, visiting the city, paid Halleck a personal call. Their conversation was wholly private, but soon the General in Chief was writing Meade to say: "You may well be proud of that battle." Lincoln, Halleck added as if to explain matters, "thought that Lee's defeat was so certain that he felt no little impatience at his unexpected escape." He acknowledged that Meade, too, was disappointed, but still it may have been from no fault of his own. "Take it altogether," Halleck summed up, "your short campaign has proved your superior generalship, and you merit, as you will receive, the confidence of the Government and the gratitude of the country."[16]

Meade continued to watch his opponent, who was well screened west of the upper Blue Ridge Mountains and the Shenandoah River. After strongly fortifying Winchester and a town near by, Lee waited behind extensive earthworks for flood waters in near-by streams to subside. Meade could not leave his defensive position to flush him out, but strong cavalry forces were sent to occupy the mountain passes and

[13] Howard to Lincoln, July 18, 1863, O.R., XXVII, pt. 1, 700.

[14] Nicolay and Hay, Abraham Lincoln, VII, 278.

[15] Meade, II, 138; Complete Works of Abraham Lincoln, IX, 39.

[16] Meade-Halleck correspondence, July 28, 30, 1863, O.R., XXVII, pt. 1, 104, 108; Pennypacker, Meade, 220–22. Reviewing the entire campaign in his long letter, Meade stated, "Perhaps I erred in judgement," although it is difficult to see just where. General Hunt saw no error in judgment save for Meade's idea of attack on July 13 at Williamsport.

to watch the main roads running south. Now that Lee really intended to retreat, he could not linger. Soon Longstreet's corps was seen moving down, and then Hill, while Ewell remained behind to protect the wagon trains. It was perhaps possible to slice the enemy columns in two. On July 21, Federal signal officers saw telltale dust clouds rising from two wagon trains and an infantry column. The larger train, moving by an inside road, was thought to be six miles long.[17]

Meade made his flank secure against a turning movement by Longstreet should he come through one of the gaps. The offensive was assigned General French and his Third Corps. Hilly roads were almost impassable for artillery, but after a struggle, French threaded the Blue Ridge, leaving his best work behind him. After leisurely taking position on July 22, he cautiously skirmished with a mere brigade or two thrown out to delay him. Meade realized too late that the corps leader in front was fumbling. From east of the mountains he galloped over for a closer look but could not arrive in time to mend matters that day.[18]

True it was that the Federal army was on unfamiliar ground, but had Reynolds or Hancock been left to the army, another tale would have been told. Delaying action by the enemy not only saved the inner road for the wagon train but enabled all of Ewell's force to escape. Part of his corps was already safe, and the rest withdrew to Front Royal under cover of darkness then marched down the inner road early next day. Soon after, Federals arriving at Front Royal found only an artillery battery and some cavalry covering the enemy rear. Not until this game had been played had Lee escaped intact. Meade, testified Humphreys, was more disappointed than he had been at Williamsport.

When Lee halted his army south of the Rappahannock River, it was to end his longest retreat of the war. Meade selected Warrenton, near the upper fords, as his headquarters, and recognizing the importance of supply lines, he recommended to Halleck a march into the Shenandoah Valley to destroy growing crops. Lincoln and the War Office preferred direct action. "Lee's army," it was insisted, "is the objective point."[19] Meade then inquired what type of campaign he was expected to pursue, but no definite reply was forthcoming.

[17] *O.R.*, XXVII, pt. 3, 745.
[18] Humphreys, *Andrew Atkinson Humphreys*, 204; Warren Lee Goss, *Recollections of a Private*, 236; Pennypacker, *Meade*, 217–18; *O.R.*, XXVII, pt. 1, 98–99; pt. 3, 753.
[19] *O.R.*, XXVII, pt. 1, 101–102.

General Halleck had a personal liking for Meade and could act as a buffer, but his primary function was to transmit messages. The General in Chief, noted Navy Secretary Welles, "originates nothing, anticipates nothing . . . plans nothing, suggests nothing, is good for nothing."[20] Halleck was frequently tactless, and one of his acts placed Meade temporarily in a bad light with Lincoln. After agreeing with the President's suggestion that a place be found for Hooker in the Army of the Potomac, Meade received a War Office letter signed by the Adjutant General. Reappointment of Hooker, it declared in effect, would not be tolerated. Meade therefore turned cool when Lincoln asked that action be taken and was set down as displaying "want of candor or failure of memory."[21]

Lincoln may not have realized it, but he had in Meade a dissatisfied general seldom in accord with administration strategy. In the West, Grant had been allowed to conduct the Vicksburg campaign in his own way and with navy help had cut off enemy supply lines before taking the city. In the East, the army leader could act only if plans were approved. Above all, Meade had to keep his army between the enemy and Washington. Lee, too, was advised by his government to act in similar fashion to protect the Confederate capital. For a few months now, in the limited area allowed them, each of these leaders would turn to frustrating the other, sometimes declining to fight if the position was poor.

Whatever was done now would be indecisive, even though Lee could be forced back. The night of July 31–August 1, Meade sent cavalry and infantry across the Rappahannock to threaten the enemy flank. Lee chose safety south of the Rapidan as troop morale sank. His army was now about where it had been before it started north to Second Bull Run. Meade and Humphreys worked out plans for an advance upon the indicated enemy base, but Lincoln did not approve. It did Meade no good to protest. Halted north of the Rapidan, he was told that a large force from his army would be required to help enforce

[20] Welles, *Diary*, I, 384.

[21] Meade-Lincoln correspondence, July 27, August 11 and 12, 1863, *Complete Works of Abraham Lincoln*, IX, 44–45, 71; *Meade*, II, 142; Hebert, *Fighting Joe Hooker*, 248, 346; *Harper's Magazine*, Vol. CXXX (December, 1914); Tyler Dennett, *Lincoln and the Civil War*, 80. The deleted name in *Meade*, II, 142, is "Thom," referring to Adjutant General Lorenzo Thomas of the War Office. Original Meade letters in the New York Historical Society, New York City.

the draft laws in New York, where rioting and bloodshed terrorized the city.

Though urging that delay would mean more to Lee than to himself, Meade could easily spare the 1,600 men first sent. But several thousand others had been discharged as enlistments expired, and a Twelfth Corps division was withdrawn to assist in siege operations in South Carolina. By August 5, promised reinforcements failing, Meade was left with scarcely two-thirds of the force he had with him at Williamsport. "Therefore," Lincoln notified Halleck, "if Meade could not safely engage Lee at Williamsport, it seems absurd to suppose he can safely engage him now."[22]

The message was relayed by the General in Chief with no constructive words of his own. Meade retorted that he had simply delayed his attack at Williamsport until he could scout the enemy position and, secondly, that he still had enough men. "Keep up a threatening attitude but do not advance," Halleck responded,[23] and military effort was quieted until the army could be rebuilt. Yet even if troops were to be sent, no amount of reinforcement, observed Lieutenant George Washington Roebling, would compensate for lack of action at a time when Lee was still retreating.[24]

Forced to remain inactive, Meade had to shoulder the inevitable public criticism, but with the draft suspended in New York City, Lincoln could not risk a defeat. On August 13, he summoned Meade to Washington to discuss the New York situation. Meeting face to face, both men agreed that the draft should be renewed and that some of the best-discipline troops should be sent. Meade picked the regiments of U. S. regulars from the Fifth Corps and a brigade from the Sixth, nearly 10,000 men. Now actually short of man power, he could do little but occupy the fords of the Rappahannock and patrol the country beyond.

Daily drills and frequent inspections helped keep the troops active, but army morale was low. Cheap whiskey spawned trouble among new recruits; desertions began to run high, and complaints were made of pillaging and plunder of civilians. To check military crimes, Meade ordered courts-martial to meet in every division. For willful desertion

[22] *Complete Works of Abraham Lincoln*, IX, 46–47.
[23] *O.R.*, XXVII, pt. 1, 108.
[24] Steinman, *Builders of the Bridge*, 260.

the sentence was death, and the same penalty was inflicted for sleeping on post, for robbery, murder, rape, and insubordination in the face of the enemy. Each corps was provided with a gallows and shooting ground for Friday executions, an unpopular detail but routine.[25]

The outlook dim for military action, many officers were permitted to go home on leave. The camp still had its diversions. A turf committee scheduled racing programs on a course laid out near Warrenton, and fetes on presentation days drew crowds. Promoted to major general and placed over the Second Corps, General Warren received a fine sword, the popular Sedgwick a war horse and sword.

At a much-postponed event long anticipated by the Pennsylvania Reserves, Meade was honored by the gift of a Damascus steel sword with scabbard of gold, a sash, belt, and golden spurs. Beautifully engraved in all its details, the gift sword was so finely wrought as to be impractical for ordinary purposes, but such was the prevailing custom. Another, purchased for Reynolds, had been sent to his family.

General Crawford's camp was decorated for the occasion with a wealth of evergreens, wild flowers, flags, and guidons. Officers were brilliant in dress uniforms; several regimental bands played. Robert Lincoln, the President's son, on vacation from Harvard, was among the spectators. Opportunity to appear was not neglected by Pennsylvania's Governor Curtin and Colonel John W. Forney, an administration newspaper publisher who sought to give the affair a political tinge. With Curtin running for re-election, Forney asked Meade to say something to help him. "You know I have nothing to do with politics," the soldier rejoined in his blunt way. Responding to the presentation speech made by General Crawford, Meade lauded the battle actions of his former command and was careful to restrict any reference to Curtin to brief thanks for his past aid in raising and supplying the Pennsylvania Reserves. Talks by Forney and others, however, were more pointed, and General Sedgwick came away complaining that the affair had been made the occasion of a great political rally. Meade in turn was embarrassed by a garbled account of his speech printed in Forney's newspaper which held him up as a campaigner for Curtin.[26] He took

[25] Thomson and Rauch, *History of the Bucktails*, 279; *Antietam to Appomattox*, 296–300.

[26] Pennypacker, *Meade*, 257; Sypher, *The Pennsylvania Reserves*, 490; Abner R. Small, *The Sixteenth Maine Regiment*, 141; Sedgwick, *Correspondence*, II, 156;

pains thereafter to avoid even the slightest reference to public figures and to partisan politics.

Toward the end of the month, two Union gunboats were surprised and captured near the mouth of the Rappahannock River. An aroused War Office indicated that Meade might act. He responded by moving General Judson Kilpatrick's cavalry division down-river while infantry marched to the lower fords to prevent his being cut off. Happening upon the boats about twenty miles below Fredericksburg, Kilpatrick destroyed them by artillery fire. "This has stirred us up a little," Meade commented on September 3.[27] Scouts were sent to check a War Office report that Lee had been reinforcing General Bragg in Tennessee. "No change," he wired Halleck,[28] whose spy system may have reported that Lee, visiting in Richmond, had been discussing that very move. Meade's wire was sent on September 8, and during the next two days Longstreet's Corps was withdrawn. Two brigades departed for Charleston, South Carolina, while 12,000 other troops boarded freight cars, some swarming over the top, for a long trip west via Georgia. Never had so many men been carried so far.

That a move of some sort was in progress became apparent when enemy pickets were replaced by cavalry. Scouts brought back word of a southerly movement on a large scale. "I shall tomorrow push my cavalry to the front to try to find out something," Meade notified the War Office.[29] Supported by the Second Corps, General Pleasonton forced enemy cavalry back across the Rapidan, Warren occupying Culpeper Court House nine miles below the Rappahannock. Weighing conflicting reports, Meade concluded that Longstreet's Corps had left its position in his front.

Now if ever was the time to turn on Lee's right flank to gain the railroad connecting the Potomac River with Fredericksburg and extending to Richmond. Meade was anchored, and not by his own choice, to the single-track Orange and Alexandria line, but coastal shipping as well as railroad service would be needed. The prime difficulty lay in military organization, for instead of one man as a leader, the army had three—Lincoln, a statesman; Halleck, a bureaucrat with limited views;

*Meade*, II, 145–46, 313–15; MS letters of August 21, September 4 and 5 to wife, Meade Papers.

[27] *Meade*, II, 146.
[28] *O.R.*, XXIX, pt. 2, 160.
[29] *Ibid.*, 172.

and Meade, who was being thwarted. Dispatches from Washington reflected vague thinking. Halleck asked in his fumbling way that some portion of Lee's force be cut off, or that "something . . . be done to weaken him or force him still further back."[30] The President believed that the army "should move upon Lee at once in the manner of general attack, leaving it to developments whether he will make it a real attack."[31] Pushing down to Culpeper, Meade asked for more positive instructions on the ground that those with authority should give them.[32]

On his immediate front along the south bank of the Rapidan were numerous earthworks, rifle pits, and entrenched batteries that could be defended for months. He did not think the Army of the Potomac, with its numerous untrained recruits, was in shape to force the enemy back to Richmond. Lincoln responded sharply that Lee's army, not Richmond, was the objective point—Meade should "fall upon the enemy and hurt him where he is."[33]

These seem to be but casual ideas. The hurt-the-enemy plan would be tried by General Grant in the spring of 1864 and then abandoned. The proper move now was to head southeast toward the Richmond, Fredericksburg and Potomac Railroad and tidewater, flanking Lee's army all the way to the James. But the administration was wed to the army's present position.

Meade had a new volunteer aide, the genial and personable Theodore Lyman of Boston, whom he first met while directing lighthouse construction off Key West, Florida. Witnessing his chief's mounting irritation over the stalemate on the strategic front, Lyman went to the heart of the matter: "Your bricks and mortar may be of the best; but if there are three or four chief architects, none of whom can agree where to lay the first brick, the house will rise slowly."[34]

It was left to Meade to decide on which flank he would move. On September 21, he called in General John Buford, First Cavalry Division, a ready soldier wearing old corduroy trousers, cowhide boots, and a blouse full of holes. The two officers discussed possibilities and exchanged views. Buford then left to inspect the upper Rapidan along

[30] *Ibid.*, 186–87.
[31] *Ibid.*, 187.
[32] Meade to wife, September 19, 1863, Meade Papers.
[33] Lincoln to Halleck, September 19, 1863, *O.R.*, XXIX, pt. 2, 207–208. Much of this letter comprises an attempt to define strategy, but the suggestions are negative.
[34] *Meade's Headquarters*, 22.

the Federal right. Meade next day was awaiting this officer's report when a War Office cipher telegram arrived: "Come at once."[35]

Meade dropped everything and hurried away, reaching the Capital at 11:00 P.M. Faces were lengthening over bad news. The telegraph had been clicking off messages from the West telling of a rout at Chickamauga Creek in northern Georgia. On the second day of the battle, Longstreet's men had poured through a gap in the Federal line. General William S. Rosecrans, commanding, had retreated to Chattanooga, where he was hemmed in and the city besieged.

Lincoln, Stanton, and Halleck had been discussing whether troops should not be transferred from the East to help Rosecrans. No decision was reached at that late hour. Meade pointed out that he had a movement pending and that Buford might discover some weakness on the enemy left.

In the morning, a telegram from Humphreys reported that Buford had driven enemy cavalry across the Rapidan. Lincoln and Halleck were now willing that Meade pursue his advantage, and he left Washington that day feeling that he could do so, but matters were actually decided by Secretary Stanton, backed by Secretary of State William Seward and Treasury Secretary Chase. Their plan, which under the circumstances was wise, was to send the Eleventh and Twelfth Corps west to rescue the army under siege at Chattanooga. Fighting Joe Hooker, the favorite of Chase and the political Radicals, was chosen to command.[36]

Since the army was in a position to march, Howard's Eleventh Corps got into line promptly; it took a little longer to bring up Slocum's Twelfth, which was stationed along the Rapidan. Meade moved First Corps troops into that advanced position and sent Slocum directly after Howard to Washington where freight trains were waiting. Some 16,300 men climbed aboard for a 1,200-mile journey to a railhead in northeastern Alabama. All along the route, railroad personnel toiled night and day to get changes of equipment ready and to clear the way. The roads used were of three different gauges, and there would have to be two crossings of the Ohio River—one by ferry and one by a pontoon bridge supported by coal barges. The five-day rail journey via Indianapolis, Cincinnati, Louisville, and Nashville to Bridgeport, Ala-

[35] *Ibid.*, 21; *O.R.*, XXIX, pt. 2, 220.
[36] David Donald (ed.), *Inside Lincoln's Cabinet*, 203; Williams, *Lincoln and His Generals*, 283.

bama, was the war's greatest single troop movement, supplanting Longstreet's.[37]

The September days drifted by. No more than in August had any concerted movement of the whole army been allowed. Early in October the troops which had been sent to New York returned, and more recruits came in. Thus reinforced, Meade revived plans to penetrate the enemy left. Lee, however, also appeared to be stirring. Each army commander issued his orders. Lee, according to Federal scouts reading enemy flags from a mountaintop, had a cavalry division draw three days' rations of hardtack and bacon. On October 9, soon after receiving this report, Meade told his corps commanders to issue five days' rations and get ready to march. On that same day he rode with Humphreys up Cedar Mountain to examine the country beyond. General Sedgwick's pickets, who were near by, believed that enemy infantry and cavalry were moving north along the Federal right, and Meade was able to see this for himself before leaving the mountain.[38]

It was cavalry leader Pleasonton's idea that Lee was simply making a feint before withdrawing to Richmond—certainly an optimistic view in the light of the loss of the Eleventh and Twelfth Corps. Meade thought it more likely that he might be heading toward Culpeper or Warrenton, or possibly into the Shenandoah Valley. It was up to Pleasonton to find out—Buford's division was sent south of the Rapidan while Kilpatrick rode west.

Next day Kilpatrick reported that Lee appeared to be moving north as if to turn the Federal right. Meade acted at once. A stand could be made at a Rappahannock River crossing to intercept enemy passage. Leaving their comfortable quarters around Culpeper Court House at three o'clock on the morning of October 11, the Federals hurried north.

This was the beginning of a campaign in which Lee got off first to carry on to a surprising finish. It would be similar to one that Meade would attempt toward the end of November, and the two could well be studied together save that they were separated by several weeks chronologically. The fact that Lee had marched first would prove no detriment to the Federal cause.

---

[37] F. P. Summers, *The Baltimore & Ohio Railroad in the Civil War*, 167–69; James A. Van Fleet, *Rail Transport and the Winning of Wars* (pamphlet), 15; *O.R.*, XXIX, pt. 1, 147.

[38] Humphreys, *From Gettysburg to the Rapidan*, 12–13.

First, find the enemy. Meade impatiently awaited reports from his cavalry. Assigned solely to watch the roads and warned against fighting, General Gregg's division was somehow drawn into battle with infantry and cavalry. If this was the main enemy column, as Gregg reported upon his escape, then Lee's army had not yet advanced very far.[39]

Only one mistake had to be made to lose contact with the cavalry-screened foe in wooded Culpeper County. The Federals had marched swiftly and were already well ahead of the Confederate position as reported by Gregg. If Lee was behind him, Meade speculated, he might get around his rear. Three corps—more than one-half of his army—were hurried back along the road they had come. These were anxious hours at headquarters. Too late came the actual facts—that Lee was already crossing the Rappahannock at the very fords where Meade had planned to fight. And at least part of the Confederate Army was extended closer to Washington than were its defenders.

Colonel Lyman once remarked that he never saw Meade in such fits as during this defensive campaign. So far nothing had gone right, and for violating instructions not to fight, declared Humphreys, Gregg should have been tried (and apparently convicted) and shot. All that could be done now was to send riders pounding through the darkness with orders for the three corps in the rear to march night and day to catch up with those already heading north.

Recalling the hard race to Gettysburg, plodding soldiers making the most of each minute opined that this one was even more difficult. Already they had been on the move for twenty-eight hours and until after midnight; now they faced about to resume the march early on the afternoon of October 12. About midnight again they were permitted to rest, only to be awakened, as it seemed, almost as soon as they had turned in. The march for those in the van was continuous on that day, October 13, until five-thirty, and for others until nine or ten o'clock at night. It was a heroic if dusty performance. "Legs won," affirmed Humphreys in recalling that crisis. "Without them we should have been lost."[40]

[39] *Ibid.,* 17.

[40] *O.R.,* XXIX, pt. 2, 288–300; H. H. Humphreys, *A Critical Examination of Pennypacker's Life of General George G. Meade,* 5–6; Humphreys, *From Gettysburg to the Rapidan,* 31.

That night one column was approaching Bristoe Station just south of Manassas with another just west on a connecting road. Little was known of Lee's position except that he was somewhere off to the left and apparently was marching northward to fight. Wisely by-passing unlucky Bull Run, Meade selected favorable high ground at Centreville. He was hurrying not only to get ahead of the enemy but also to seize the heights before Lee could arrive. Since Centreville, a crossroads town, was only about twenty-two miles from Washington, a calculated risk was assumed.

The average citizen aside, nervous Washington officials could hardly appreciate Meade's strategy, which happened to be backed by Humphreys. General Halleck, for one, feared the city lost. Army leaves were canceled, fortifications doubly manned. New York City was called upon to send all troops that could be spared. A warning went out to the Baltimore and Ohio Railroad, which had been ripped apart in past invasions: "Look well to your rolling stock. . . . Expect new cavalry raids."[41]

Still in a great hurry, Meade continued to spur his men on. At 2:00 P.M. on October 14, Sykes of the Fifth Corps notified Warren, Second, in the army rear that General French had reached Manassas Heights and that he was waiting at Bristoe "to see the head of your column," whereupon he would move along to close the gap.[42] Sykes lost no time in making good his intentions. Informed that the Second Corps was not far behind, he hastened from Bristoe and across Broad Run. He had been forced to wait only because Warren had been halted by a morning skirmish with Jeb Stuart's cavalry; arriving at Bristoe seven or eight miles farther on, Warren discovered an interesting situation.

Musketry in front told him that enemy troops were firing into the Fifth Corps rear, although Sykes, charging on under the spur, did not even realize that his rear was being attacked.[43] Damage, however, was slight. As Warren's weary-legged men hurried up from the blind side, their approach screened by woods, their leader could see that the enemy (Heth's division of A. P. Hill's corps) appeared eager and confident. The way was open to revise this attitude. Warren called out from the saddle, "Tell General Hays to move by the left flank, at the double-quick, to the railroad cut,"[44] and everyone bolted for the shelter of the

[41] *O.R.*, XXIX, pt. 2, 307.
[42] Walker, *History of the Second Corps*, 343.
[43] *Ibid.*, 347–48.

embankment, a perfect position. Although Heth's troops had reached Bristoe first, they lay well out in the open. It was a collision at about a right angle.

Mounted officers galloped up and down the railroad to inspirit riflemen who had plodded a long way for this. Two field batteries whirled into place, orders were shouted, and white smoke billowed along the concealed line. The air was burdened with lead from individual pieces. Within a very few minutes, gray-clads in front were dropping at a rate too rapid to withstand. Before the next enemy division following could arrive and get into position, the battle was over, Heth moving off. The fighting had lasted perhaps forty minutes, but his toll was as many as 1,360 killed, wounded, and missing. Warren lost fewer than 350.

Had the action been more prolonged, other troops on both sides would have been engaged. Meade, as soon as notified, recalled both the Fifth and Third Corps, but dusk had fallen by the time they reached the vicinity of Bristoe. Although Sykes's men clamored to be sent in, Meade could not risk the result of an impromptu battle so close to the capital he was sworn to defend. If the enemy were to fight in a body, it would have to be on ground of his own choosing.

Next day the dirt flew at Centreville, and General Hunt meticulously placed his guns as Meade made ready to meet an attack. Lee's cavalry and pickets approached and began examining the position. The situation as it had existed at Williamsport was now reversed; Meade, criticized for not fighting there, waited to see what his opponent would do. Next day a drenching northeaster held both forces motionless. Concerned that Lee might head for the Shenandoah Valley or push for the Potomac to make a crossing, Meade sent cavalry units to occupy the mountain gaps and ordered up a pontoon bridge to get over the river himself if necessary.

Whatever Lee might be doing or planning, Meade could not remain entirely on the defensive. On the seventeenth, the weather clearing, supply trains blocking the roads were moved into open fields. Meade searched for the enemy's front. Both infantry and cavalry movements were reported near Chantilly, the next town north, as well as south of the Federal position. Somewhat needlessly, he retorted to Halleck, who was pressing him, that he could not move his army until he knew exactly where Lee was.

[44] *Ibid.*, 349.

Doubtless feeling the strain, Halleck continued to clamor for action of some kind. "Lee is unquestionably bullying you," Meade read as his temper rose. "If you cannot ascertain his movements I certainly cannot. If you pursue and fight him, I think you will find out where he is."[45] Meade's tone in reply was as sharp as if he were addressing a subordinate: "If you have any orders to give me, I am prepared to receive and obey them, but I must insist on being spared the infliction of such truisms in the guise of opinions as you have recently honored me with, particularly as they were not asked for. . . . I ought to be . . . and desire to be, relieved from command."[46] To Margaret he wrote that an end to his military career might soon be expected.[47]

Wounded feelings aside, the real issue was Lee's strategy, which Meade was making every effort to discover. Lee could flank Centreville on the left and march for the Potomac, or he could attack or withdraw. But with the lesson of Gettysburg in mind and with a vulnerable supply line, Lee could no longer afford to take chances. Early on the morning of October 18, he began to withdraw behind his cavalry screen.

As the enemy was seen retreating to recross an almost barren country, Humphreys and Meade looked at each other. Lee was turning back without a fight—a significant change in affairs since the palmy days of invasion. For the Federals, rapidity of movement and choice of position had won.

Lee would not attempt again to gain ground with his whole army. With the retreat from Gettysburg he had seen his last of Union soil, and Centreville now marked the turning point. Thereafter he would be almost wholly on the defensive, although easily able to damage and disrupt an attacking foe. Despite Meade's enforced inaction for much of the time since Gettysburg, he had demonstrated at last that Lee could not with safety advance very far.

[45] *O.R.*, XXIX, pt. 2, 345.
[46] *Meade's Headquarters*, 36; Meade to Halleck, October 18, 1863, *O.R.*, XXIX, pt. 2, 346.
[47] Meade to wife, October 21, 1863, Meade Papers.

# 16. Checkmate
## (October 18-December 2, 1863)

MINUS A LEG as the result of his Gettysburg wound, General Dan Sickles rode over from Washington that day to ask that he be restored to the Third Corps. But it had been said of Sickles that he had been circulating petitions to get the high command for himself and had inspired some tall Gettysburg tales glorifying himself and reflecting upon army leadership.[1] Irrespective of his own feelings, Meade knew that Sickles no more than Hooker was considered eligible for reappointment. Sickles was permitted to posture before his old command, which marched in review, and to make his farewell to the army. Otherwise he got nowhere with Meade, who declined his request on the ground of disability. Returning to Washington, Sickles began arguing that Lee should have been attacked at Centreville, and newspapers in consequence began saying that Meade had received imperative orders to give battle.[2] "Not a word of truth in it!" stormed Colonel Lyman. "[And] you might as well give imperative orders to catch a sea-gull with a pinch of salt."[3]

True, the administration had tried to force Meade to give battle, but even if he had been able to fight and win a victory which could have been no more than partial, Lee could hardly have retreated faster or farther than he now did in withdrawing again to the Rappahannock. With but a single exception, no longer would Lee even attack a Federal army in position, nor indeed would Meade open battle unless some visible advantage was to be gained. There would be no contest as long as the enemy moved behind protective woods and hills. "If Bob Lee will go into those fields there and fight me . . . I will do it this after-

[1] Meade to wife, August 27, 1863, Meade papers; editorial in Wilkes' *Spirit of the Times*, August 29, 1863, reprinted in *Meade*, II, 316–17.

[2] Dennett, *Lincoln and the Civil War*, 101; *Report of Joint Committee on the Conduct of the War*, I, 303–304.

[3] *Meade's Headquarters*, 38.

noon," Lyman heard Meade declare,[4] but Lee would fight only behind cover or strong works.

Administration weakness was reflected in an apologetic message from Halleck, who explained that in trying to hurry Meade into battle he had merely been conveying official wishes. If in so doing he had been unpleasant, then he sincerely regretted it. It was hardly the thing for a superior officer to apologize to a junior on such grounds; Meade would have cooled off. He, however, "accepted" the explanation and thanked Halleck for it,[5] but both men seemed to be corresponding too much.

Called to Washington, Meade had a long talk with Halleck, who, although "very urgent that something should be done," could not say what. Meade also saw Lincoln, whom he found "as he always is, very considerate and kind."[6] The President, however, was obviously still disappointed that no battle had been fought. Meade reported no other military ideas forthcoming from Washington, Secretary of War Stanton then being absent in the West.

Washington acquaintances could see that Meade's hair and beard were growing prematurely gray and that he was looking a little worn. His military problem was unchanged—the defeat of Lee's forces by an army acting in defense of the capital and held to a line not approved by himself. This was the Orange and Alexandria Railroad, which could not be abandoned until Grant made the decision.

Because Lee had destroyed much of this railroad during his retreat, Meade found himself hung up near Warrenton until repairs could be made. For the present, provisions for troops, horses, and mules had to be hauled by wagon. A greater problem was just how to get at General Lee once the army was able to move. Talking with Humphreys and with his supply officers, Meade would stride up and down before the campfire, his head bent well forward, hands clasped behind him, cigar in his mouth, hat down over his eyes.

Digesting reports from cavalry scouts, he wrote Halleck on November 2 of his decision. Since Lee's forces were massed between the Rappahannock River and Culpeper Court House with the two main fords well guarded, he favored neither a frontal attack nor an advance on the

[4] *Ibid.*, 31.
[5] Meade-Halleck correspondence, October 18, 1863, *O.R.*, XXIX, pt. 2, 346, 354.
[6] *Meade*, II, 154.

enemy left where the country was rough and broken, with few main roads. He would prefer to throw the whole army "rapidly and secretly" to his far left and across the Rapidan at Banks Ford to gain the heights below Fredericksburg.[7] This position could be supplied both by a rail line—the Richmond, Fredericksburg and Potomac—and by navigable waters once the road to Aquia Creek, which entered the wide Potomac, was opened.

Meade sent this important message to the War Office by a trusted aide. The administration could signify in reply whether it wanted a military offensive along a more favorable line. But after showing Meade's note to the President, Halleck responded: "He does not see that the proposed change of base is likely to produce favorable result while its disadvantages are manifest. I have fully concurred. An entire change of base I can neither advise or approve."[8]

No constructive ideas were submitted. The administration would not get its eyes open for another six months, and in the meantime Meade would be tied to a defensive position. He could, however, regain ground previously held—the area between the Rappahannock and the Rapidan—as soon as railroad repairs were finished. As the work progressed, a way was devised to take the nearest fortified positions. The enemy had strengthened two hilltop forts on the Rappahannock's north bank, and together with these would go clusters of newly built log huts erected as snug winter quarters.

For the movement planned for November 7, 1863, the army was divided into two wings. Sedgwick, commanding the right, was to take the two fords located at Rappahannock Station. Four or five miles below, across Kelly's Ford, were two semicircular works to which French and the left wing were assigned. One cavalry division above and another below were to ford the Rappahannock with French while artillery blasted the opposite shore.

After the day dawned cloudy and foggy, a breeze helped clear the air as the sun shone through. Reaching the river, Sedgwick's artillery opened soon after midday and was echoed by the left wing at Kelly's Ford. A division ordered on by French splashed across in such spirit as to seize three hundred prisoners with but small loss. The Federal guns frustrated an enemy counterattack.

[7] Meade to Halleck, November 2, 1863, *O.R.*, XXIX, pt. 2, 409.
[8] Halleck to Meade, November 3, 1863, *ibid.*, 412.

Sedgwick meanwhile had continued to hammer without much effect. Not much November daylight was left when he asked for another look at his orders. Meade, then with French, was awaiting results. Sedgwick called to General Horatio G. Wright, who was temporarily in charge of his corps. Their terse exchange of views was reported by a watchful aide.

"Wright, what do you think are the chances for an assault with infantry on that position?"

"Just as you say, General."

Sedgwick turned to General David A. Russell, commanding the leading division. "Do you think you can carry those works?"

"I think I can, sir."

"Go ahead and do it."[9]

The Sixth Maine and Fifth Wisconsin were aligned in front, with the Fifth Maine and 121st New York in support. Daylight was fading as the four regiments dashed up the rocky slope. From the forts came derisive yells and an annoying but irregular fire. Half-concealed by smoke and the dusk, the skirmishers threw themselves at the works to capture in one blow some 1,500 prisoners and "all the guns." First among prizes which appeal to men's hearts were eight enemy flags and, of practical use, a pontoon bridge. Federal losses were fewer than 300 men of an attacking party of about 3,000. Prisoners admitted it was a brilliant affair. "You'n Yanks are getting doggone smart!" said one, eying the snug log huts built for the winter.[10]

Although hoping to renew the battle in the morning wherever Lee might make a stand, Meade was held up by fog. For several hours, Sedgwick was unable to discover whether the enemy had actually retreated. When it became apparent that he had withdrawn, a pontoon bridge was thrown over the Rappahannock, and the entire army moved across that afternoon. Early on the ninth Federals moved in pursuit along two roads. It was expected that Lee had retired only as far as the hills near Brandy Station about six miles on, but as Meade and his staff dashed from one corps headquarters to another, they could find no one who had seen more than a trace of the enemy.[11]

[9] *Battles and Leaders*, IV, 86.

[10] Goss, *Recollections*, 244–45; *Meade's Headquarters*, 46; Humphreys, *From Gettysburg to the Rapidan*, 44–46. Colonel Lyman said the loss was about 400 men.

[11] *Meade's Headquarters*, 44.

Again Lee had declined to fight, dodging behind the Rapidan for safety. "What a disappointment we have gone through," mourned Humphreys. "We counted fully upon having a battle."[12] However, news of the second Federal triumph within a month was generally well received. The *Evening Star* of Washington heralded the November 7 affair as "one of the most signal victories of the war." Meade may have been surprised when, from Abraham Lincoln, came the first direct word of praise yet received: "I wish to say well done." This, perhaps, was for the whole army, but Meade was one man in it. Copies of this portion of the telegram were sent to all corps commanders without comment. Lincoln also had inquired about the number of prisoners taken—about 1,900, including 400 by French, as reported. More important, some twenty miles of ground had been regained at small expense. Meade could now reoccupy a line of camps and patrols extending for forty miles along the Rapidan's north bank.[13]

Headquarters were taken up at Brandy Station near Lee's former base at Culpeper, but Brandy was a long way from a more useful Fredericksburg, which was at least twenty-five miles nearer Richmond. The remote hamlet comprised three or four houses and a small unpainted building for receiving freight. Thrown forward to the Rapidan, the troops had to build many of their own winter huts. In one of those military ceremonies that warmed men's hearts, the Fourth and Fifth Maine, the Fifth Wisconsin, and the 121st New York presented the captured battle flags to their commander in chief. After complimenting the victors, Meade authorized General Russell to take the trophies to Washington to present to the Secretary of War. It was a little disheartening when the man behind the desk said he was too busy to see Russell when he arrived.[14]

Army quartermasters and wagon trains were kept busy. Little food or forage would be found between the Rappahannock and the Rapidan. Engineers were laboring day and night on a bridge which, by the middle of November, was opened for Rappahannock passage of freight. The railroad line was then extended to Brandy with sidings built for

---

[12] Humphreys, *Andrew Atkinson Humphreys*, 210.

[13] *Washington Evening Star*, November 9, 1863; Margaret Leech, *Reveille in Washington*, 271; Lincoln to Meade, November 9, 1863, *O.R.*, XXIX, pt. 2, 443; *Battles and Leaders*, IV, 87–88. This last source mentions "more than 1,600 prisoners" taken by Sedgwick.

[14] *New York World*, November 12, 1863; *Battles and Leaders*, IV, 87–88 n.

unloading supplies. Without an adequate supply line and supply base the army could not move, although the Abolitionist press was crying for action.

Inasmuch as the men in the field knew and understood conditions, this editorial clamor was one of their pet hates. "The disgust . . . on account of these tirades was unspeakable," remarked an artillery veteran. "The editors . . . exploited their 'patriotism' by urging gallant soldiers on to useless slaughter."[15] Meade was quite aware that the administration, as usual, was looking for another battle.

He did not intend that his own views be published, but Judge Cortlandt Parker, a family connection and an administration friend, took one of his letters to the press, although withholding his own name. To Abolitionists the sentiments which Meade expressed were inflammatory. He would not be influenced, he said, by the view that it was better for the army to be destroyed than to remain inactive. No blood would be shed needlessly if he could help it, nor would a battle be fought unless considered a justifiable risk. As soon as Editor Horace Greeley of the *New York Tribune* read the letter, he declared that Meade was corresponding with General McClellan. Upon being set right, Greeley apologized, and Judge Parker then let it be known that he had been satisfied with Meade's conduct from the beginning.[16]

One year earlier, Meade had cited the army's true position, and cavalry Colonel Charles Francis Adams, Jr., now waxed sarcastic: "We *must* cover Washington and we *must* threaten Richmond, so we rush to the Rapidan and actually hear Lee laugh from the heights beyond. If once the President would shove us onto the south bank of the James, Lee would stop laughing."[17] General Sedgwick declared Meade was always willing to fight, but added that some risk was involved with the army lodged too far in the interior of the enemy country.[18] Meanwhile the Confederate guerrilla Colonel John S. Mosby, a thorn in the flesh, would now and again tear up the army's only railroad supply line.

[15] Buell, *The Cannoneer*, 137.
[16] Meade "To a Friend in New Jersey," *New York World*, December 16, 1863; *Meade*, II, 162; Judge Cortlandt Parker to H. A. Crane, December 16, 1863, Meade Papers.
[17] W. C. Ford (ed.), *A Cycle of Adams Letters*, II, 105. See *Meade*, I, 330 for his views on "the James River being the true and only practicable line of approach to Richmond . . . [which] need not and should not be attacked at all."
[18] Sedgwick, *Correspondence*, II, 160.

Despite numerical advantage, 60,000 Federals, many of them raw recruits, would not be superior to Lee's 40,000 in an unfamiliar and broken country. Meade, however, believed it might be possible to turn the enemy right, which was the nearer to the Federal line. If no time was lost on the march, the attack might succeed before support from the left could arrive, he advised the War Office, and was ordered to go ahead. Planned for the last week in November, the movement would co-ordinate with a thrust by General Grant, who was about to strike the Confederate Army of Tennessee on the heights below Chattanooga.

The chances for a successful march to a given point in wooded enemy country were never good. Great pains were taken therefore to forestall error. Sketches of the route were given each of the five corps leaders, and the plan was gone over in detail at headquarters. French was to move on the right, Sedgwick and Warren in the center, Newton and Sykes on the left. On the assumption that the Federal right would be attacked, one fateful change was made. While French retained the lead, Sedgwick was placed just behind him. The army was to travel as light as possible with only ammunition, medical, and ambulance wagons allowed. Cavalry forces were assigned to each of the three columns.[19]

Everyone was sworn to secrecy. Newspapermen trying to discover what lay behind busy preparations could only surmise what Meade was up to. A *New York Herald* man gave the opinion that no word could be expected from him "until he shall have arrived in Richmond or been disastrously defeated en route. . . . He does not fear to meet Lee anywhere."[20] Mrs. Meade was duly informed, Captain George writing his mother on the twenty-third: "We move again tomorrow. I think everything is coming out all right, the Army was never in better condition."[21] Although somewhat reluctant to leave their warm huts, the troops appeared in their usual good spirits.

But now the weather, that greatest of military hazards, turned bad. When two days of rain held up the march, it was not at all difficult for the enemy to learn that Meade had issued extra rations, signaling an offensive. And it was not enough that General French was two hours late in starting on November 26, delaying the rest of the army. The

[19] Humphreys, *From Gettysburg to the Rapidan*, 52.
[20] Whiteley-Hudson correspondence in *American Historical Review*, Vol. XXXIX (January, 1934), 294–95.
[21] MS letter, November 23, 1863, Meade Papers.

Rapidan River became so swollen that bridging pontoons fell short of the far bank.

Meanwhile great events were taking place elsewhere. On November 24–25, General Grant, aided by Sherman, Hooker, and Rock-of-Chickamauga Thomas, dislodged the Confederate Army of Tennessee from its strong position behind Chattanooga. By Grant's order, pursuit of the enemy was halted after only one day. No note of disappointment or disapproval came from the White House. Chattanooga was hailed as a great victory, as indeed it was.

Meade already had lost some advantage in time. More valuable hours were lost in erecting trestles to span the gap between pontoons and river bank. Next it was learned that the artillery of Sedgwick and French could not be hauled up the steep riverbank just across Jacob's Ford. The guns were moved over a narrow and rutted woods road to Germanna Ford below, and not until the next morning were they all safely across. Now they had to be guided along the far bank to rejoin their own columns.

With the movement thrown badly off schedule, Meade, then with Warren, anxiously awaited news from French. The Federal right was attacked as had been expected, but French made it easier for the enemy's delaying action by getting a portion of his command on the wrong road. Argument by one of his better-informed division leaders availed nothing. The turn to the right naturally brought him that much closer to a command identified as General Edward Johnson's division of Ewell's corps, which had been sent to divert the invaders until Hill could arrive from the Confederate left. If successful, this tactic alone would disrupt Meade's plan.

The error in placing Sedgwick behind French was now clear. French had been assigned the advance, and in fact probably had claimed it as senior commander, but the unhappy reality was that he was bungling his work just as he had done in the Blue Mountains. With the Third Corps immobilized, the main road was blocked, and Sedgwick with nearly 15,000 men was unable to get through. Very unhappy now, Meade could see the entire effort going to pieces.

Urgent appeals were rushed to French in an effort to get him to join Warren promptly on the east-west Orange Turnpike. Confused and "obfusticated," as his disgusted soldiers bore witness, French maddeningly sent back word that he was engaged with the enemy and was

waiting for Warren. Sedgwick would later deny that French, with
whom he talked during the fighting, was "in the slightest degree under
the influence of liquor,"[22] but he could say nothing at all for his tactics.
Not until French had held up the advance for almost an entire day did
he respond to persuasion and get on the right road. Bad news also came
from the left wing, which lost most of its ammunition train to enemy
cavalry. Although Warren also was attacked during the late afternoon,
Meade got the First Corps on the scene to make everything safe about
twilight.

Lee, of course, had all the time that he needed to select a defensive
position as Hill hurried over to join him. And as the wagons remaining
with the Federal left were seen turning westward, it was apparent that
Meade intended to fight rather than seize the Fredericksburg Railroad, which had been denied him by the War Office.

November 28, a dismal and rainy day, was spent in forming the
army along the Orange Turnpike. "This was a tremendous job in the
narrow wood-roads, deep with mud," Colonel Lyman bore witness.
"These long columns cannot move over two miles in an hour, often not
so much."[23] Mud-stained troops turned to confront an enemy occupying the far bank of Mine Run, a Rapidan tributary, where "in an incredibly short time" stout fieldworks and barricades were made ready.[24]
The position selected by Lee was indeed formidable. Behind the steep
banks of Mine Run, rising ground had been cleared for more than one
thousand yards. Heavy timber flanked an open space well up the slope.
The summit was crowned with tree slashings, infantry breastworks,
and earthworks for batteries. Skirmish fire rattled among the hills and
ravines as cavalry and infantry units scouted in several directions.

Yes, Lee had retreated from Centreville under similar although
less discouraging conditions. Now what would Meade do?

On November 29 the weather turned cold and icy. Soldiers who
had tossed away their overcoats during the march expressed regret.
Superseding discomfort, the plain and disagreeable fact was that the
army had made another tiresome march only to find the enemy stoutly
guarded and comfortably fixed along a high-banked stream. Taking

[22] J. T. Headley, *Grant and Sherman*, 429; Hays, *Under the Red Patch*, 215;
Humphreys, *From Gettysburg to the Rapidan*, 58–60.
[23] *Meade's Headquarters*, 55.
[24] Freeman, *R. E. Lee*, III, 200.

shelter at Robertson's Tavern on the Orange Turnpike, Meade reinforced Warren with a Sixth Corps division for the purpose of turning
the enemy right at some vulnerable point.

To reach his assigned goal, Warren had a roundabout route east
and then south to the Plank road paralleling the turnpike, then west to
Mine Run. The roads were still heavy under a covering of frost, slowing the march. When a courier breathlessly reported that Gregg's
cavalry, acting in support, had been cut in two and its train captured,
Warren halted his men while he discussed the possibility of an enemy
trap.[25] No one could know what might lie ahead in the woods. But taking his chances, Warren sent an infantry brigade to support Gregg,
who, as it turned out, had encountered only cavalry, beating off the
attack. Time, however, was running out. After Warren had crossed
Mine Run below Lee's position and reached a point where the enemy
works, withdrawn from the stream, looked a little thin, an hour or two
more of daylight was needed to organize and launch an attack. This
was not allowed him; the sun soon dipped below the Wilderness
horizon.

By the end of this fourth day, provisions were more than half gone.
As the corps commanders met with Meade that night in the old tavern,
Sedgwick proposed an attack along his own position, the Federal right.
Meade could agree, but as he was shaping plans for three concerted
assaults, back came Warren to argue that he could carry everything before him on the far left and that the entire movement should pivot on
him. Meade inquired about enemy defenses, which Warren could say
were weak at that point.

Warren's record was good; he had demonstrated promptness and
vigor at both Bristoe Station and Gettysburg. Although General French
and some of the other veterans disapproved, Meade agreed to the plan
and assigned Warren two additional divisions from the Third Corps.[26]
After making the long ride back to his command, Warren labored all
the rest of that night. Pickets and skirmish lines were advanced, assaulting regiments drawn up just behind. Supports and reserves were posted,
the flanks strengthened, the artillery carefully placed.

That night was bitterly cold. Pickets were changed every half-hour,
yet a few froze to death. Troops behind picket lines stuck their muskets

[25] Walker, *History of the Second Corps*, 377.
[26] Taylor, *Warren*, 160.

in the ground, slapped their hands together, and ran up and down. Wrapped in his cloak, Warren crept beyond his lines just before sunrise to reconnoiter. He suddenly became aware that he was on enemy ground where the men in gray seemed too busy to take notice. He was able to withdraw safely after spotting a formidable new defense line. Pale dawn and a rising sun revealed "breastworks, epaulements and abatis perfected."[27] Startled Federals were confronted by the muzzles of newly placed guns. As Warren, now ashy, well realized, the situation had abruptly changed between sunset and sunrise.

A rider arrived from Meade with a message: "Attack at once or whenever ready." But the men who had confidently marched into place were piling their knapsacks on the ground and were writing their names on pieces of paper to pin to their blouses. Money, valuables, and keepsakes were turned over to regimental chaplains and other noncombatants. Some, remembering Fredericksburg, were saying their prayers. Colonel Thomas L. Livermore of the Eighteenth New Hampshire felt that he never saw a sight more impressive.[28]

Men were scanning Warren's face to fathom his thoughts. Fatigued with his long labors, their leader appeared anxious and careworn.[29] Continuing on foot, Warren strode to his headquarters, where he gave his aides instructions to order each division commander to charge. The couriers dashed off, but after only a few moments Warren himself was seen riding to the front. There was an unexplained delay. The troops lay down in their places and waited.

Anxiously awaiting the sound of Second Corps guns, Meade ordered a battery in the Federal center to open. On both right and left, Sedgwick and Sykes joined in with 32-pounders. Troops were massed for the attack with storming parties ready. French pushed his skirmish line to within three hundreds yards of the enemy and tauntingly inquired as Meade stood near by, "Where are your young Napoleon's guns; why doesn't he open?"[30] It was shortly after nine o'clock when Captain Roebling of Warren's staff rode up. Roebling bore "rather a troubled air" and a message which caused Meade to exclaim: "My

[27] *O.R.*, XXIX, pt. 1, 698.

[28] Livermore, *Days and Events*, 302; Goss, *Recollections*, 247; *Antietam to Appomattox*, 271.

[29] Charles D. Page, *History of the 14th Connecticut Regiment*, 204.

[30] Livermore, *Days and Events*, 304.

God! General Warren has half my army at his disposal."[31] Some moments later, Colonel Livermore, who was seeking his ambulance train, saw Meade riding hard toward Warren's position "looking as savage as anyone could."[32]

Others saw Captain George Meade racing in the opposite direction with a message for Sedgwick. Half a mile out, his galloping mount took fright at an exploding shell and failed to clear a deep mudhole, throwing the rider under and crushing him in the cold slime. George was pulled out gasping, "I'm General Meade's son. Send to the right and say the order to attack is countermanded. Quick, quick!"[33] An officer mounted and dashed off, but George, recovering quickly, also soon got to Sedgwick.

Confronting Warren, who was full of apologies, Meade was given food for thought. Occupying the enemy right, A. P. Hill's troops had extended their line well past Warren's during the night and had strongly fortified the position. Would any advantage be gained then in sacrificing thousands of men on the cold, bristling slopes? The question answered itself, and, moreover, rations and forage were running quite low. Should he remain where he was, Lee might then cut him off at one of the fords, splitting the army from its main supply train.

Those who saw deep lines in Meade's face as the army retreated thought him never more discouraged. In the light of Grant's sweeping triumph before Chattanooga, the Mine Run campaign was sheer fiasco. Perhaps Meade had placed too much trust in Warren.

"I am conscious that my head is off," Meade ruminated after reaching the old camp above the Rapidan. "There will be a great howl."[34] In Washington and elsewhere the feeling was growing that he would now be relieved. But hardly a voice was raised against him in the Federal Army. Quoting the couplet about the King of France and 40,000 men, Colonel Lyman declared himself astonished "at the extraordinary moral courage of General Meade."[35] It was pointed out that some officers would have been tempted to make it a dashing fight, however strong the enemy position. "The army, perhaps the Union cause," said

[31] *Meade's Headquarters*, 56.

[32] Livermore, *Days and Events*, 303.

[33] Abner R. Small, *The Road to Richmond*, 118.

[34] Testimony of General Marsena R. Patrick. *Report of Joint Committee on the Conduct of the War*, I, 474; *Meade*, II, 158.

[35] *Meade's Headquarters*, 57.

Colonel William C. Talley of the First Pennsylvania, "was saved due to the clear judgment and military skill of those ground officers, Meade and Warren. If officers less cautious and less able had been in command, the battle likely would have been fought then and there. Thus would have ended the remainder of the 1st Reserves."[36]

There was still another side to the story. Although it was a very bitter pill for Meade, General Lee was no less disappointed. After the Federals had declined to attack, he had decided to wait until the next day before attempting an offensive. Then, overnight, Meade had quietly cleared out, skillfully withdrawing from his untenable position. "I am too old to command this army!" Lee ruefully declared to his officers. "We should never have permitted those people to get away."[37]

[36] Stine, *The Army of the Potomac*, 592.
[37] Col. Charles S. Venable of General Lee's staff in *Battles and Leaders*, IV, 240.

# 17. The Political Battle Front
## (December 2, 1863-March 8, 1864)

NEWSPAPER COMMENT on the Mine Run affair reflected upon leadership in the field. Failure was sneered at. There were calls for the return of the Radical favorite, Fighting Joe Hooker. Save in his official report, which was private, Meade was unable to present his own case and so painfully shouldered the blame. Although he had withdrawn to avoid disaster, he could not argue the point. "Officers here know . . . what we have a reasonable expectation of taking, and what not," Colonel Lyman said. "It should be remembered, also, as a fundamental fact, that this line is *not* approved as a line of operations and *never has been* but we are forced to work on it."[1]

Naturally sensitive whenever his name was assailed, Meade was concerned over his reputation as a soldier. "I do not want to lose this entirely," he wrote Margaret.[2] He was heartened by letters from the convalescing Gibbon and Hancock, who reaffirmed their confidence in him as the army commander. Mingling with armchair strategists in Washington, Gibbon found it vain to attempt to convince them that Meade was conforming to sound military principles, which would be the same in any case regardless of politics. The objective view would win no converts. Gibbon was stared at, was wryly congratulated on being "such a staunch friend of McClellan," and was informed that the test of a man's military soundness was whether in his *talk* he supported "the true policy of the war."[3] If not, he was obviously unworthy of his command.

---

[1] *Meade's Headquarters*, 61. "But for the restrictions imposed upon me, I should in retiring have taken a position in front of Fredericksburg, and I cannot but think that substantial advantages would have resulted," Meade wrote Halleck after Mine Run. *O.R.*, XXIX, pt. 1, 18. This position, of course, would have permitted easier access to the James River and would have precluded a march through the Wilderness.

[2] MS letter of December 11, 1863, Meade Papers.

[3] Gibbon, *Personal Recollections*, 206–207.

There was a possibility, Meade thought, of either Hooker or Thomas being brought east to succeed him. Hancock, who was both able and popular, would surely be considered. After the death of Reynolds, he was the officer closest to Meade, who now warned him that under existing conditions, the post was "not to be desired by any reasonable man."[4] "I would sooner command a corps under you than have the supreme command," Hancock warmly responded. "I have faith in you. I would not like to serve under a bad commander . . . [but] if the command was put on me, I suppose I would feel and act as you did."[5]

General Grant had been sounded out some months before, but after making his excuses, was grateful to be passed over.[6] The *New York Herald* surprisingly had it that Pleasonton of the cavalry would be the man.[7] Next to the remote possibility that French, the senior corps commander, would be chosen, this was probably the longest shot. Meade's worst fear was that he might be transferred to some remote post where he would be even farther removed from his family. After several days of uncertainty he had the assurance of Colonel Forney's newspaper, the *Washington Chronicle*, that he would not be relieved. Soon the *New York World* and other journals had the news: "General Meade will retain his position . . . all rumors to the contrary notwithstanding."[8]

Allotment of the honors of war was one of the most important matters before the new Congress, which spent considerable time in satisfying the prejudices of the Radical majority. Sponsored by the politically able Elihu B. Washburne from his own state, General Grant was voted a gold medal for his western successes, and a joint House-Senate resolution of thanks was unanimously passed. While Grant well merited all due thanks and his medal, a resolution was dragged in honoring General Nathaniel P. Banks, a political general from Massachusetts, for compelling the surrender of Fort Hudson farther below. The achievement of General Banks was actually slight; isolated Fort Hudson had fallen into his hands as the natural result of the surrender at

---

[4] Almira R. Hancock, *Reminiscences of Winfield Scott Hancock*, 292.

[5] *Ibid.*, 292. Original Hancock and Gibbon letters are in the Meade Papers.

[6] Williams, *Lincoln and His Generals*, 275; Grant to Charles A. Dana, August 5, 1863, Dana MSS; "I should beg very hard to be excused before accepting that command," Grant wrote.

[7] *Meade's Headquarters*, 60.

[8] *Washington Chronicle*, December 12, 1863; *New York World*, December 14, 1863.

Vicksburg and a stratagem of Grant's. Next on the agenda were the exploits of General Burnside, who had been sent west after Fredericksburg. In a wholly defensive action, he had saved Knoxville from assault by Longstreet toward the last of November. More of an easygoing politician than a good general, Burnside was voted the thanks of Congress without serious dissent.

Of those who came next, General Hooker of Massachusetts had long been sponsored by Treasury Secretary Chase and the inner Radical group, while General Howard of Maine was an avowed Abolitionist backed by Vice President Hannibal Hamlin of his own state. The formula in Hooker's case was not difficult to arrive at. It was asserted that he had done all the planning for the Gettysburg campaign and that Chief of Staff Butterfield had arranged the marches each day as the army advanced under Meade. Any astuteness shown could not be claimed for the new army commander. As for the actual fighting, the several corps commanders had taken care of that. Meade, upon hearing the news, allowed that it soon would be proved that either he was not at Gettysburg at all or that his presence there had been a positive detriment.[9]

Senator and chairman of the Committee on Military Affairs Henry Wilson of Massachusetts sponsored the resolution which complimented Fighting Joe for the "skill, energy, and endurance which first covered Washington and Baltimore from the meditated blow." Hooker at least had marched as far as Frederick. In view of the prevailing mood, George Gordon Meade could be awarded only secondary mention "for skill and heroic valor."

Even at that, the resolution lingered for several weeks in committee while friends of General Howard spoke up and General Sickles tried to have Meade's name eliminated in favor of his own. It was General Howard with himself, asserted Sickles, who had selected the position at Gettysburg while Meade had merely followed their advice or had been forced to go along as the fighting broke out. Sickles could say that he had led the fighting with his Third Corps until disabled. It was implied that had he not been wounded, Gettysburg would have been won in two days instead of three. But there were some who could

[9] *Meade*, II, 160. "General Sickles asserts that Hancock selected the position and that he (Sickles), with his corps, did all the fighting at Gettysburg."—*Ibid.*, 164. This should read *Howard*, not Hancock.

not stomach Sickles, a Tammany Democrat who still had enemies in Congress. Although unable to win official laurels for himself, Sickles may have helped get Howard's name included in the Gettysburg resolution, thus further overshadowing Meade. Those who voted for it in its final form apparently considered it a fair compromise to cite Hooker, Howard, and Meade in that order.[10] The names of Reynolds and Hancock, which well could have been coupled with Meade's, were passed over; none of the good Pennsylvania generals, including Humphreys, were ever able to swing very much weight on Capitol Hill.

As a matter of soldierly duty, the opposing army leaders spent Christmas Day each in his own camp. Although Mrs. Lee, now living in Richmond, was invalided by arthritis and a daughter-in-law at home was very ill, the Southern leader wished to set an example for his officers and men. Meade remained not to set an example especially but because he was absorbed in re-enlisting the veteran volunteers. Inasmuch as most of the new recruits or drafted men were deemed worthless at first hand, it was important to win back the veterans. For Meade the day was less gloomy; more of the three-year men than had been expected chose to remain in his army. Once they had signed, they received furloughs if they wished to go home, and some regiments left in a body.[11]

Two days after Christmas, still busy with his task, Meade heard an aide call out, "There's Hancock," and at once hurried out of his tent. "I'm glad to see you again, Hancock," he said in greeting, grasping that officer's hand in both of his own.[12] There was much to talk over. Hancock remarked that his commander's removal had been seriously considered after Mine Run and that he had learned of plans to assign the command to him. But Halleck stuck with Meade, suggesting that everyone wait until more was learned of the campaign. Then it had been Meade's report, combined with the opinions of officers passing through Washington, which "changed the whole aspect of the case."[13]

Hancock appeared well satisfied with the result. Since General

---

[10] *Congressional Globe*, 38 Cong., 1 sess., 17, 134, 257, 343, 361, 421. Amended on January 20, 1864, to include General Howard, the resolution became law on February 1, some six weeks after its introduction. The *Army and Navy Journal* (February 20, 1864) commented scathingly on the precedence given Howard over Hancock.

[11] Walker, *History of the Second Corps*, 393.

[12] Schaff, *Battle of the Wilderness*, 42.

[13] *Meade*, II, 164.

Warren was on leave, Meade could not do less than reassign him to the Second Corps, but since it was much reduced in strength, Hancock soon left camp to recruit volunteers. Other officers, recovering from wounds, were undertaking the same enlistment duty. Throughout the winter and spring the army would have to be built up by every possible means for its most rigorous campaign.

In its busy recruiting, the government dipped into the dregs of the cities and into the criminal class. Bounties offered for enlistment tempted men to desert and re-enlist under other names, and often two or three bounties were collected. Problems arose from a rising proportion of habitual deserters, bounty jumpers, and men who would never make soldiers. In and about the front, military crimes became so numerous that the courts-martial handled cases in groups, and executions were sometimes carried out in the same manner. A sad and depressing sight was the shooting of four deserters by a Fifth Corps detail on an otherwise pleasant afternoon.[14]

A sympathetic President Lincoln, however, could be seen by almost anyone, and relatives of condemned men soon learned to whom they should go. The troops were not merely soldiers—they were his boys. Soon he and Meade were exchanging messages directly as he asked for particulars and issued quick pardons. In an emotional atmosphere, conditions were not well understood. "General Meade is very active in shooting his own men, and, it would appear, rather carelessly,"[15] newspaper comment ran when actually it was only the friendless offender or the more flagrant deserter or criminal who was shot. Provost marshals, the army police, frowned at a low ratio of executions compared with actual sentences.

The common soldier was asking himself: "Does it pay to be faithful to duty or is the skulker better served?"[16] Colonel Lyman asserted that relaxation of camp discipline and further outrages on civilians stemmed directly from the uncertainty of the death penalty "through the false merciful policy of the President."[17] On the last day of the year Meade discussed this side of the case directly with Lincoln, but

[14] Buell, *The Cannoneer*, 138–40. Death by firing squad was not abandoned until 1938.

[15] Quoted in Sandburg, *Abraham Lincoln*, III, 518.

[16] Buell, *The Cannoneer*, 138–39.

[17] *Meade's Headquarters*, 117.

save in the most flagrant cases the President continued to issue pardons. Meade could expect a telegram at almost any hour, and staff officers soon learned the quickest routes to the execution grounds of each corps.[18] Occasionally, when names were garbled, they would have to rush to two or three. Tiring of the game, Meade asked and received permission to commute death sentences to hard labor on the Dry Tortugas Islands off Florida. On its face, this may have seemed more merciful, but not to many unfortunates shipped to this remote and barren prison camp.

Meade's trip to Washington to see the President was made memorable when Margaret came down from Philadelphia to attend the New Year's Day reception.[19] Both of them thoroughly enjoyed the White House affair. Meade gracefully paid his respects to Mrs. Lincoln, who appeared with white flowers in her hair and a black lace shawl draped over her silk gown. "How elegantly Mrs. L. looked and how affable the Sec^y [Stanton] was to you," he recalled to Margaret[20] when memories of the trip were still vivid.

Home on leave by mid-January, the General was overtaken by a cold followed by pneumonia, which kept him confined for nearly three weeks. Mrs. Meade was kept busy answering inquiries, and when it was learned that he was up and about, a group of convalescent soldiers and musicians from the military hospitals made up a brass band. "We want you all to return and bring all you can with you," Meade called out from his doorway after the concert. "May you all live to see this struggle brought to a speedy and glorious end. It is but a question of numbers and time." More music was heard as a city band brought up a delegation from the loyal Union League Club. Meade went on with his recruiting. "What we need is men," he told his visitors. "I want all of you here, every man of you, to send recruits to the army."[21] When he was able to leave the house, he exhorted an audience gathered at Independence Hall, where the City Council had arranged a reception: "The war can be closed only by desperate and bloody fighting. What we

---

[18] Robert T. Lincoln collection of Lincoln Papers, vol. CXXXVI; *Complete Works of Abraham Lincoln*, IX, X; Benjamin P. Thomas, *Abraham Lincoln*, 462–63, 465; *O.R.*, XXXIII, 98.

[19] Leech, *Reveille In Washington*, 285.

[20] MS letter of January 5, 1864, Meade Papers.

[21] Pennypacker, *Meade*, 257–58.

want is fighting men to destroy the military power of the Rebels."[22] Not yet in perfect health, he was hurried home early to escape the crowd which would have detained him.

Two days later, February 11, 1864, his doctor permitted him to leave the city. Reaching Washington the next day, he took tea upon arriving at Willard's Hotel and got to bed early. His morning round took him first to the War Office to see Secretary Stanton, who wished to discuss changes in army organization. Meade was a little surprised to hear him say that he knew certain corps leaders to be a positive handicap in military operations. In that case, he would offer no objection to their removal, Meade replied.

In dead earnest, Stanton asked him to call again next day, when he revealed his plan. The First and Third Corps between them had lost some 10,200 officers and men at Gettysburg and were still greatly reduced in strength. Stanton proposed to combine the remainder with other units, thus eliminating the two corps commanders. Besides French and Newton, Pleasonton of the cavalry was apparently on his way out. At later meetings it was decided that Hancock should permanently resume his Second Corps command while Warren replaced Sykes of the Fifth.

Meade usually stood by the regulars. He put in a word or two for all of these men but later withdrew his objection in Pleasonton's case upon learning that the cavalryman, a braggart, was taking a patronizing view of his superior in testimony before the Committee on the Conduct of the War. Meade was also resigned to the loss of Newton and French, particularly the latter, but he would regret parting with Sykes, "an excellent soldier."[23] At least Sykes had saved the army left at Gettysburg.

Stanton was even insisting that General Sedgwick, who had been in charge in Meade's absence, should be permanently relieved. From his own point of view, he had a strong reason. Meade knew part although not all of the story, and he hurried back to camp to hear it from Hum-

[22] John T. Scharf and Thompson Westcott, *History of Philadelphia*, I, 84; *Meade*, II, 208, 251; *Meade's Headquarters*, 79–80.

[23] *Meade*, II, 165, 182–85; *Meade's Headquarters*, 180. Meade complimented Pleasonton for good work in the Gettysburg campaign (*O.R.*, XXVII, pt. 1, 90), but on March 9, 1864, he wrote his wife, "His vanity is over-weening."—Meade Papers. Pleasonton's exalted views concerning himself are found in *Annals of the War*, 447–59, *Battles and Leaders*, III, 172–82; the view of others in MHSM *Papers*, Vol. III, 202–17, Ford (ed.), *A Cycle of Adams Letters*, II, 44–45. Incidentally, all four officers under discussion were born south of the Mason and Dixon's line. General Sedgwick was from Connecticut.

phreys. It seems that Benjamin F. Butler, a political general answerable to Lincoln and the War Office only, had advanced the idea of a surprise raid upon Richmond from his base at Fortress Monroe near the mouth of the James River. Both Sedgwick and Humphreys thought the plan impractical and a little silly under winter conditions, but Butler was calling the turn and Halleck writing the orders.

Asked to co-operate, Sedgwick was given very short notice. His protests that a flank movement was more or less useless over winter-rutted roads and in unfavorable weather were passed over. On February 7, the Second Corps, the nearest available, was swung across the Rapidan River at Morton's Ford on the extreme Federal right as a diversion. Surprised enemy skirmishers were driven back for some distance, but since Butler failed to get very far, the corps was withdrawn. About the only result of the move was that strong new defensive works were quickly thrown up by the enemy. Sedgwick therefore made the point that the advance at Morton's Ford had only spoiled the chances for an enemy surprise at that place when it might be of real value. His report was not well received at the War Office.[24]

In Washington again on the twentieth, Meade so strongly objected to Sedgwick's removal that Stanton allowed him a concession. Sedgwick, he suggested could be transferred to military operations in the Shenandoah Valley, an independent command. In that case, Meade preferred John Gibbon to succeed him with the Sixth Corps. But Lincoln interposed with an order directing that General Franz Sigel be assigned to the Shenandoah. Although he never proved much of a general, Sigel had organized the Third Missouri Volunteers and had won some early successes in his state. Brought east, he had fought in the Shenandoah and at Second Bull Run. His command was later given the dignity of an Eleventh Corps, as designated, but he could never get along with Halleck and therefore asked to be relieved. After several radical German delegations pressed for his reappointment, Lincoln acted. As a result, Meade was able to retain an officer whom army men considered one of his best soldiers.[25] Otherwise, only Hancock, among his former corps leaders, would have been left.

[24] *O.R.*, XXXIII, 524, 532, 554; *Magazine of American History*, Vol. XVI, 359; Humphreys, *From Gettysburg to the Rapidan*, 72–74. Meade was not present at the action as some accounts state.
[25] Gibbon, *Personal Recollections*, 209.

The "on-to-Richmond" idea still persisted, and to reduce it to an absurdity the right man presented himself. This was General Judson Kilpatrick, Third Cavalry Division, a flamboyant twenty-seven-year-old brigadier. Familiarly known as "Kill-Cavalry" for his rash tactics, he was regarded in infantry circles at least as not well endowed with judgment or good sense.[26] Since his immediate superior, General Pleasonton, was then in official disfavor, he felt himself free to advance a plan of his own by visiting Washington and talking even with Lincoln, who failed to call Meade in. As military affairs were then being run, almost anyone with an idea—Ben Butler, for example—could have his way, since the White House and the War Office were making the decisions.

Meade did not even know that the plan was being discussed in Washington until he was visited by Colonel Ulric Dahlgren, a cavalryman who had lost a leg just after Gettysburg. With an artificial limb in place, young Dahlgren was eager to accompany Kilpatrick on a literally desperate mission, which, however had some ingenuity about it. Lincoln, of course, sent Kilpatrick to Meade, who had to accept the idea that a cavalry force dashing into Richmond might throw open the prisons where 15,000 Federals were confined, and, with their aid, seize and hold the city until other help arrived.

Meade wasted no time in vain correspondence with the War Office but got to work. Since he needed those 15,000 men, he was not without hope that the plan might succeed. The details of the march were left to General Humphreys, who outlined a two-pronged approach to Richmond from the army left. With 4,000 men, Kilpatrick was to cross the Rapidan at Ely's Ford and proceed on his long journey—perhaps seventy-five miles—more or less directly south. Dahlgren with 500 men was to swing off and make an end run which would bring him down to the James River west of Richmond, and the forces would be joined in forcing an entrance from two sides. Elaborate diversionary movements were planned. Sedgwick was ordered to lead his corps upstream while General George Custer with 2,000 cavalry would ride on past toward the Orange and Alexandria Railway as it curved past Gordonsville to the southwest. A Third Corps division was also detached in the effort to show that the real attack was to be made on the enemy's left flank.[27]

---

[26] *Meade's Headquarters*, 79; Virgil Carrington Jones, *Eight Hours before Richmond*, 33–34, 153.

[27] *Battles and Leaders*, IV, 93, 95.

And so the power of the army was brought into play on the far side as Kilpatrick slipped away on the evening of February 28, 1864, toward Spotsylvania Court House. The cavalryman had nearly twenty-four hours of good weather for marching, looting, and burning, but rain and felled trees impeded the advance as he neared Richmond's defenses. Drawing close to the city on March 1, the third day, Kilpatrick heard or saw no signs of Dahlgren, and confronted by only a small force with six field guns he reluctantly retreated. Dahlgren, toward evening, was thrown back by musketry and, after withdrawing, was assailed by a strong cavalry force late that night. In the black darkness his command was split in two, but the direct cause of his failure seems to have been lack of familiarity with the ground. The penalty was paid: Dahlgren was slain and his body mutilated. About 300 of his men were able to join Kilpatrick, who sought safety within General Butler's lines near Williamsburg.

Until the news came, headquarters had been anxious and hopeful. Meade, however, was heard to remark that he hadn't expected much. Knowing Kilpatrick, Humphreys was plainly disgusted. "The great raid was a great failure," Sedgwick summed up.[28] Losses totaled 340 men and 1,000 horses, but now that the lunatic fringe of Butler and Kilpatrick had been given its chance, perhaps the army could get down to work.

One result of the raid was some official correspondence between Meade and Lee. Headquarters was startled to learn that Confederate newspapers were ablaze with furious comment over instructions found on Dahlgren's body ordering the burning of Richmond and the slaying of Jefferson Davis and his cabinet. Meade termed it "a pretty ugly piece of business,"[29] and having grounds for suspicion sent for Kilpatrick, who flatly denied that the paper was official. Soon, however, he received a formal inquiry from Lee. Meade again sent for Kilpatrick, who in a carefully written statement cleared everyone superior in rank to Dahlgren, a dead hero unable to testify.

Apparently Meade knew something which could not be divulged, for he could hardly make an issue of any Federal wrongdoing. He suggested privately that someone in authority was to blame, mentioning

---

[28] Humphreys, *From Gettysburg to the Rapidan*, 76–80; Sedgwick, *Correspondence*, II, 177–78; Humphreys, *Andrew Atkinson Humphreys*, 216; *Meade*, II, 169–70.
[29] *Meade*, II, 190–91.

certain "collateral evidence" that was in his possession and calling attention to Kilpatrick's reputation. But with Kilpatrick's denial before him, he could only assure Lee that no one had ever sanctioned the burning of Richmond or the murder of civilian officials "or any other act not required by military necessity and in accordance with the usages of war."[30] It was, as he knew, a tawdry episode, but the original plan had not come from him. The natural result was a hardening of feeling in the South and a bitter reproach upon the Federal army. General Josiah Gorgas, Confederate chief of ordnance, mildly suggested that any Union prisoners taken thereafter should be murdered.[31]

One of President Lincoln's favorite ideas was that an easy way to beat General Lee was to fight him near Washington.[32] He, however, took the first step toward the proper tactics because he was the only one who could. It was a roundabout means. Sworn to uphold the Constitution, Lincoln could tolerate no one in power who might find himself tempted to interfere with the government or seize the reins himself, but after learning that Grant had rejected suggestions that he run for president, the Chief Executive began to consider higher rank for that officer and a post of authority in Washington.

It was known that Grant would not serve as head of the Army of the Potomac under Halleck, who had been unfriendly since the days of his own service in the West. Lincoln, however, could get around that. On February 26, he asked Congress to revive the rank of lieutenant general, and within three days the bill was passed. Lieutenant General Grant, which he became on March 3, was soon named to the command of all the armies. Now the Army of the Potomac had a leader empowered to plan and execute his own campaigns, probably a necessary step if the war was not to be unreasonably prolonged. Although Grant would not be directly in command, it was his decision to stay out of Washington and to make his headquarters with Meade's troops.

First of all, the appointment meant a change for General in Chief Halleck, who would now be kept on as a military chief of staff, although

---

[30] *Ibid.*, 191; Freeman, *R. E. Lee*, III, 219; Humphreys, *From Gettysburg to the Rapidan*, 81–86. Some of the originals of the Meade-Lee correspondence are in the New York Historical Society.

[31] *Civil War Diary of General Josiah Gorgas* (ed. by Frank A. Vandiver), 85–86.

[32] Williams, *Lincoln and His Generals*, 297.

actually he would have little to do. Grant was not disposed to retain Meade in his present position but had tentatively decided that General William F. Smith, who had done good work in opening up a supply line for the besieged troops in Chattanooga, should have the Army of the Potomac to command.[33] However, Radical circles were stirring. Their perennial candidate was Fighting Joe Hooker, who had regained some lost stature by winning the Battle of Lookout Mountain during the Chattanooga campaign. Without first sounding out Grant about his chances, the Committee on the Conduct of the War sought to clear the way by criticizing Meade's record in the Gettysburg campaign.

"My enemies," the General wrote a family connection in New York, "consist of certain politicians who wish me removed to restore Hooker; then of certain subordinates whose military reputations are involved in the destruction of mine; finally a class of vultures who in Hooker's day preyed upon the army, and who sigh for a return to those glorious days. I expect to retain my place, but I am anxious about my reputation."[34]

Whatever the committee's hearings were meant to reveal, it became obvious that certain army officers had behaved as mere spies—a view advanced by the *New York Times*.[35] The *New York Tribune*, a radical organ, labored the familiar thesis that the Gettysburg campaign and battle had been conducted not by Meade but by others and that Sickles had saved the entire army in the second day's fight.[36] Besides Sickles, another disgruntled officer was Doubleday, whom Meade had displaced as temporary First Corps commander when he named Newton. Doubleday was claiming that the pro-McClellan and proslavery clique, with which he linked Meade, was in full control of the army, and such leadership would have nothing to do with anyone of loyal views; hence, presumably, his present inactive situation.

Another deponent was General Albion P. Howe, a former Sixth Corps brigadier removed for some cause but useful to the committee

---

[33] *Ibid.*, 292–93; Sandburg, *Abraham Lincoln* (one-volume edition), 459–60; Cyrus B. Comstock, MS Diary, entry of March 11, 1864. Lincoln, in December, did "not think it would do to bring Grant away from the West."—See Williams, *Lincoln and His Generals*, 290.

[34] *Meade*, II, 179.

[35] *Ibid.*, 180.

[36] *Ibid.*, 320–21.

in testimony charging both Sedgwick and Meade with lack of vigor and alertness. Three successive days of sworn views unfavorable to the army command appeared to give the committee all that it wanted. On March 3, Chairman Benjamin F. Wade of Ohio and Michigan's Senator Zachariah Chandler, whom Meade once called his bitterest foe, went to the White House to suggest his removal. President Lincoln thought it proper to inquire whom they might prefer instead. After citing General Hooker as their first choice, they considerately left the door open. The statement was made that "if there was any general whom the President considered more competent for the command, then let him be appointed."[37]

Lincoln thought that the other side of the case should be presented, but in any event he would not interfere with Grant, who had been named lieutenant general that day. In Washington to arrange final details of the merger of the First and Third Corps with others, Meade took the stand on March 5 and rode down his critics. They were refuted in detail by the official dispatches which he read into the record, but as Meade remarked to Stanton, he could not but feel that he was losing his military reputation. Stanton, who knew Meade to be oversensitive, urged that he really had no cause for worry.[38] It seemed as though reputation meant more to Meade than the army command.

The decision in his case, however, would not be Stanton's or Lincoln's, for by promoting Grant and giving him the high command, the President had rid himself of the Hooker problem. What Treasury Secretary Chase and Hooker's other Radical backers did not realize was that Fighting Joe stood absolutely no chance with Grant.[39] Lincoln, however, must have known it, as no one was ever sharper in matters of this kind.

Yet the true significance of Grant's stepping into high office was that he would be the first general with the military authority that operations against General Lee and his army required. No longer would there be any restrictions or artificial conditions imposed by the admin-

[37] *Ibid.*, 172. The complete testimony appears in volume one of the Committee's *Report*. See also J. G. Randall, *Lincoln the President*, II, 289.

[38] *Meade*, II, 169.

[39] "His [Hooker's] friends are working like heavens to get this place for him."— Meade to wife, March 14, 1864, Meade Papers. "I . . . regarded him [Hooker] as a dangerous man."—U. S. Grant, *Personal Memoirs*, II, 539.

istration; now the commander in the field could move as he saw fit. The decision of President Lincoln himself, it was a happy turning point in war policy. Once Grant took the reins, the Washington administration could no longer indulge in military errors, and some already made would be undone. Whatever errors might now be committed would not be on the side of defensive caution.

## 18. Grant Tests His Strategy
## (March 10-May 6, 1864)

AT THE REQUEST of the President, Grant came to Washington to visit at the White House. It was a cordial meeting of two men from almost the same countryside. Grant listened carefully to what Lincoln had to say concerning military strategy but refrained from offering any plan of his own. Probably little if any time was spent on the findings of the Committee on the Conduct of the War, which was still sitting. General Pleasonton had taken the stand to testify that *he* had suggested Gettysburg as the proper battleground and that Meade never had the confidence of the Cavalry Corps, when Grant left the city to visit field headquarters.

Whether or not Grant would elevate Baldy Smith, who had testified that military leadership in the East could be improved, Meade did not especially care. He was inwardly prepared for whatever might happen and for whatever Grant might decide. "I hear . . . that the ultra-radicals are determined to have me out," he wearily wrote Margaret. "God knows I shall be satisfied if any better or more successful man can be found." Pleasonton's testimony, he said, had made him "very heartsick," and he admitted also to a bad cold and severe cough.[1]

All eyes were turned on Grant as he arrived in camp on March 10. Men around headquarters saw a short-statured, plain-looking individual who rode his horse well. General Sedgwick, upon meeting him, marked his "straightforward, common-sense view of matters"; Colonel Lyman, a good judge, noted an "extreme determination, grant simplicity and calmness."[2] Lieutenant Morris Schaff of Ordnance was happy that the new man did not appear to be the chieftain type. "What did I see?" Schaff later looked back. "A medium-sized, mild, unob-

1 *Meade,* II, 172; MS letters of March 8-9, Meade Papers.
2 Sedgwick, *Correspondence,* II, 177; *Meade's Headquarters,* 80.

trusive, inconspicuously dressed, modest and naturally silent man. He had a low, gently vibrant voice, and steady, thoughtful blue eyes."[3]

Meade was genuinely glad to see him, rushing up to shake hands before he could dismount. The two men disappeared inside a headquarters tent to smoke together and to recall Mexican War days. Apparently there was a meeting of minds. Meade later reported to Margaret, who had been critical of the newcomer, that Grant "showed more capacity and character than I had expected."[4] He was disappointed, however, in Grant's decision to remain in the field with the army, of which he was informed, and he barely mentioned the fact that his own proffered resignation was declined. Grant had heard Meade say that the success of the cause was of first importance. Coming from this man, the words were sincere. As Grant looked back on the situation, Meade "spoke so patriotically and unselfishly that even if I had had any intention of relieving him, I should have been inclined to change my mind after the manly attitude he assumed in this frank interview."[5]

Grant nevertheless kept his counsel. Hearing no official word, newspapers said that recurrent weakness from pneumonia would prevent Meade from taking the field. Editor Horace Greeley, visiting Washington, demanded his outright removal. Grant, who had returned to the Capital after a brief visit, rejoined that if he saw Greeley, "he should tell him that when he wanted the advice of a political editor in selecting generals, he would call on him."[6]

But had Grant spoken out in Meade's favor, fewer stories might have been told. There was no more widely read newspaper than the *New York Herald*, which on March 12 carried a highly colored account of the second day at Gettysburg. Artfully signed "Historicus," it was from the pen of one John B. Bachelder, formerly of Sickles' headquar-

---

[3] Schaff, *Battle of the Wilderness*, 47. Schaff's character portrayals are excellent, and good personal analyses of many army leaders are to be found in this work. Schaff discovered in Meade a "noble, fiery nature," but he bore hardest on General Burnside, who was set down as an utter failure although "noted for a soldierly bearing."—*Ibid.*, 111–12, 126.

[4] *Meade*, II, 178.

[5] Horace Porter, *Campaigning with Grant*, 29. "This incident gave me even a more favorable opinion of Meade than did his great victory at Gettysburg," Grant wrote in his *Personal Memoirs*. "I assured him that I had no thought of substituting any one for him."—Grant, *Personal Memoirs*, II, 117.

[6] Andrews, *The North Reports the Civil War*, 524; *Meade*, II, 187.

ters. The theme was that Sykes's Fifth Corps had done no rescue work at Gettysburg but had only got in the way of the heroic Third. "My only motive," wrote Historicus, "is to vindicate history, do honor to the fallen, and justice to the survivors when unfairly impeached."[7]

Astonished and indignant Fifth Corps soldiers replied with the facts as they knew them. For the most part, the tempest was their battle, but Meade, too, had been deprecated and assailed. He had no idea who Historicus might be; it was years later that a loyal Fifth Corps man identified him, "a loud-mouthed, blatant artist-photographer . . . and henchman of Sickles," as the writer. But he well realized that Sickles was concerned. Perhaps thanking his stars that Grant had not permitted him to resign in the face of this new storm, Meade wrote to several officers to obtain true accounts of the rout of the Third Corps and of the timely possession and defense of Little Round Top. Secretary Stanton was urged to confront Sickles with the letter signed "Historicus." If Sickles acknowledged or endorsed these sentiments, Meade suggested, then a Court of Inquiry should be named. Stanton sensibly declined to consider the idea. "No attention should be paid to such a person as Sickles," he remarked to his old legal associate George Harding of Philadelphia, brother of the *Inquirer* publisher and a Meade supporter.[8] However, he did pass on the request to Lincoln, who urged that Meade overlook the criticism. "The country knows that, at all events, you have done good service," the President wrote him candidly.[9]

A few words from Grant might have saved Meade some trouble, but with all of the negative testimony in, he was again called before the Committee on the Conduct of the War for another rebuttal. He notified his wife that Chairman Ben Wade "took great pains to convince me that the committee was not responsible for the newspaper attacks,"[10]

---

[7] *New York Herald*, March 12, 1864, reprinted in *Meade*, II, 323–31. Bachelder is so characterized by soldier and author R. G. Carter in a letter quoted in W. A. Graham, *The Custer Myth*, 318. It is ironic that Bachelder, through Sickles' influence, should have been named the official historian of Gettysburg. This, of course, was to Meade's detriment because of the peculiar slant of Bachelder's chronicles, which were used as the source for other comment, including lectures.

[8] *Meade*, II, 184; MS letter to wife, August 8, 1864, Meade Papers.

[9] Lincoln to Meade, March 29, 1864, *Meade*, II, 336; original in New York Historical Society.

[10] Meade to wife, March 4, 1864, *Meade*, II, 177.

but nothing was said to show that they were regretted. Placed on the stand, he had to point out that routine orders issued for the purpose of getting an army out of a bad place did not necessarily mean that retreat was the original intention.[11] If Meade had been allowed a choice between Gettysburg and Pipe Creek, he would naturally have fought on the latter ground, which he considered best suited. However, a major political issue was made of the fact that Gettysburg had been selected by someone other than Meade. And yet it had been Meade's own decision as of late afternoon, July 1.

The effort to convict him of bungling was even more prolonged. When the War Office denied a request from General Butterfield that he be allowed to leave his post and testify, he nevertheless appeared before the committee by subpoena at lawyer Sickles' suggestion. Stanton angrily ordered him back to his post, but not before Butterfield had gone on record as stating that Meade had been so timid that he had prepared an order to retreat from the Gettysburg battlefield.[12]

That General Meade would remain as head of the Army of the Potomac was a *New York Herald* exclusive as of March 21. The changes to be made would affect not Meade but certain corps commanders. The army commander, not Grant or the War Office, was apparently responsible for these changes. Meade's name was on the order reducing the five army corps to three, but even as he had sought to save Sykes, French, and Pleasonton, he tried to temper the blow: "The First and Third Corps will retain their badges and distinctive marks, and the major general commanding indulges in the hope that the ranks of the Army will be filled at an early date so that those corps can again be reorganized."[13] But although the badges were temporarily retained, the sweeping changes were not easily accepted either by the men in the ranks or by individual officers who long had been bound by close associ-

---

[11] Meade appeared before the Joint Committee on March 5 and 11 and finally on April 4, 1864, when he gave an extended rebuttal to General Butterfield's testimony. *Meade*, II, 354–95.

[12] *Meade*, II, 188; Sickles to Chandler, March 10, 1864, Chandler Papers. Generals Hunt, Hancock, Gibbon, and Warren testified in Meade's behalf, but the weight of the evidence was disregarded. Inasmuch as the Committee tried to get Hunt to admit that an order to withdraw from Gettysburg "might have been issued without his knowing anything about it," Meade feared that "Butterfield's perjury is to outweigh the testimony of all others."

[13] *O.R.*, XXX, pt. 1, 722.

ation with their old corps. And since Meade had signed the order, it was he who was held responsible.

Hancock again resumed leadership of the Second Corps, now increased to four divisions, and Warren took the Fifth, also of four divisions. Each received troops from dissolved units, as also did Sedgwick. Cavalry chief Pleasonton, whom Grant as well as Stanton did not wish to be retained, went west with Sykes and Newton, the latter joining Sherman's army, while French was returned to a Maryland post.

Although none of the four officers let go were of high caliber, General Humphreys questioned the wisdom of the reorganization. In the heavily wooded country in which the army would have to strike, a single corps commander with four division leaders would face the difficulty of getting his orders quickly to each and of controlling his lines of battle. Rather than three corps of well over 20,000 men each, five of 15,000, declared Humphreys, would have been more desirable.[14] He had the advantage of hindsight in his criticism, but officers experienced in campaigning against an enemy both wily and audacious could probably foresee his point.

Grant's choice to command the cavalry was an infantry officer from the West who had served under Thomas in the Army of the Cumberland. This was General Philip H. Sheridan, a ruddy, coarse-fibered, contentious apostle of violence with "a genius for war."[15] Sheridan, arriving, declared the condition of the horses deplorable, but Kill-Cavalry Kilpatrick also was transferred, and Meade obligingly contracted the picket lines to relieve the mounted arm of much of this work.

Grant's strategy as outlined on April 9 linked outworn ideas with some of his own thinking. "Lee's army will be your objective point," his order to Meade ran. "Wherever Lee goes, there will you go also."[16] (Actually, Grant would do better than this.) Above all else, he planned for co-ordination both in the East and in the West, all armies moving together. While the Army of the Potomac advanced, General Butler, with 40,000 troops, would push forward from the mouth of the James along its south bank. One army or the other would then cross over, and the two would be united. "I will . . . operate directly against Lee's army, wherever it may be found," Grant notified Sherman, who was

---

14 Humphreys, *Virginia Campaign*, 3–4.
15 Schaff, *Battle of the Wilderness*, 43.
16 Grant, *Personal Memoirs*, II, 134–37.

to march into Georgia as the Army of the Potomac headed south. "Get into the interior of the enemy's country as far as you can, inflicting all the damage you can."[17]

The order to Meade showed that Grant was not yet decided whether to move to right or left, but after further talks at field headquarters, the General in Chief agreed that the army should march by the left flank, which would bring it closer to the Fredericksburg railroad. The rail line now occupied at the behest of the War Office would be abandoned as useless. Below Fredericksburg, which Meade, the preceding fall, had asked to be allowed to occupy, the country was fairly open, permitting ease of maneuver, but Grant would have to cut through the Wilderness in heading south and southeast from Brandy Station. Denied to Meade, Fredericksburg could not be used as a base, but the army would still be moving nearer to navigable waters previously used by McClellan. Wagon routes to be utilized between them would not be difficult, or, as Humphreys remarked, "No protecting force would be necessary to cover these short land routes."[18] And the wounded could be more easily and comfortably moved by land and by water rather than by long hauls over the Alexandria railroad, to which Meade had been held.

Meade's troops, many of them green, had been regularly drilled during the winter. Early spring days brought exhibition drills, dress parades, and reviews on the best available ground. Returning from a visit with Sherman, Grant watched the massed men with great interest and declared himself satisfied.[19] The easterners always looked better than the western troops, yet the impression lingered at Grant's headquarters that the Army of the Potomac had never been fought to the limit and that this could only be accomplished through western leadership. Colonel Lyman sensed a saucy air among Grant's staff officers, who "talked and laughed flippantly about Lee and his army."[20] While some of this was sheer ebullience, Lyman also could detect a shade of overconfidence which, after hard experience, would disappear.

The army continued to flex its muscles and demonstrate its skill.

[17] Grant to Butler, April 2, 1864, *ibid.*, 560–61; to Sherman, April 4, *ibid.*, 130–32.

[18] Humphreys, *Virginia Campaign*, 10.

[19] *Meade's Headquarters*, 84; Gibbon, *Personal Recollections*, 211.

[20] *Meade's Headquarters*, 87; Douglas, *I Rode with Stonewall*, 276; Schaff, *Battle of the Wilderness*, 106.

The infantry practiced with seven-shot Spencer carbines, a new weapon; artillerists perfected their maneuvers; and, under Sheridan, the spirit of the cavalry improved. Meade prepared himself for hard campaigning by purchasing a large brown Morgan to replace the veteran Baldy, who was retired to the green pastures of Captain Sam Ringwalt's farm. A newspaperman caught sight of him on "the ideal war-horse, tall and powerful . . . a picture of helmeted knight of old."[21] Grant, who was always well mounted, had one of the handsomest horses, said Colonel Lyman, that he had seen. The man, too, was remarked upon: "He sits firmly in the saddle and looks straight ahead, as if only intent on getting to some particular point."[22] The two army leaders were co-operating very well, and the more that Meade saw of Grant the better he liked him, considering him cut from the pattern of Old Zack.[23]

Margaret Meade would have to be persuaded that all was right, Grant being visibly in charge. Acutely sensitive regarding her husband's military position, she even urged that he resign. Meade was moved to warn her to be careful and not to criticize his superior or indicate any feeling that anyone might have cause to resent. "I *am* in command of a large army in the field about to meet the enemy," he reminded his helpmate. "It is my duty to do all that I can. I say moreover that my personal interests are identified in remaining. All will come out right in the end." Of course, it was lonely in camp, and if Meade missed his wife and family, he should say so. "How I wish," his letter went on, "I could go home & be quiet with you & the children. To accomplish this object I would willingly let Grant gain victories, have all the credit & be made Presid^t. Perhaps before long all this will come about."[24] In mentioning the Presidency, Meade was referring to Grant.

By the last week in April, General Humphreys was busy writing orders in his crisp, efficient manner for the army movement directly across the enemy right. Directly under Meade were the Second, Fifth, and Sixth Corps; General Burnside's Ninth, arriving from the West, began to replace the Fifth above Rappahannock Station as Warren moved off. Thinking to spare Burnside's feelings, Grant had permitted him to retain the Ninth as a separate command instead of taking orders

[21] Charles A. Page, *Letters of a War Correspondent*, 111.
[22] *Meade's Headquarters*, 83.
[23] *Meade*, II, 191.
[24] Meade to wife, April 26, 1864, Meade Papers.

from Meade. The gesture was unnecessary, however. Some weeks before, when Meade was under political attack, Burnside had generously assured him that he would be willing to serve under him as a corps leader.[25] Later on he would.

"May God bless this undertaking at last and give an end to this war!"[26] wrote Colonel Lyman in one of his frequent letters to his wife, Elizabeth. Meade was sure that the desired end could be attained if hard fighting would do it. He could, he believed, rely on his men for that. His official message read to the troops carried a high tone. "Keep your ranks on the march and on the battlefield," Meade reminded them, "and let each man earnestly implore God's blessing and endeavor by his thoughts and actions to render himself worthy of the favor he seeks. Victory under God's blessing must and will attend our effort."[27]

The appeal to the Almighty was being heard from the pulpits both North and South. General Lee likewise invoked divine aid in his letters and messages. "The Army of Northern Virginia," he wrote a member of his family, ". . . is preparing for a great struggle, but I pray and trust that the great God, mighty to deliver, will spread over it His almighty arms, and drive its enemies before it."[28] One thing was certain—the unfettered Army of the Potomac was poised to win the war that spring, and if God was on the side of the biggest battalions, it was clear that He favored the North. Both sides had used every resource in recruiting, corralling even fat boys. But Lee had fewer than 65,000 men of all arms, Grant probably some 116,000, a force so much superior in strength that it could go where it would.

Leading the way across the Rapidan, Sheridan's cavalry broke camp on Monday, May 3, and laid bridges for the passage of wagons at Ely's and Germanna fords. Shortly after the following midnight, the Second Corps started out under the stars; then came Warren, followed by Sedgwick around 4:00 A.M. Within a few hours, men, artillery, ambulances, and ammunition wagons were pouring across the fords. In contrast to the difficulties of the previous November, warm and dry weather favored the march; the sun was warm; the grass was green; and dogwoods and spring flowers in bloom fringed the roadsides. The

[25] Same to same, March 8, 1864, *ibid.*
[26] *Meade's Headquarters,* 84.
[27] *Meade,* II, 192–93.
[28] Freeman, *R. E. Lee,* III, 268.

mood of the troops as they sang their campfire songs or hallooed to infrequent bystanders was almost merry, although veteran officers were less carefree.

At midmorning, Meade and his aides crossed Germanna Ford and halted for a few hours to watch the steady passage of the river. Everything seemed to be going well. Because the roads were dry and hard and the route more familiar, the errors of the advance to Mine Run were avoided. Well remembered was loss of part of the wagon train to the enemy. Now the trains were carrying all the army's ready supplies and had to be all the more closely guarded; otherwise the troops could have marched much farther down the Germanna plank road. Long before sunset, Warren, in advance, bivouacked near the junction of the east-west Orange Turnpike and the plank road. Farther back, Sedgwick made camp on the heights beyond Germanna Ford. Occupying the left, Hancock pitched his tents on part of the old Chancellorsville battleground, where men mused over whitened skulls and skeletons peeping from shallow graves.[29] Because the Ninth Corps was too far back when it started, Grant had to wire Burnside to make forced marches to cross the river.

Headquarters tents were pitched near the lower bank, Meade raising a magenta-hued, swallow-tailed banner with a silver wreath enclosing an eagle of gold. His letters fail to record the origin of the emblem, but no one could possibly have foretold Grant's remark when he first saw it. "What great Caesar is this?" he was said to inquire after crossing the river next morning. Meade soon resumed the use of a small American flag that had been abandoned because the General in Chief also flew the national colors.[30]

What General Lee might be doing in the shadowy and tangled Wilderness could only be surmised. There had been no resistance at the river crossings and no attempt on the long wagon train. Only small parties had been seen by mounted patrols, which, reconnoitering the Orange Turnpike, rejoined their division near sunset as ordered.

[29] Schaff, *Battle of the Wilderness*, 75–101, describes the march, also MHSM *Papers*, Vol. IV, 14–24, with orders quoted in the text. W. F. Dawson (ed.), *A Civil War Artist at the Front*, 33, tells of each soldier carrying a six-day ration of hardtack, coffee, sugar, and salt and of supply trains carrying a ten-day ration with enough salt pork for one day, while beef to feed more than 100,000 men for 13 days was driven over separate roads so as not to impede the march. See also Humphreys, *Virginia Campaign*, 18–22.

[30] Pennypacker, *Meade*, 267; John D. Billings, *Hardtack and Coffee*, 340.

Nevertheless, the corps of General Richard S. Ewell quietly paused within three miles of Warren, who was spread out on the Federal right. Other enemy forces were not far away. Hill with the Confederate Third Corps occupied a lower east-west road, and Longstreet with the First was hastening from a westerly railroad junction to join Lee. Since the areas which Hill and Longstreet would penetrate lay south of the Orange Turnpike, the farther the Federal army marched into the Wilderness, the greater resistance it would meet.[31]

There was no sign, observed Humphreys, that Grant expected a battle next day (May 5),[32] nor in all likelihood did Meade anticipate a concerted attack by an enemy which had shown almost no aggressiveness since Gettysburg. But about 7:00 A.M., he and his staff halted at the Wilderness Tavern, at the junction of the Germanna plank road and Orange Turnpike, and inquired what might be in Warren's front. Griffin, who could be relied upon, was two miles out on the turnpike, and a cavalry feeler was extended in the same direction along a lower east-west road, the Orange plank. There was no doubt but that enemy forces would somewhere be struck, but Meade could not read their intentions. Soon word came that Griffin's skirmishers were engaged and that the cavalry was being thrown back. The forces of both Ewell and Hill were in motion.

Prompt to act at the sound of firing, Meade rode quickly to Warren and was heard to exclaim, "If there is to be any fighting this side of Mine Run let us do it right off."[33] The Army of the Potomac would have to appear at its best in this first battle under Grant's eye. Aides were hurried off in several directions. Sedgwick was asked to send a division down a diagonal road to join Warren, who was told to attack with his whole force. A courier raced to Hancock to see that he did not march too far that morning as further orders would have to be awaited, and another rode back to Grant with a note telling him what had been done within the last fifteen minutes. "I think the enemy is trying to delay our movements and will not give battle, but of this we shall soon see," Meade advised.[34] Grant characteristically replied by urging prompt measures before the enemy could get set, but the entire army

[31] Schaff, *Battle of the Wilderness*, 114–18.
[32] Humphreys, *Virginia Campaign*, 56.
[33] Schaff, *Battle of the Wilderness*, 128.
[34] *Ibid.*, 128.

was then in motion or forming for battle, although for a time only Griffin was carrying the fight. Wadsworth's Fifth Corps division plunged into some woods on Griffin's left, to its cost, and after forcing his way along for nearly a mile, Griffin had to retreat for lack of support. That truculent officer complained angrily to Meade in Grant's presence. His language was so emphatic that Meade had to assure his superior, "It's only his way of talking." He made the Orange plank road safe by bringing Getty's Sixth Corps division down, and Hancock was swung around in support as the entire army faced an almost hidden enemy, which, in the woods and brush, could easily overcome the difference in numbers. "There were many places," noted Colonel Lyman, "where a line of troops could with difficulty be seen at fifty yards."[35]

Little in fact could be accomplished as originally designed. Sedgwick had been unable to connect with Warren, nor could Hancock, who, to protect his front while the divisions in the rear stumbled forward, threw up three lines of log and earth breastworks. There were any number of individual battles in which isolated bands of troops fought almost leaderless, and although casualties were piling up in that crackling storm, densely growing saplings and tree limbs stopped countless bullets and saved many lives. About midafternoon Meade abandoned hope for a concerted attack and ordered Getty to move out alone. Musketry was obstinate even in the dense thicket, and as Getty began to run out of cartridges, he appealed directly to Hancock, who got several brigades up only to lose General Alexander Hays, shot in the head. A battery poorly placed in those blind surroundings was seized by the enemy and then retaken during the fight. Given one more hour of daylight, Hancock would have driven Hill from the field, in the opinion of General Humphreys,[36] but by eight o'clock the hard day's work in the tangle was over; troops seeking water began to wander into enemy lines.

It was no more than a drawn battle, and Federal progress had been delayed. Grant's order for the next day could easily be surmised: Attack all along the line. In the continued absence of Burnside, the disadvantage of a divided command became manifest—Grant's chief of staff, not Humphreys, had failed to get him up on time. Burnside was

---

[35] *Meade's Headquarters*, 89. Lyman relates the Griffin incident in *ibid.*, 91 n., and in MHSM *Papers*, Vol. IV, 168.

[36] Humphreys, *Virginia Campaign*, 33.

ordered to get into position by daylight between Hancock and Warren, but he required several hours to do it even with the assistance of some of Grant's aides. Longstreet appeared with the advance of his corps on the Confederate right just in time to check Hancock, who had been driving a part of Hill's force into disorderly retreat. On the Federal right, neither Warren nor Sedgwick could dislodge Ewell from field-works strengthened during the night.

Artillery moved to high ground thickened the din. Infantry lines were so twisted and shade and shadow so misleading that rifle bullets were flying in all directions through the trees. As Longstreet started a flank movement against Hancock, a ball fired by one of his own men struck him in the throat. Severely and painfully wounded, he would not return to the field for nearly six months; yet he had not been so unfortunate as Stonewall Jackson at Chancellorsville. Meade's corps commanders survived without harm, but the Fifth Corps would feel the loss of division leader James Wadsworth, a hero of Gettysburg, who in the forefront against Hill had scorned caution for his own person.

Although together throughout most of that day, Grant and Meade could do little to direct the action effectively. It was unmistakably a crisis when, toward evening, Sedgwick was surprised and struck on his right flank. This was at the far or northerly end of the Federal line. Visibility was so poor at that hour that concerted charges failed to carry very far, but damage was done as several hundred panicky troops raced for safety toward the Rapidan River. Alarmed couriers galloped to Meade to spread the report that the corps had been utterly broken, that the army right had been turned, and that Sedgwick and division leader Wright had been captured. Noting that Meade's disposition "was always to grow calmer and calmer as others got more excited," Colonel Lyman heard him ask coolly, "And where are Upton's and Shaler's brigades that Sedgwick said he could spare me this morning?" "I don't know, sir." "Do you mean to tell me that the Sixth Corps is not to do any more fighting this campaign?" "I'm afraid not, sir." This was sheer nonsense, but after ordering up reinforcements from Warren, Meade had to take the news to Grant, who was disturbed.[37] But neither Sedgwick nor Wright had been taken prisoner, and after the Pennsylvania Reserves and even some armed teamsters had been moved into

[37] MHSM *Papers*, Vol. IV, 170; Schaff, *Battle of the Wilderness*, 318; Porter, *Campaigning with Grant*, 68–69. Porter declared Grant unshaken, but others say he was.

place, the enemy retired into the night. Save for the brigade hardest hit, Wright's own division had stood firm.

It had not been an easy day for anyone, nor could a victory be claimed to lighten the burden. Little ground had been gained and some had been lost, so that planned marching routes would have to be altered. The army nevertheless had proven itself. Grant declared himself satisfied with it in the most desperate fighting he had known.[38] Captain George Meade stressed one or two points in a brief summary of the action. The infantry firing, he wrote his mother, was "the most incessant I ever heard, it was fearfull." And whether or not the General in Chief had been present, "*Papa* has fought this army, and they have fought magnificently."[39]

For those who had never witnessed Lee's army in action the two days' experience was something of an actual shock. Colonel Lyman noted that Grant's "very foolish" officers who had "talked and laughed flippantly about Lee and his army" soon changed their note.[40] What thoughts passed through Grant's mind cannot be fathomed, but after all proper measures had been taken, he threw himself down on his cot and "something like stifled, subdued sobs were heard."[41] Too much had been shut up within his own heart, but soon he recovered and again became his calm self, chatting with Sylvanus Cadwallader of the *New York Herald* "upon indifferent subjects."[42]

Two days of the kind of fighting which Grant described seemed to prove that Lee could not be driven out of the Wilderness. Federal losses amounted to some 18,000 killed, wounded, and missing out of more than 102,000 effectives.[43] The tally from Lee's army is not known, but in view of Longstreet's severe injury and the loss of five of his brigade leaders, the damage was not inconsiderable.

[38] Grant, *Personal Memoirs*, II, 204. Captain George Meade to his mother, May 7, 1864, Meade Papers. Said Grant to Meade: "[General] Joe Johnston would have retreated after two such days' punishment."—MHSM *Papers*, Vol. IV, 171.

[39] George Meade to his mother, May 7, 1864, Meade Papers.

[40] *Meade's Headquarters*, 87.

[41] Schaff, *Battle of the Wilderness*, 327.

[42] Sylvanus Cadwallader, *Three Years with Grant* (ed. by Benjamin P. Thomas), 181.

[43] MHSM *Papers*, Vol. IV, 431; Thomas L. Livermore, *Numbers and Losses in the Civil War in America*, 110.

# 19. Reaction to Ugly Rumor
## (May 7-June 8, 1864)

GRANT NOW EXPECTED that Lee would retreat, but the war in the woods persisted next day as positions were shifted to partially encircle the enemy. From the movement of Meade's wagon trains, which began leaving the roads that afternoon to let the infantry through, Lee divined that the Federals would march by the left flank to Spotsylvania Court House. Should they take and hold Spotsylvania, important as a road junction, they would be able to get between the Confederate army and Richmond. Lee ordered General Richard H. Anderson, succeeding Longstreet, to act on that assumption, and the corps moved early to escape a woods fire.

Federal ignorance of the enemy's advance during the night of May 7 was never more costly, and officers were plagued by confusing delays along the road. At 8:30 P.M. the Fifth Corps began moving down, to be followed by Hancock, and after seeing the advance columns start, Grant and Meade rode ahead to await Warren. They soon found the road occupied and blocked by wagons and headquarters escorts, including mounted troops. The infantry, meanwhile, was making very slow progress.

With Warren some miles back, in his proper position, watching the withdrawal, Meade took steps to remove the obstruction. The high command and its escort turned into a side road to avoid a woods fire, and after getting lost in the darkness they regained the direct route and about midnight halted at Todd's Tavern.[1] There in bivouac awaiting orders from Sheridan was the mounted division of General David McMurtrie Gregg, who with Wesley Merritt's brigade had cleared the area of enemy cavalry by driving it into Spotsylvania. In the absence of the cavalry commander, Meade ordered Merritt to open up the road ahead for Warren and to take a position beyond Spotsylvania.

[1] Porter, *Campaigning with Grant*, 80-81; *Meade's Headquarters*, 103.

Gregg was posted along a right-hand road leading to the one by which the enemy was now known to be marching so that he might relay information.

Sheridan actively resented what he considered interference. Although duly notified of the steps taken, he would loudly claim that no word ever reached him. In any event, his own orders soon arrived, in which the hour of the cavalry movement was set for 5:00 A.M. on May 8, or entirely too late for execution on the roads specified. Advancing enemy infantry would have been able to block the movement by that time, and because opposing cavalry forces had filtered back from Spotsylvania, reoccupying the road to Todd's Tavern, Meade's orders for Merritt were also too late.

No one had foreseen the celerity of Lee's new corps commander, who had started out even before the hour cited in orders. Had Sheridan kept the road to Spotsylvania open until Warren came up, the race might have been won, but Merritt was unable to do anything effective in the darkness. At daybreak he gave way to advancing Federal infantry, and the result would have been the same whichever set of orders had been followed.[2] Meade and Sheridan, two men of temper, argued it out after the movement had failed. Angry because Sheridan had not kept the road open, Meade in fairness apologized when the cavalryman declared he had received no order to do so. However, "one word brought on another," Sheridan related, "until, finally, I told him that I could whip Stuart if he [Meade] would only let me, but since he insisted on giving the cavalry directions without consulting or even notifying me, he could henceforth command the Cavalry Corps himself—that I would not give it another order."[3]

This, of course, was not only insubordinate but stretching the truth; however, Sheridan could brook no checkrein.[4] Whether or not it was unwise to leave the army without adequate cavalry protection and without a strong mobile force for scouting, Sheridan in effect was asking

[2] Humphreys, *Virginia Campaign*, 68–70; Carswell McClellan, *Personal Memoirs and Military History of U. S. Grant*, 64; MHSM *Papers*, Vol. IV, 217–18. Humphreys and McClellan refute Badeau, Sheridan, and Grant.

[3] MHSM *Papers*, IV, 218–19; Philip H. Sheridan, *Personal Memoirs*, I, 368–69; *Meade's Headquarters*, 105–106 n.

[4] Richard O'Connor, *Sheridan the Inevitable*, 35–36, cites Sheridan's early difficulties with officer-cadets at West Point. Sheridan "had to be in chief control, tolerating no restraint from equals."—Schaff, *Battle of the Wilderness*, 282.

for an independent command with which to fight separate engagements. Although Meade went to Grant in no mood of compliance, nevertheless he reported Sheridan's proposal. Since Sheridan was always a great favorite with Grant and because he could fight, the General in Chief nodded assent. New orders made out by Meade at one o'clock that day provided for independent operations against enemy cavalry.[5]

Enemy soldiers hurriedly taking positions within Spotsylvania slowed and ultimately checked Warren's advance. The few who reached there first were still too many. As the rest of the Federal army closed up with most of Lee's forces in front, Grant settled down to the hammering tactics that had won in the West. The wisdom of this strategy was questioned by Humphreys. Good roads lay open on either side by which "we could have moved to turn either flank," he pointed out. Spotsylvania itself could not be considered as of "special military strength."[6]

There were, of course, more "frightful losses"—Meade's words.[7] As the toll mounted, the thousands of wounded followed those of the Wilderness to Fredericksburg and Washington, where the first steamer, bearing six hundred, "as dark as a sepulchre" and as silent, arrived on the night of May 9.[8] Mourned among the Spotsylvania dead was General John Sedgwick, felled by a sharpshooter. (His loss, said Grant, was worse than losing an entire division.) He was replaced by division leader Horatio Wright of the Twelfth Corps, a former Department of the Ohio commander and a veteran of Gettysburg.

The ledger was balanced by the fatal wounding of Jeb Stuart by Sheridan's men in a fight at Yellow Tavern near Richmond. Then, on May 12, a Federal thrust swept up General Edward Johnson, division commander, among other prisoners. As Johnson, a former West Pointer, was brought to Federal headquarters, Meade cordially grasped his hand and took him to Grant. "It's a long time since we have met," the latter remarked. He offered his visitor a chair and a cigar and spoke of events, familiar to both, of years ago in Mexico.[9]

[5] Sheridan, *Personal Memoirs*, I, 369. The orders were also given verbally by Grant.

[6] Humphreys, *Virginia Campaign*, 71.

[7] *Meade*, II, 195. "Our losses have been frightful; I do not like to estimate them. Those of the enemy fully as great." Letter of May 13, 1864, to wife.

[8] William H. Reed, *Hospital Life In the Army of the Potomac*, 11.

[9] Porter, *Campaigning with Grant*, 104.

Lee's line was temporarily broken, first by a single brigade and then by a corps. Had both breaks occurred near together in time or place, Spotsylvania might have been taken, but it was always the supporting end that failed against Lee.[10] After Colonel Emory Upton's Sixth Corps brigade rushed up a slope to win a hand-to-hand fight, the advantage was not followed up. One of Hancock's divisions ordered to pitch in was halted by artillery, and it was then considered rather late in the day for much further fighting.

Probably an entire corps rather than a division should have been sent to support Upton, but inasmuch as a single brigade had prevailed, a surprise assault by Hancock was decided upon for the fifth day of fighting at Spotsylvania. It was a foggy, wet morning when Hancock, after moving by night over a narrow and difficult road, surprised and swept over an enemy salient. Brisk rifle fire sparkled through the rain, many prisoners were taken, and captured guns were turned on the enemy. Repelling bloody counterattacks, Unionists struggled fitfully over piled logs, massed tree stumps, heavy brush, and the heaped-up bodies of uncounted dead and wounded. Front-line fighters lay within fifty feet of one another and even much closer as rifles were discharged directly into men's faces. "Never since the discovery of gunpowder has such a mass of lead been hurled into a space so narrow," recounted an officer with Hancock.[11] At one point in the famed "Bloody Angle," men were clubbing each other over piles of mangled dead.

But neither Burnside on the left nor Warren or Wright on the other side was able to dent Lee's entire first line, nor could a break-through be made anywhere along the second. Again Federal co-ordination was faulty. Meade's temper was aroused by Warren, who, after getting close to enemy works, failed under positive instructions to drive farther. When a division commander reported to Warren that he could not carry a hill, the entire corps came to a stop, and Meade was not notified promptly. Toward noon, Grant authorized Meade to relieve Warren if necessary, but the Fifth Corps now seemed to be doing better, although no more successful than the others.[12]

[10] MHSM *Papers*, Vol. V, 169–70.

[11] Walker, *General Hancock*, 200–201. "There was not a more desperate struggle during the war." MHSM *Papers*, Vol. V, 266. But practically all of the fighting during May and June, 1864, was of the same character.

[12] *O.R.*, XXXVI, pt. 2, 671; Porter, *Campaigning with Grant*, 108; Walker, *His-*

Results were reviewed at Grant's headquarters that night. Execution had been so deadly that there was confidence that Lee was already beaten. Present as Stanton's observer, Assistant Secretary of War Charles A. Dana notified his chief that the enemy was actually retreating.[13] Better schooled in Lee's ways, Colonel Lyman wrote that "my own experiences [have] taught me a little more skepticism."[14] Lee had withdrawn only to the base of the blood-drenched Salient where a new line now barred Federal progress.

Lack of success fomented inquiry at Grant's headquarters whether there was not something amiss in the chain of command. As the two armies buried their dead and fought occasional battles next day, Grant was urged by his aides to transmit his orders directly to the corps leaders, by-passing Meade. This would have meant Meade's resignation, and Grant, who had a liking for his honest and efficient lieutenant, raised a practical objection. He already, he said, had a great deal of work to handle, since his entire command embraced not only the Army of the Potomac and Burnside's separate corps but the armies of Ben Butler, Franz Sigel in the Shenandoah, and Sherman and others in the West. He and Meade were usually together or close to each other in the field, and each always knew and understood what the other was doing. "Capable and perfectly subordinate," in Grant's words, Meade had relieved him of much responsibility.[15]

Nevertheless, through orders written in greater detail at national headquarters, Grant gradually assumed more control. This made Chief of Staff Humphreys more of a figurehead, but Meade could raise no objection, remarking simply that "it would be injurious to the army to have two heads."[16] Outsiders had always been a little confused over the dual leadership. One news correspondent tried to explain by observing that Grant administered the grand strategy, Meade the grand tactics.[17] But to forestall any damage done by Dana, who was always criticizing, Grant wired Stanton that day, "General Meade has more than met my most sanguine expectations." Promotion to major general in the regular

---

*tory of the Second Corps*, 474; Meade to Chief of Staff Rawlins, June 21, 1864, Meade Papers.

[13] Dana to Stanton, May 13, 1864, Stanton Papers.
[14] *Meade's Headquarters*, 110.
[15] Porter, *Campaigning with Grant*, 114–15.
[16] *Meade*, II, 197.
[17] *Ibid.*, 197.

army was suggested for both him and Sherman.[18] Nor was Stanton's attitude unfriendly; recently he had wired Meade and his command congratulations and official thanks for military achievement.

It was the thirteenth of May, the ninth day of fighting since the start of the campaign, yet no important post had been taken and the army was still in the Wilderness, "a most fearfully discouraging place."[19] That night Grant began his move to by-pass Lee's fortified works. Floundering through mud and darkness, the Fifth Corps slid past the enemy right to emerge from the woods and gain cultivated green fields as storm clouds gave way to the sun. "It was for this, and all this, that the army breathed freer," remarked a spent soldier.

A minor affair of the fourteenth was the recapture of a small hill under Meade's personal direction,[20] and on that night the "Bloody Angle" of the Salient was evacuated. Wright and Hancock followed Warren as closely as possible, but wretched marching conditions prevented their union in time for an effective assault on Lee's flank just outside Spotsylvania. For a few brief days the fighting eased, and the men rested as roads began drying under a warm sun. Volunteers whose three-year terms had expired were permitted to leave, and the gaps were filled by new troops. On May 16, the Second Corps welcomed four heavy-artillery regiments and other troops to be organized into a new Fourth Division of infantry. Other arrivals, mostly green, made their debut.

Shakily reinforced, Hancock was moved back for another assault at the "Bloody Angle," but the artillery and infantry of Ewell were waiting. Rapid gunfire alone—canister added to shrapnel—broke up a running charge, and Grant concluded that this was enough. The sorry affair of May 18 led Meade to remark, "Even Grant thought it useless to knock our heads against a brick wall."[21] Meade, however, was not questioning Grant's leadership nor did he revert to the idea that the war could only be won by cutting enemy supply lines south of the James. It was agreeable to maneuver to draw Lee out of his works so as to fight again on better terms, if possible.

[18] *Ibid.*, 196; *O.R.*, XXVI, pt. 2, 695. "I would not like to see one of these promotions at this time without seeing both," Grant wrote.

[19] Ford (ed.), *A Cycle of Adams Letters*, II, 134.

[20] *Antietam to Appomattox*, 426; J. L. Bowen, *History of the 37th Massachusetts Regiment*, 314–15; Bicknell, *History of the Fifth Maine*, 324; Porter, *Campaigning with Grant*, 118.

[21] *Meade*, II, 197.

So it was tried. On May 20, Hancock led the way south but worked toward the right according to plan to lure the enemy into the open if possible. But instead of attacking Hancock, offered as a pawn, Lee pushed toward the North Anna River, always keeping between Grant and the city of Richmond. It now became Grant's turn to complain that he could never catch Lee out of his works and meet him in open battle.[22] Lee still refused to fight unless behind strong entrenchments.

Worn and battle sore, both armies moved south. Good progress was made through country as yet untouched by war. Ripening fruits, fragrant clover, and waving fields of grain greeted the eye in fertile and prosperous Caroline County. Rural stores were still open, a few grist- and sawmills were running, but pillared and porticoed mansions were tightly shut against the invader.[23] Private property and civilians as persons were legally inviolate, but fears of pillage were not entirely groundless. Some officers, notably Barlow and Birney, severely punished offenders. Meade always took action, whether in protection of property or in the specific instance of some careless soldiers who had wounded a small boy armed with a shotgun. Happening upon a poorly dressed woman fringed by several crying children—a family which the cavalry had robbed—he pulled out a five-dollar bill and also saw that food was provided for the day's neediest. "The soft-hearted General . . . thought of his own small children," Colonel Lyman reflected. "He is a tender-hearted man."[24]

The idea that the war could be won only through western leadership and strength could never be safely bespoken in Meade's presence, but Assistant Secretary Dana could never resist playing the gadfly. In characteristic mean spirit he took delight in reading aloud to both Meade and Grant a message which General Sherman had sent Stanton. It was Sherman's inspiration that: "If General Grant can sustain the confidence, the esprit, the pluck of his army and impress the Virginians with the knowledge that the Yankees can and will fight them fair and square, he will do more good than to capture Richmond or any strategic advantage. This moral result must precede all mere advantage of strategic movements, and this is what Grant is doing. Out here the

---

[22] *Meade's Headquarters*, 31; Porter, *Campaigning with Grant*, 131, 134; Charles A. Dana, *Recollections of the Civil War*, 214–15.

[23] O. R. Prowell, *History of the 87th Pennsylvania Volunteer Regiment*, 144.

[24] *Meade's Headquarters*, 129.

enemy knows we can and will fight like the devil; therefore he maneuvers for advantage of ground."[25]

Sherman had seen some warfare but not all, and his interpretation was faulty. For the Confederates in the West to maneuver was proper strategy since they were heavily outnumbered. But Lee also had been maneuvering ever since Gettysburg, and in his only offensive he had turned back without fighting. Meade, however, did not pause to reflect; he, who had driven the Army of the Potomac on its swift marches and seen it engage in the most desperate fighting ever witnessed on the North American continent, was so agitated, observed his chief aide, that his eyes "stood out about one inch as he said, in a voice like cutting an iron bar with a handsaw: 'Sir! I consider that despatch an insult to the army I command and to me personally. The Army of the Potomac does not require General Grant's inspiration or anybody else's inspiration to make it fight!' He did not get over it all day, and at dinner spoke of the western army as 'an armed rabble.'"[26]

Colonel Lyman was thinking that Grant had said more than once that the fighting in Virginia was much more desperate than in the West and that he had expected no such resistance. Nevertheless, the sectional rivalry between the East and the West pervaded the armed forces, the halls of Congress, and, of course, the War Office. Meade could see that he was being passed over in all official dispatches and in the news columns. The fact was that he had been placed in an awkward position as operating head of an army under a constantly present General in Chief. Grant would be mentioned, and the corps, division, and brigade leaders who saw action. There was little necessity of crediting Meade with any specific action, even had indifferent newspapermen been disposed to do so. They were in no way encouraged to become friendly.

It was a giant stride to the North Anna River, where the Fifth Corps battered A. P. Hill on May 23. Because of recurring illness, Hill was not then at his best, nor was Ewell, who appeared about to collapse, and an intestinal disorder kept General Lee out of action. Otherwise, since he had been reinforced by Pickett's division fresh from a repulse of Ben Butler on the James River, he probably would have counterattacked. Yet Lee seriously embarrassed his opponent. As Grant got astride the North Anna, the corps of Hancock, Warren, and Wright

---

[25] Quoted in Lloyd Lewis, *Sherman: Fighting Prophet*, 361.
[26] *Meade's Headquarters*, 126; Grant, *Personal Memoirs*, II, 204.

lay below, but most of Burnside's remained above. Hancock was separated from Warren and Wright by Anderson's corps, which occupied
a peninsula between these two Federal wings. If Lee had been able to
press his advantage by attacking anywhere, each wing on the south side
would have had to cross the river twice to reinforce the other. On May
24, therefore, Grant permanently assigned Burnside to Meade's command "to give more unity to the movement."[27] The army pulled out
by recrossing the river to the north side and resuming the march by the
left flank.

Another long stride brought Grant and Meade to the Pamunkey
River, a confluence of the North and South Anna. Meade told of crossing the Pamunkey to get within only eighteen miles of Richmond or
within striking distance if that was Grant's goal. "We are getting on
very well," he assured Margaret, "and . . . will continue to maneuvre
till we compel Lee to retire into the defenses of Richmond when the
grand decisive fight will come off."[28] Pressing toward Gaines's Mill
and other old scenes, army veterans were reminiscent. They could
recall several of McClellan's division commanders, all now absent
or dead, although Baldy Smith, now with Butler, still remained in
the East.

A flare-up occurred between Warren and Sheridan, who, returning
from his forays, was expected to co-operate with Meade's infantry.
With no personal liking for Warren, with whom he had clashed before,
Sheridan neglected to protect the Fifth Corps flank, as ordered, on
May 29. When Warren's protests reached cavalry headquarters, Sheridan retorted: "I have had troops on the left of General Warren's corps
all day and connected with him." But since Lee's forces had got around
his flank, Warren also had a tale to tell.[29] Meade sent in Hancock when
Warren was attacked next day near Totopotomoy Creek, and troops
under Early were hurled back "with considerable slaughter."[30]

That day, May 30, marked the last fight of the Fifth Corps brigade
known as the Pennsylvania Reserves. Their 10,000 of June, 1862, had

[27] Porter, *Campaigning with Grant*, 144. The situation at the North Anna is discussed in *ibid.*, 145–46; in Freeman, *R. E. Lee*, III, 358, and *Lee's Lieutenants*, III,
496–97.

[28] *Meade*, II, 199.

[29] *O.R.*, XXXVI, pt. 3, 336, 339, 341, 361, and Pennypacker, *Meade*, 306–307,
give details.

[30] *O.R.*, XXXVI, pt. 3, 375.

shrunk to only 2,000, but in their last fight only a few miles from the scene of Beaver Dam Creek, they took seventy prisoners and held the ground won.[31] On the thirty-first, their enlistments expired, although not all went home; the Eleventh Pennsylvania still proudly survived as a unit.

The *New York Herald* announced that Lee's army had been routed at Spotsylvania. "That army cannot be routed, and neither can this one," retorted Captain George Meade. "You can whip them every day in the week, they will merely take up another position not at all discouraged."[32] Grant had cited an alternative if the push toward Richmond failed—army movement to south of the James—but that was still a second choice when a celebrated dispatch was written at Spotsylvania: "I propose to fight it out on this line if it takes all summer."[33] He could now look back on some one hundred miles of ground gained.

On May 31, when Sheridan took and held the crossroads hamlet of Old Cold Harbor, both Grant and Meade were saying that another flank movement would have to be made to push the enemy into its Richmond defenses, and then, added Meade, "will begin the tedious process of a quasi-siege."[34] Meade thought that the siege would last as long as that at Sevastopol in the Crimea, or eleven months, "unless we can get hold of their railroads and cut off their supplies, when they must come out and fight."[35] Incidents near at hand would amend the idea of besieging Richmond. Along a line facing west between Old and New Cold Harbor, Wright took position, followed by Hancock who marched past him. On the army right, some 10,000 troops under Baldy Smith, withdrawn from Butler, got into line. Driving the enemy through woods, Wright and Smith dug in along a new line, but Warren and Burnside stood farther off to the right where no enemy was. The battle, then, would be fought by only part of the army. No time was allowed to examine the ground. Grant's order for 4:30 A.M., June 3, called for an immediate assault all along the line, i.e., from Smith to Hancock. Meade obtained a brief postponement to permit Hancock to get into position, but to attack Lee behind strong works when other

---

[31] MHSM *Papers*, Vol. IV, 314.

[32] MS letter of May 20, 1864, Meade Papers.

[33] Grant to Halleck, May 11, 1864; reproduced in Porter, *Campaigning with Grant*, opposite page 104.

[34] *Meade*, II, 200.

[35] *Ibid.*, 200.

roads south could be found seemed ill advised and in effect an obsolete method of warfare.

These works had been built along rough and uneven ground varying from swamp, which required little defense, to small hills. Well realizing what lay in front, men in the Federal ranks could be seen scribbling their names on slips of paper and pinning them to the backs of their jackets, a scene reminiscent of Mine Run (but there a restraining hand had been felt.) When General Upton of Wright's corps called Cold Harbor "a murderous engagement because we were recklessly ordered to assault the enemy's entrenchments knowing neither their strength and position,"[36] he gauged the situation precisely. Grant, who had not yet learned all about war in the East, was expending too many men's lives.

Swampy ground was belatedly discovered in front of Gibbon, Second Corps, and the vital importance of a hill temporarily gained by Barlow was not recognized until too late.[37] As the result of Grant's haste, the few acres of ground gained were covered with bodies "about as thickly as they could be laid," numbering between 6,000 and 7,000 trained officers and soldiers.[38] Meade said little and blamed no one, but reflecting upon the costly result, Grant himself sounded the right note: "I regret this assault more than any one I have ever ordered." He would not again fight that same battle over, he stated.[39] A parallel and contrast with Meade's position at Williamsport, Maryland, is suggested.

Now that the army had been stopped short of a position from which Richmond could be besieged, perhaps the alternate route would be suggested. Grant was now seen wearing an "intent, abstracted look" as if thinking very hard,[40] but while he debated what to do next, the army uncomfortably remained at Cold Harbor. It was a particularly bad time for those in the front lines. Sharp skirmishes were engaged in

[36] Peter S. Michie, *Life and Letters of Emory Upton*, 108–109. Following his successful assault of May 10, Upton was promoted from colonel to brigadier general.

[37] MHSM *Papers*, Vol. IV, 339.

[38] *Ibid.*, 445; W. C. Oates, *The War between the Union and the Confederacy*, 386.

[39] Porter, *Campaigning with Grant*, 179; *Battles and Leaders*, IV, 220. Grant wrote in his *Personal Memoirs*, II, 276, "I have always regretted that the last assault at Cold Harbor was ever made. . . . No advantage whatever was gained for the heavy loss we sustained."

[40] Ford (ed.), *A Cycle of Adams Letters*, II, 135.

daily, with the usual artillery duels at night. Fatigue, heat, dust, blood, the sight of the pitiful unattended wounded, the stench of dead men and horses left unburied, and the plain misery of war harried men's minds. General Warren, a basically humane man, was visibly affected; Meade had occasional irascible fits; and other officers were always snapping at each other. With army affairs at this low point, the General in Chief was stigmatized as a butcher by an angry and grieving North.

It was during these dismal and uncertain days that Meade made a damaging error which affected him personally. Aside from loyal Governor Curtin of Pennsylvania, few men in the political arena could expect to derive advantage from association with Meade in the field, and the less so after Grant had been assigned the high command. Foreign military observers were usually shunted off to the Meade camp, where they had to be entertained at the General's expense—an inescapable nuisance[41]—but visitors from Washington came to see Grant. The most prompt was Congressman Elihu B. Washburne from the General's home district. Washburne could have no doubt of his welcome. He had helped advance Grant's fortunes since his early days with the Illinois militia and had introduced the bill in Congress which made his man a lieutenant general.

Attaching himself to Grant's headquarters before the start of the campaign, the black-clothed civilian aroused whimsical speculation among the troops as to his calling.[42] In truth, he may have come to protect Grant from the so-called McClellan influence. Washburne may have originated, and at least he helped circulate, a story that Meade favored withdrawal of the army across the Rapidan on the night of May 6.[43] A partial withdrawal, which both Grant and Meade agreed on, was made, although Meade had favored swinging both wings back still more, the better to resume an orderly march.[44] However the story originated, every man knew it next day, one soldier declaring that he had heard it fifty times.[45]

A staff officer was confident that Meade's attitude was simply (as he was heard to remark), "By God! the army is across now and it has

[41] *Meade*, II, 162–63; *Meade's Headquarters*, 23, 49, 62–63, 178.
[42] Porter, *Campaigning with Grant*, 42–43. The men debated whether he was a parson or Grant's private undertaker.
[43] Pennypacker, *Meade*, 318. Grant was notified of Washburne's conduct.
[44] *Meade's Headquarters*, 98.
[45] Frank Wilkeson, *Recollections of a Private Soldier*, 79.

got to stay across";[46] but whatever may have been said, Meade in his letters discounted failure, made much of small successes, and held out the hope that the war would be ended that summer. With Halleck displaced and Grant leading, the mood at Meade's headquarters was sanguine. Had the retreat story been dropped then and there, little damage would have resulted, but on his return to Washington, Congressman Washburne saw fit to make use of it.[47] He talked there with a *Philadelphia Inquirer* reporter who had once lived in his Illinois district. This was correspondent Edward Cropsey, whose family Grant also knew.[48]

The offending article written in Washington had doubtless not been intended to arouse the storm which it did in the Meade camp when read through to the end. Cropsey wrote after seeing Washburne,

> . . . Let me say a word of Meade's position. He is as much the Commander of the Army of the Potomac as he ever was. Grant plans and exercises a supervisory control . . . but to Meade belongs everything of detail. He is entitled to great credit for the magnificent movement of the army since we left Brandy. . . . In battle he puts troops into action and controls their movements; in a word, he commands the army. General Grant is here only because he deems the present campaign the vital one of the war and wishes to decide on the spot all questions that would be referred to him as General-in-Chief.

So far, so good, but Cropsey ran on. "History will record that on one eventful night during the present campaign Grant's presence saved the army and the nation, too. Not that General Meade was on the point of committing a great blunder unwittingly, but his devotion to his country made him loath to lose her last army on what he deemed a last chance. Grant assumed the responsibility and we are still 'On to Richmond!' "[49]

Not only the story itself but the wide circulation given it deepened the injury. Newspapers then reprinted each other freely, and the daily press had a wide circulation in the Army of the Potomac. Meade, who

---

[46] Schaff, *Battle of the Wilderness*, 323.

[47] Pennypacker, *Meade*, 218; Meade to wife, June 9, 1864, Meade Papers.

[48] *Meade*, II, 203. Usually misspelled "Crapsey," the name appears as "Cropsey" in Meade's own handwriting and in *Philadelphia Inquirer* by-lines.

[49] *Philadelphia Inquirer*, June 2, 1864; reprinted in part in *Meade*, II, 341.

could feel his authority weakening, went to Grant, who strongly upheld him by wiring Secretary Stanton that he had never counseled
retreat "nor once intimated a doubt." The Secretary wired back re-
assurance that the "lying report" was not for a moment believed, but
apparently this was not enough.

At Cold Harbor a mounted guard sought out Cropsey, who had
returned to the army. Where, inquired Meade, had his story come
from? "It was the talk of the camp," Cropsey responded. "It was a
base and wicked lie," Meade rejoined.[50] In a mood to take punitive
action, he consulted with Provost Marshal Marsena R. Patrick, who,
since he hated all war correspondents, was the wrong man. Patrick
suggested the punishment, and Grant nodded approval as Meade wrote
out the order. Apparently Meade wished "to draw attention to the
falsehood and the truth,"[51] but the means chosen defeated the end.
Sandwiched between two placards inscribed "Libeler of the Press," the
unfortunate Cropsey was mounted backwards on a sorry-looking mule
and exposed to the jeers of the troops. A trumpeter riding in advance
heralded his disgrace as a drum corps beat out "The Rogue's March."[52]

General Sherman, who had treated certain newspapermen roughly,
had been set down in print as stark crazy,[53] but a meeting of correspondents voted the silent treatment for Meade. "It was soon noticed,"
reported Sylvanus Cadwallader of the *New York Herald*, "that Gen.
Meade's name never appeared . . . if it could be omitted. If he issued
an official or general order of such importance as to require publication,
it would be printed without his signature."[54] If a signature appeared to

[50] Porter, *Campaigning with Grant*, 191; *Meade*, II, 202.

[51] Meade to wife, June 17, 1864, Meade Papers.

[52] *Meade*, II, 203; *O.R.*, XXXVI, pt. 3, 670; Wilkeson, *Recollections*, 146;
MHSM *Papers*, Vol. V, 16; Pennypacker, *Meade*, 318–19; Cadwallader, *Three Years
with Grant*, 207. A garbled account appears in Poore, Ben: Perley, *Perley's Reminiscences*, II, 153. Cropsey was dismissed from the army on June 8, 1864, a bad day all
around.

[53] Andrews, *The North Reports the Civil War*, 116–17.

[54] Cadwallader, *Three Years with Grant*, 209. The Cropsey affair hung over Meade
for some time. On June 22, 1864, Grant replied to a Boston correspondent, "General
Meade on no occasion advised or counseled falling back towards, much less across, the
Rapidan. There has been no word or act of his from the beginning of this Campaign
which indicated even a belief on his part that such a step would ever become necessary.
Such rumors as you speak of are entirely idle and without the shadow of a foundation."
The letter of inquiry was from one Isaac P. Clark, who himself had expressed doubt of
the story's validity: "Not believing that the gallant Meade volunteered any such advice,"

be required, then Grant's name was substituted. And so while war history was being made and the names of Grant, Sherman, Sheridan, Hancock, and others loomed in the headlines, Meade's work was withheld from public notice unless it could be presented unfavorably. It did not take him long to realize that he had made a bad error and that he should have taken his complaint to the *Inquirer* editor. He was William Harding, a brother of George Harding, who had the ear of Secretary Stanton and had helped Meade in the past. Never friendly with more than one or two war correspondents,[55] Meade by a single act had made himself hated.

he wrote Grant, "I have taken the liberty of informing you of the report which, if untrue, you will not require . . . laurels forced upon you at the discredit of the hero of Gettysburg."—Meade Papers.

[55] One of these was Joseph R. Sypher of the *New York Tribune* whom Meade assisted in his *History of the Pennsylvania Reserves* by making available wartime manuscripts which he had at his home.

# 20. Errors at Petersburg
## (June 7-18, 1864)

IT WAS OBSERVED that the army was tired and down at the heel. Battle-worn troops in the front lines had much the worst of it as Grant clung to Cold Harbor. Burned by the sun, unwashed, their clothing stained with mud, perspiration, and blood, they required more food and water than could actually be supplied within range of active enemy snipers. Toward the army rear, life was much easier; but, aware that the campaign had bogged down, men argued uncertainly over what Grant might do next. One theory was that the army would swing north of Richmond to occupy ground above the Chickahominy Swamp, where the Federal left was miserably lodged. This idea may have been de-rived from the withdrawal of Sheridan and two cavalry divisions, which on June 7 turned north. But orders to Sheridan mainly concerned destruction of the Virginia Central Railroad near Gordonsville, a junc-tion point for supply lines to Lee's army.[1]

General Halleck thought that Grant should occupy a position north-east of Richmond—the old formula which would have kept the army on a direct line with Washington—and if the War Office had prevailed, the army would have been pinned down there. After Gettysburg, Lin-coln had thought that the war could be won north of the Potomac and that only a little more effort would be needed to defeat Lee. His dis-appointment that Lee had managed otherwise was remembered now only vaguely, and what it actually would take to win was becoming plainer. Following unpleasant experience, Grant began to realize that the war could not be won north of the Chickahominy or even above the greater barrier of the James. This was by no means a new strategic idea, but only a leader suitably invested with authority could carry the war into the South.[2]

[1] Humphreys, *Virginia Campaign*, 194; Sheridan, *Personal Memoirs*, I, 414–16.
[2] "The proper mode to reduce Richmond is to take possession of the great lines of

If Grant appeared to be thinking hard, it was because he was pondering the outcome of strategy being plotted. A detachment from General Butler's Army of the James was sent to take Petersburg, a railroad center on the Appomattox River, but decisive leadership was lacking, and little more was done than to examine discouragingly strong works held by the Meade family kinsman, Confederate General Henry A. Wise. Meanwhile, on June 6, Grant pointed the way forward by sending aides Horace Porter and Cyrus B. Comstock to locate suitable crossings of the James River. With the navy in control of the lower James, a crossing could be made if the enemy were deceived about intentions. Sheridan's raid to Trevilian Station would keep most of the cavalry away, and Lee could be occupied by a demonstration toward Richmond on the Federal right.

Meade hinted at a flank movement in a letter written Margaret on June 9 but withheld details. He had spent most of two days inspecting the entire position and making ready for secret evacuation of Cold Harbor. Soldiers began digging hidden passages by which they could move out. Meanwhile some fresh vegetables and clean clothing arrived, a shipment never more welcome and the last of its kind for more than a month.

Grant had already made up his mind. On June 11, before Porter and Comstock returned, he sent off Warren's corps and General James H. Wilson's cavalry division, which had been retained for outpost duty and to guard trains. Moving from the army right toward the Chickahominy, Warren and Wilson forced a crossing at Long's bridge, a demolished structure which was replaced by pontoons. The incursion had the men whooping it up for an attack on Richmond itself, an idea not at all discouraged. Lee had to be persuaded to cover the city, as of course he did.

Early on June 12, Porter and Comstock returned to a nervous and anxious leader. As they talked of their mission, Grant fitfully smoked and kept saying, "Yes, yes," whenever the words didn't come fast enough.[3] One crossing selected was at Wyanoke Landing, where

railroad leading to it from the South and Southwest."—Meade to wife, November 22, 1862, *Meade*, I, 330. "In the latter part of May [1864] . . . General Smith had proposed to capture Petersburg."—Humphreys, *Virginia Campaign*, 206 n. See also MHSM *Papers*, Vol. V, 115.

[3] Porter, *Campaigning with Grant*, 189.

Charles City County projected into the James. Between this blunt peninsula and a spit of land opposite, the mile-wide stream was narrowed to about 2,100 feet. This distance could be spanned by anchored rafts and pontoons.

Meade had everything ready for a hurried and secret march by Hancock, Burnside, and Wright. At 3:00 p.m., headquarters broke camp to ride in advance, and Cold Harbor was gradually vacated during the night. Baldy Smith's troops got away unobserved after dark to march rapidly east to the White House, the new supply base on the Pamunkey. Picking up more of his men there, Smith embarked on a voyage down the coast and up the James River, and he would get past the point of intended crossing before the bridge was laid.

For ten days no rain had thickened the soil. Clouds of dust arose, stifling the soldiers and slowing the march. It was a bad omen next morning when Meade, joining a Second Corps column, found Hancock in misery from his old Gettysburg wound, which had painfully reopened as fragments of bone worked to the surface. Resting as he could on the ground, Hancock was bathing it with water from his army canteen.[4]

The rumble of artillery echoed from a 1,700-foot pontoon bridge laid for passage across the Chickahominy River. Here immense cypresses bent over the banks, and enormous pine trees and spreading white oaks caught the eye of nature-loving General Humphreys.[5] Soon the men entered open plantation country, the cultivated fields extending down to the James. At midafternoon of June 13, dismounting at Clarke's house one mile from the river, Meade sent Colonel Lyman and Major James C. Duane of the Engineers to examine the selected crossing and choose a position to cover the army right wing.

The officers gained the high-banked river at Wilcox's Wharf and looked diagonally across to Fort Powhatan, a Revolutionary work rebuilt during the War of 1812. A signal officer was flagging a message to the occupied fort and to steamers anchored near by. As the day waned, long lines of troops trailed by artillery batteries, ammunition trains, supply wagons, ambulances, and wagons filled with medical stores filed into the broad fields along the river. Negroes in sole charge

[4] MHSM *Papers*, Vol. V, 19.
[5] Humphreys, *Andrew Atkinson Humphreys*, 231.

of the John Tyler plantation supplied green peas and fresh milk for a memorable supper at headquarters.[6]

Wilcox's Wharf was selected for the passage of troops crossing the river by ferry. For the approach to the projected bridge site, a road passable for artillery was cut down the steep bluff near Wyanoke Landing. Felled cypresses were split and laid along the swampy margin. A fleet of ironclads and gunboats under Rear Admiral Samuel P. Lee stood by in the river; smaller craft bearing supplies and dispatches darted between ship and shore. Army veterans recalled similar busy scenes of almost two years before, but there was an important difference. Upon General McClellan's withdrawal from Harrison's Landing in July, 1862, the veterans of the Seven Days were depressed, whereas the mood now was one of cheerfulness and hope.[7]

As Smith's troops passed up the river on their way to join Butler at Bermuda Hundred, army engineers working from each side began to join pontoons and rafts. Since the tidal current was strong, three naval schooners were moored fast in the center to brace eighty-two floating units. Meade and Humphreys kept things moving, while Grant talked with Butler, returning in the afternoon. One hour before midnight the 2,100-foot structure, "an exploit in bridge building that has never been equaled,"[8] was declared ready.

Just above, busy ferries crowded with Hancock's troops plied back and forth from Wilcox's Wharf to Windmill Point nearly opposite. Since boats were too few, the work went on through most of the night while "hundreds of happy Doughboys," Lyman wrote, seized the occasion to bathe in the river.[9] By 3:30 A.M. on June 15, the Second Corps of some 21,000 men was entirely over. Artillery and wagon trains were crossing the great bridge. At various intervals behind came the other three corps by direct and roundabout routes. When Crawford's Fifth Corps division, feinting toward the right, had a skirmish down the Long's Bridge road, Warren gathered that Lee had extended his defensive line from Malvern Hill near the river to White Oak Swamp some distance above. He was still between Grant and Rich-

---

[6] MHSM *Papers*, Vol. V, 27. John Tyler, tenth U. S. President, died early in 1862.
[7] Chas. H. Banes, *History of the Philadelphia Brigade*, 277–78.
[8] *Meade*, II, 204.
[9] Colonel Lyman in MHSM *Papers*, Vol. V, 22.

mond, but Federal leaders no longer cared. The crossing went on smoothly and quite undisturbed.

"All goes like a miracle," Secretary Stanton was informed by Charles Dana.[10] The message lifted a burden of care from Lincoln. "I begin to see it; you will succeed,"[11] he buoyantly wired the General in Chief. The administration was falling into line nicely. Coming from Grant, the idea of a suitable change of position had begun to take hold, for this was the primary essential if the war was to be won by methods other than attacking entrenched lines. Lincoln well understood the cost of war by attrition of man power. The onetime prevailing "smash-'em-up" policy advocated by an officer close to Grant—Colonel Comstock—had finally been discredited by Cold Harbor, and the present campaign was, happily, of a new character.[12]

Without a doubt, the crossing of the James on June 14–15, 1864, was one of Grant's most splendid achievements, and possibly for this reason the important end to be gained was subordinated to the means. Everyone was so occupied in the mass exodus from Lee's front that the vital necessity of immediate capture of Petersburg was neglected. Error twice compounded played its part, as did prevailing secrecy. But it was not expected that Petersburg, which lay about ten miles southwest of already occupied City Point near the junction of the James and the Appomattox, would present any great problem.

If anyone is to be blamed for lack of foresight and preparation, General Butler is the first to be named. It is true that he could not have known everything in Grant's mind, but he continued to act as an independent commander, in effect neglecting orders. Inasmuch as Grant returned to the army on the fourteenth before Smith arrived at Bermuda Hundred, Smith received only Butler's version of an order for another attack on Petersburg. Grant had asked that Smith start that same night, but instead arrangements were made for the next morning.[13] Grant had also asked Butler to supply Hancock, who also was to

[10] Dana to Stanton, June 15, 1864, O.R., XL, pt. 1, 19–20. Dana cites the pontoon bridge at Fort Powhatan, the far end being lodged just above the fort.

[11] Porter, *Campaigning with Grant*, 199.

[12] "It is useless and needless for the admirers of General Grant to say that his movement across the James was a continuation of the Wilderness Campaign. . . . When he began the movement he abandoned the attempt to reach Richmond or to draw out the enemy by menacing Richmond."—Col. Thomas L. Livermore in MHSM *Papers*, Vol. V, 37.

move toward Petersburg, with 6,000 rations, for "without this precaution the services of the corps cannot be had for an emergency tomorrow."[14] The term "emergency" is vague; yet all Butler had to do was to obey orders. However, he would not deplete his stores for an army he believed undeserving, nor was he writing a passport to glory for any rival, including Baldy Smith, if he could possibly help it. Meade meanwhile was busy getting Hancock off and the bridge completed while keeping in constant touch with the other three corps. He never did learn that Petersburg was to be attacked, nor did Hancock, who on that point was emphatic.[15]

Grant had given Smith the lead because of his good work at Chattanooga. But, as he later discovered, Smith became practically useless the moment he differed with a superior. Although a friend of Meade's during prewar Detroit days, he had failed to respond to his orders during infrequent contacts after Gettysburg and was exiled to Fortress Monroe. Recalled to Cold Harbor, he again found himself under Meade, "much to his [Smith's] disgust," and when leaving to rejoin Butler, he wrote his wife, "I am once more away from the Army of the Potomac, and Meade is, I suppose, as glad as I am."[16] Thus the effort would suffer from a divided command. Butler was advised by Grant that Hancock would march toward Petersburg and await further orders, but apparently this information was not passed on to Smith.

A damaging delay was caused by Butler's neglecting to send rations. Since Hancock had supplies for only two days, Meade permitted him to wait after 6:00 A.M. on June 15, the time set for the march. When a vessel was seen unloading supplies near by, Hancock continued to wait, supposing them to be from Butler. When it was found otherwise, Hancock, at nine o'clock, was ordered to start. But signal officers wigwagging Meade's order failed to understand each other, and a boat carrying a messenger with the same order ran aground. Ultimately, at 10:30 A.M., after a loss of four and one-half hours, the columns started out in the heat of the day. Hancock had about twenty-two miles to go by the most direct route, but he had the ill luck to be provided with a faulty map and instructions based on data received from Butler's headquarters

[13] *Ibid.*, 46; *O.R.*, XL, pt. 2, 36.

[14] *Ibid.*, *O.R.*, XL, pt. 2, 36.

[15] Walker, *History of the Second Corps*, 528, and *General Hancock*, 232; Pennypacker, *Meade*, 322.

[16] Meade to wife, June 4, 1864, Meade Papers; MHSM *Papers*, Vol. V, 108.

proved misleading. The march was dusty and fatiguing. After canteens were drunk dry, no water could be found, and by midafternoon fainting soldiers began to drop from the ranks.

Hancock's instructions as stated by Grant were to move "direct for Petersburg with directions to halt at the point on the road nearest City Point unless he receives further orders."[17] He approached Petersburg roughly from the northeast, Smith more from the north. Along the way there was some communication between them when Smith discovered that he was to be reinforced. The latter got away early, and after forcing his way through occasional resistance for eight or nine miles, he arrived before noonday at a position a little northeast of the field-works which widely ringed Petersburg. Hurrying from Butler's front, General Pierre G. T. Beauregard had taken up these lines with only a few thousand troops, and although the works were regarded as strong, they were but weakly manned. After slow and careful reconnaissance, Smith ordered his gunners to blast the enemy line and then sent in foot troops, who captured part of the works by a bold dash. Smith again halted and later renewed the attack, but the works carried were still some distance from Petersburg. Toward evening Birney's and Gibbon's divisions began to arrive, and when Hancock deferred to the officer already on the ground, he was asked merely to occupy the works while Smith and his command rested. General Francis C. Barlow's division lost its way entirely and did not arrive until toward morning.

By asking Hancock simply to take over ground won, Smith had fallen well short of a determined drive to capture the city that day— and, indeed, he had not been ordered to do so. Although the troops of Birney and Gibbon had been under physical strain nearly all day, they were thrilled by the spontaneous idea that they might take over and push straight into the city. Hope gave way to disappointment and anger when orders made no reference to that kind of action. "The rage of the enlisted men," one of them wrote, "was devilish . . . the whole corps was furiously excited."[18]

Meade and Admiral Samuel P. Lee of the United States fleet were having supper together when news of a successful early skirmish arrived by land and water from Smith.[19] That fighting below had already

[17] Grant to Butler, June 14, 1864, *O.R.*, L, pt. 2, 36.
[18] Quoted in Bruce Catton, *A Stillness at Appomattox*, 191, 410, note 12.
[19] *Meade's Headquarters*, 161; MHSM *Papers*, Vol. V, 28.

started called for a quick change in the army's marching order. Meade shunted aside artillery still crossing the bridge to permit passage of Burnside's Ninth Corps. Directly behind came Warren, who was advised to ferry his troops over the river starting at 4:00 A.M. next day. Both corps were then to hasten directly to Petersburg. The Sixth Corps, which was serving as a rear guard behind entrenchments, was to remain where it was until all other troops and trains had crossed the James, and then it would follow, taking care to salvage the bridge. General James H. Wilson's Third Cavalry Division was occupied in guarding the wagon train, and since Sheridan remained absent on one of those independent missions so dear to his heart, he had not been nor could he be of any use in the effort to capture the all-important rail center of Petersburg. In the main, the foot troops would have to do their own scouting, although some 2,400 cavalry accompanying Smith would be of some use. On the sixteenth, directly after breakfast, Grant and his staff embarked for City Point; and, confident that all was going well, Meade, Humphreys, and two staff officers followed on the navy steamer *Powell*.

Riding from City Point toward the Federal line drawn around one small sector of outer Petersburg, Meade met Grant returning from the front. The two men stopped to talk astride their horses. Grant made no mention of plans in case of failure to take Petersburg, nor, indeed, had the possibility of failure even occurred to him. Smith, he said, had taken a line of works "stronger than anything we have seen this campaign," and Hancock was now probing an inner enemy line. Unworried over the chances of capturing the city, Grant told Meade, "If it is a possible thing, I want an attack made at six o'clock this evening." The enemy should be driven straight across the Appomattox that night.[20]

Meade's little cavalcade rode on, meeting next a dusty, sun-scorched brigade which made room for it to pass. This was part of Burnside's advance as it looked near the end of a night and day march—hot, thirsty, and with weary feet. The road then led past Smith's command, which appeared in good spirits, and then to Hancock, who was testing enemy fieldworks in front with artillery fire.

Meade asked that skirmishers be called in while Humphreys, Barlow, and himself reconnoitered the ground. Just ahead, trees had been felled to clear an area about nine hundred yards wide in front of the

[20] MHSM *Papers*, Vol. V, 96; Porter, *Campaigning with Grant*, 206.

next line of enemy works. Small hills, farmhouses, and all available fences were linked with the defense barrier, and a railroad leading to City Point had been cut off about two miles from the city. The enemy left was securely anchored on high ground along the Appomattox, the right guarded by dismounted cavalry behind piled dirt and brush. From rising ground, Colonel Lyman caught his first view of the spires of Petersburg, which lay some miles off in a hollow,[21] but not much more could be seen or learned than that the enemy had been reinforced. Although he still lacked troops to occupy all the prepared works, particularly those on the Federal left, Beauregard had between 14,000 and 15,000 men. Meade had more than twice this number, but the accepted military formula was that one man defending breastworks was equal to three making the attack.

Escaping an enemy round shot which bounded close to his group, Meade counted the artillery bursts. He turned to Hancock, who, getting his men up, cleaned out some woods and took over a few scattered farmhouses. Captain Horace Porter arrived from Grant to ask that the assault be pushed strongly to distract enemy attention from Bermuda Hundred. It was learned that General Pickett's division of 4,500 from Lee's army had retaken works temporarily yielded there as two small divisions hurried to reinforce Beauregard—the new troops received earlier. Then Pickett would arrive later that day, to be followed by others, as General Lee, recovering from a rare surprise, located his new front.

Porter related in his memoirs that he found Meade directing the battle in his usual intense manner. All told, three enemy ramparts and connecting earthworks were taken, though at a cost of 2,500 casualties, and it was still a long way into Petersburg. The enemy even launched a limited offensive by moonlight amid much din. Colonel Lyman rode to City Point meanwhile to take Meade's report to Grant, who was still unworried. "I think it is pretty well to get across a great river," Lyman heard him remark, "and come up here and attack Lee in his rear before he is ready for us!"[22]

Warren's men began to move in, arriving through the night and the next morning, then a Sixth Corps division, Grant turning two others toward Bermuda Hundred. Instead of combining all forces before

[21] *Meade's Headquarters*, 165.
[22] *Ibid.*, 166.

Petersburg, he also sent Baldy Smith with a single division to join Butler. Using one of Burnside's divisions, Meade extended his front toward Warren on the left, but the men were so exhausted by the long march from north of the James that many fell asleep whenever ordered to halt. Nevertheless, they would fight well. Ably led by General Robert B. Potter, son of the Episcopal Bishop of Pennsylvania, the division rushed across a gully and climbed a ravine to surprise some entrenched Tennesseans and capture four guns, several colors, many small arms, and a few hundred prisoners.

It was a favorable start for the third day, June 17. Yet so much energy had been spent and so much of the best blood spilled between the Rapidan and the James that anything done now seemed to require a great deal of effort. About one mile above Potter, where Second Corps lines had been pushed closer to the city, a house and its hill were occupied, but supports all along the line were grievously weak or unready, and the stubborn defenders had still other prepared works in depth. Warren got a division into position on Burnside's left and massed two in the rear, but did little else that day. More "ifs" appear in connection with the Petersburg campaign than any other of the war except Gettysburg. General Hancock, Colonel Lyman, and others would declare that if it had been known on June 15 that the city was to be attacked, then it would have fallen. Lyman used a stark metaphor: "It would have gone like a rotten branch."[23] Beauregard, too, would testify that it "was clearly at the mercy of the Federal commander who had all but captured it."[24] And it was said of Warren that if he had marched promptly up the winding north-south highway known as the Jerusalem plank road (from the Virginia town then called Jerusalem), as he was expected to do, without stopping to reconnoiter, then Beauregard would have been flanked and "Petersburg would have been taken."[25]

Physical ailments attendant on both Smith and Hancock may have played some part in the result. The former suffered from an old malarial weakness; Hancock was having trouble with his Gettysburg wound, which began discharging pieces of bone. The *New York Tribune* entered the fight by denouncing both Meade and Hancock for

[23] *Ibid.*, 162.

[24] *Battles and Leaders*, IV, 541.

[25] MHSM *Papers*, Vol. V, 182. Jerusalem, in Southampton County, was later renamed Courtland.

"refusing" or failing to co-operate with Smith, an Abolitionist favorite because his command included a division of Negro troops. Hancock at once asked for an official investigation, but the whole thing fell to the ground. Neither Smith nor Meade nor Grant could find any cause for censure, and save for an attempt to place the *Tribune* reporter under arrest, the matter was soon dropped.[26] Forced into inactivity because of his old wound, Hancock temporarily handed the Second Corps over to Birney.

Early up on June 18, the fourth day, Meade appeared in a great hurry and in no pleasant mood. He jarred even his correct and affable aide, Colonel Lyman, who nevertheless excused him by observing that no one was in a very good humor. Regardless of enemy movements, of which Meade knew little, he relied on the Fifth Corps to attack promptly at 4:00 A.M. in conjunction with Burnside, and "with all the force you can put into it."[27] Whatever was to be done had to be done quickly.

The day began well. On the Federal right a strange silence hung over the arena as the troops cautiously emerged from their shelters and entered Confederate works. Birney's troops and the remainder of Smith's under General John Martindale then skirmished through some woods only to find the enemy withdrawn to another fortified line about one mile from the city. Elsewhere, however, the troops would have farther to go to reach the new line, and the ground to be covered was more broken. The movement took the form of a right wheel as the Federals closed in, but almost from the start Burnside and Warren faced punishing artillery and soon ran into musketry.

What both Grant and Meade wanted was concerted action in storming the enemy works wherever found, but now the right wing would have to wait until the center and left had come far enough to batter the new line. Starting early, two of Burnside's divisions had forced their way through woods and driven enemy skirmishers as far as the curving line of the Norfolk and Petersburg Railroad, where a long, sweeping ridge had been cut to accommodate it. Although Burnside could report progress, this was still short of the mark, and his troops were "much wearied"[28] from the effects of day and night marches, tactical move-

[26] Walker, *General Hancock*, 235, and *History of the Second Corps*, 527–32; MHSM *Papers*, Vol. X, 43, 88; *New York Tribune*, June 27, 1864. Smith complained that the article was unjust. *O.R.*, XL, pt. 3, 89.

[27] *O.R.*, XL, pt. 2, 192.

[28] *Ibid.*, 191.

ments, and fighting. Warren had to circle around some deep ravines, a feat difficult enough under artillery fire, but instead of hurrying his men over the ridge in conjunction with Burnside, he stopped to entrench while he brought up his guns and looked the ground over. Probably more than any other officer Warren hated to sacrifice lives, and his disposition was to reconnoiter the ground ahead thoroughly.

Meade continued to try to inspire his corps leaders, who "so soon as dispositions could be made" were to assault. "I have moved the whole army forward and directed the officers on your right and left to communicate with you," he notified Birney by field telegraph. "It is of great importance that the enemy be pressed, and, if possible, forced across the Appomattox. I can not ascertain there is any force in our front but Beauregard's. . . . They can not be over 30,000, and we have 55,000."[29] But on this day, as on each of the others, a few precious hours were lost. The last statement of Meade's may have been true as of 7:30 P.M., but conditions behind Beauregard's lines were rapidly changing. By withdrawing to his new position, which by hard work was strengthened that night, and by checking the Federal left, Beauregard had bartered a mile or more of ground for a delay of a few hours. With his exhausted soldiers at almost the breaking point, he discovered that the tactic had served its purpose. Sometime before eight o'clock, General Joseph B. Kershaw's division of Anderson's corps was sighted approaching, a timely relief, and another division would arrive later. Farther away but coming on fast was A. P. Hill's corps.

Nowhere on the Federal side was there much co-ordination that day, and without it very little could be done. By midmorning, most of the line was ready for another thrust, but Warren still asked for more time. When Meade inquired when he expected to be ready, Warren could not say. Forcing the issue, Meade called for a general assault at noonday, but only the right of the line became active, and only Martindale had much success.

When neither Warren nor Burnside made a move, not even at one o'clock as Meade required, all that could be done was to order each corps leader to assault without reference to the other. At this point, another message came from Warren, who could be troublesome at times. Not hearing any firing at one o'clock, he had not attacked, and following this astonishing remark he suggested that the simultaneous

[29] Walker, *History of the Second Corps*, 540.

movement be made at three, when, if the others were not ready, he would attack alone.[30]

As Grant's observer, Captain Horace Porter told of Meade's "earnest and vigorous action" that day as he sent "ringing despatches to all points of the line, and paced up and down upon the field in his nervous, restless manner."[31] But there was obviously a limit to what men could do. Standing with Meade in an open field toward the left of the line, Colonel Lyman witnessed the work of that afternoon and revealed why it failed. Burnside's men finally pushed the enemy out of the railroad cut only to be checked before reaching the more formidable line. Colonel Lyman related,

> In front was a broad expanse, quite flat, then the railroad cut with a fringe of bushes, and then a gradual rise crowned by the Rebel rifle-pits and batteries, which were distant perhaps half a mile. Close to us, on each side, were our batteries, firing as fast as they could, and the Rebels were sending back shot, shell, and shrapnel as hard as they could. Half a mile is no good with minié rifles; and, as soon as we attacked, the balls came tolerably numerous, cutting up little puffs of sand on the dry field . . . I can't say it was pleasant, though it is a help to have others cool and brave. It was as I expected—forty-five days of constant marching, assaulting, and trenching are a poor preparation for a rush! The men went in, but not with spirit; received by a withering fire, they sullenly fell back a few paces to a slight crest and lay down . . . The slopes covered with dead and wounded bore testimony that they were willing to give proof of courage even in circumstances that they deemed desperate. Another attack at six resulted no better, save that the lines were at all points pressed close in on those of the enemy . . . I returned after dark, feeling pretty sad. General Meade was much disappointed, but . . . you cannot strike a full blow with a wounded hand.[32]

As darkness came on, Meade ordered the troops to form the best line they could and hold it. Like everyone else, he could see that impetus had been lost and spirit had deteriorated. Many seasoned vet-

[30] *O.R.*, XL, pt. 2, 179, 209; Meade to Rawlins, June 21, 1864, Meade Papers.

[31] Porter, *Campaigning with Grant*, 209–10, adds: "His aquiline nose and piercing eyes gave him something of the eagle's look and added to the interest of his personality. He had much to try him on this occasion, and if he was severe in his reprimands and showed faults of temper, he certainly displayed no faults as a commander."

[32] *Meade's Headquarters*, 169–70.

erans who had started the march from the Rapidan were dead or in hospitals, and their places had been taken by recruits for whom there was no time for training, nor was there time for the careful selection of officers to replace the fallen.[33] Given the army he had at the start of the campaign, Meade asserted, he would have succeeded with one-half the losses, which from June 15 to 18 totaled nearly 10,000 killed, wounded, and missing.[34]

There were other reasons why Petersburg was not taken,[35] but basically the effort had failed at the start because attention had been concentrated on the river crossing on June 14-15 while the bastioned city lay only dimly beyond. Neither Grant nor Meade at their remote posts, nor even Hancock or Smith had considered immediate capture. That became the obsession only of the common soldier who reached the scene late on the fifteenth, and he could not execute orders which were never given.

[33] "Grant had not moulded one man in this vast mob."—Wilkeson, *Recollections*, 193. This, too, was Meade's responsibility, but no time was allowed.

[34] *Meade*, II, 206–207.

[35] MHSM *Papers*, Vol. V, 182. Smith complained that Grant "had no well-defined project for an attack when he planned the flank march."—*Ibid.*, 113.

## 21. Defeat at Its Worst
## (June 22–July 30, 1864)

PRESIDENT LINCOLN UNEXPECTEDLY ARRIVED in camp, coming by boat with his son Tad and Caleb Willard, the hotel proprietor of Washington. "No one knows what he came for," complained Captain George Meade when army headquarters was paid no special attention.[1] But at least the President could show that he was mindful of the welfare of his fighting men, and he could relax in the informal atmosphere of General Grant's camp, the national headquarters. He had no strategic ideas to offer, but when more fighting was mentioned, he earnestly remarked, "I cannot pretend to advise, but I do sincerely hope that all may be accomplished with as little bloodshed as possible."[2] Saddened by the heavy casualty lists, Lincoln had lost interest in battles as such. Nevertheless, perfect faith still prevailed between him and his General in Chief, a great alliance in history.

Although the great effort to take Petersburg had failed, attempts would be made to edge closer on the left, where the lines were farthest away from the city. Fighting was resumed on a warm June 22 when the Federal left crossed the Jerusalem road and wheeled toward the enemy defenses. The woods and broken terrain were confusing; officers were sighting the sun and scanning their compasses in an effort to keep the lines straight and in contact. Wright's Sixth Corps, returned from Butler, had been placed on the left of the Second and was pivoting. Barlow, Second Corps, was to follow up closely in the grand right wheel. As soon as enemy fire began dropping his men, however, Wright cautiously halted his advance and dug in.

Still moving, the Second Corps division somehow lost contact. "You cannot connect with both; keep . . . with the right,"[3] Meade advised

[1] Letter to Mrs. George G. Meade, June 24, 1864, Meade Papers; Humphreys, *Andrew Atkinson Humphreys*, 236.
[2] Porter, *Campaigning with Grant*, 223.

Barlow; but the enemy chose this critical moment to strike the unprotected Second Corps flank, which gave way in panic. Enemy troops which hardly could be seen struck at the next division in turn—Mott's—and then at Gibbon's. The action was brief but decisive. Although casualties were not many, the humiliated Second Corps lost several hundred prisoners as well as four guns, which were turned toward them. Gibbon, very angry, ordered a brigade leader to retake the guns at once, then put him under arrest for being too slow. But Confederate troops under General William Mahone lingered not a moment too long, disappearing into the brush before Gibbon could retrieve his artillery. For the proud Second Corps to lose guns was unprecedented.[4]

"I have ordered a general advance at daylight," Meade informed Grant that evening,[5] but on June 23 the Second Corps found only skirmishers in front, and Wright could find nothing. Of course some ground was gained, but Colonel Lyman, an observer with Wright, deemed the two-day action faulty in execution. "There was everywhere, high and low, feebleness, confusion, poor judgment," he wrote his wife. "The only person who kept his plans and judgment clear was General Meade himself. On this particular occasion, Wright showed himself totally unfit to command a corps."[6]

This was a little hard on Wright, a good soldier unaccustomed to woods fighting. General Warren, who had been assigned no part in the movement, also was under a cloud. Much had been expected of him on June 18, and after his failure Meade had drawn up charges only to withhold them after the actions of others, including Burnside, seemed to look almost as bad.[7] Meade took notice at least that his corps leaders were laboring under difficulties in broken and unfamiliar terrain. To his wife he had written, "The army is exhausted and absolutely requires rest."[8]

Since morale was noticeably shaken, Meade asked Grant to come to the front. The decision then made marked another turn in strategic policy. Active field operations, Grant decided, would be replaced by

[3] *O.R.*, XL, pt. 1, 328.
[4] *Ibid.*, 367. Walker, *History of the Second Corps*, 544–45.
[5] *O.R.*, XL, pt. 2, 304.
[6] *Meade's Headquarters*, 176 n.
[7] Meade to Rawlins, June 21, 1864, Meade Papers; Porter, *Campaigning with Grant*, 252.
[8] June 21, 1864, *Meade*, II, 206.

siege. Engineers began to busy themselves in constructing emplacements for guns, redoubts and bombproofs for shelter, and passages
deep enough for horse and rider to pass along safely. Guns from the
army's siege train, which had been abandoned as an encumbrance on
the long march, were to be returned from Washington.

The Fourth of July passed peaceably with bands playing and artillery salutes, although mortar fire was exchanged where the lines were
close together on the right. But when a brigade band with Warren's
corps played "Hail Columbia," a North Carolina regiment "rose as a
man and gave three cheers."[9] At his camp on the Jerusalem road,
Meade went over some reports during the day and welcomed a Sani-
tary Commission wagon which halted at headquarters to unload some
mutton, canned fruit, and other delicacies calculated to sustain officer
morale. A gay evening was enjoyed at Gibbon's headquarters, where
that officer's promotion to major general was celebrated.[10] General
Hancock, apparently recovered from the effects of his wound, had resumed his Second Corps command. Jocular chaffing was heard between
him and Meade—both had been recommended for promotion at the
same time as Gibbon, and they both were still waiting.

Since the army was well settled and convenient to reach, visitors in
camp were becoming more numerous. Several Englishmen and Canadians came and went, and Meade also found himself host to two
French artillery officers sent to U. S. shores as official observers. As he
was then situated, he was being penalized for a good command of the
French language, of which Grant confessed he knew nothing.[11] The
foreigners, however, were delighted to be with Meade, a cosmopolitan
type and good host. Received with less ceremony were Senators Chandler of Michigan and Morton S. Wilkinson of Minnesota, two Radical
members of Congress. Meade could recall that Wilkinson had delivered a lengthy tirade in the Senate against him when Gettysburg honors
were being reallocated. Ostensibly this pair had come to inspect the
army, but their actual mission, as Meade learned from Hancock, was
to persuade Grant to remove him. He himself had been approached,
Hancock said, with the idea of taking over the army, but he knew that
Grant firmly opposed any change. Quite uninterested himself, as he

---

[9] *Meade's Headquarters*, 182.
[10] J. R. C. Ward, *History of the 106th Pennsylvania Volunteers*, 233.
[11] *Meade's Headquarters*, 178.

always had been, Hancock passed the matter off as mere political intrigue.[12]

Actively campaigning for the post, however, was the more ambitious and outspoken Baldy Smith, who, returning to the army after a quarrel with Butler, began to insist on the removal of Meade. Smith, however, had lost prestige, and his eager criticism of his immediate superiors made Grant feel that he would always make trouble. After speaking out to Grant, Smith departed on sick leave, an absence considered unnecessary, as in fact it was unwise.[13] Grant looked about for a permanent replacement and picked the reliable Edward O. C. Ord, who back in 1862 had served with Meade and Reynolds with the Pennsylvania Reserves and who was later at Vicksburg.

The usual camp rumors meanwhile went the rounds, some reaching the newspapers. "The stories you hear . . . are mere canards," Meade reassured his wife, who apparently had shown concern. "I have never had any quarrel with either General Hancock or Smith. Hancock is an honest man. . . . I never doubt his statements, and I am sure I have for him the most friendly feelings . . . I am perfectly willing at any time to turn over to him the Army of the Potomac, and wish him joy of his promotion. . . . The camp is full of . . . intrigue and reports of all kinds, but I keep myself free from them all . . . mind my own business, and stand prepared to obey orders and do my duty."[14] Hancock's position seems to have been the same as that of his friend Meade, while Smith, who spawned difficulties, would not be permitted to return.

Perhaps Petersburg would prove as difficult a problem as had Vicksburg, which had occupied Grant for ten months. By July 10, 1864, the opposing armies had made themselves solid and secure around the perimeter with double lines of fortified works backed up in some places by a third line. The only action of consequence occurred some distance away, Wright's corps, the least worn, being sent. Lee had detached a roving corps—about 20,000 men—under General Jubal Early to counter Federal forces in the Shenandoah Valley, and, victorious there, Early moved through Harpers Ferry, Sharpsburg, and on to Washing-

[12] *Meade*, II, 212 and MS letter of July 12 to wife, Meade Papers. Probably also involved in the cabal was Assistant Secretary of War Dana. See Dana, *Recollections*, 226–27; *O.R.*, XL, pt. 1, 35.

[13] Col. Cyrus B. Comstock called it "an unnecessary leave of ten days."—MS Diary, July 17, 1864, entry.

[14] Meade to wife, July 23 and 26, 1864, *Meade*, II, 215–16.

ton. Arriving just in time, Wright threw him back, but panic had been created in the city in its first real contact with war.

Not greatly concerned over Washington, Grant was debating where the next blow should be struck south of the Appomattox. Meade carefully read his written inquiry and passed it along to his corps commanders. Their feeling was that further direct attacks against enemy fieldworks would be futile. Meade observed that the Federal lines could be slowly advanced so that the heavy siege guns could be brought to bear at short range on enemy positions, but another and more novel idea came from General Burnside. In front of his works east of Petersburg, soldiers who had once labored in Pennsylvania's coal mines had been digging since June 25 with the idea of placing a powerful land mine under an enemy salient.

The moving spirits of the work were Colonel Henry Pleasants, who led the burrowing regiment, the Forty-eighth Pennsylvania, and General Potter, his division chief. Burnside, too, had become interested. The idea had a precedent in a mine touched off under an enemy work at Vicksburg, but only a sixty-foot tunnel had been dug there to explode two thousand pounds of powder, whereas the tunnel mapped by Pleasants would have to be some five hundred feet long. The charge to be exploded, therefore, could be much greater.

Meade was skeptical at first. The officer who could have made the work much easier, Chief Engineer James C. Duane, openly scoffed, and so Pleasants and his miners were left to forage for their own materials and do the best they could. No instruments for sighting and measuring were made available, and only cracker boxes reinforced by salvaged scrap iron could be used to remove the tons of loosened earth. But after two weeks of confining and often perilous labor, the effort was officially recognized when Meade sent General Hunt and Major Duane to examine the ground and submit a plan for a Ninth Corps offensive.

Their report clung to traditional lines and followed Meade's own suggestion of the use of siege guns, but it was added significantly that if the tunnel and mine were successfully finished, then that device might also be utilized. After talking with Grant, Meade ordered work begun on emplacements for the big guns and on redoubts and rifle pits bearing on the prospective point of attack. This was known as Elliott's Salient, from the name of the brigade commander there. Just beyond, a low ridge, which would have to be taken, rose above the enemy's first defense line.[15]

As the mine began to loom larger in the general scheme of attack, action was postponed until its completion. On July 23, when the tunnel but not the mine was ready, Grant visited the work in company with Meade. The maximum distance penetrated, he was informed, was 510.8 feet, easily a new record for a work of this kind, and the diggers had worked to the right and left at the far end to make room for the explosive. After sleeping on the problem, Grant agreed that the mine should be used.[16] Countermining by a suspicious foe failed to disturb the workers as powder loading was begun, eight thousand pounds being stored directly under the salient.

What results this massive weapon might effect was sheer guesswork. Burnside, indeed, had wanted to use twice as much powder, but army engineers believed the smaller charge would be more effective. Whether any Federal troops when moved up close would be hurt was a moot question as elaborate plans were made to divert the enemy and to push directly forward after the blast. There could be no test explosion for this 1864 equivalent of an atomic bomb.

On July 26, therefore, while powder was still being carried into the mine's distant chambers, the Second Corps was moved across the Appomattox and past Butler's position on the far left as if to threaten Richmond. Sheridan, who had rejoined the army, was in a position to make a dash for the Confederate capital should Hancock advance to a point from which the city's defenses might be broken. The painstaking labor of the sweating miners had thus given rise to a far-reaching plan.

Hancock, however, did not get very far. Somehow aware of Second Corps activity, Lee already had sent troops across the Appomattox to hold the James River bridge which Hancock had expected to use. When he crossed over another bridge a short distance east, the fortified banks of a stream known as Deep Bottom stood in his way. When Grant learned that the Second Corps faced fieldworks, he notified Meade, "I do not want Hancock to attack entrenched lines,"[17] and so ended

[15] *O.R.*, XL, pt. 1, 159–60, 286–87. General Stephen Elliott, Jr. of Bushrod Johnson's division was in command.

[16] *O.R.*, XL, pt. 3, 424, 438. Pleasants said the mine was finished on July 18; Humphreys, July 23.—MHSM *Papers*, Vol. V, 226 n.

[17] Walker, *History of the Second Corps*, 555–56.

the flank march aimed at Richmond's defenses. Before the mine was exploded on July 30 as scheduled, Hancock would have to return.

Meanwhile Burnside, who was to direct the attack after the explosion, had made his own plans, of which he informed Meade on the day that Hancock marched. Since three of his four divisions had been almost constantly on the front line, then the next in turn would lead the assault. This was General Edward Ferrero's command of 4,300 men who had been specially trained for the grand stroke, but Meade gaped in surprise when he realized that the division was a Negro unit with no fighting experience.

For a regular army officer with no desire to glorify the Negro, the question of capacity was foremost. Here were the Negroes, willing soldiers who were in high fettle over the great opportunity within their grasp, but they were still new in the army and largely untried, and their courage and stamina under fire were questioned. They had been tested on June 15 when a Negro division with Smith had carried a part of the outer Petersburg defenses, a feat widely hailed in the Abolitionist press, but it was learned that the works had been weakly manned. Few officers in fact would use Negroes in the same way as other troops. Their work was chiefly the guarding of trains, the felling of trees, and trench digging. General Burnside, who was politically wise, never losing an election in his postwar career, may have thought it expedient to use Negroes for this operation, or perhaps he only wished to give them a chance to fight and prove themselves soldiers.

Meade's position regarding the Negro was similar to that of his own politics—about center. When, more than one year before, the idea of using the newly emancipated Negroes in the ranks was being discussed, he silenced a critic in his blunt fashion by observing that "if the nigger were going into the field and really could be brought heartily to fight, I was ready to command them and should prefer such duty to others that might be assigned me."[18] This seemed to be going pretty far, and observing that Meade looked out for the Negro soldiers' physical welfare and was punctilious in returning salutes, Colonel Lyman remarked that if his superior had any bias at all, it was for and not against the colored men in uniform.[19] But when it came to putting

[18] *Meade*, I, 356. Meade, however, was generally believed unfavorably disposed toward Negro troops. Augustus Woodbury, *Major General Ambrose E. Burnside and the Ninth Army Corps*, 471.

these inexperienced soldiers in front on what seemed a desperate chance, Meade declined to allow it.

Burnside protested so strongly against this decision that Meade went to Grant. If the attack failed, he was reported as saying, "it would then be said, and very properly, that we were shoving these people ahead to get killed because we did not care anything about them. But that could not be said if we put white troops in front."[20] Grant, who usually agreed with Meade, did so in this case. Yet there was another element in the situation that probably was not given enough weight. With the elimination of the unit that had been trained to go in first after the explosion, the spark behind the enterprise was lost. General Henry G. Thomas, commanding one of the Negro brigades, was mindful of this when he said, "It is an axiom in military art that there are times when the ardor, hopefulness and enthusiasm of new troops, not yet rendered doubtful by reverses or chilled by defeat, more than compensate, in a dash, for training and experience."[21]

It was also a little late for a change. Burnside made no effort to drill other troops for the July 30 assignment. Conferring with Ninth Corps officers on the preceding day, Meade asked that he put in the best troops he had, with the brigadiers leading in person if necessary.[22] Burnside, however, had about given up. Instead of following orders to the letter, he left it to the three remaining division leaders to draw lots. Meade was not notified of this whimsicality, and as luck would have it, the command fell to the weakest of the three brigadiers.

This was General James H. Ledlie of New York, who, a civil engineer before the war, lacked military training. He had an untimely fondness for the bottle, and had Meade known it, Ledlie would have been deprived of his command. ("His total unfitness," General Humphreys tartly observed after it was all over, "ought to have been known to General Burnside. . . . It was not known to General Meade."[23]) It was also urged at the conference that prompt advantage be taken of enemy confusion after the explosion to gain the ridge or crest beyond the salient. Should the attack fail, Meade emphasized, the troops were to be withdrawn at once.

[19] *Meade's Headquarters*, 256–57.
[20] *Battles and Leaders*, IV, 548.
[21] *Ibid.*, 563.
[22] *Meade's Headquarters*, 214.
[23] Humphreys, *Virginia Campaign*, 252.

Orders written by Humphreys for July 30 were perfectly clear. Ledlie's troops and the others to follow were to be formed by brigades, and the parapets opened to permit the free passage of men and artillery. Warren's Fifth Corps and the Eighteenth (formerly Smith's) under Ord were to lend support on each side, keeping the flanks well protected. The mine was to go up at 3:30 A.M., whereupon Federal artillery would join in as Ledlie's troops rushed forward on each side of the crater to seize the crest and "effect a lodgement there." Returning from Deep Bottom, Hancock was to fill in for the Eighteenth Corps as Ord formed next to Burnside. Copies of each order went to every corps leader so that all would know what the others were doing. The best efforts of everyone were asked. "Promptitude, rapidity of execution, and cordial co-operation are essential for success," Meade counseled.[24]

On the night of July 29, the whole army was in motion. Concealing his weakness from a reinforced enemy, Hancock crept back from Deep Bottom after devising elaborate ruses to show that he was moving the other way. The Ninth Corps left its extensive trench system and took front-line posts. On Burnside's left, Warren pressed closer; on the right, Ord. Sheridan, too, was assigned an active role, but since he had a longer distance to travel, he excused himself on account of lack of time.

General Hunt had siege guns, field artillery, and mortars ready. Grant, two aides, and an orderly rode over from City Point to bivouac near Burnside's regular station one mile from the front. Up at 2:30 A.M. on the thirtieth, Meade rode in early to take his post at the same Ninth Corps headquarters from which a telegraph wire had been run to Burnside's temporary position near the front. The hours ticked away slowly as the troops moved into their places. Those in position up front had lain down, and all was quiet as Colonel Pleasants entered the tunnel up to ninety-eight feet, where he ignited the long fuse at 3:15 A.M. From the end of the fuse, which had been spliced to give it length, a narrow trail of powder would carry the flame into the two magazines.

Pleasants, his pulse bounding, hurried back to a protective earthwork and counted off the seconds, watch in hand. Minutes then went by as men looked at each other, then a long and wearisome half-hour. Vowed one observer: "Pleasants became like a maniac,"[25] but he was

[24] *Ibid.*, 429–30.
[25] O. C. Bosbyshell, *The 48th* [Pennsylvania] *in the War,* 169.

still able to decide that the probable source of the difficulty was the spliced fuse.

Probably a little too remote from the scene, Grant and Meade were waiting together near the telegraph wire. Since no messages were being received despite the inquiries that Meade sent, two staff officers were sent to Burnside to ask the reason for the delay. Grant kept looking at his watch—it was now after four o'clock.

"What's the matter with the mine?" he asked Meade.

"I don't know—guess the fuse has gone out."[26]

"Is there any difficulty in exploding the mine?" the telegraph operator asked Burnside. Grant continued to examine his watch.

At 4:20 A.M. another message was sent: "Is General Burnside at his [temporary] headquarters?"[27]

Grant himself now asked that the assault be launched at once even if the mine had failed. The lonely telegraph clicked on.

Up front in the glowing dawn, Pleasants was talking with Sergeant Henry Reese and Lieutenant Jacob Douty, two dauntless helpers. Reese, who was permitted to enter the mine at about 4:15 A.M., slashed away the taping over the burned fuse until the spliced part was reached, then cut it through above the charred portion. Douty appeared bringing more fuse. The two ends were spliced and the new length carried to the front to be lighted. At sixteen minutes of five, just as Grant had placed his watch back in his pocket, the earth trembled, tongues of lurid flame lit up the area, and a dull-sounding roar reached the ears of the army leaders one mile in the rear.[28]

Dazed witnesses near the front saw white smoke atop a great black cloud. A huge mass of clay, rocks, guns, caissons, timbers, ammunition, wagons, tents, and mangled bodies was lifted upward. Troops nearest broke for the rear in disorder as the chaotic mass thudded to earth. In their front, a South Carolina regiment and a four-gun battery had been hurled into the air and then nearly buried. There was left a great hole, in rough dimension nearly 200 feet long, 50 or 60 feet wide, and 25 or 30 feet deep. Federal cannon, eighty-one guns and mortars, "burst forth in one roar"[29] as if applauding the most awesome spectacle of the war.

[26] *Meade's Headquarters,* 198.

[27] *O.R.,* XL, pt. 1, 47.

[28] Porter, *Campaigning with Grant,* 251; Joseph Gould, *Story of the 48th Pennsylvania Regiment,* 169.

[29] *Meade's Headquarters,* 198.

Almost at once, disregard for orders and lack of training became apparent. Ledlie's leading brigade pulled itself together and gave a reassuring yell, but contrary to orders, the way forward had not been cleared. A few men could get through a space perhaps ten feet wide, but most had to struggle over logs and heaped-up sandbags. Bayonets were shoved between the logs so the troops could climb up, but as the straggling line stumbled over the barrier and started running across uneven ground, formations could not be held.

Worse, many soldiers paused at the crater's edge to stare at the debris, and some gave a hand to half-buried enemy troops. Along came Ledlie's Second Brigade to mix in with the First. Instead of racing around the crater and heading for the crest, most of the men jumped or slid into the wide hole. Fresh arrivals only heightened the confusion by thrusting themselves into the mass. "The men could not be got forward," reported Captain Stephen Weld of the First Brigade. "It was a perfect mob. . . . To ask men to go forward in such a condition was useless. . . . Moral backing . . . was wanting."[30]

Other than a few plucky but exasperated brigade and regimental commanders, no one seemed to be leading. General Ledlie, who had been ordered to stay with his men, had made himself comfortable in a sand-bagged shelter and was fortifying himself with the bottle. He was joined there by General Ferrero, Fourth Division, who also was neglecting his work. Burnside was in an earthwork battery too far from the scene to understand what was going on, and Meade and Grant were still farther away. Not the Federals but the Confederates were beginning to rally amid the welter of dust, smoke, and debris. Enemy riflemen began picking off obvious targets, taking officers first. Troops trying to skirt the broad crater were staggered by canister shot. The fire was then turned on the blood-dampened hole.

Unable to get much information out of Burnside even after the explosion, Meade turned to Warren and Ord, who replied that little was stirring in their immediate front. An optimistic report now arrived from Burnside. The enemy's first line, he wired, had been carried. "Please report frequently," Meade wired back. "Push your men forward at all hazards. . . . Rush for the crest."[31] There followed another long silence. At about 5:30 A.M., Grant, becoming impatient, mounted

[30] MHSM *Papers*, Vol. V, 209.
[31] *O.R.*, XL, pt. 1, 140.

his horse to ride to the front. Soon afterward Meade read a message signed by Burnside's inspector general. It had been intended for Burnside alone, but, in error, had been brought to the regular corps headquarters. Inspector C. G. Loring, who had witnessed the debacle, reported that Ledlie's men could not be made to advance.

In that event, Burnside was supposed to order a retreat, but he never could admit failure. "If possible we will carry the crest," he was telegraphing. "It is hard work but we hope to accomplish it." Meade shot back a personal message: "Do you mean to say your officers and men will not obey your orders to advance? If not, what is the obstacle? I wish to know the truth and desire an immediate answer."[32]

Grant rode toward the reeking front with Captain Porter and an orderly. Dismounting beside a clump of trees, he hurried on foot through waiting files of soldiers. Porter could see sweat pouring from his face from the exertion and the heat. After asking a few questions along the way, Grant joined Burnside in the battery earthwork, and speaking rapidly, he told that preoccupied leader, "There is now no chance of success. These troops must be immediately withdrawn."[33] Without awaiting a reply, he turned away and went back to his horse.

Then engaged in a quarrel with Meade, Burnside had paid him little attention. "I have never in any report said anything different from what I conceived to be the truth," he retorted awkwardly to Meade's last dispatch. "Were it not insubordinate I would say that the latter remark of your note was unofficerlike and ungentlemanly."[34] The tone of this message caused Meade to request a copy of the note which he had previously sent. Burnside might have to face a formal inquiry.

At the moment, he was still putting in all his men, some moving forward even after Grant's call. The last was Ferrero's division of Negro troops, who, drawn up in two columns, raced around the crater as they had been drilled, swarmed over enemy breastworks, and charged an interior line. Prisoners and a stand of colors were taken, but retaliation was swift. Maddened by the sight of a Negro enemy, Southerners cleaned out a trench and flung back terror-stricken hundreds. Six Confederate brigades arrived from a camp beyond the town as the tide of battle turned. Canister from batteries on both flanks and

[32] *Ibid.*, 48; pt. 3, 660; *Meade's Headquarters*, 200.
[33] Porter, *Campaigning with Grant*, 267.
[34] *O.R.*, XL, pt. 3, 660.

infantry fire in front shattered the only line that had been formed. Most of the Negro troops fell back into the crater, which actually offered no protection. Others fled into near-by woods and were hours finding their way back. Infuriated Southerners slew many wounded Negroes where they lay, making them their first target.[35] Several score were seized and marched away as trophies of war.

As Grant returned to tell what he had seen, Meade repeated the order to withdraw. Burnside could not bring himself to forward the order promptly, possibly realizing that to withdraw from the trap would be difficult. While Federal guns and musketry held the enemy in check, shovels and pickaxes were tossed into the crater. Both within and without, men began digging furiously to open up a trench to safety. Troops who could be rallied formed a line around the rim of the hole to defend it with bayonets, gun butts, sticks, and stones until the interior had been cleared of everyone but the helpless and the dead.[36] As the order to withdraw was passed along, the able-bodied began scrambling over the sides to seek the nearest shelter while others scurried through the freshly dug trench. The Federal loss in this unsettling defeat was reckoned at nearly 3,500 killed, wounded, and missing.

His florid face reddened from heat and anger, Burnside returned to his own headquarters, where he began arguing with Meade. Whatever his excuses, orders as both stated and written had been practically disregarded. Meade brushed off his "extremely insubordinate language"[37] and took his leave as soon as he could. Grant, who did not wish to remain a party to a scene, had already gone.

Colonel Comstock, who tried to quiet the aggrieved Ninth Corps leader, commented sympathetically after his own fashion: "He is not competent to command a corps. . . . Poor Burn."[38] As the crater itself and a full brigade of prisoners fell to the enemy, anger and disappointment spread through the ranks. It had been a black and bitter day

[35] C. M. Clark, *History of the 39th Illinois Regiment,* 208; MHSM *Papers,* Vol. V, 211. General Stephen M. Weld related, "A wounded negro, shot through the body, was just in front of me . . . hardly able to stagger along. Two Confederate soldiers in succession ran up to him and shot him, the last one killing him." Some unarmed Negroes who had surrendered were shot dead.—*Ibid.*

[36] "Carnage at the Crater," *Confederate Veteran,* April, 1894 (supplement), 32–33.

[37] *Meade's Headquarters,* 200.

[38] MS Diary of Cyrus B. Comstock, July 30, 1864, entry.

for the veteran Ninth Corps, and as a result there were "scowls and frowns in the camps."[39]

A recounting of errors committed would require the attention of a formal Court of Inquiry and of the Committee on the Conduct of the War, which, of course, would defend Burnside. Viewing the sad result objectively, Colonel Lyman thought the day had been lost because the men did not fight hard enough,[40] which was true, but leadership could not have been worse. Yet no fault could be found with Meade's orders, Grant contended. "So fair an opportunity probably will never occur again," he wrote his subordinate. "The crest beyond the mine could have been carried. This would have given us Petersburg with all its artillery."[41]

The achievements of the Army of the Potomac were perhaps four in number. It had stood off Lee at Antietam and had won at Gettysburg. In October, 1863, it demonstrated at Centerville that Lee could no longer assume the offensive. In mid-June, 1864, it crossed the James and Appomattox. But it never won any smashing success in offensive warfare, particularly when the enemy stood ready and waiting. Perhaps Grant could find some other way to score.

[39] MS Journal of William H. Harris, July 30, 1864.
[40] *Meade's Headquarters*, 201.
[41] To Meade. *O.R.*, XL, pt. 1, 134.

## 22. The Fighting on the Flanks
## (July 31-November 17, 1864)

THE CRATER AFFAIR GAVE the newspapers an opportunity for a fling at Meade, who had earlier expelled two war correspondents at the request of Grant and Hancock. Defending its own William Swinton, who had been caught eavesdropping on Grant, the *New York Times* coldly cited "the general temper he [Meade] exhibits toward the press."[1] Hancock's complaint dealt with a *New York Tribune* story which Grant declared "false and slanderous upon a portion of the Army [Second Corps] now in the field."[2] But since the order expelling both Swinton of the *Times* and William Kent of the *Tribune* had been issued by Meade, it was he who was blamed.[3]

"It is disgusting to see the Papers put our failure on Papa's shoulders after having credited all the successes to Grant," complained Captain George Meade.[4] Some newspapers indeed were praising both Grant and Burnside. Always first with the news, the *New York Herald* predicted that Meade would be relieved and have no further command.

[1] *New York Times*, July 14, 1864. "They [the newspapermen] do not dare to address him. With other generals, how different."—*Meade's Headquarters*, 359.

[2] *O.R.*, XL, pt. 2, 593.

[3] Although acknowledging that the expulsion order had been made "by direction of the Lieutenant-General commanding," the *Times* concentrated its editorial attack upon Meade. Swinton, it declared, "is one of the most intelligent, impartial and competent of correspondents." Sylvanus Cadwallader of the *New York Herald*, who was close to Grant, held a different view. Swinton, he wrote, was "cold-blooded, conceited and prejudiced to a surprising extent. . . . So far as he had sympathy for any person, or any cause, he was heartily in sympathy with the Southern Confederacy."—Swinton's role of eavesdropper as Grant talked privately with Meade, an order of Burnside's to have him shot, and related episodes are detailed in Cadwallader, *Three Years with Grant*, 210–13. William Kent of the *Tribune* also was ordered to leave the lines after Hancock had complained of an article, printed June 27, implying that he had declined to co-operate with Smith in the attack on Petersburg. A *New York Herald* story of June 30, incidentally, offended General Wright, etc., etc.—*O.R.*, XL, pt. 2, 559; pt. 3, 40–41.

[4] Letter of August 7, 1864, Meade Papers.

Hooker again was advanced as his successor despite the fact that he would stand no chance with Grant. Sardonic comment was heard at the Confederate capital: "Meade being as near a gentleman as a Yankee comes, he's probably become distasteful to the Washington concern."[5]

Public opinion and the Crater defeat may have affected the selection of a military head for the newly organized Middle Division. Combining operations in West Virginia, the Shenandoah Valley, and other areas north of the Potomac, the post had become an important one. In late July, Lincoln had temporarily named Halleck, whom Grant did not want, and the President demurred over the suggestion that either Franklin, Grant's first choice, or Meade be sent.[6] Franklin had once quarreled with Burnside, who could swing political weight, and now Meade and Burnside were at odds.

Furthermore, complaints had been made concerning Meade's temper, which Burnside, Warren, Quartermaster Rufus Ingalls, and others had felt. Captain Porter of Grant's staff believed that Meade's fits of anger "stood him at times in good stead in spurring on everyone,"[7] but in view of all circumstances the point could be made that a new man would be more acceptable politically. While Meade debated with himself whether he wanted to be sent north to oppose General Jubal Early, who was raiding as far north as Chambersburg, Pennsylvania, Grant talked with Lincoln at an unheralded meeting at Fortress Monroe. When he turned to Sheridan as a compromise candidate, the President approved.[8]

Meade learned of the selection with mixed feelings. As Grant later explained matters, the President did not wish to separate him from the Army of the Potomac, since that action might be viewed as disapproval. This explanation did not go down easily, and Meade felt that other factors were involved. If it was a matter of temper, a choice could hardly be made between him and Sheridan, who was known as hair-trigger.[9]

[5] *New York Herald*, August 3, 1864; Robert G. H. Kean, *Inside the Confederate Government* (ed. by Edward Younger), 169.

[6] *Meade*, II, 216; Sandburg, *Abraham Lincoln*, 529; Richard O'Connor, *Sheridan the Inevitable* (Indianapolis, 1953), 189; *O.R.*, XXVII, pt. 3, 374, 408, 433–34.

[7] Porter, *Campaigning with Grant*, 209.

[8] *Meade*, II, 218–19.

[9] O'Connor, in *Sheridan the Inevitable*, contends that following expulsion from the Military Academy, Sheridan never again let his temper get out of hand. See pages 35–36, 105. Cadwallader believed that Sherman, who, he said, "was often beside him-

If it was felt that the younger man would be quicker, there would be misgivings on this score as the campaign haltingly progressed. But Sheridan received a hint of the political importance of his selection when he heard it intimated in Washington "that the defeat of my army might be followed by the overthrow of the party in power."[10] Lincoln was hopeful for him, Secretary Stanton doubtful, believing him too young at thirty-three years of age.

Knowing Sheridan to be an ambitious man, Meade could not warm to the assignment of the Sixth Corps to his army. Sheridan also received most of the cavalry, a small-sized Eighth Corps, formerly the Army of West Virginia, and Nineteenth Corps troops sent from Louisiana. This would give him about 36,000 men, or a heavy balance over the invader, but both sides would be reinforced. On August 7, 1864, Sheridan took over the so-called Middle Military Division with a mixed force later known as the Army of the Shenandoah.[11]

Something more of significance came out of Washington. The War Office attitude toward any proposed field strategy was brought home to Grant after he had notified Halleck that Sheridan was "to put himself south of the enemy and follow him to the death." South of the enemy? When Lincoln saw the message, he wired Grant, who was seeking to cut Early off: "It will neither be done nor attempted unless you watch every day and hour and force it."[12] At least Lincoln was aware of what the War Office might be doing. As Grant explained the matter in later years, "It was impossible for him [Stanton] to avoid interference with armies covering the Capital when it was sought to defend it by an offensive movement,"[13] and he cited the Secretary's physical timidity. Had Lincoln shown Meade this same confidence by advising him likewise in midsummer, 1863, instead of holding him up, it might have helped matters; but the President could not then act

---

self with anger and wrath," had more of a temper than Meade, who "rarely gave offense to subordinates or superiors." Cadwallader, *Three Years with Grant*, 344. This is an interesting view.

[10] Sheridan, *Personal Memoirs*, I, 500.

[11] *Battles and Leaders*, IV, 501.

[12] Grant, *Personal Memoirs*, II, 318.

[13] *Ibid.*, 537. As Grant further analyzed the situation, he saw Halleck "a little afraid to have a decisive battle fought . . . for fear it might go against us and have a bad effect on the November elections."—*Ibid.*, 332. See also comment on "timid, restrictive caution" in Catton, *A Stillness at Appomattox*, 271.

independently of the War Office, as he was now doing and persuading Grant to do.

Casualties, illness, desertion, and the withdrawal of Wright reduced Meade's infantry to only about 33,700 effectives. These comprised forces under Warren, Hancock, and John G. Parke, lately Ninth Corps chief of staff and now successor to Burnside. The Eighteenth Corps was technically under General Butler, but Ord, commanding, was invariably co-operative.

At least the Ninth Corps would be more capably led. If Parke, a clear-headed adviser and good liaison man, had not been absent on sick leave, the affair of July 30 would have resulted less disastrously and perhaps even favorably. A military court presided over by Hancock decided that Burnside had failed to obey orders, and he received a thirty-day leave which would be indefinitely extended. Ledlie and Ferrero were cited for neglect of duty. All three went their separate ways following a farewell party. Riding over to Ninth Corps headquarters on business, Colonel Lyman heard "the sound of minstrelsy and playing upon the psaltry [*sic*] and upon the harp; to wit, a brass band tooting away at a great rate."[14] Although conviviality was the keynote, Lyman detected an appearance of leave-taking.

As usual, Meade sympathized with the fallen leader, although he was rather plain-spoken about it. "I feel sorry for Burnside because I really believe the man half the time don't know what he is about and is hardly responsible for his acts," he wrote Margaret.[15] It was simply a case of a round peg in a square hole; as a postwar senator from Rhode Island, Burnside would end his days with a surfeit of honors won.

One of Petersburg's chief attractions for the Federal army was its railroads. Of the three main lines radiating out to the southeast, southwest, and south, only the Norfolk and Petersburg was within the works drawn east of the city. Late in June, cavalry led by General James H. Wilson had destroyed sixty miles of other road, some in remote areas such as Burkeville, a junction for the Petersburg and Lynchburg and the Danville Railroad to Richmond. The cost was excessive—1,501 casualties, twelve guns, and the wagon train—and all roads remained in enemy hands. After repairs, trains were soon running and again bringing supplies to Lee's army.

14 *Meade's Headquarters*, 211.
15 *Meade*, II, 221.

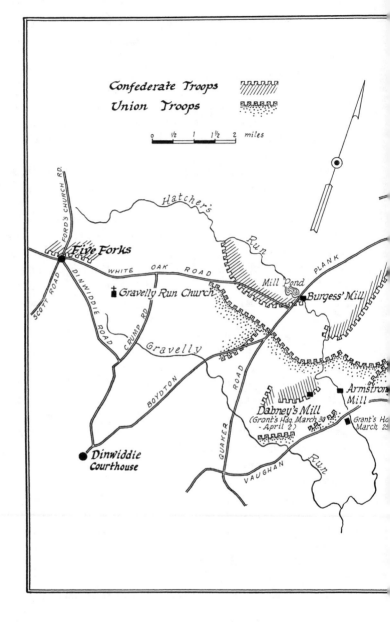

Confederate Troops
Union Troops

0    ½    1    1½    2    miles

FORD'S CHURCH RD.

Hatcher's Run

Five Forks

SCOTT ROAD

DINWIDDIE ROAD

WHITE    OAK    ROAD

CRUMP RD.

† Gravelly Run Church

Gravelly

Mill Pond

PLANK

Burgess' Mill

BOYDTON

Run

QUAKER    ROAD

Dabney's Mill
(Grant's Hdq. March 30
- April 2)

Armstrong
Mill

Grant's Ha
March 29

Dinwiddie
Courthouse

VAUGHAN    Run

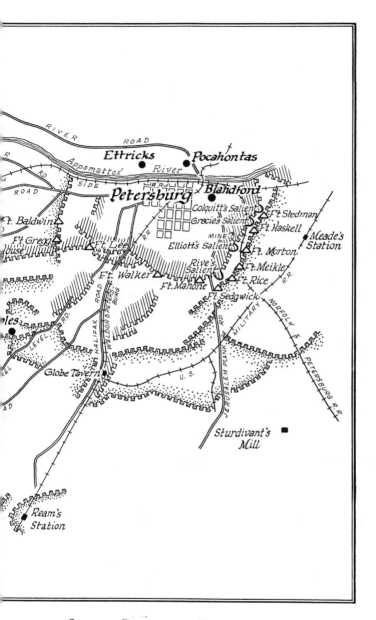

SIEGE OF PETERSBURG, VIRGINIA

Grant backed into a regular campaign against the railroads after again sending Hancock north of the James to threaten Richmond's defenses, a move for which Lee was amply prepared. It had been reported that three divisions (actually only one) had been sent to support Early, and thinking of Sheridan, Grant sought to induce Lee to bring some back.[16] After Hancock lost a hard fight at Deep Bottom, Meade, who had been reconnoitering, suggested another means. Toward the Federal left, Lee's defense line looked a little thin. It was decided that Warren should seize and hold a portion of the Weldon and Petersburg Railroad, a sensitive Confederate artery leading south from the city. On August 19, Warren won his first engagement since Bristow Station by holding a position at Globe Tavern on the Halifax Road which paralleled the rail line. "I am delighted to hear the good news . . . and most heartily congratulate you and the brave officers and men,"[17] Meade wired him in relief, and rode through a downpour of rain to join him next day. Aided by the Ninth Corps on his right, Warren held on, although not without serious loss when a resourceful foe found his right flank uncovered. On August 20, as the fighting continued, Hancock was summoned from north of the James.

Of Hancock's many campaigns, this would prove the most difficult. For eight days his troops had marched and fought with varying success, and now they plodded all night over roads deep in mud. They rested only long enough to boil coffee and have breakfast, then hurried on again toward the Weldon Railroad. When the weather turned hot after the rain, hundreds "fell helpless."[18]

Meade notified Grant that the Second Corps was so exhausted that nothing more could be expected of it for the rest of that day, August 21, but since Warren's fieldworks were stout, he needed no immediate aid. Next morning, Second Corps parties shielded by cavalry began tearing up track as far as Reams Station, about fifteen miles south of Globe Tavern. Each day more track was destroyed, and on the twenty-fifth men were still hacking away when word reached Hancock that enemy troops were passing southward. But no one erred on the side of caution until later that day. Nothing was done to strengthen some old field-

[16] *O.R.*, XXXXII, pt. 2, 244.
[17] *Ibid.*, 309.
[18] MHSM *Papers*, Vol. V, 271.

works at Reams Station, and although Hancock beat off one assault, when attacked later that day, his ranks could not be rallied. The strength had gone out of his corps.[19]

Meade sent two Ninth Corps divisions to help, but by a roundabout route to avoid any enemy forces waiting along the railroad. General O. B. Willcox, who arrived too late, heard a despairing Hancock avow that he could have won easily had his men been as staunch as he had known them. And had the reinforcements been sent directly down the railroad, "we would have whipped him." A Petersburg newspaper quoted Lee as claiming nine guns, seven flags, and two thousand prisoners, a fairly accurate count. Reams Station had to be given up permanently, but the Fifth Corps was still astride the railroad near Globe Tavern.[20]

Two days before Hancock's defeat, President Lincoln had written, "It seems exceedingly probable that this Administration will not be re-elected."[21] In the Shenandoah Valley, Sheridan had retired to a defensive line without dealing a hard blow. Below Petersburg, Grant seemed to fumble, but he nevertheless had arrived on the direct road to victory. The loss of the Weldon and Petersburg was serious for the Confederates—Lee now would have to haul his supplies around the area Warren had fortified. Should more supply routes be lost, his men could be starved out.

Action not all along the line but along Lee's sensitive flanks could close out the war, even though Grant should win only one battle in three. Food and clothing in almost unlimited supply assured Yankee recovery after defeat. Barring setbacks from campaign fatigue and hot weather, the troops were generally healthy. "Old Meade," wrote one who ate regularly, "certainly fed, clothed and paid his troops better and more promptly than any other commander the Army of the Potomac

---

[19] "We can beat them yet! Don't leave me, for God's sake," Hancock was heard to shout in the heat of the fighting.—John D. Billings, *History of the Tenth Massachusetts Battery,* 253.

[20] *Battles and Leaders,* II, 573; *O.R.,* XXXXII, pt. 2, 556; Walker, *History of the Second Corps,* 546, 563, 598. For the Corps to retain all its guns and colors had been a matter of honor. The defeat, wrote General Walker, was but the logical result of the system of "attacking all along the line" as at Cold Harbor where Hancock lost heavily.—*Ibid.,* 521, 605.

[21] Sandburg, *Abraham Lincoln,* 543.

ever had. The way he would sometimes whoop up his Quartermasters and Commissaries was a caution."[22]

While Meade had something tangible and nourishing to work with, Lee could not supply his men properly.[23] When Warren got astride the Weldon Railroad, the tide definitely turned, and no doubt of final victory could be entertained as Atlanta fell to Sherman on September 3. Bands played patriotic airs, and shotted salutes broke out in celebration all along the Federal front.

Meade's thoughts, however, were diverted by personal cares, a labored topic in the almost daily letters to Margaret. His oldest son, who had been studying law, was losing ground to tuberculosis. A sea voyage in company with a physician was debated. Meade snatched some time to go home for four days, and leaving Philadelphia "very sad and dispirited," he was gratified by an offer from Secretary Stanton to place a government steamer at his wife's disposal should the trip be decided upon. It was decided finally that Sergeant was not well enough to make the trip.[24]

With Meade back in camp, Grant left to talk with Sheridan in the Shenandoah. That officer fortunately had arrived at a plan which on September 19 brought initial victory at Opequon Creek near Winchester. Meade's responsive guns blasted away for an hour, enemy artillery joining in. Hundreds of bursting shells deepened the roar, and echoes under low cloud formations were prolonged. "Such a grand cannonade from several hundred guns would be esteemed in Europe a sight and sound so well worth seeing and hearing that a long journey would be undertaken to be present," wrote General Humphreys. "Yet several at our headquarters, waking at the first guns, fell asleep again in a few minutes."[25]

Grant continued to postpone further action around Petersburg. Meade hailed another victory by Sheridan, at Fisher's Hill, as "very great news . . . a very great feat,"[26] and again the guns thundered at sunrise, raining shot and shell upon an unelated foe. Even without

[22] Buell, *The Cannoneer*, 250. "Since we have left Culpeper, I have not seen troops look so healthy."—Colonel Lyman to wife, October 2, 1864, *Meade's Headquarters*, 238.

[23] Freeman, *R. E. Lee*, III, 491.

[24] Meade to wife, September 8 and 10, 1864, *Meade*, II, 226–27; also MS letters of September 16, October 9 and 11, Meade Papers.

[25] Humphreys, *Andrew Atkinson Humphreys*, 252–53.

[26] *Meade*, II, 230.

another battle on his immediate front, Meade could sense that the enemy was reeling. "The Rebels are being exhausted and now is the time to strike heavy blows," he wrote Captain Sam Ringwalt, who was caring for Old Baldy on his Pennsylvania farm.[27]

His army leaders successful on other fronts, Grant planned a double blow north and south of the rivers, not only to gain ground below Richmond but to stride nearer the single railroad left open to Lee. To the troops under Butler was assigned the task of surprising enemy defenses across the James, while Meade pushed along the right of Lee's attenuated line. A part of Richmond's outer defenses, Fort Harrison had the advantage of open country in its front but was weakly manned. On September 29, Ord and Birney, the latter now with Butler, led the attack, surprising and taking it early, then turning to the next post near by. There they were beaten off, but Meade moved that day to extend the line already drawn across the Weldon Railroad.

A short distance west of the road, enemy redoubts tapered off at a place known as Peeble's Farm. September 30 and October 1 were battle days, Griffin and Romeyn B. Ayres of Warren's Corps seizing two of the barriers as enemy bullets flew high.[28] On the right, General Potter, Ninth Corps, was rapped on the flank by an enemy familiar with paths and positions, but the line was restored before nightfall. Next day, sweeping west and north, Meade extended the Federal line to within a few miles of the Petersburg and Lynchburg Railroad, more familiarly known as South Side.

Engineers marked out positions for fieldworks connecting with the Weldon Railroad on the right, and the ground was made secure with redoubts and heavy batteries. For the next several days, Meade spent most of his time inspecting the works and getting lines into their true position.[29] When completed, the entire fortified system stretched for twenty miles from the Appomattox River to Fort Fisher southwest of Petersburg. Never on any European field had fortified lines been so widely extended or made so complete.[30]

[27] MS letter of September 24, Meade family collection. Old Baldy's care cost $3 per week during the fall and winter when oats were supplied; $1 during the grazing season.

[28] *Meade's Headquarters*, 235.

[29] *Ibid.*, 243.

[30] *Ibid.*, 244–45; *Meade*, II, 233. Lyman cites a visiting British officer who in his amazement frequently exclaimed: "Bless my soul."

With the presidential election only a few weeks away, success on all major fronts brightened the outlook for Lincoln. In the shadow were known admirers of General McClellan, who had been named by the Democrats. Little Mac was pronounced by Meade "very unfortunate in his friends and backers,"[31] but it could have been the other way around. "A soldier who don't agree with the Administration must be got rid of," gibed Colonel Lyman. "It is nothing in his favor that he has exposed his life in twenty different actions." The War Office was taking due heed in awarding brevet commissions. Recently, three had gone to officers from the "uncertain state of Pennsylvania," only one of which had been suggested by Meade.[32]

He had been wondering when his own promotion, suggested by Grant in May, might be ordered. Hancock had received his, and Sheridan also had been made a brigadier in the regular army, which brought them even with Meade except for seniority. Failure to act spawned loose talk. The *Washington Chronicle* reported that Meade, normally a Lincoln man, had been driven by mistreatment into the camp of the opposition. Elsewhere it was said that he was delivering the army vote to McClellan.[33] Of course, in no way did Meade, any more than Grant, give any sign that he favored either candidate. He could speak his mind in his letters to Margaret, yet hardly did so except in confessing to a difference with Gibbon, who backed McClellan, "because I decline acceding to all his views." Gibbon, he thought, had talked most unwisely.[34]

In one way or another, political use could be made of a general's fame, and thus the Reverend Henry Ward Beecher's *Independent* weekly compared Meade with three Radical favorites, Sheridan, Butler, and Grant. It was naturally disturbing to be set down as the officer

who in the campaign from the Rapidan to the James under Grant annulled the genius of his chief by his own executive incapacity, who lost the prize of Petersburg by martinet delay on the south bank of the James; who lost it again in succeeding contests by tactical incompetence; who lost it again by inconceivable follies . . . when the mine was exploded; who insulted his corps commanders and his army by attributing them

31 *Meade*, II, 232.
32 *Meade's Headquarters*, 248.
33 *Meade*, II, 232.
34 Meade to wife, October 9, 1864, Meade Papers.

that inability to co-operate . . . which was traceable solely to the unmilitary slovenliness of their general; who, in a word, holds his place by virtue of no personal qualification but in deference to a presumed, fictitious, perverted, political necessity, and who hangs upon the neck of Gen. Grant like an Old Man of the Sea whom he longs to be got rid of, and whom he retains solely in deference to the weak complaisance of his constitutional Commander-in-Chief. Be other voices muzzled, if they must be, ours, at least shall speak out.

The polemicist hailed Sheridan's victories as "brilliant" and asserted that Butler had done his part "promptly and thoroughly." It was asked "that Grant's hands may be strengthened by the removal of Meade." But even under the alleged handicap, "Grant presses with irresistible steadiness toward the rebel capital."[35]

The theory that Butler could do better than Meade and that it took Grant to insure victory would be given a field test late in October. On the twentieth, meanwhile, came news of another Sheridan victory, at Cedar Creek, and again the guns boomed at Meade's order. Once more Grant prepared to strike both north and south of the rivers. North of the James, Butler's army faced General Longstreet, who, battle scars healed, had recently returned to the saddle. He properly read a heavy skirmish line facing his right as covering an attempt on his left flank, and Butler was thrown back defeated.

Below Petersburg, on the Federal left, picked troops from three corps threaded pine woods and forced small streams in a wide turning movement to gain the South Side Railroad. The weather on October 27 could hardly have been gloomier. Roads were muddy under a steady rain, and felled trees, woodland thickets, and swampy rivulets impeded the marchers. Fords had been dammed up to form water barriers. As in earlier excursions, little was known of the country. Either the Army of the Potomac could reconnoiter expertly in such country, or Sheridan could have his cavalry do so, and that decision already had been made. "Nothing could be accomplished with the cavalry force I had in my advance," Hancock stated flatly.[36]

It could be seen, however, that enemy fieldworks had been ex-

[35] *The Independent*, October 13, 1864, quoted in *Meade*, II, 341–43. Meade's comments will be found in *ibid.*, 236. Grant, to whom he complained, said that he "felt as much pained as you."—*O.R.*, XXXII, pt. 3, 317.

[36] Quoted in MHSM *Papers*, Vol. V, 325—General Walker's account.

tended, whatever their strength. Both Parke and Warren were checked when they came upon bristling nests too difficult to carry. Toward the left of the confused line, Grant, Meade, and Hancock rode within range of enemy guns to try to see something, but the group made an excellent target. Bursting shell fire which killed one of Grant's orderlies and wounded two others caused Meade to remark, "This is pretty hot; it will kill some of our horses."[37] To hear him speak came as a relief to Captain Porter, who had thought for a moment that he had been killed by a shell which erupted close by, but Hancock alone happened to be stung by flying gravel.[38] Thinned by its casualties, the official party moved off.

The main highway in that wilderness country, the Boydton plank road leading to Petersburg, crossed the main stream, Hatcher's Run, just above the area then being explored. Hancock and a cavalry force held the road, but neither he nor others could keep the near-by woods clear. When General William Mahone, Hill's corps, a troublemaker in previous fights, forded Hatcher's Run behind the Federals and came out of the woods, Hancock faced a bad moment. Badly mauled at the outset, he rallied his men and counterattacked, but the thrust failed when Fifth Corps troops—Crawford's division—were unable to get up to support him. Virtually lost in the woods, Crawford was baffled for some hours by small forces thrown in his path. Later in the day, after he appeared, Hancock hit the enemy flank and, aided also by a portion of Gregg's cavalry, took nine hundred prisoners, but was unable to turn the entire defense line. It was conceded that Mahone had the advantage of position, but he and his guides also knew the woods.

Since the army had tried to make an end run, the South Side Railroad was still ten miles away. Spirits were dampened by a heavy downpour that evening. The high command left the field early, leaving orders for the sodden troops also to withdraw. Officially termed a "reconnaissance in force," the affair at Hatcher's Run was reported by both Grant and Meade as a success with credit to Hancock, but Colonel Lyman saw nothing more than a "well-conducted fizzle."[39] *Inquirer* reporter Edward Cropsey, whom Meade had permitted to return to the army, let it be known that the movement was never called a recon-

[37] *Meade's Headquarters*, 251.
[38] Porter, *Campaigning with Grant*, 310.
[39] *Meade's Headquarters*, 251; O.R., XXXII, pt. 3, 402.

naissance until after it failed and that it "was not so intended."[40] Assuming it to be a reconnaissance, there was some gain. The nature of the ground and of the enemy's fortifications in that direction had been revealed—knowledge to be used another day.

Election day, November 8, had its amusing side. Meade found it necessary to restrain some accredited political agents, in this instance Democrats, who were supplying the soldiers with ballot forms on which the names of Republican electors were misspelled or omitted. Arrests were made politely and quietly, but no sooner was Secretary Stanton informed than a strong infantry guard was dispatched by special boat to escort the party to Washington.

Otherwise the day passed without incident, interest being lukewarm. Meade did not vote, nor did Grant, and there were some who felt that the country's safety rested more on the success of their own efforts than on that of either political group. Nearly complete returns showed only 19,219 votes cast by the Army of the Potomac, but Lincoln had a majority of better than two to one, which was about as Meade had anticipated.[41] To quiet his wife's doubts, he had written her in September, "I fancy we shall be happy, never mind who is President if God will only spare my life, restore me to you and the children, and graciously permit dear Sergeant's health to be re-established." With the election now past, he earnestly hoped that enough men would be raised to assure "an irresistible onward movement." The effects of the three years' war were apparent in the enemy camp, he wrote Sergeant, and the suggestion was added that his son might well divert himself with Owen Meredith's *Lucile*.[42]

[40] Quoted in Andrews, *The North Reports the Civil War*, 611.

[41] *O.R.*, XXXII, pt. 3, 570; *Meade*, II, 240; *New York Times*, November 12, 1864.

[42] *Meade*, II, 228–29, 242.

# 23. Southern Strength Ebbs
## (October 19, 1864-April 1, 1865)

MILITARY LAURELS ELUDED the Army of the Potomac and its leaders as honors were distributed elsewhere. A much-publicized victory at Cedar Creek on October 19 won another promotion for Sheridan, and it began to be said that Sherman's star was eclipsing Grant's.[1] Although Correspondent Sylvanus Cadwallader of the *New York Herald,* who was close to Grant, became friendly with Meade after hearing it frankly confessed that the Cropsey affair was "one of the greatest mistakes of [my] life,"[2] the Army of the Potomac chief was little heard of save disparagingly.

Promotion was given to Sheridan over Grant's head, nor was Grant notified until some weeks after it had been done. On October 22, Secretary Stanton obtained Lincoln's signature on the document and hurried it to Army of the Shenandoah headquarters by Assistant Secretary Dana. Sheridan was thus advanced ahead of Meade, his senior as regular brigadier general by some fifteen months. Stanton waited until after McClellan resigned on November 8 and after the election news was off the front pages, then let it be known that hero Sheridan would fill the vacancy. Although Meade considered the promotion just and deserved, he defined the maneuver as "a coup-de-théâtre to annihilate McClellan for which Sheridan was very available because of his popularity and recent successes."[3] Otherwise, he himself, who had the backing of Grant but not of the Radical press, might have been named. What Meade felt most keenly was that, with only one exception, all his officers who had been recommended for promotion had received it, and he, the army commander, was that exception.[4]

---

[1] Meade to wife, November 24, 1864, Meade Papers.
[2] Cadwallader, *Three Years with Grant,* 257.
[3] Meade to wife, November 20, 1864, Meade Papers.
[4] Printed extracts from *ibid.* in *Meade,* II, 244.

"It is hard on Meade and I think he feels it," thought Colonel Lyman, who had clear insight into affairs affecting his chief. No one, Lyman was confident, had worked harder or done better in a difficult post. He wrote his wife,

> During a long campaign he has handled an army . . . under circumstances very trying . . . that is to say, obliged to take the orders and tactics of a superior, but made responsible for all the trying and difficult performance. . . . I undertake to say that his handling of the troops . . . has been a wonder, without exaggeration, a wonder. His movements and those of Lee are only to be compared to two exquisite swordsmen, each perfectly instructed and never erring a hair in attack or defence. . . . He has done better with the Army of the Potomac than McClellan, Pope, Burnside, or Hooker; and—I will add boldly and without disparagement to the Lieutenant-General—better than Grant! . . . I don't say he is Napoleon, Caesar, and Alexander in one, only that he can handle 100,-000 men and do it easy—a rare gift! General Grant, as far as I can hear, thinks everything of General Meade, and it is said will have him promoted like the others.[5]

Lyman, who saw Meade at his best and at his worst, was a man of conviction.

One effect of Sheridan's promotion was to make Margaret Meade angry with Grant, whom she readily believed responsible. Since she had always been quick to criticize him, her husband had to remind her to be careful what she said openly. "I know all your views are based on pride in me and love for me," he acknowledged and suggested that she regard Grant more favorably.[6] On occasion, he had sent her evidence of the kindness of Grant's heart, saying, too, that he reminded him of Old Zack and that he was a man above littleness. He could say now that Grant had "expressed regret at not having insisted on my appointment when Sherman was appointed," and had "assured me my not being assigned to the Middle Military Division was accidental, as he always intended I should go there, until it was too late." And finally, "he assured me . . . he had never entertained or expressed any but the strongest feeling in my favor . . . Now, I believe Grant."[7]

Within a short time he was able to furnish evidence of his superior's

[5] *Meade's Headquarters*, 271–73.
[6] Meade to wife, November 5 and 25, 1864, Meade Papers.
[7] *Meade*, II, 244.

"truthfulness and sincerity."[8] Feeling that an injustice had been done, Grant had spoken to Lincoln in Washington concerning the promotion recommended for Meade six months before. A regular major general's commission was then ordered as of November 24, an innocuous post-election date. That hurdle cleared, the new rank was made effective as of August 18, date of the seizure of the Weldon Railroad, which made Meade senior to Sheridan by about two months, although junior to Sherman by six days. The next step now would have to be confirmation by Congress, a slow mover in matters of this special kind.

Since a leader must plot his own path and take it almost alone, high rank is ill conducive to close friendship. Nearest to Meade now that Reynolds was gone were Hancock and Colonel Lyman, although he could confide only in his helpmate at home. It was all the more regrettable that incidents which touched upon Hancock's military honor found Meade unable to mollify that proud officer's feelings. There were unhappy sequels to the defeat at Reams Station and to Hatcher's Run.

A military custom long established but often overlooked was depriving regiments of the right to carry colors if they had lost them in battle. Gibbon had ordered this done to three regiments after Reams Station, and Hancock had approved, but he asked that the stigma rest not on these three alone, for other regiments which had lost their colors at Reams Station and in action since had not been penalized. Concurring in regard to future battles, Meade had ignored the point raised. Although some Ninth Corps regiments had lost their colors at Peeble's Farm, they were composed of green troops and were altogether untried.

General Grant upheld the decision, but complaints soon reached politicians, who went to Lincoln. The President referred everything to Stanton, and so back went the papers to Grant and through channels to Gibbon. Again it was argued that the offending regiments—two from New York and one from Wisconsin—had been deprived of their colors for due cause. "I will not yield," Gibbon protested, "to Governor Randall"—this was A. W. Randall, a former governor of Wisconsin and now first assistant postmaster general. Apparent coolness existing between Hancock and Meade was only slightly eased when the colors were formally restored after Hatcher's Run.[9]

[8] *Ibid.*, 247.

Hancock had experienced some difficult days since he had been flayed by the *New York Tribune* for not trying to seize Petersburg on June 15. Since he was affected, too, by his long-troublesome wound and by being overweight, his physical condition must be taken into account. It is reasonable to suppose, the then approaching election aside, that one reason Grant and Meade put Hatcher's Run in the best possible light was to spare his feelings, although there could be no question regarding his leadership. Correspondent Cropsey sent a more objective account to the *Philadelphia Inquirer* but tried to be fair. After witnessing Mahone's charge on Hancock's right while enemy cavalry swept around the left, he wrote feelingly: "Under circumstances like these, even the splendid skill of Hancock and the soldierly ability of Mott and Gibbon could avail but little. The Corps was forced back, and for an hour and a half the contest was desperate, and the safety of the Corps for a moment or two was doubtful."[10] Not precisely agreeing, Hancock urged Meade to take punitive action again, but in view of the storm which swirled up after the previous expulsion, and that too of Swinton (*Times*) and Kent (*Tribune*), he declined to act unless formal charges were brought.

By the time that the discussion between Hancock and Meade had been thoroughly aired, it was late in November, and a change had been ordered in Second Corps leadership. The warrior who had earned the title "The Superb" in the Peninsula Campaign, who had fought in every major battle through Gettysburg and again from the Wilderness through Hatcher's Run, was about to yield the reins to General Humphreys, who was eager to return to the field. His new task would be the recruiting of discharged veteran soldiers for a projected new First Corps. Time was lacking to prepare charges against Cropsey, "nor do I think it necessary to do now," Hancock informed his superior. Meade's response was a little brusque, but apparently he, too, was vexed. "Your orders," he stated in a businesslike way, "will be issued in a few days. In the meantime, if you wish it, you can go on leave."[11] Hancock waited only long enough to draft an order praising his troops as having won "an imperishable renown."[12] Meade remarked that he

[9] Correspondence, orders, etc. are in *O.R.*, XXXXII, pt. 2, 595, 981, 1071; pt. 3, 14, 40, 494–99, 542–43. The affair seems to have taken up a great deal of time.
[10] *Philadelphia Inquirer*, October 31, 1864.
[11] *O.R.*, XXXXII, pt. 3, 484–85, 699, 705–706, 713.
[12] Walker, *General Hancock*, 290.

went off in a huff, which may have described his attitude fairly well. The departure witnessed no handclasp between the two men.

Since his regular duties had been gradually taken over by Grant's chief of staff, Humphreys was glad of the chance. General Gibbon, who had considered himself next in line, now took offense and stiffly asked to be relieved. Meade, who liked Gibbon personally, could see no end to the affair. "I am the most unfortunate of men," he began to complain. "Humphreys is the senior & entitled to the place."[13] If someone had to be offended, it could hardly be he.

Appearing jaunty and well fed, General Wright's tested veterans returned from their Shenandoah Valley adventure, leaving Sheridan to follow. Save for a Fifth Corps raid along the Weldon Railroad almost to the North Carolina border, the war simmered down to artillery exchanges with the enemy and routine drill. The next phase of strategy as Grant defined it would be for the Army of the Potomac to swing to the left, cutting the South Side Railroad to "make Lee's position untenable,"[14] but this could best be done early in the spring. Meanwhile, in far-off Nashville, a point of anxious interest because of being threatened by General John B. Hood's Army of Tennessee, Rock-of-Chickamauga Thomas soundly defeated and scattered the invader. Fought December 15–16 along the hills just outside the city, the two-day battle virtually ended the war in the West. Meade wired congratulations and ordered the usual artillery salutes. Then came the news that Sherman had taken the city of Savannah with its cotton, which he dramatically offered to President Lincoln as a Christmas gift. The military exploits of others still overshadowed the entangled Army of the Potomac.

With no compensatory laurels to sustain him, Meade had a difficult time with four members of the Committee on the Conduct of the War who wished to restore General Burnside's military reputation. Like Fighting Joe Hooker, Burnside was berthed in a sensitive political area which the arbitrary legislators had vowed to defend. The testimony of Burnside's known friends in camp was invited, but Meade's official report interested the members only insofar as they could search with their questions for flaws. Permitted finally to leave, Meade requested that the committee hear General Hunt and Chief of Engineers

---

13 Meade to wife, November 29, 1864, Meade Papers.
14 Porter, *Campaigning with Grant*, 312.

Duane. After only a brief appearance "these officers came out laughing and said as soon as they began to say anything that was unfavorable to Burnside they [the committee] stopped them and said that was enough."[15] But even though only information of the proper kind was admissible, it still would be impossible to rehabilitate Burnside.

Christmas approached, the fourth in this war that Meade had spent away from home. Headquarters was almost deserted—Humphreys had not been replaced, and four aides had gone home on leave, in one instance to get married. An early gift was a box of cigars from Mrs. Lyman, and savoring the smoke, Meade remarked to his volunteer aide, "I have a Christmas present . . . whom I shall send home to her,"[16] the Colonel straightway departing. Meade welcomed leave to visit home on his twenty-fourth wedding anniversary and forty-ninth birthday, when he found Margaret depressed and grieving over Sergeant's weakened condition. Hushed conferences with doctors and almost constant watch by his son's side occupied him until his reluctant leave-taking on January 9, 1865. There seemed little hope for his son.

An accident on the return trip delayed him several hours. The boat out of Baltimore was groping through ice, fog, and darkness when it crashed into a schooner near the mouth of the Potomac. As Meade went about quieting the alarmed and excited passengers, the vessel stopped at Annapolis for an examination of its damaged superstructure, but was able to continue on to Fortress Monroe.[17] Toward the last of the month, when Sergeant became worse, he was summoned home, where there was little he could do except sustain Margaret. It seemed doubtful that Sergeant could outlast the winter, but because Grant was frequently away, Meade had to notify his wife after his return that he would not be able to leave again soon. "Let me rely on your exhibiting in this, the greatest trial you have had in life, true Christian fortitude," he pleaded and sent the letter home by his son and aide.[18] George arrived in Philadelphia early next day, but death had come at the same hour the letter had been written. Informed of Meade's loss, Grant ordered a steamer to take the saddened father to Fortress Monroe, where connection was made with the Baltimore boat.

[15] *Meade*, II, 254.

[16] *Ibid.*, II, 253; *Meade's Headquarters*, 303.

[17] *Meade*, II, 255; Bache, *Meade*, 272.

[18] Meade to wife, February 21, 1865, *Meade*, II, 263–64.

The higher rank for Sheridan and also for Thomas, promoted for Nashville, was promptly confirmed by the Senate. Meade was still awaiting action nearly two months after his own nomination when Grant went to Washington to lobby in behalf of an action sponsored by himself. Letters received by Meade showed he was actively working. A friendly note from Senator William Sprague of Rhode Island, Burnside's home state, explained that most of the opposition seemed based on that officer's enforced retirement.[19] Senator Henry Wilson of Massachusetts, chairman of the Committee on Military Affairs, wrote that he had reported on the nomination favorably and had no doubt of the result.[20] Grant, who had told Wilson that recognition of Meade's services was well merited, nudged Senator Washburne on the same day. "General Meade," he set down on the record, "is one of our truest and ablest officers. . . . I defy anyone to name a commander who could do more than he has done with the same chances."[21] Grant had not wasted his time. By the end of January, the opposition had been reduced to a handful, and on February 2 he was happy to reveal that confirmation had been carried by a heavy majority.[22]

A series of shifts now uprooted General Butler, who after the election was easily expendable, and put Ord in his place as head of the Army of the James. Assigned to Ord's old command, John Gibbon took over a newly-organized Twenty-Fourth Corps replacing the Eighteenth. Meade was relieved that he was again in good humor as he came to say good-bye. When the effort to recruit a new First Corps failed, Hancock was named to take Sheridan's place with the Middle Military Division. Upon completing his work in the field by laying waste much of the upper Shenandoah Valley, Sheridan was ordered to join Sherman, who had entered North Carolina on his sweep up the coast. Carefully estimating his chances, which probably would have been poor under the well-organized Sherman, Sheridan disregarded the order and directed his march to the White House landing on the Pamunkey River, where he would be able to requisition forage and

[19] William Sprague to Meade, January 22, 1865, Meade Papers.

[20] Henry Wilson to Meade, January 21, 1865, Meade Papers.

[21] Grant to Wilson and to Washburne, January 23, 1865, *O.R.*, XXXXVI, pt. 2, 206; *Meade*, II, 343–44.

[22] Alexander Webb to wife, February 1, 1865, Webb Papers; Meade to wife, February 2, 1865, *Meade*, II, 260.

rations.[23] He thereby served notice that he was returning to the Army of the Potomac, and the chances were that he would be able to retain his separate command.

For his new chief of staff, Meade picked a West Pointer who had been wounded at Gettysburg and Spotsylvania. Son of a famous New York newspaper publisher and Lincoln's minister to Brazil, Alexander S. Webb was only in his late twenties but was a major general of volunteers by brevet. After being felled at Spotsylvania, he had read his own published obituary in a Fredericksburg hospital,[24] a laudatory article which he probably could not have improved. He had served Meade before as Fifth Corps chief of staff, and at Gettysburg had exhibited high courage as a brigade leader. He had a high opinion of his chief, considering both Meade and Sherman as superior to Grant, and he in turn was regarded by Colonel Lyman as "a thorough soldier, wide-awake, quick and attentive to detail."[25]

Even more than battle losses, pinched supply lines and winter's chill were sapping enemy strength. Soldiers who had deserted to Lee's army during the summer were streaming back and bringing others with them. It was appreciated that most of the deserters from the Confederate side were veterans, both officers and men in the ranks, and still others were quitting to go home. Weighing Lee's prospects, Meade could foresee probable victory in the spring and no hope for the South.

A conference between Lincoln and Confederate leaders at Fortress Monroe came to nothing; instead, at the President's urging, the war was to be pressed "to the utmost."[26] On February 5, the day after the emissaries returned to Richmond, Meade moved Humphreys and Warren some distance west of the occupied Weldon Railroad and within the area occupied during the October thrust toward Lee's South Side Railroad. Enemy defiance was successfully countered until toward evening, when Warren was thrown back in disorderly retreat. Meade rode over to help re-form the lines and next day applauded a successful push forward. Extended outward three miles, the Federal line now bridged

[23] O'Connor, *Sheridan the Inevitable*, 238. The author comments, "No one thought to accuse him [Sheridan] of insubordination."

[24] *New York Evening Post*, May 9, 1864; MS copy in Webb Papers.

[25] *Meade's Headquarters*, 307.

[26] Stanton to Grant, March 5, 1865, *O.R.*, XXXXVI, pt. 2, 802. "You are to press to the utmost your military advantages," ran Lincoln's message which Stanton sent Grant.

Hatcher's Run and extended to a road just east of the October arena.[27] This Battle of Dabney's Mill or Rowanty Creek finds no conspicuous place in the chronicles of the war, but as the Army of the Potomac crept farther toward Lee's last remaining railroad, the rank and file began to talk of the beginning of the end. Soon after Meade's return from his son's funeral, he was asked to prepare to move on short notice should Petersburg be evacuated.

A few weeks passed quietly as the army made ready for offensive action. Lee, however, made an audacious decision, and on the morning of March 25 he succeeded in an effective surprise. Distinguished company was then with the Federal army. Late on the twenty-fourth, President and Mrs. Lincoln had arrived, and two days before them, a party of twenty-nine led by Mrs. Meade wearing mourning, son George, Mrs. Joseph Hopkinson of Philadelphia society, and Mrs. Theodore Lyman of Boston. They enjoyed a boat ride on the James, toured the camps, witnessed corps reviews, and were regaled with patriotic band concerts.[28] On the twenty-fourth, the eve of the scheduled departure from City Point, Grant invited Meade to stay over instead of returning to camp. The hour was then late, Meade and his wife retiring, and his absence therefore was not known at the front. General Ord also remained at City Point to watch the arrival of the presidential steamer *River Queen,* which dropped anchor near by.

Wherever the opposing lines were close together along the front, deserters and spies flitted back and forth between the two sides. Whether or not General Lee was advised of the preoccupation of the Federal leaders, his assault on Fort Stedman was very well timed. The work lay within the Ninth Corps area toward the Federal right, and only about 150 yards separated it from the enemy line, with pickets perhaps one-third of that distance apart. For the attack of March 25, a Federal order permitting deserters to bring their arms with them was put to practical use. Enemy commandos waving rifles overran picket posts to surprise and storm the strong outpost.[29] Within the work, surprised Federals fired a few shots and hastily gave way. Breastworks both to the right and left were abandoned.

[27] *Meade,* II, 261; MHSM *Papers,* Vol. X, 90.
[28] George Meade Diary, Meade Papers; *Meade's Headquarters,* 321–22.
[29] *O.R.,* XXXXVI, pt. 1, 317, 332.

Staff officers relayed messages to City Point, where both Meade and Grant were aroused. Grant, who occupied a headquarters room with his wife, was awakened by an aide who tapped on the door and read a message from General Parke saying that the Federal right had been broken. Up and dressed, Grant found Meade pacing up and down outside as he dictated orders to Webb. The tone of his voice, recounted Captain Porter, who was somewhere within hearing, "showed very forcibly the intensity of his feelings."[30] The one thing which Meade had always dreaded was absence from the front during enemy action.

Lee had taken a long chance in an effort to improve morale through victory. Admittedly surprised but not unduly alarmed, Parke rushed up supports from adjacent posts to hem in the intruders. The din of war spread as artillery joined in after daybreak. A Fifth Corps division reinforced Parke on the left at Meade's order, and Sixth Corps troops also pressed in. So hot was the fire from three sides that enemy intruders holding the fort were unable to get out or reinforcements to get in. The Yankees swooped down from a near-by slope in a counter-surprise, retaking two batteries and then another as fresh forces struck. Casualties were heavy among Southerners trying to regain their own lines. At a relatively small loss to the Federals, nine stands of colors and nearly two thousand prisoners were taken. "It was just the 'Mine' turned the other way," Colonel Lyman exulted.[31]

The Fifth Corps division returned in triumph to parade past the presidential party, which had ridden in to watch the show. Driving in enemy pickets in a dash, Wright carried an entrenched line as the fighting spread. Humphreys, too, was given his chance, and after gaining some ground, he smartly repelled counterattacks.

When all the returns had come in, Webb totted up 2,783 prisoners. Including deserters who came in later that night after dark, the enemy losses were put at some 5,000 men against 2,080 for the Federals.[32] His good humor restored, Meade collected his thoughts in a message which closely followed Margaret home. "I am very glad you came," he wrote reassuringly, "[but] I do expect to be pitched into by the *Tribune* for sleeping with you when Lee attacked our lines." Her visit,

[30] Porter, *Campaigning with Grant*, 403.
[31] *Meade's Headquarters*, 323.
[32] *O.R.*, XXXXVI, pt. 1, 155–56; pt. 3, 172–73.

he added, had been a happy one for him, and he had been gratified by the attention she had received.[33]

The surprise attack of March 25 was Lee's final stroke. Hunger and exposure had sapped the life of his army; in some brigades desertions were running as high as 10 or 12 per cent as troops deserted to Meade's army or quietly returned to their stricken homes in the blackened area of Sherman's invasion. All over the North the scent of victory was in the air. Politicians galloping to glory would contend for the honors of war. Already western newspapers were saying that victory could never be won without Sherman's help and the support of the troops from north of the Ohio River. Realizing that he must do what he could to quench sectional rivalry, Grant issued his orders for the spring campaign early.[34] Instead of the first week in May, as in 1864, the last week in March was chosen.

A turning movement toward the left would squeeze Lee out of Petersburg. Grant could then cut loose from his main base, leaving but a small force behind. He had at hand the combined strength of Meade, Ord, and Sheridan, an overwhelming 124,700 good troops, including the 36,700 with Ord and Sheridan's 13,000 cavalry. Lee had possibly 45,000 ragged and roughly-bearded die-hards who no longer bore the outward appearance of soldiers, although there was no question of their courage.

Ord, who was farthest away, would have to move first. On the night of March 27, with his 1,700 cavalry and about half his infantry, he made a secret march to occupy Second Corps fieldworks the following evening. Humphreys was sent across Hatcher's Run on that second day, and Sheridan to the extreme left.[35] From right to left the detached line would be formed by Ord, Humphreys, Warren, and Sheridan in that order, with the Second and Ninth Corps holding the works before Petersburg.

West and north lay the sensitive area, commanding as it did the approaches to the South Side Railroad. The main southerly road left to Lee was the Boydton plank, which crossed Hatcher's Run beyond

[33] Meade to wife, March 26 and 29, 1865, Meade Papers; *Meade*, II, 268. Commenting further, Meade wrote, "Mrs. Lincoln spoke very handsomely of you and referred in feeling terms to our sad bereavement. The President also spoke of you, and expressed regret that your visit should have been so abruptly terminated."

[34] Coffin, *The Boys of '61*, 488; Porter, *Campaigning with Grant*, 450–51.

[35] Humphreys, *Virginia Campaign*, 323–24; MHSM *Papers*, Vol. VI, 213.

GEORGE MEADE, LIEUTENANT, SIXTH PENNSYLVANIA CAVALRY, *1863*

"General Meade expressed regret that George did not accept an appointment in the veteran Third Pennsylvania Cavalry. . . . a place was found where social standing, as well as other qualities, was a requirement." From a portrait in the possession of Mrs. H. H. Francine.

PHIL SHERIDAN'S RIDE TO THE FRONT, *October 19, 1864*

"A much-publicized victory at Cedar Creek on October 19 won another promotion for Sheridan." From a wood engraving in *Harper's,* November 5, 1864.

the Federal line. Just below the Run, the westerly White Oak Road joined the Boydton plank close to fortified works which Lee would have to defend. Other roads would be mentioned in battle reports—the north-south Vaughan, on which Meade took up temporary headquarters near Gravelly Run, and the Quaker, which, running almost due north, diagonally approached the Boydton plank from the right. Swollen by heavy rains to several times its usual size, Gravelly Run swept over both the Quaker and Boydton plank roads, carrying bridges away.

Comfortable winter quarters were abandoned on March 29 as Meade and his staff rode through peach trees in blossom along the line of the Second Corps. They witnessed the rout of a small enemy party from rifle pits near Dabney's Mill, now marked only by a large pile of sawdust, then hastened to join Warren, whose work was more arduous. Fighting its way through a rough wilderness, the Fifth Corps came upon the Quaker Road, and as Meade looked on, wheeled to the right toward the Boydton plank, skirmishers well out. Now too deep for fording, Gravelly Run had to be bridged, and the forcing of enemy works farther along cost the leading brigade one man in every four. But by that night, which was cold, rainy, and cheerless, Warren's front was lodged in the woods within striking distance of the Quaker–Boydton plank junction.[36]

Humphreys, too, had pushed on close to Warren's right, and on the far side Sheridan rounded out the wide clockwise movement. Five miles from Warren's position, he brushed aside a small mounted force at Dinwiddie Courthouse and might have gone farther but for badly mired wagon trains held up in the rear. Meade reported progress to Grant, whom he visited at his bivouac on Gravelly Run, and the General in Chief wrote Sheridan that evening: "I now feel like ending the matter if it is possible to do so before going back. I do not want you, therefore, to cut loose and go after the enemy's roads at present. . . . We will act together as one army here until it is seen what can be done with the enemy."[37]

Another note sent Sheridan next morning advised a complete halt because of persistent rains and soft roads. Withdrawal of as much cavalry as could be spared was urged so that horses and men could be fed

[36] *Meade's Headquarters,* 328–30; Chamberlain, *The Passing of the Armies,* 54; *O.R.,* XXXXVI, pt. 1, 801. This was known as the Engagement at Lewis' Farm.
[37] *Ibid.,* pt. 3, 266.

at the nearest railroad point in the rear. These two messages brought Sheridan to Grant's headquarters to argue against the "one army" formation. In earnest talk, with aides standing outside, he contended that he could easily drive in the enemy's cavalry, and with infantry added to his command could either crush Lee's right or force him to weaken his line in front of Petersburg so that the city would fall. "I tell you, I'm ready to strike out tomorrow and go to smashing things,"[38] declared Sheridan, and after talking privately with Grant he went on his way, apparently satisfied.

Informed that the South Side Railroad would be Sheridan's objective, Meade told Warren that apparently he must act without cavalry assistance. Grant had fallen in with the idea of sending Sheridan an "entirely detached" infantry corps, but realizing that a five-mile gap separated him and Warren, the Commander in Chief did request that Sheridan be prepared to assist the Fifth Corps should it be attacked.[39] This suggestion, however, was not acknowledged at Dinwiddie. Despite heavy rains, Warren skirmished up the Quaker Road that day, March 30, reached the Boydton plank, and pushed one division farther. Disregarding the situation in his rear, Sheridan sent some cavalry to Five Forks, five miles northwest of Dinwiddie, but a mounted force under General Fitzhugh Lee began driving it back. Army engineers struggled with wagon trains throughout the day but covered only short distances.

Enemy movements signified that Federal cavalry and infantry on the army left should get together. Five infantry brigades under Pickett marched to defend the South Side, and four under Lee himself were approaching Warren. Next morning, as he was talking with Grant, Meade started off at the sound of heavy firing in Warren's direction. The first sight of stragglers told the story. Within the first hour of fighting, the divisions of Generals Romeyn B. Ayres and Crawford on the uncovered left were thrown back across Gravelly Run. Meade hurried in Humphrey's leading division, which with Griffin's, the last in the Fifth Corps line, struck the enemy front and left, carried the woods, and seized prisoners. The recoil carried the Federal line some three hundred yards across the White Oak Road extending west, and Lee was driven into the works from which he had started.

[38] Porter, *Campaigning with Grant*, 429.
[39] *O.R.*, XXXXVI, pt. 3, 1325; MHSM *Papers*, Vol. VI, 287.

Although the sun had come out after midmorning, it had been a bad day for Federal forces unprotected by cavalry and for Sheridan himself. Further dividing the army, Sheridan had struck out early for Five Forks, only to be driven back by Fitzhugh Lee and Pickett to Dinwiddie. His maneuver served notice that Warren would not have the cavalry support that had been ordered.[40]

Grant did advise Sheridan that he hoped the cavalry was up where it could be of assistance, but apparently he left any final decisions to Sheridan. "Let me know how matters stand now with the cavalry, where they are, what their orders, etc.," he wrote late that day, March 31. "If it had been possible to have had a division or two well up . . . they could have fallen on the enemy's rear as they were pursuing Ayres and Crawford."[41] Finally, upon the receipt of unfavorable news from Dinwiddie, it became apparent that help would have to be sent Sheridan.[42]

Too, the lines had been extended beyond easy communication. Sheridan was five miles from Warren, who was five miles from Meade, and from Meade to Grant it was two and one-half miles, with the former closer to Sheridan. Since the field telegraph was working badly, riders had to be used to carry some messages, and there was no line west of Warren's old headquarters on the Quaker Road. As head of the Army of the Potomac, Meade could communicate with Warren but not with Sheridan, who had made himself answerable only to Grant. Furthermore, the General in Chief would have to send instructions for Warren through Meade and be advised of results through the same channel.

Now that the cavalry was unable to smash things, Warren had to deal with a variety of orders and suggestions: first, to send a brigade along the White Oak Road toward Sheridan, then the same brigade down the Boydton plank, then to withdraw entirely to the plank road and send a division to Sheridan. Later, all three divisions were to be sent by this road or that.

Some of the orders serve as clues to grave difficulties. Again a drizzle set in, and, for the hard-working Fifth Corps, fatigue. At 8:45 P.M., greatly concerned over Sheridan's safety, Grant asked Warren to with-

[40] *O.R.*, XXXXVI, pt. 3, 324.
[41] *Ibid.*, 380–81.
[42] Chamberlain, *The Passing of the Armies*, 118.

draw from the Quaker Road to the Boydton plank and send a division to aid the cavalry. Ord's mounted troops, who had been guarding Meade's trains, were asked to get ready. One hour later, Meade acted upon a suggestion from Warren that the entire Fifth Corps be sent to engage in what promised to be an open field fight. "Let Warren move in the way you propose," Grant responded; but with little appreciation of the time the movement would take, he gave Sheridan to understand that he would be reinforced by midnight.[43]

This was carrying anxiety a little too far. To have reached Sheridan by midnight via the Boydton plank road was hardly possible even with dry footing. In view of routine preparations and inevitable delays, including downed bridges, the march would take considerably longer. Timed at 10:15 P.M., Meade's final instructions were not received by Warren until thirty-three minutes later, or an hour and twelve minutes before midnight. Even then there was not yet an end to advice and suggestions.

At Grant's headquarters the thought occurred that Sheridan should be notified of his complete authority over Warren and the infantry. At 10:30 P.M., Grant asked Meade to convey this assurance. "The messenger to Sheridan has gone now so I cannot send what you desire about his taking command," Meade replied as patiently as possible. "I take it for granted he will do so as he is the senior."[44] Grant then made notification certain by sending a messenger directly to Sheridan.

Consideration and execution of this and that consumed a great deal of time. Warren's own orders had to be written and carried to each division commander, then to the brigades, regiments, and companies, and orally to the individual troops (in subdued tones so as not to alert the enemy just in front). In making the movement as finally decided upon, Warren would have to turn his men around and march south, then by winding roads west, then north. Capping all this hurry-scurry was the news that the enemy, after its victory, had withdrawn toward Five Forks, so that Sheridan was in no immediate danger. Any headlong rush through the night to reinforce him was therefore unnecessary.

Later reporting that Warren had found the bridge across forty-foot wide Gravelly Run destroyed and that it would take some time to rebuild it, Meade said he had suggested that Warren now take the

---

[43] O.R., XXXXVI, pt. 3, 365–68, 381; MHSM *Papers*, Vol. VI, 345.
[44] MHSM *Papers*, Vol. VI, 342.

more roundabout Quaker Road, or both roads if necessary. Actually the decision was left to Warren's judgment, but "every exertion to re-enforce Sheridan at the earliest moment and the vital importance of it has been impressed upon him,"[45] Grant was advised, and Meade went to bed about midnight suffering from a bad cold.

About 1:30 A.M., April 1, the bridge over Gravelly Run was completed, and Ayres passed over without delay. A halt for ten minutes in each hour was permitted the tired troops, who at once fell asleep, to be aroused only by shaking or slapping. Approaching Sheridan's position by dim light, Ayres was directed about one mile out of his way before he reached his goal near daybreak and formally reported. Permission was given for the troops to rest and make coffee, and for several hours the advance remained undisturbed. Warren marched the other two divisions across country and farther along by dirt roads, arriving from about seven o'clock on.

In view of Warren's arrival several hours after the time that Grant had set, he was held accountable, and when an observer had reported him far to the rear of where he actually was, Sheridan was notified that he could replace him should he fail to be prompt and amenable to orders. Up early on April 1, Meade moved near Grant's headquarters at Dabney's Mill and placed a Second Corps division in the position vacated by Warren.

As the day wore on, sounds of battle drifted in from the southwest. Scant news followed in its wake, but in the area between Dinwiddie and Five Forks, as Sheridan charged on the left, Warren, misguided at first so as almost to miss the enemy, belatedly got all his men into the fight on the other side, and the isolated force of Pickett was broken. Active throughout the day, Warren repaired a break in his line resulting from an order given by one of Sheridan's aides, yet was not permitted to share in the honors of war. Sheridan loudly declared on the field, "He was not in the fight," and ordered him replaced by Griffin. He later shifted his ground by asserting that Warren "did not exert himself to get up his corps as rapidly as he might have done" and that he "did not exert himself to inspire the troops."[46] However, most of the Fifth Corps officers and men stood by their commander. One of

[45] *Ibid.*, 343.

[46] Chamberlain, *The Passing of the Armies*, 142; Sheridan's report, *O.R.*, XXXXVI, pt. 1, 1105.

them felt his removal "a mystery"; another "heard only expressions of disapproval" at Sheridan's arbitrary action.[47] The Fifth Corps had always fought well under Warren.

Army headquarters was awaiting some word from the cavalry leader when at 10:00 P.M. on that April 1 a staff officer brought news that lighted up haggard faces. No credit, however, was accorded Army of the Potomac forces. It was reported verbatim in the newspapers: "Sheridan's Cavalry and Infantry have carried all before them."[48] Meade was moved to inquire softly, "What part did Warren take? I take it for granted he was engaged."[49] Toward midnight, accompanied by a single staff officer, a sad-faced rider appeared at army headquarters, where he was fed by Colonel Lyman. Aroused from his bed, Meade talked in a friendly way with Warren, but was frank in reviewing his past. It could not be denied that the record had been marred by Warren's questioning of orders and his tardiness in action unless in agreement with their intent.

Meade well knew this failing, and he made allowances for it, but Warren had been most unfortunate in being assigned to the hair-trigger Sheridan, who so disliked him. And as long as official feeling against Warren ran high, Meade could do nothing. Soon after the end of the war, he would ask of Grant, although in vain, that Sheridan's victim be reinstated.[50] And not as long as Grant was president could anything be done. After seventeen years, in 1882, a Court of Inquiry calmly decided that although Warren "should have started earlier," still "no unnecessary delay" had occurred on the road, and, again, that the Fifth Corps leader had continuously exerted himself on the field.[51]

[47] Taylor, *Warren*, 233; R. E. M'Bride, *In the Ranks*, 266.

[48] *Philadelphia Inquirer* and other dailies of April 3, 1865. Sheridan, who helped the war correspondents to obtain his own account of the battle, was prominently headlined in the *Inquirer*, the *New York World*, etc. and also received editorial mention.

[49] *O.R.*, XXXXVI, pt. 3, 397–98; Pennypacker, *Meade*, 31.

[50] *Meade's Headquarters*, 333; Meade to Grant, April 18, 1865, *O.R.*, XXXXVI, pt. 3, 822. Warren was then in charge of the defenses of City Point and Bermuda Hundred.

[51] Humphreys, *Virginia Campaign*, 359, 361; *Record of Warren Court of Inquiry*, II, 1559–61; *Battles and Leaders*, IV, 723–24. One who took part in the fight summed up: "From midnight March 28 to 2 A.M. April 1 was 98 hours, during which not to exceed 18 had been devoted to rest or refreshment while 80 hours had been spent in the most toilsome and distressing marches in mud and rain, by night and by day, and in fighting three battles of which the combined casualties had been about 2,000 out of a corps numbering about 13,000. Under these circumstances the wonder is not that they

Formerly, in army experience, cavalry had been used to protect the flanks and the wagon train, to reconnoiter the ground, and to discover the enemy's presence and numbers. General Lee, after arriving at Gettysburg, had reproached General Jeb Stuart for a prolonged absence that had left the main army without cavalry services for more than one week. Confronted by a similar situation, Grant could not have complained, since Sheridan's time was largely his own, and the June, 1864, attempt to take Petersburg was made without thought of his aid. Because of the sheer willfulness of one man, the Army of the Potomac had had to learn to do without cavalry. Nevertheless, had Sheridan and Warren been closer together on March 31, 1865, neither would have been so roughly used, nor would the hard night march after two days of fighting have been necessary.

should have required some time to make the march to Five Forks and effect the dispositions for that attack, but that they should have been able to move at all."—Buell, *The Cannoneer*, 348. Sheridan, of course, had been unwilling to move the other way, as ordered.

## 24. *"The Hills Fairly Shook"*
## *(April 1-9, 1865)*

WARREN'S REMOVAL was but an incident during a night of purposeful activity. Artillery fire rumbled along the Petersburg front; skirmishers were active; and battle lines were either on the move or getting ready. The tension of a fateful hour was felt by forward troops confronting strong works, who lay sleepless and shivering on the cold earth as they awaited the signal. Several days previously, General Wright had extended his line to an area commanding fairly open ground in front of a Federal work erected near Peeble's Farm the previous October. After looking over the ground, Meade had approved a plan of attack which would strike the opposing line in the center.[1] Should the blow be carried through, Petersburg would fall.

Both sides had thinned their ranks in the fieldworks before Petersburg. The Ninth Corps of Parke now held all the ground from the Appomattox River to Fort Wadsworth four miles south of the city, and from this point Wright's Sixth Corps extended out toward Lee's attenuated right. Ord was posted just behind Wright to connect with Humphreys farther down. Orders for Wright and Parke to go forward at 4:00 A.M. on April 2 were agreeably decisive, but disagreement would arise between the army leaders concerning assigned movements.

More eager than Grant, who urged caution, Meade bade Wright follow up his assault "with all the force at your command." No, said Grant, let Wright and Parke open with artillery and push out cautiously to see if the enemy gives way.[2] Even though the lines in front were bristling with all the known arts of fortification, Wright himself was in a hurry. "The corps will go in solid and I am sure will make the fur fly," he wired Meade. "If the corps does half as well as I expect we will have broken through the rebel lines in fifteen minutes from the

[1] MHSM *Papers*, Vol. VI, 419.
[2] *O.R.*, XXXXVI, pt. 3, 498.

word 'go.' "³ While still anxiously waiting to hear from Sheridan late on April 1, Grant suspended a Meade order for Humphreys to attack a bastion at the Crow house east of the Boydton plank road, and this action would delay Second Corps progress next morning. Commanding Humphreys' First Division, General Nelson A. Miles marched that night to reinforce Sheridan, who still had the Fifth Corps at his disposal, but no special orders went out to the man of strong temperament on the far Union left.

His heavy cold still troublesome, Meade was taking the prescriptions of Colonel Thomas A. McParlin, chief surgical officer, which he believed were doing him some good. Although the night was noisy with artillery and occasional musketry, he managed a few hours' sleep before returning to the saddle as the crash of Wright's guns rolled back. Creeping toward enemy picket lines near the main point of attack, Getty's division was met by a scattered volley, then by heavy musketry and shell. Cheering Federals paid little heed to weakened resistance as they raced forward to sweep over the works. In their momentum, all formation was lost. One of Getty's staff officers was agreeably surprised to see troops "without halting or re-forming, regardless of order, rush in from crest to crest, the foremost firing on the fugitives, all cheering, until it seemed as if all bonds of discipline were broken. It was only by galloping ahead and stopping the foremost and throwing them into a line to check the others that the troops were finally halted and re-formed over a mile beyond the captured works."⁴

At last the army had broken through. News from Wright which Meade hurried to Grant revealed that it had taken less than the predicted fifteen minutes to sweep over the enemy line. Soon came another report: "We have captured 2 guns, 3 caissons, 3 flags, and several hundred prisoners."⁵ Parke was having a more difficult time before even stronger works, the first that the enemy had built, but by hard fighting the Ninth Corps managed to penetrate as far as the inner line, taking twelve guns and eight hundred prisoners. Their own losses, however, were not small, and in view of Wright's ability to smash through, it is questionable whether it was necessary for Parke to do more than blast away with his guns.

So was decided the fate of the city that had held out for nearly ten

³ *Ibid.*, 398.
⁴ MHSM *Papers*, Vol. VI, 424.
⁵ *O.R.*, XXXVI, pt. 3, 453.

months. For the defenders, tragedy and disaster blackened the day. Jubilant Federals had come into view some distance off when Lee left his headquarters that morning. Soon afterward he learned that corps leader Hill had been shot by invaders roving about in mere twos, threes, or dozens. Lee summoned division leader Harry Heth, then opposing Humphreys, to replace him. With the help of the best men he had left, he would have to fight holding actions to stem the Federal tide.

Already cut off from Petersburg was Heth's division of Hill's corps, two divisions under Anderson, and Fitzhugh Lee's cavalry. Because the enemy was both north and west of Federal lines, Meade was moving in both directions. Successful above, although Parke was still fighting, he put his order of the previous evening to Humphreys into effect, sending him against Heth in the Crow house redoubts sometime after six o'clock. The position and most of the garrison taken, Humphreys moved Mott's division against Burgess' Mill, also held by Heth forces which previously had made trouble for Warren on the Boydton plank road.[6] About 8:30 A.M., this detachment, now led by General John R. Cooke, began to leave the works, though maintaining a troublesome fire. Wright meanwhile was brought down toward Humphreys, a squeeze on any enemy brigades remaining in the pocket. Most escaped toward the northwest, and upon reaching Hatcher's Run at about nine o'clock, Wright again turned toward Petersburg, supported on the east side of the road by one of Ord's divisions, Gibbon commanding.

Lee was now bargaining for time to evacuate. Facing heavy shell fire, Wright slowly worked his way back and at length pushed his left to the river. Ord and Gibbon fought their hardest engagements below Petersburg at Forts Gregg and Baldwin, then occupied by Anderson with orders to hold out to the last man. The enemy also fought stubbornly before Parke, but not many hours would be left to the defenders of Petersburg. Meade and Humphreys believed that enemy remnants on the far left could be hemmed in between the Second Corps and the forces under Sheridan.

There was both strength and weakness on the Federal left. General Sheridan was probably as good a battlefield fighter as the Union Army possessed, but he had not been under the control of any superior for

---

[6] Mott's Second Division, Second Corps, took this strong work. Humphreys, *Virginia Campaign*, 367; MHSM *Papers*, Vol. VI, 429.

some months, nor was he at this time. Insisting upon independence of action, he acted on his own initiative, and if the main infantry force marched in one direction, he was likely to move in another. Nor was he interested in help from infantry not directly assigned to his command. The Second Corps had been split for this purpose, Miles's division marching early to aid him; but since Humphreys still retained control over it, back it was sent.[7]

Humphreys, after notifying Meade, turned from Burgess' Mill to meet Miles with his remaining divisions, for as soon as the corps was united, it could pursue enemy remnants toward the railroad and river. Sheridan had moved forward that morning and was tearing up track, and the assumption was that he could easily form the upper half of the vise. Meade, who thought he might be farther above but had no means of knowing, sent him a message at ten o'clock requesting him to move toward Humphreys to trap the three reduced brigades of Cooke, but Grant intervened by ordering the Second Corps, except Miles, to push directly toward Petersburg.

As Sheridan turned back toward Five Forks, Miles was left isolated. So instead of concerted action by the Second Corps and the cavalry plus the Fifth Corps, Humphreys would be marching north, Sheridan in another direction, and Miles would find himself immobilized before an improvised enemy work. After sending two divisions away, Humphreys and a staff officer rode off to make certain that Miles was all right. Finding that young officer in a confident mood, the corps leader rejoined his command.

With Humphreys, Wright, and Ord facing Petersburg, Meade rode up the Boydton plank road at 11:00 a.m. to overtake Grant, who had gone ahead. As open country was reached, Colonel Lyman saw the road full of soldiers, "who, catching sight of the General trotting briskly by, began to cheer and wave their caps enthusiastically."[8] The presence of Grant and Meade near points of greatest resistance, thought Sergeant Fred C. Floyd of the Fortieth New York, inspired and encouraged the men, who were confident that they were being safely directed.[9] Cheered all along the way, Meade drew up at a weather-

---

[7] MHSM *Papers*, Vol. X, 91; Humphreys, *Virginia Campaign*, 369; O.R., XXXXVI, pt. 1, 839; Pennypacker, *Meade*, 367–68.

[8] *Meade's Headquarters*, 338.

[9] Fred C. Floyd, *History of the 40th New York* [Mozart] *Regiment*, 246.

worn farmhouse where Grant and his aides were seated on the porch watching Wright and Ord maneuvering some distance away.

Meade probably suggested at this time that Sheridan get into the fight, Grant wiring him at 12:30: "I would like you to get the 5th Corps and all the cavalry except [Ranald S.] MacKenzie across the Appomattox as soon as you can. You may cross where you please. . . . All we want is to capture or beat the enemy." A movement north of the river might well have put an end to the war then and there, but Sheridan would act only according to his own lights. Replying, he contended that enemy troops and wagons were already moving west. "With these impressions," he stated, "I am in some doubt as to the result of my moving north of the Appomattox."[10] Lee's inner defenses, however, were still intact, and it was not until after sheltering darkness had fallen that his main force began to leave Petersburg. Miles had a three-hour battle that afternoon in dislodging Cooke from Sutherland Station, but he was unable to force retreat in Sheridan's direction. "It is a pity," Meade later told Grant, "that Sheridan did not move as I suggested . . . for had he done so, those fellows would have been cut off." Sheridan and the Fifth Corps did engage some dismounted cavalry and tear up some more track that afternoon, but the South Side Railroad, which they had worked over so diligently, was no longer of any use to the enemy.[11]

It is difficult to account for Sheridan's actions unless he was trying to run away from the Army of the Potomac and defy it to overtake him. Toward evening, Meade suggested that a pontoon bridge be placed so that Humphreys could cross the river to stand in Lee's way, but Grant now had a message from Sheridan that the enemy already had escaped up the river and that only a few troops still remained in the city. Then permit Humphreys, Meade rejoined, to take over the Fifth Corps as well as the two divisions with him, cross the river at a point well above Petersburg, and "co-operate with or take orders from Sheridan."[12] Grant then temporarily placed Humphreys under Sheridan, but Miles's fight remained the only action of any account on the Federal left that day.

[10] O.R., XXXXVI, pt. 3, 488–89.

[11] Ibid., 458, pt. 1, 711–12, 1106; Chamberlain, The Passing of the Armies, 186–88, 193–94; Carswell McClellan, Notes on the Personal Memoirs of Philip H. Sheridan, 74–76; Pennypacker, Meade, 368.

Yet the total collapse of Confederate military power could not be much longer delayed. In quiet resignation, Lee rode out of Petersburg with his army that night to join troops leaving Richmond. Pressing against the Confederate capital, Ord's Twenty-fifth Corps, which had been left north of the James River, breached inner works impregnable ever since the temporary threat of McClellan. An eighteen-year-old aide to General Godfrey Weitzel, commanding, slept that night with the flag he expected to raise over the Capitol next day.[13]

Jubilantly awaiting a morning ride into Petersburg, Colonel Lyman printed a terse note to his wife: "The rebellion has gone up."[14] At early dawn wild Yankee cheering was heard, and because of high jinks elsewhere the news from Richmond, which fell at 8:15 A.M., did not reach Grant until almost midafternoon. Slowly at first and then with all speed, over humming wires the word went out from Washington. When the greatest news of the century reached New York about ten o'clock, the city "went off at once into fits," remarked Dr. Morgan Dix of downtown Trinity Church. In Wall Street, which Trinity faced, "there was an immense gathering . . . at which between 5,000 and 10,000 people sang the Doxology, and the bells of Trinity clattered and clanged as loud, as hard and as fast as three raw hands c^d make them go, for the bellringer, Ayliffe, was absent from town."[15] In Washington, D. C., nine hundred guns were fired in a conspicuous waste of ammunition while "oratory burst spontaneously."[16]

Grant and Meade rode through the subdued hostility of storm-racked Petersburg. Greetings were exchanged with President Lincoln, an early visitor with his son Tad. Talking with Grant, the President alluded to sectional feeling extending itself to the spoils of war. Grant himself was still thinking that unless the eastern armies conquered Lee single-handedly before Sherman came up, then credit might be claimed by the Westerners. Lincoln replied that he had not thought of it in exactly that light; uppermost in the President's mind were larger problems.[17]

[12] *Ibid.*, 370.
[13] Humphreys, *Virginia Campaign*, 372 n. Lieutenant J. L. de Peyster of New York City raised the flag.
[14] *Meade's Headquarters*, 339.
[15] *Guide Book to Trinity Church, New York* (1950 edition), 14.
[16] Leech, *Reveille in Washington*, 378.
[17] Porter, *Campaigning with Grant*, 450–51.

But to spur on soldiers marching hard after Lee, the idea was spread that unless every effort was made, then "old Sherman and his bummers will catch him and get all the glory."[18] Sheridan with the cavalry and the Fifth Corps was given the right of way, to be followed by Humphrey's command, now returned to Meade, and General Wright. The western route to be followed would strike the Richmond and Danville Railroad, the only line now left open to Lee. Ord was to follow the South Side line with Parke just behind him.

To reach Burkeville, the junction of the South Side and the railroad from Richmond, the pursuers would have a slightly shorter distance to travel. That focal point was fifty-five miles away as Lee would march, less than fifty for the Federals. Grant and Meade could not tell whether Lee would head west or southwest from Burkeville, but scanning maps later that day at Sutherland Station, they hoped to cut him off before he reached the rail junction.

A start had been made on April 3 following entry into the city. Next morning the two leaders parted, Grant joining Ord. Meade's route ran along the Appomattox until the stream made an enormous bend to the right, where it was lost in the distance. He had hoped that the Second Corps, the advance, would make a long march that day, but it was held up by one of Ord's divisions, which had taken a wrong turn, and then by cavalry entering the road. Humphreys was blocked from 11:00 A.M. until dark. When Sheridan's trains sank in the mud, Meade ordered the road rebuilt and helped them along.[19]

Although suffering from a bad cough and fever made worse by a chill, Meade kept well ahead of his mess wagon and trains. He might have gone supperless had not the resourceful Humphreys provided food, getting him then early to bed.[20] Bivouacking a little east of Deep Creek, Meade was then almost thirty miles from the city, with Lee on an occasionally parallel east-west road only eight or ten miles above him. Enemy cavalry under Fitzhugh Lee was well up, closely followed by Longstreet.

Both pursued and pursuers were then heading for Jetersville Station on the Richmond and Danville, only fifteen miles from Meade's bivouac. Since Sheridan had gone ahead, a collision of some sort was

[18] Buell, *The Cannoneer*, 365.
[19] Pennypacker, *Meade*, 372; *O.R.*, XXXXVI, pt. 1, 681.
[20] *Meade's Headquarters*, 385.

inevitable. That same evening, Sheridan's flankers struck troops approaching Jetersville from Amelia Courthouse, the next station northeast, where Lee had arrived. Riders galloped back to Meade to relate that Lee's main force was only a few miles from Sheridan's front. If the infantry would only hurry, Sheridan urged, "we will have sufficient strength."[21]

Instead of following Sheridan to Jetersville, Meade had intended to pass below it, which would have given him a better advantage. Now he changed his orders: "The troops of the Second Corps and the Sixth Corps will be put in motion tomorrow by 3 A.M. regardless of every consideration but . . . finishing the war; will move toward Jetersville. . . . The major-general commanding impresses upon all officers and men the necessity of promptitude and of undergoing . . . privations."[22] Rations might not be available since the wagon train would have to be left far back in the rear.

General Humphreys, who hardly slept, was off at 1:00 A.M. on April 5, but after covering only a few miles was halted by Merritt's cavalry division filing in from a side road. Since the cavalry had the right of way, Humphreys waited. The delay, however, permitted time for some wagons to come up and for Meade to send on a stiffly worded note timed at 4:30 A.M. If infantry support is needed, Sheridan was reminded, then the road should be cleared.[23] It had been kept open for the hard-marching Fifth Corps, which had waded through mud sometimes ankle-deep to reach Jetersville late on the previous day.

So instead of about noon as expected, the Second Corps began to enter the little village at 2:30 P.M., followed after a long interval by Wright. Without scruple, Sheridan falsely reported the incident in his *Personal Memoirs*: "Although the Fifth Corps arrived at Jetersville the evening of April 4, as did also Crook's and Merritt's cavalry, yet none of the Army of the Potomac came up till about 3 o'clock the afternoon of the 5th."[24] Colonel Lyman, who was fed up with cavalry high jinks, detailed the situation as otherwise viewed:

[21] *O.R.*, XXXXVI, pt. 3, 557.

[22] *Ibid.*, 549. In a dispatch of 8:30 A.M., April 5, Meade notified Grant that he would continue toward Farmville and was told, "Your movements are all right."—*Ibid.*, 576.

[23] *Ibid.*, 581.

[24] Sheridan, *Personal Memoirs*, II, 176.

These cavalry bucks . . . howl about infantry not being up to support them, and they are precisely the same people who always are blocking up the way; it was so at Todd's Tavern, and here again, a year after. They are arrant boasters, and, to hear Sheridan's Staff talk, you would suppose his ten thousand mounted carbineers had crushed the entire Rebellion. . . . The plain truth is, they are useful and energetic fellows but commit the error of thinking they *can* do everything and that no one else *does* do anything. Well, Humphreys could not stir a step till seven.[25]

Pounding over a rough and uncertain road in an ambulance drawn by four horses, Meade found the Fifth Corps, Griffin commanding, strongly posted along a line a mile and a half long with cavalry on the flanks facing the road to Amelia. The arrival of Humphreys made the position so strong that Lee turned away some miles out to follow a wide arc north and west. Had the reinforcement not arrived in time, he might have tried to force his way through to Burkeville, a route now abandoned. The forced march, therefore, had the specific result of changing enemy plans.[26]

Ill as he was, Meade mounted a horse and rode to see Sheridan. He offered to let the cavalry leader place Wright's troops where he wished when they arrived, but as senior officer on the ground he resumed command of the Fifth Corps. Wright's troops, however, did not begin to come in until early evening, the last division not until 10:00 P.M. Unwilling to move without Wright, Meade wrote Grant that he would march against Lee at six o'clock the next morning with all the infantry and with Sheridan,[27] but the latter would make his own plans. Earlier, he had advised Grant, "I feel confident of capturing the Army of Northern Virginia if we exert ourselves," and suggested a conference.[28] Sixteen miles away at Nottaway Courthouse on the South Side Railroad, Grant directed Ord to take and hold Burkeville, then rode to join Sheridan.

The night journey by back roads from Nottaway to Jetersville was not without its perils, especially since a perplexed guide almost lost his

[25] *Meade's Headquarters*, 346.

[26] *Ibid.*, 348. It was no part of Lee's plan, as General Chamberlain put it, to be attacked by the whole Federal Army. Chamberlain, *The Passing of the Armies*, 206.

[27] Humphreys, *Virginia Campaign*, 377; *O.R.*, XXXXVI, pt. 3, 577. Meade's orders were timed at 7:00 P.M., April 5, 1865.

[28] *O.R.*, XXXXVI, pt. 3, 582.

*Courtesy Yale University*

General Ulysses S. Grant to Congressman Elihu B. Washburne. Written January 23, 1865, the letter was misdated December 23, 1864. From the Webb Papers, Yale University Library.

GENERALS GRANT AND LEE AT APPOMATTOX, *April, 1865*

The two leaders discussed terms of surrender at Appomattox Court-house. From a lithograph by C. Inger, 1872, after a drawing by Edgar Klemroth, Sixth Pennsylvania Cavalry, April 9 and 10, 1865.

way close to enemy campfires. Grant's arrival was, of course, a surprise to all except Sheridan, who obviously was seeking a way out. After talking with him, Grant wrote Meade at 10:30 P.M. that although he believed Lee might retreat during the night, the orders to march on Amelia Courthouse would be left unchanged. That they were changed, as asserted in sometimes inaccurate memoirs, or that Grant had an interview with Meade is clearly untrue. "I would go over to see you this evening but it is late, and I have rode a long distance today," Grant's message concluded.[29] Sheridan, however, had gained his point, being permitted to separate himself from the main army and ride directly west. When the infantry headed northeast toward Amelia, it would have no cavalry scouts.

After the alarm had been given, Lee's advance had continued only a short distance toward Jetersville. Taking a right-hand road scarcely more than a mile from the village, the Confederate army turned toward Amelia Springs, the only practicable route of escape. With the exception of Humphreys' Second Division, whose hapless leader, found asleep at 6:30 A.M., was immediately relieved,[30] the Army of the Potomac got off to a good start in the morning. Threading dense woods without regard for roads, Humphreys, on the left, spotted wagons and a long infantry column moving past his front. Had Sheridan's cavalry been up, the movement might have been discovered in time.

Humphreys sent a brigade in pursuit and a courier to Meade, who quickly altered the course of the army, but after Grant had been notified, a message came back asking that Wright, who was Sheridan's choice, move via Jetersville to join the cavalry. In a sweeping move-

---

[29] *Ibid.*, 577. Grant adhered to Meade's orders although he might well have changed them. Sheridan's version of the incident is as follows: "Grant did not reach us till near midnight. . . . We went over to see Meade whom he then directed to advance early in the morning to Amelia Courthouse. . . . Grant also stated that the orders Meade had already issued would permit Lee's escape and therefore must be changed. . . . When on the morning of the 6th Meade advanced toward Amelia Courthouse, he found, as predicted, that Lee was gone."—Sheridan, *Personal Memoirs*, II, 178–79. Whose prediction? Grant, although "strongly of the opinion" that Lee might move out that night, was not certain, and therefore Meade's orders stood.—See Grant to Ord, 10:10 P.M, April 5, 1865, *O.R.*, XXXXVI, pt. 3, 583. Grant was then at Jetersville. In his *Personal Memoirs*, II, 469, Grant also mentions a conference with Meade, but no one at Meade's headquarters ever made any reference then or later to such a meeting.

[30] General William Hays was relieved by General Francis C. Barlow who had rejoined the army after an absence of nearly eight months. *O.R.*, XXXXVI, pt. 3, 597–98.

ment executed with precision, Wright was guided past the rear of the other two corps. Griffin with the Fifth was now on the right of the army, continuing directly north with orders to attack anything found. Humphreys was marching with all speed for Amelia Springs and Deatonsville, the next town.

From an upstairs window at Jetersville headquarters, Colonel Lyman witnessed the fighting four miles away as Humphreys shattered Lee's wagon train and rear guard.[31] After taking a ridge, he kept up a running fight close behind and was making distance almost as fast as any troops could even if not in contact with the enemy. After a final sharp contest near the mouth of Sayler's Creek,[32] the day's yield to Humphreys was conservatively put at 1,700 prisoners, 13 flags, and 4 guns.[33] Darkness put an end to the pursuit.

Humphreys' fight was against the fleeing General John B. Gordon, who was mistakenly following the wagon train instead of the infantry of Anderson and Ewell, which turned south. The pursued were thus separated, and when Wright came upon Ewell lower down on Sayler's Creek, he heard no reply to his guns. Lacking artillery, the enemy waited, then poured in a volley that buckled the Federal line. A gallant and unexpected counter-assault sent Wright again to his guns, but neither Ewell nor Anderson could prevail against heavy infantry odds plus Sheridan's cavalry, which swept over each flank in turn. His entire corps routed and as a unit destroyed, Ewell surrendered to Wright[34] and was himself taken prisoner. So was brigade leader Custis Lee, oldest son of the Commander in Chief. The day's casualty list was overwhelmingly in favor of the pursuers, who lost probably fewer than one thousand in the two battles, Lee nearly eight thousand.[35] Only the blotting out of a detachment sent by Ord to destroy a bridge in his front marred the day. Longstreet was there, and the Federal force was too small.

Detailing the action along Sayler's Creek as a victory all his own, Sheridan reported to Grant through Meade's headquarters: "The enemy made a stand . . . I attacked them with two divisions of the Sixth Army Corps and routed them handsomely. . . . I am still pressing on."[36]

[31] *Meade's Headquarters*, 349–50.
[32] Written "Sailor's" in most accounts (but not in Freeman, *R. E. Lee*), this spelling is taken from the U. S. Geological Survey map *Farmville*, Sheet 1889.
[33] *O.R.*, XXXXVI, pt. 3, 600; Humphreys, *Virginia Campaign*, 381.
[34] Alexander Webb to wife, April 10, 1865, Webb Papers.
[35] Humphreys, *Virginia Campaign*, 384; Freeman, *R. E. Lee*, IV, 93.

Meade briefly scanned the first person singular and turned a cold eye on the bearer. "Oh! So General Wright wasn't there." "Oh yes," responded Colonel Redwood Price, staff officer from Sheridan, "General *Wright* was there."[37] Meade turned away abruptly. At a later hour, when he received the reports of Humphreys and Wright, he sent the originals directly to Grant. Wouldn't it be possible for these officers to receive some credit for the day's victory? he asked. Grant was quite willing, forwarding all the dispatches to Stanton, who released them to the press, but Sheridan's apparently had the advantage of time. As the newspaper stories were made up, the names of Sheridan and Grant blazed in the headlines. Meade was not mentioned, and anything from Humphreys and Wright was obscurely buried in the late editions.[38]

Humphreys, as a consequence, never learning that his dispatch had appeared, always felt certain that Stanton had suppressed it so as to favor Sheridan. It was possible, of course, that it had been held up at some point. Scanning the newspapers in his usual sober mood, Colonel Lyman remarked that if the public could be deceived by telegrams and dispatches, then that would be done. A laudatory review of Sheridan's career was even then making the rounds of the newspapers. The result was such common observations as this: "The generals of the Army of the Potomac are laggards. It required Sheridan and Grant to overtake and beat Lee."[39]

It was April 7, the fourth day after the fall of Petersburg. The Fifth Corps, which had encountered only a cavalry rear guard, was placed on the left flank of the army as Meade gathered Wright in. Humphreys was still racing on at a furious pace, keeping almost the same distance from Sheridan. That morning, the army crossed the blackened path of battle, where abandoned wagons, gun carriages, ammunition of all kinds, tents, and officers' baggage lay. Colonel Lyman saw a hillside at Deatonsville "white with Adjutant-General's

---

[36] *O.R.*, XXXXVI, pt. 3, 610.

[37] *Meade's Headquarters*, 351. In his *Sunset of the Confederacy*, 155, Morris Schaff comments, "Had Wright been one of the smooth foxy men of the world, he would have started an aide to Meade before the smoke had drifted from the victorious field . . . but he was of that other class of old-time West Point men, men who did not boast, and who shunned newspaper fame."

[38] *Philadelphia Inquirer*, April 8, 1865. Previous editions carried the implication that Sheridan was Lee's only pursuer.—*Ibid.*, April 6.

[39] *Magazine of American History*, Vol. XVI (October, 1886), 368.

papers scattered from several waggons of that department; here and there lay a wounded Rebel."[40] To Humphreys fell the honor of checking the survivors at a road junction near Farmville in Prince Edward County, around which battle again swirled. This delay helped Sheridan to gain ground as he moved ahead almost unimpeded south of Meade's route. Since Longstreet, who had suffered no defeat during the chase, was ahead, Sheridan again was permitted to take over the Fifth Corps. Ord and his Twenty-fourth Corps were also accompanying him along roads leading to the town of Appomattox and to Lynchburg, where it was possible that Lee might escape.

Chasing other survivors after crossing to the north bank of the river, Humphreys and Wright had the longer route but kept doggedly at it. From what Meade could learn from captured Confederate officers, the pursuit seemed to be near its end. "They . . . say they believe Lee is prepared to surrender,"[41] he cheerfully wrote Margaret from his farmhouse bivouac that evening. Late that same day, Grant, then at Farmville, sent Adjutant General Seth Williams through Humphreys' lines with a flag. The historic note carried plainly requested surrender. But Lee's reply cautiously inquiring about terms might only mean that he was sparring for time.

Excitement spread next day as another note was forwarded. "Men and officers surrendered," Lee was instructed, "shall be disqualified for taking up arms against the Government of the United States until properly exchanged."[42] Coming up with the army, Grant gave Meade a friendly hail as he overtook his ambulance among Second Corps trains and rode with the column. Toward sundown the rumble of artillery fire drifted back from Appomattox Station a dozen miles southwest.

That the strength of forces in Sheridan's front was unknown gave Grant concern, but he could go no farther that day. Miles away from any village, Meade and Grant lodged at or near a farmhouse known as Stute's, according to Lyman's notes of that same day, and since his own wagons were far in the rear, the General in Chief and his staff partook of Army of the Potomac fare.[43] Grant also had been feeling far from

[40] *Meade's Headquarters,* 351–52.

[41] *Meade,* II, 270.

[42] *O.R.,* XXXXVI, pt. 3, 619; Humphreys, *Virginia Campaign,* 439.

[43] *Meade's Headquarters,* 354–55; Porter, *Campaigning with Grant,* 462. These two varying accounts can perhaps be reconciled. Lyman says that Meade and Grant halted at the Stute house for the night and stayed near there. Porter gives details of a

well. Attempts to remedy a lingering headache by bathing his feet in hot water and mustard, with mustard plaster applied to his wrists and the back of his neck, gave little relief—nor did a second note from Lee. Toward midnight, a staff officer awakened him with a message from the enemy suggesting peace proposals but not outright surrender. Grant was unable to read Lee's mind, and his headache still persisted. "We thought it was all over and fight we must,"[44] Captain George Meade wrote his mother after overhearing a breakfast-table discussion next morning, Sunday, April 9. Taking coffee with Meade at the Stute house, Grant reiterated in a third note that the South must lay down its arms. Feeling a little more comfortable, he rode with the army as far as the village of New Store, then turned left at a crossroads to join Sheridan. Wagons of a dozen war correspondents raised a cloud of dust behind him.

His cold much improved, Meade appeared in good spirits, but he was sorry to lose Grant in the midst of a parley. Lee's notes would continue to come to him and would have to be forwarded. This would mean the loss of much time. Believing peace close at hand, the troops marched almost gaily that morning over the Lynchburg plank road. Just beyond New Store, Meade overtook the Sixth Corps, which cut in behind Humphreys after turning south from a parellel road. His forces intact, he could now deal the finishing blow as he came up with the enemy. Two wandering Negroes brought news; Lee's army, they said, was cut off near Appomattox.[45]

Another note from Lee handed on by one of Humphreys' staff officers reflected this latest turn of events. Although the message was addressed to Grant, Meade immediately tore it open. "I now request an interview," Lee stated in an epoch-making decision, "in accordance with the offer contained in your letter of yesterday."[46] Meade turned to Chief of Staff Webb and began dictating letters to both Grant and Lee while two aides made copies.

It probably would expedite matters, Lee was advised, if duplicate notes were sent through to some other part of the Federal line to reach

bivouac "at a large white farmhouse a few hundred yards from Meade's camp." This was some distance south of Curdsville and on Humphreys' route. On the next road north, Wright was then passing west through Curdsville.

[44] April 9, 1865, Meade Papers.
[45] *Meade's Headquarters*, 356.
[46] *O.R.*, XXXXVI, pt. 3, 664.

the General in Chief, whose present location was not accurately known. In a message to Grant, Meade suggested that a parley be held. Then a copy of the message to Lee together with the original note to Grant from behind the lines went off down the nearest road to Appomattox Station.[47] Still no truce had been asked or agreed upon,[48] and Sheridan's artillery was still booming. Meade spurred the pursuit, first calling on Humphreys to hurry, then sending Webb and a bugler ahead to clear the road of wagons so that Wright could close up.

Meade's ambulance swayed and careened along the crowded plank road. Within a few miles of Appomattox Courthouse, which lay almost due west, he overtook Humphreys. Troops were advanced to assail an enemy skirmish line detected in front. Humphreys had given his orders and was about to hurl his men forward when someone called out that a flag of truce was approaching. "Receive the flag but push on the skirmishers," rejoined Humphreys, who like Meade was willing to end the war then and there, but a group of riders came rushing up with a courier from Lee. In his fourth note to Grant, Lee requested that arms be laid down "pending the adjustment of terms."

Was this still a ruse to gain time? Lyman heard Meade cry out: "Hey! What! I have no authority to grant such suspension. . . . Advance your skirmishers, Humphreys. . . . We will pitch into them at once."[49] But almost as if it were a scene in a play, action was again halted as Colonel James W. Forsyth of Sheridan's staff came on with a Confederate officer to say that a truce was actually in effect. Meade recalled that toward noon, only a few minutes before, the sound of artillery in the distance had ceased. So persuaded, he now advised Lee: "I have no

[47] *Ibid.*, 667–69. The context of Meade's note is indicated in Lee's second letter of April 9 to Grant.—*Ibid.*, 665. But there is an error in the recorded time of Meade's note to Grant. Instead of 10:00 A.M., the time should be either 10:30 A.M. or possibly eleven o'clock. All letters were chronologically entered in Meade's *Letterbook*, and the fact that the note timed at 1:00 P.M. follows one of 10:30 A.M. in the book is indicative of error. Letterbook—Letters Sent, 1865, Meade Papers. Colonel George Meade remarks upon the error in a letter to Adam Badeau, December 16, 1880, Webb Papers.

[48] Eyewitness accounts agree that the only truce granted on Meade's front was one of two hours which went into effect at about twelve noon and was later extended. *O.R.*, XXXXVI, pt. 3, 605 (Meade's report), 666; George Meade Diary, April 9, 1865, entry, Meade Papers. Another version of events appears in Freeman, *R. E. Lee*, IV, 129, 513–15, but this was taken almost entirely from foggy reminiscences written long years after the event. There is plenty of contemporary evidence available.

[49] *Meade's Headquarters*, 357.

authority to suspend hostilities unless it is with the distinct understanding that you are prepared to accept the terms . . . sent you yesterday. Your letter will be at once forwarded. . . . To enable . . . Forsyth to return and report my action, I agree to a suspension of hostilities until 2 P.M. this day, and shall be glad to prolong it on being advised by you that you agree to General Grant's terms."[50] Colonel Forsyth speedily departed.

There was a large and receptive audience to all these proceedings, but nothing was made clear. The men in the ranks who had been so suddenly halted began asking each other just what was up. When an order was given for them to move from the road into the fields and make their coffee, it became all the more mysterious. "The troops knew enough to get breakfast without orders," a veteran remarked scathingly.[51] Many, however, were too tired to care, relaxing at full length to get some lost sleep. But active minds began to circulate rumors.

Someone was saying that stacked rifles had been seen within the enemy lines and that this could mean outright surrender. On the other hand, Sergeant S. D. Hunter of the 116th Pennsylvania heard it said that Lee would make a last rally and die at the head of his troops rather than surrender to Grant. More important, Hunter saw and heard much that actually took place—events he never forgot. "In the midst of conjectures," he later narrated,

> there was heard cheering . . . and soon we saw that modest hero of Gettysburg, General George G. Meade and staff, coming up on a gallop, passing through our lines and over into the enemy's stronghold. Now for surmising! What will Lee do? What great suspense now hung over us. We talked of nothing but the return of our great leader Meade. Soon an officer . . . galloped back to headquarters. Soon after, the order was given to fall in. We marched to within 100 yards of the Rebels' breastworks. . . . When the regiment was properly aligned, another was placed on the opposite side of the road in like manner, and so continued the entire corps. . . . Standing at attention we "Order Arms." Could it be that Lee was going to surrender?
>
> It was about 4 P.M. when we heard the clatter of horses coming from within the Johnnies lines. The order "Attention, carry arms!" was given, and we awaited their approach. As General Meade . . . stopped in front

[50] *O.R.*, XXXXVI, pt. 3, 666.
[51] Page, *History of the 14th Connecticut*, 334.

of our Regiment no salute was given except the dipping of the colors. Taking his cap in his hand he bowed and announced: "General Lee has surrendered to General Grant!" Turning to the regiment on the opposite side of the road he repeated the message and so on. . . . It now seemed as if the hand of God's life had been suspended for several minutes. Not a word was spoken, not a movement was made. Officers and men stood like regiments of statues in the perfect silence. Then like an electric shock there broke forth one grand shout, and cheer after cheer rent the air. The Lynchburg Plank Road became one swaying mass of joyful Yankees.[52]

Genuine exultation soared to rare heights. Caps, coats, shoes, knapsacks, and canteens were sent flying. Completely beside themselves, the Yankees were dancing, laughing, shouting, crying, hopping up and down, rolling on the ground, and thumping the earth with their fists. Batteries were run out, and the big guns thundered in triumph. Banners by the score were raised, and for the very first time the Old Man himself was seen waving his cap. As the wild uproar vibrated over the enemy lines, even the Confederates joined in.

A Massachusetts gunner thought it amazing and so reported: "I have never seen such a sight. . . . The men hurrahed as if their throats would split. Soon after General Meade came riding through the lines, all the flags were given to the breeze and the men crowded around them and cheered lustily, rushing after General Meade all the time. . . . Everyone had a smile on his face though they had been without rations for a day and a half."[53]

"Such yelling and cheering," George Meade wrote his mother, "I never heard . . . it is the grandest day of my life. . . . Papa is a great deal better."[54] General Webb saw men crazy with joy throw their caps under the horses' hoofs as Meade passed. "His name was yelled and screamed in a way I never dreamt any man's could be,"[55] he wrote home after the great day had passed. To a soldier of the 140th Pennsylvania it was an earth-shaking scene:

All the pent-up emotion of our hearts burst forth in one mighty shout

[52] St. Clair Mulholland, *Story of the 116th Pennsylvania Regiment*, 313–15.

[53] Alfred S. Roe and Charles Nutt, *History of the First Regiment of Heavy Artillery, Massachusetts Volunteers*, 212.

[54] April 9, 1865, Meade Papers.

[55] April 10, 1865, Webb Papers.

. . . while the bands struck up our national airs and the artillery broke forth in salutes. How the hats of the boys flew skyward and *the hills fairly shook* with the cheers of massed thousands as General Meade, with uncovered head and beaming face, rode down the lines with the glorious news.[56]

The last several days had been hard. Hungry and footsore from the forced marches, the victors in the chase were quite as weary as the unfortunate pursued. Some had declared that another step was impossible, and yet as the band struck up "Yankee Doodle," the men joyfully marched from the field "with steps as light as boys just out of school."[57]

[56] Stewart, *History of the 140th Pennsylvania*, 270–71.
[57] Page, *History of the 14th Connecticut*, 335.

## 25. End of Days
## (April 10, 1865-November 11, 1872)

"VICTORY! PEACE!" sang the headlines on Monday, the tenth. In Northern towns and cities eager hands grasped bell ropes; cannon wherever found had to be fired whether serviceable or not. Joviality and gloom prevailed on the opposite sides at Appomattox, although Yankee rations unloaded from freight cars brought down the South Side Railroad improved the lot of the defeated. The troops had been forbidden to mingle, but where the lines were closest, coffee was exchanged for tobacco, the one staple left to the Southerners.

Former West Pointers and Mexican War veterans could exchange visits for the first time in four years. Both Longstreet and General Cadmus M. Wilcox of Hill's corps, who had attended Grant's wedding back in 1848, came to national headquarters with other Confederate officers, including Pickett and Heth. Wanting especially to see Lee, Meade obtained permission from one of Longstreet's generals for himself and his staff to pass through the lines. Along the way, hearing a Southerner remark that he looked like one of them, he declared it a compliment. Bravery had to be admired, he observed to his Confederate guide; say what you would, such men had to be respected.[1] Lee and his aides were seen approaching the little cavalcade. Meade bowed and removed his cap. "Good morning, General," he said in his best manner, but as Lee had not seen him since Veracruz eighteen years before, he had to explain who he was. "What are you doing with all that gray in your beard?' the Confederate leader inquired. "You," Meade responded, "have to answer for most of it."[2] He accepted an invitation to enter Lee's tent, where the two men discussed the long siege at Petersburg. Meade was surprised to learn that only 33,000 defenders

[1] Southern Historical Society *Papers*, Vol. XIV, 562. Meade was accompanied by General Charles W. Field.
[2] *Meade's Headquarters*, 360.

334

had been in the works at the very end, while the Federals up front had numbered about 50,000.

Near by lingered General Henry A. Wise, an embittered, unreconciled old man full of hate but still Margaret Meade's brother-in-law. Meade greeted him warmly as an old friend and tried to make conversation. The former Governor of Virginia looked little different from any impoverished backwoodsman. Calling at his quartermaster's upon his return, Meade ordered a pair of mules and an ambulance loaded with supplies sent to the Wise family in Richmond and also transmitted $50 in cash, which had to be considered a loan. Already repaid was a sum advanced to a son, Colonel Peyton Wise, whom Meade had helped some months before when he learned that the youth was a prisoner. Bitterness was less intense in the soldier; other members of the family whom Meade later saw never wished to forgive or be forgiven.[3]

As soon as possible the troops began moving out to an encampment at Burkeville. On the eleventh, the Second Corps quit camp, then the Sixth, followed by most of the Fifth, which left a division behind for the April 12 formal surrender. From its extended position along the South Side Railroad, the Ninth Corps turned back to Sutherland Station, later embarking for Washington.

Could it have been expected that jubilation would prevail and that banners would wave gaily during the long marches? On the contrary, everyone felt numb both inside and out. First of all, the April weather was bad. A cold downpour drenched the troops as they plodded "with less of display than they had marched from many a field of defeat."[4] Too, they felt disappointed because Grant had gone to Washington without saying a word, even of thanks. But worst of all, laurels had been snatched away from the Army of the Potomac. Few newspapers arrived in camp, but those that did were tossed disgustedly aside. Humphreys' battle on April 6 had gone practically unnoticed, and it was he who had checked the enemy flank, enabling Sheridan to get ahead. General Wright had been effectively smothered by Sheridan, and feelings were rankled by the fact that no officer from the Army of the Potomac had been invited to the treaty council with Lee. As General

---

[3] Wise, *Life of Henry A. Wise*, 368; E. M. Woodward, *History of the 198th Pennsylvania Regiment*, 61; *Meade*, II, 238, 270; Meade to wife, April 18, 23, 29, Meade Papers.

[4] William H. Powell, *The Fifth Army Corps*, 870.

Webb observed sourly, no one tried very hard to get Meade,[5] but Sheridan, of course, was there. Finally, when a Federal division had been selected to receive enemy arms and to parole prisoners at the formal surrender, it had been one under the temporary command of the cavalry leader.

Bound to his chief by long personal friendship, Colonel Lyman found himself "boiling and fuming over the personal neglect of General Meade and the totally undeserved prominence given to Sheridan."[6] Son George declared the whole army thoroughly disgusted. Officers of the Sixth Corps, he wrote his mother, were planning to organize to remedy matters,[7] and this corps had been closest to Sheridan. Meade, too, raged against newspapers "full of falsehood and undue and exaggerated praise of certain individuals who take pains to be on the right side of the reporters." Mrs. Meade in turn was upset and had to be told not to worry, but her husband could say little to make her feel better. "I don't believe the truth ever will be known, and I have a great contempt for History," he wrote pessimistically.[8] A cavalry general who had once served under Sheridan had a similar thought after reading the official reports: "How difficult it is to believe in any History after seeing a page or two of our own made!"[9]

Sheridan was ordered to take a force into North Carolina and make contact with Sherman, and now that the war was over, he consented to go. Wright and the Sixth Corps marched with him, but that officer decided not to send Sheridan his Sayler's Creek battle report as the latter had requested. "I was under the orders of Major-General Meade to whose army my corps belonged," he contended, but Sheridan at once reported the incident to Grant, who would never refuse him. General Theodore S. Bowers of national headquarters wrote to tell Wright what to do, and so from the campaign report already sent Meade, the extract dealing with Sayler's Creek was copied and sent to the unyielding cavalry leader.[10]

Burkeville was a miserable place for soldiers impatiently awaiting

[5] Webb to wife, April 10, 1865, Webb Papers.

[6] *Meade's Headquarters*, 358.

[7] George Meade to his mother, April 22, 1865, Meade Papers.

[8] To wife, April 10, 1865, *Meade*, II, 271.

[9] Gen. W. W. Averill to William B. Franklin, January 22, 1866, New York Public Library MSS.

[10] *O.R.*, XXXVI, pt. 3, 933, 1102. Wright's report is in *ibid.*, pt. 1, 905–908.

orders to turn homeward. The worst of news, which had to be told them, turned their minds from themselves. On the night of Friday, the fourteenth, Lincoln was shot by an assassin at Ford's Theater in Washington, and Secretary of State Seward was knifed as he lay in his bed. Notified of the tragedy while en route to his home in Burlington, New Jersey, Grant returned to Philadelphia that same night to board a special train for Washington. Saddened and shocked officers gathered at Meade's headquarters next morning. Some were heard to declare that if the government were destroyed, then the army would have to take over the Capitol, where Grant would sit as dictator until civilian power could be restored.[11] Meade's formal message to the troops bade them realize that even this horror should not be allowed to interfere with the country's future prosperity and happiness. In words precisely defining Lincoln's role in the war, he recalled the President's active interest in the welfare of the army, his frequent visits to the front, and the deep regard he had won from officers and soldiers. "A generous friend . . . an honest man, a noble patriot and sagacious statesman has fallen! No greater loss, at this particular moment, could have befallen our Country."[12] In Philadelphia, Margaret Meade enwreathed her windows with black and hung out the old battle flags of the Pennsylvania Reserves at half-mast.

On April 17, just before leaving for North Carolina, Sixth Corps troops presented captured Confederate flags to Meade's headquarters. The response to their toil and successes on two fronts was generous and gratifying, and they were credited with the decisive movement of the campaign—the capture of Petersburg. "Gen[l] M—— made a remarkably good speech," reported General Webb. "He speaks with great fluency & uses elegant language."[13]

Grant, who originally had intended to return to the army after a few days, remained at the War Office to aid in the hunt for the assassin and conspirators. He also had to deal with a morose character in General Halleck, who no longer had much to do except to occupy his worn armchair.[14] In former years, when with a leading law firm in San Fran-

---

[11] Chamberlain, *The Passing of the Armies*, 281.

[12] General Orders No. 15, April 16, 1865, *Meade*, II, 273–74.

[13] Webb to wife, April 18, 1864, Webb Papers. The gist of Meade's talk is in *O.R.*, XXXXVI, pt. 1, 909.

[14] As Sherman later wrote Meade, "He was always harsh and boorish . . . and more especially at the end of the war." Letter of November 8, 1871, Meade Papers.

cisco, Halleck had helped write California's constitution and had compiled *Mining Laws of Spain and Mexico*. His *Elements of Military Art and Science*, an outgrowth of a West Point education and Mexican War service, had been generally useful during the late war. Until Grant had been placed above him, he had been the senior major general in the regular army, but although an able organizer, he was poor in execution. Because he had always been personally unfriendly and quite impossible to work with, Grant now sent him to Richmond to head a new Department of Virginia and give orders to Meade. As usual, the Lieutenant General said nothing to others directly affected, and since the change was made suddenly, Meade felt sore in spirit and humiliated.[15]

The action, however, signaled the end of a miserable and idle existence at Burkeville, and marching orders which arrived on May 1 found Meade ready. Military parades in Richmond and Washington were high on the program, and visiting the Confederate capital some days before the army was due to arrive, he paid his respects to Halleck and helped make arrangements. As soon as he could, Meade visited the Wise family and made the most of an opportunity to talk again with General Lee. No longer could anything be decided between them, although Meade did try to persuade the Confederate to take the oath of allegiance as a necessary step toward the renewal of citizenship. The point was that Lee would thus set an example.

Thinking, however, of his own proud people, Lee demurred on the ground that he would not wish to change his status as a paroled prisoner of war until he knew what Federal policy would be toward the defeated. Southern leaders, Meade answered, could help shape such policy by taking the oath and satisfying the government of their allegiance. Yet Lee could take no step that might be considered against public opinion as well as his own conscience. They talked of the Negro, "the great and formidable question of the day,"[16] but Meade could not make any useful suggestions. He admitted himself sad at heart in leaving this once powerful figure. Lee himself was a forceful reason why the North and South should arrive at amicable terms, but with Lincoln gone, there was no guidance. Some days later, when talking with civic leaders

[15] Meade to wife, April 23, 1865, and George Meade Diary, April 23 entry, Meade Papers. "If I was in General Meade's place I would tender my resignation and let them shift for themselves," George wrote.

[16] *Meade*, II, 278–79.

in Fredericksburg, Meade asked if Virginians would not like General Lee for their governor. Assured that everyone would be pleased, Meade heartily responded, "That is my idea of a restoration."[17]

For many the triumphal parade through Richmond's crowded streets on May 6 was but an incident of the long march to Falls Church, only a few miles south of the Potomac. For the last time company streets were laid out and marked. On the heights about near-by Alexandria, Sherman's army was tented, with much booty and many strange mementoes. Each camp sought to outdo the other in ceremonial pomp.[18] Visitors walking the streets delighted in the cadenced beat of the drum and the shrill notes of bugle and fife. Bands played patriotic airs as assembled soldiers sang. After dark the tents dotting the hillsides were lighted by thousands of candles, a scene that left unforgettable impressions. Among army guests were Meade's younger sons, Spencer, now nearly seventeen years old, and Willie, aged nine, who had a tent to themselves and horses to ride. When it was definitely settled that the grand review of the army would be held on May 23, Mrs. Meade and the other children arrived in camp and were promised seats in the reviewing stand in front of the White House.

Sheridan and Wright were still absent, but two cavalry divisions were on hand to lead the Second, Fifth, and Ninth Corps of the Army of the Potomac. In his place in front and facing the massed spectators, Meade rode Blackie, his show horse, accompanied by his entire staff except Lyman, who as an unpaid volunteer aide had been permitted to go home. From the Capitol to the White House, Pennsylvania Avenue was bedecked with bright flags and bunting. Bearing garlands thrown by eager onlookers, Blackie halted in front of the stands, where Meade dismounted to watch the parade with his family. He shook hands with General Sherman, who said, "I'm afraid my poor tatterdemalion corps will make a poor appearance tomorrow when contrasted with yours." Until late afternoon the regiments and their bands continued to file past in the greatest military pageant the country had yet seen.[19]

Save for the routine duty of paying and mustering out most of the

[17] *Magazine of American History,* Vol. XVII (June, 1887), 469.

[18] *Antietam to Appomattox,* 604.

[19] Lewis, *Sherman,* 373; Leech, *Reveille in Washington,* 415–16; William T. Sherman, *Memoirs* (New York, 1875), II, 376; Porter, *Campaigning with Grant,* 506–507; O. L. Hein, *Memories of Long Ago,* 37–38; Pennypacker, *Meade,* 3.

volunteer troops, this was the last duty with the Army of the Potomac. Unlike many who would fill the halls of Congress, gubernatorial posts, and the Presidency, Meade had not the slightest political ambition, but he made sure of an understanding with Grant. It was perfectly agreeable for Halleck to be sent to the Pacific Coast, where he had lived before the war. Third in rank, Sherman would command in the West, while the South was divided among Thomas, Sheridan, and others. This left the Division of the Atlantic to Meade, who ranked fourth, and headquarters at his suggestion would be in Philadelphia.

In many large cities, soldiers formed in more parades as they reached their mustering-out stations. Philadelphia had its great day on June 10 as Meade and Humphreys led the disbanding Pennsylvania regiments through densely lined streets in a downpour of rain. The lions of the day attended a reception and banquet and the theater that evening and later appeared at the "Union Volunteers Refreshment Saloon," where Meade surprised the crowd by nearly fainting from lack of air. Windows were hurriedly opened to revive an outdoors man unaccustomed to a scarcity of oxygen.[20]

That Meade had to return to Washington to organize his division gave Philadelphia time to prepare another round of public and private receptions which he found generally agreeable. Colonel Lyman, meanwhile, summoned him to Boston, where the Meade banner had been raised in a newspaper article detailing events leading up to Lee's surrender. Sitting with the Lymans at Harvard's commencement exercises, Mrs. Meade saw the purple hood of a Doctor of Laws thrown over her husband's shoulders as President Hill read a laudatory citation in Latin. Students of that language were reminded that George Gordon Meade by his courage and sagacity had restored the fortunes of his country at the most hazardous crisis of the war.[21] He was taken into the ancient and aristocratic Porcellian Club, and as an after-dinner

[20] Taylor, *Philadelphia in the Civil War*, 313; *Philadelphia Inquirer*, June 12, 1865; George Meade Diary, June 10, 1865, entry, Meade Papers.

[21] The citation read, "*Illum exercitus Americani Imperatorem, qui periculosissima belli discrimine res patriae virtute et consilio restituit, Georgium Gordon Meade,*" or translated, "That Commander of the American Army who at the most hazardous crisis of the war by his courage and sagacity restored the fortunes of his country, George Gordon Meade." *Army and Navy Journal* (July 29 ,1865), 77; Ferris Greenslet, *The Lowells and Their Seven Worlds*, 306–307. Andrew Jackson and Winfield Scott were the generals previously honored, and Grant would be the following year.

speaker at Harvard he praised the valor and fidelity of the Massachusetts troops.

In every military district of the South, frightening incidents were being reported. Meade's first mission to such scenes followed forced entry into a house and the violation of women by Negro troops at Pocotaligo, South Carolina. General Quincy A. Gillmore, commanding in the state, had some of the offenders executed, but Northerners who held that Negroes were more sinned against than sinning were disturbed and angry. In an attempt to quiet Southern rage, Meade let it be known that he was trying to rid the army of Negroes, but that he had to move cautiously so as not to offend Northern opinion. Returning to Washington, he submitted his view that military control should be exercised with discretion, whereupon Grant ordered a reduction in the number of interior posts and *white* volunteers discharged. While little could be done openly to offend Negroes, Federal officers of moderate views began relieving them also from regular duty. Their status was later restored by enrollment as militia by carpetbag governments as the ideological warfare continued.[22]

For quite another reason, a firm hand was required along the Canadian border. Bonds of friendship with Canada had been weakened by her cool attitude toward the North during the war and by newspaper references to "the late Union." A favorite topic of conservation around Federal campfires had been an invasion of Canada after the close of the war, but since most soldiers wished only to go quietly home, it took a great cause to rally public opinion. The American Fenians, a sturdy branch of the Irish Fenian Society, had a ready-made cause, and an invasion plan was drawn up by veteran General Thomas W. Sweeny. Money and volunteers had to be raised. As thousands responded, a Fenian congress meeting in Philadelphia named Sweeny to the supreme command—secretary of war of the Irish Republic, a salaried position. Sweeny obtained a leave of absence from the regular army and began organizing war veterans of Irish descent into regiments, brigades, and divisions.

The winter of 1865–66 was enlivened with public dinners and fundraising. Some of the money, passing from hand to hand, ultimately

[22] Stanton to Meade, August 21, 1865, Meade Letters, War Department Files, National Archives; Myrta Lockett Avary, *Dixie After the War*, 378; *O.R.*, Series 3, V, 212; *Meade*, II, 284.

reached party coffers. Politicians found it rather worthwhile to con-
tribute, even Speaker Schuyler Colfax of the national House and Postmaster General William Dennison, Jr. Arms were purchased from
overstocked government arsenals. Federal officials, Sweeny could truth-
fully say, were "perfectly aware of the purpose for which they were
intended."[23]

With the coming of spring, men left their firesides and entrained
for the border. Great crowds were seen passing through Boston and
Portland, Maine. From Eastport, a landing was made on Campobello
Island, owned by the outlying province of New Brunswick. Storehouses
were destroyed on an island near by and a flag torn from its custom-
house staff.

Diplomats in Washington began to lodge protests. As three British
warships and the U. S. S. *Winoosky* drew near, several hundred
Fenians returned to Eastport to await the arrival of a steamer bringing
munitions. This vessel, the *Ocean Spray*, was held up by the *Winoosky*,
which awaited instructions. Badgered by protesting Canadians and British, President Andrew Johnson talked with Grant, who ordered Meade
to Eastport to safeguard the border. Picking up two artillery companies
at Boston and other troops along the way, Meade ordered the munitions
ship seized and directed the placing of troops along the St. Croix River.

Shaping his tactics to meet an extraordinary situation, Meade was
able to check the Fenial right wing, but changeable spring weather
brought on an attack of pneumonia that kept him in bed for three
weeks.[24] When he stopped off at Portland and Boston on his return to
Philadelphia, he was hailed as both a hero and a blackguard, yet because
he was known to be only carrying out orders, most Fenians were able
to overlook his personal part in the intervention. Attention was drawn
to another frontier as forces from the Middle West began converging
upon Buffalo.

Ground was gained across the Niagara River before Meade was
able to get there. Toward the last of May, 1866, General Sweeny threw
a column across the river from Buffalo, and cheering Fenians raised the

[23] Campaign report of General Thomas W. Sweeny, Sweeny Papers, New York
Public Library.

[24] *Meade*, II, 285; Welles, *Diary*, II, 486; R. W. Winston, *Andrew Johnson*, 463–
64; Ellis Paxson Oberholtzer, *History of the United States Since the Civil War*, I, 530;
*Canadian Magazine*, Vol. X (November, 1897), 41; (March, 1898), 411–13.

Green Flag over Fort Erie near the far shore. Canada, whose defenses were weak, found herself in actual danger. Two volunteer regiments sent in to defend native soil were defeated in the Battle of Limeridge. Veterans of the Peninsula and the Wilderness campaigns were not to be checked by "the spluttering of a few rifles."[25]

Hurrying to Buffalo, Meade found the city a scene of much excitement. Reinforced, the Queen's Own managed to drive the Fenians to their flatboats, which were escorted across the Niagara by the waiting U. S. S. *Michigan*. Meade placed his guards along the river, banned Fenian meetings, and urged the absentees from home to rejoin their families. Some accepted his offer of transportation at government expense and did so, but several hundred cut loose for other border towns in New York State and Vermont. Meade and his escort had no choice but to follow. He kept so close to Sweeny that on one occasion both traveled on the same train, but Meade stopped off at Potsdam and Malone, while the Fenian leader went on.[26]

Seeing friendly Fenians crowd around the tall bearded figure and hail him as one they had known in the war, townspeople began to mistake Meade for Sweeny. At first annoyed, Meade decided to accept the situation good-naturedly.[27] He continued to urge everyone to go home and threatened to use force if compelled to. On June 7, arriving at St. Albans, Vermont, he had Sweeny arrested and held for trial on $20,000 bail. When alert Federal officials seized large shipments of arms on trains en route for the border, prospects for invasion grew dim. A few die-hards managed to scramble across to engage in scattered clashes, but they could not be reinforced by either men or arms. It was conceded, however, that had quantities of arms and supplies been landed, Canada's soil would have been turned red with blood.[28] Returning to Buffalo to sweep other Fenians from the city, Meade reported them dispersed as of June 15. General Sweeny, after formal trial, was freed. Some months later Meade visited Canada, where he received the honors due a veteran of two wars.

Again, conflict. Georgia happened to be a sore spot in the South, where each state had to write a new constitution under the Reconstruc-

---

[25] *Army and Navy Journal* (June 16, 1866).
[26] *North American & U. S. Gazette,* June 5, 1866.
[27] *Philadelphia Press,* November 12, 1872.
[28] *Army and Navy Journal* (June 16, 1866).

tion acts. Delegates to a constitutional convention had been elected in Georgia, but most were Radicals or anti-South. When the Governor and State Treasurer withheld funds for expenses, General John Pope, who ruled the Third Military District, sought their removal.

President Johnson was entertaining suggestions that Meade be named arbitrator in executing the laws. Meade himself had received similar suggestions. He was very well satisfied, however, to remain in Philadelphia. "Political passion is again assuming the ascendency," he wrote a friend in the South. "Blinded by this malign influence, both sides are plunging into the same evil courses which originated the war."[29]

At odds with the Radicals, Johnson would not uphold Pope. Called to Washington in December, 1867, Meade, as the replacement, was expected to reflect the President's views. Johnson knew him to be well liked in the South. It was a matter, first of all, of the velvet glove. An Atlanta newspaper, hailing the appointment, placed Meade on a high pedestal. He was "more like a Virginia gentleman" than a tyrannical soldier—a reference to Pope.[30]

Nevertheless, he was sworn to uphold the acts of Congress, however extreme, and after talking with Grant, who did not see eye to eye with the President, Meade went to Atlanta and carried out Pope's threat. The newspapers then quickly turned against him. In Washington, the Conservative minority was angered; President Johnson, "mortified and chagrined."[31]

Neither Radical nor Conservative but chiefly a Moderate, Meade won back some popularity by curbing the military officers he had named to take over for Georgia's governor and state treasurer. The friendship of Confederate war leaders strengthened his hand. General William J. Hardee, a veteran of western campaigns, made his own position clear by declaring Meade "emphatically a soldier and a gentleman—a man of ability, honor, and integrity." Apparently Hardee was seeking to smooth the way. "In the execution of the laws of Congress there will be as much of kindness and generosity extended to the people . . . as the

[29] *Meade*, II, 290.

[30] *Atlanta New Era*, January 20, 1868, quoted in C. M. Thompson, *Reconstruction in Georgia*, 179.

[31] Welles, *Diary*, III, 258; George Fort Milton, *The Age of Hate*, 481; Meade's report, January 13, 1868, Andrew Johnson Papers, CXXIX, 18845.

nature of his duties will permit," the Georgian explained. "I feel assured that he is free from partisanship and from personal and sectional prejudice."[32]

The ties of old soldiers could not be ignored. If a man was well liked, it made no difference where he had fought. A man who had fought on neither side once interrupted a proposed toast to Confederate General John B. Gordon, who sat near Meade at a dinner, because it was "too soon after the war to be drinking to a Rebel." As Gordon related the incident, Meade quickly got to his feet and "with a compliment to myself . . . and a rebuke to the objector, he held up his glass and said with significant emphasis: 'I propose to drink, and drink now, to my former foe but now my friend, General Gordon of Georgia.' "[33]

In Alabama, Conservatives were heartened when Meade criticized the Radical idea of placing candidates' names on the same ballot used to vote on the new constitution. None of these candidates had been nominated in a convention or a primary election. But Grant upheld the ballot as prepared and ordered the polls kept open for four days while Negroes in remote areas were brought in to vote.

Yet the constitution, in Meade's words, was "fairly rejected." Congress then ordered it adopted so that Alabama could be readmitted to the Union at once.[34] Again, in Florida, Meade sided with the Conservatives. The state convention, said he, would not be adjourned merely because a few Radicals charged that certain delegates had been unfairly elected. As the members sat and began quarreling, an inquiry showed the charges unproved. Meade offered a face-saving compromise, and it then could be voted to make way for statehood.[35]

Other acts endeared him to the Conservative wing and at the same time pleased President Johnson. Wherever legally elected Conservatives performed their duties acceptably, Meade protected them in the exercise of their powers. He freed batches of political prisoners, jailed others of whatever persuasion, and sought to protect individual rights "without reference to any consideration but that of justice and law so far as I could comprehend it."[36] A harsh policy exercised by General

[32] *New York Times*, January 31, 1868.

[33] John B. Gordon, *Reminiscences of the Civil War*, 459.

[34] John W. DuBose, *Alabama's Tragic Decade*, 138–39.

[35] *Meade*, II, 293; Robert Selph Henry, *The Story of Reconstruction*, 294–95.

[36] Meade's report, *Army and Navy Journal*, (December 5, 1868), 250.

Pope toward the press was eradicated by the opening of Conservative journals to paid official notices.

An outside interest was St. Philip's Episcopal Church in Atlanta which Federal troops had used as a commissary depot and, after the war, as a mere bowling alley. After being refitted and reconsecrated, it grew rapidly in numbers. In the newspapers and by other means, Meade appealed for funds to enlarge and furnish it. From Philadelphia, where Margaret Meade set to work, and from other Northern cities, money poured in. A new transept was added, and an organ and furniture were purchased with the $5,000 received.[37] Although General Sherman could not be forgotten, worshipers could relax in their new pews.

Such was the brighter side, but Meade had to deal with almost daily crime and disorder as Southern culture wore thin. During trials for murder, wild and exaggerated stories were told, and often he was convinced that both the accused and the aggrieved were in the wrong. When the Carolinas were added to his command, he had to move in troops to protect threatened Radical officials. That Radicals in power should be shielded and loyal Southerners arrested aroused the *Charleston Mercury*. It followed that General Meade was "still a satrap, a partisan and an unpleasant specimen" whose rule was a "hideous caricature of charity, forbearance and humanity."

Innocent citizens, the *Mercury* stormed, had been delivered up "to be tortured . . . by expedients and cruelties unheard of in any Christian country since the days of the Spanish Inquisition."[38] To Meade's defense came the *Army and Navy Journal*. This General, it had cause to affirm, had always been fair in hearing both sides and in acting judiciously. It was pointed out that no attempt had been made to suppress the *Charleston Mercury*. In Atlanta, the rector and wardens of St. Philip's Church made their gratitude known. "We shall ever remember you as an honest, unselfish and liberal Christian gentleman,"[39] they wrote as Meade wearily turned to go home.

Grant had easily won the 1868 presidential election with 214 elec-

---

[37] *Ibid.* (April 3, 1869), 518; *Meade*, II, 295. Meade made his appeal in Atlanta newspapers of April 22, 1868. See also, R. A. Palmer (compiler), *Seventy-Fifth Anniversary, St. Philip's Cathedral, Atlanta, Georgia, 1847–1922* (Atlanta, 1922), 23–24.

[38] *Army and Navy Journal* (October 31, 1869).

[39] *Ibid.* (April 3, 1869), 518.

toral votes to 80 for Horatio Seymour of New York. Since Grant never forgot a friend or a kindly act, certain appointments would be made on this basis.[40] General Rawlins, a small-town lawyer who had been his chief of staff, was named secretary of war. Benefactor Elihu B. Washburne was the choice for secretary of state. William Tecumseh Sherman, who had shown kindness in dark hours, was moved up to full general. Sheridan was never the real friend that Sherman was, but he had won Grant's admiration as a soldier. He therefore was named lieutenant general, succeeding Sherman.[41]

In defending Sheridan's promotion, Grant observed that he had been named a regular major general before Meade. This point of view took no notice of the injustice done Meade who, recommended for major general in May, 1864, had been held back until after the fall election of that year. For it was to remedy an "apparent injustice" that Lincoln, upon signing the appointment, agreed to an August date for the commission, which thus made Meade the senior of Sheridan by some two months.

Meade had been confident that he would receive higher rank until, in discussing appointments with the President-elect, he was unable to obtain any hint of his intentions. Thus there had been lingering fears, but in view of circumstances, Meade had expected too much.[42] The situation was not wholly clear. A historian of that era has observed that Grant's admiration for Sheridan was "as incomprehensible to Meade as it is to the present-day student."[43]

The first clue that Sheridan had been named was the signature of Sherman, the *General* commanding, on a message sent Meade. One of

[40] F. L. Paxson in *Dictionary of American Biography*, VII, 468.

[41] In his *Personal Memoirs*, Grant ranked Sheridan with Napoleon and Frederick and the greatest commanders of history, and he told Senator George Frisbie Hoar: "I believe General Sheridan has no superior as a general, either living or dead, and perhaps not an equal."—Hoar, *Autobiography of Seventy Years*, I, 209. Sheridan, however, had been quick to declare himself independent of Grant in trying to get Longstreet to surrender to *him* during the truce preceding the Grant-Lee council on April 9, 1865, but was promptly put in his place.—Freeman, *Lee's Lieutenants*, III, 736. His later rule in the South, where he exercised an iron hand and especially his Indian campaigns in the West were characterized by harshness and cruelty; in the destruction of native villages, men, women, children, and ponies were shot.—J. G. Randall, *Civil War and Reconstruction*, 757; O'Connor, *Sheridan the Inevitable*, 306.

[42] McClure, *Lincoln and Men of War-Times*, 361; *The Sherman Letters* (ed. by R. S. Thorndike), II, 324–25; *Meade*, II, 296–98.

[43] W. B. Hesseltine, *Ulysses S. Grant, Politician*, 43.

Sherman's first acts was to relieve Meade of onerous duties in the South and permit him to return home. News of Senate confirmation of Sheridan's new rank arrived in Atlanta late that same evening, March 5, 1869. Meade could not conceal his disappointment. "You can imagine the force of this blow, but it is useless to repine over what cannot be remedied," he wrote Margaret next day. "It is the cruelest and meanest act of injustice."[44] A Philadelphia newspaper used rather strong language: "A gross and unjustifiable act of personal favoritism."[45]

His chances for promotion gone, Meade listlessly took over the reins from General Hancock, who had replaced him at Philadelphia. He was in poor physical shape to resume his work. Doctors said it was his old battlefield wound that made him susceptible to pneumonia, which again sent him to bed, but he was obviously depressed. This third attack proved the most serious yet experienced. Not until early summer was Meade able to resume the full routine of his military division.

He did not miss the first meeting of the Society of the Army of the Potomac in New York City. That place had been chosen in anticipation of the election as president of George B. McClellan, then New York's chief engineer. Many had expected that the former army commanders would be named society president in order of service. McClellan was duly nominated, then Meade and Sheridan, and other complimentary speeches were made in behalf of Hancock, Slocum, Humphreys, and Burnside, who occupied the chair. Sheridan, who had nominated Meade, then asked to be excused, but his name was not withdrawn.

On the first ballot, McClellan led with 164 votes, but since Sheridan had 142 and Meade 111, his margin fell short of a majority. Sentiment now swung to the man sponsored by Grant, and only one more ballot was necessary for Sheridan to win. As he was escorted to the chair, McClellan and many of his supporters quietly left the hall.[46] It was recalled that Sheridan had served with the Army of the Potomac for only a little more than four months.

But when Philadelphia was selected for the second reunion in April, 1870, it was clearly understood that Meade would be honored. Grant occupied his right on the platform, and Sherman, a guest at Meade's

44 *Meade*, II, 300.
45 *Philadelphia Age*, March 8, 1869.
46 Horatio King, *The Army of the Potomac*, 4–5 n.

home, also sat near by. The balloting was routine. A visiting British historian saw Meade "almost borne down by the number of bouquets which admiring hands had thrust upon him." Justin McCarthy noted in his *Reminiscences*, "I shall never forget the sweet and genial manners, the courtly presence, the unaffected good-humour and courtesy of General Meade, one of the foremost among the Federal heroes."[47]

Secure in his position as long as Sherman was general in chief, Meade was enjoying a tranquil existence in his domestic circle and as a leader of Philadelphia society. With the nation's borders at peace within his own jurisdiction, he was free to spend some time on civilian projects. A founder and president of the Lincoln Institution, which provided a home and education for war orphans, he scoured the city and environs for funds. Growing Fairmount Park, a large area watered by the winding Schuylkill River and Wissahickon Creek, was an active interest and avocation. Meade saw that more land was acquired from the older estates to unite disjointed portions, and he rode in the park almost daily as landscaping work was done under his eye.[48] To young Philadelphians, the graying veteran on horseback seemed an anachronistic figure among the smart carriages and rigs.

Meade's interest in the national election of 1872 was as a supporter of Grant over opponent Horace Greeley of the *New York Tribune*. "Greeley has always been down on the Army and West Point and could not conceal his hostility even during the war," he wrote his son Spencer, a railroad man.[49] Early Republican sweeps in Pennsylvania and in other state contests pointed to victory for the incumbent. Also in newspaper headlines as the national election approached was the "Canadian horse disease," which was carrying off many valuable animals. No horse-drawn streetcars were running, and men were pulling delivery wagons. Old Baldy and Meade's other horses were safe on a secluded estate— Meadow Bank in near-by Jenkintown—a family resort in the summer.[50]

On October 31, Meade appeared in good spirits as he talked with a

---

[47] Justin McCarthy, *Reminiscences*, I, 247. "If ever there was an actual presentment in real life of Thackeray's Colonel Newcome, it stood before me, I thought in the noble form of General Meade," the writer narrated.

[48] *Meade*, II, 301; Pennypacker, *Meade*, 391–92. "He gave his time without stint to the labor," stated Park Commissioner George H. Boker.

[49] Meade to son Spencer (Pennie) Meade, August 3, 1872, Meade Papers.

[50] Meadow Bank, located on Fox Chase Road, Jenkintown, was on the estate of the widow of Joshua Fisher, historian and political writer.

nephew, Richard Hartman Bache, at headquarters. At noonday, when taking his customary stroll with Margaret, he began to complain of pains in his side. Turning homeward as the discomfort grew worse, he was put to bed seriously ill again with pneumonia. Colonel George Meade, absent with the First Artillery, was sent for; also son Spencer and daughter Margaret, who lived elsewhere.

Four days later when the disease took an alarming turn, Doctor John Neill called in consultants. Disregarding protests, the patient gave the family his final instructions. He received Holy Communion from Dr. Hoffman, the Episcopal minister, and then fell asleep, arousing himself at long intervals.

Because of the virtual quarantine of carriage horses and the excitement attending the November 5 election, few in the city learned that Meade was seriously ill. Late on the sixth, after it became known that Grant had won, celebrations were hushed as word was spread that Philadelphia's best-known citizen was gone. The General was not yet fifty-seven years old.

"The news fell like a bolt from a clear sky," lamented the *Philadelphia North American* in an outburst of feeling. "He died at 6 o'clock last evening at his residence, 1836 De Lancey Place. . . . Hardly any more severe blow could fall to mingle its unexpected rue with patriotic joy in the city especially, but over the whole country as well."[51] General Sherman requested Irvin McDowell, who had fought at First and Second Bull Run, to consult with the widow and see to arrangements. It soon became apparent that thousands expected to march. Meade's old corps commanders, Humphreys, Wright, and Parke, also Lieutenant General Sheridan, and four navy admirals were selected as pallbearers. On November 11, all business was suspended in a city draped in mourning. An early special train from Washington brought President Grant, Sherman, cabinet members, and ranking army and navy officers. Crowds solidly lined the streets to catch a view of the great men and to witness the solemn pageant.

Veterans of the Pennsylvania.Reserve Corps quietly assembled, and other regiments of the old army came to march in a body. National Guard and regular troops took their assigned places. The Governor and his staff, the Mayor, City Council members, and other civic officials

[51] *Philadelphia North American*, November 7, 1872. A tribute appears in *Army and Navy Journal* (November 9, 1872).

came to old St. Mark's Church. The Right Reverend Bishop Oden-
heimer, who had united George and Margaret in marriage nearly
thirty-two years before, spoke at the services.[52]

Brought out of retirement, Old Baldy, riderless, ambled with long
stride behind the caisson bearing his master. The cortege wound
through hushed streets to the banks of the Schuylkill, where the casket
was placed on a black-draped barge to be taken to East Fairmount Park.
As the *Undine* made its way upstream, wailing music came from regimental bands drawn up at intervals along the right bank. At the grave
at Laurel Hill Cemetery, Bishop H. B. Whipple of Minnesota recalled
a day when Meade summoned him from Washington to celebrate
Easter Sunday at his field headquarters in Virginia.[53] Rifles crashed in
a parting salute.

Newspapermen hurried to their offices to write detailed stories that
would take up a full page in some journals. Colonel Lyman, who was
then touring Europe, sadly read the accounts and then wrote Meade's
soldier son: "He was a man who did not strive for cheap popularity but
actually would go out of his way to frown it down, of such steel-like
honesty was he. A piece in the Philadelphia *Ledger* said with great
truth that he would have made a distinguished judge, so imperturbably
well-balanced was his mind. But when he was gone, all men said within
themselves: 'We have lost a man who did not know what it was to
be false.' "[54]

No military record appears on the Meade tombstone; instead, a
simple and commonplace phrase taken from the sermon preached at the
funeral: "He did his work bravely and is at rest." These same words
could have been said of many either of high or low estate. Meade's
work was of the long-suffering kind—a patient role for a restless and
impatient man. It had been necessary for him to subordinate himself
to war policies which he believed inadequate and wrong—policies he
could do little to change. Meager credit had been allotted him for his
achievement at Gettysburg, for his long pursuit of General Lee into
Virginia until halted by a War Office order, for the final turning back

[52] Scharf and Westcott, *History of Philadelphia*, I, 812–13; Philadelphia newspapers of November 12, 1872, especially *The Press; Meade*, II, 304–305.

[53] Military Order of the Loyal Legion of the U.S., Philadelphia, has the hand-
written MS of the funeral address by the Rt. Rev. H. B. Whipple, D. D.

[54] Lyman to George Meade, Cannes, France, December 23, 1872, Meade Papers.

of the enemy at Centreville in October, 1863, and for the furious marches his men were forced into both before and after Gettysburg, then to Centreville, and, finally, to the vicinity of Appomattox Court-house, where again he held the upper hand. He had been a familiar figure close to the front during most major battles and had won the respect of the troops, who warmed his heart with their cheers even though he gave no responsive sign. In most of the difficult places where he had trod, recollections of this plain-spoken officer were pleasant. His lighthouses along the East Coast and the Florida shore, the Great Lakes survey, and the planning of Fairmount Park were enduring. He had assumed no punitive role toward the South but had urged the quieting of sectional feeling. After Gettysburg, in responding to General Howard's letter defending Meade, Abraham Lincoln character-ized him as not only a brave and skillful officer but a true man. Perhaps these words should have been carved in stone.

# *Appendix*
## *The Meade Family*

FOR SEVERAL GENERATIONS the Meade family acquired wealth from shipping and trade. Robert, the great-grandfather of George Gordon Meade, emigrated from Ireland to the Bahamas, where he busied himself with West Indies commerce and set up a trading house in growing Philadelphia. Sparse records reveal some acquaintance with the town of St. Croix in the Danish West Indies, where on July 16, 1754, "being very sick & weak in Body but of perfect mind & memory," and likewise of tolerant spirit, Robert Meade bequeathed five pieces of eight to the Danish church there and a like sum to the English establishment.[1] He later died while on a visit to Philadelphia.

None of the three children—Garrett, George, and Catherine—had then reached maturity, but the older son continued the business in the widow's name and took it over on his twenty-first birthday as an importer of rum, sugar, and able-bodied young Negroes. In 1762, the younger son entered the firm of Garrett and George Meade. Favored trading grounds were the Windward Islands and the Barbadoes, where George was then stationed.[2] His chosen bride was Protestant-born Henrietta Worsam, daughter of Richard Worsam, Esq., of His Majesty's Council, an influential Colonial figure. George, however, was not of Worsam's religion, nor was he a supporter of Britain's system of taxation for the American colonies. It was said that sharp words passed between the two men, but opposition served only to delay the marriage. On May 5, 1768, when the wedding took place in Philadelphia, George was twenty-seven years old and his bride a young woman of twenty. In

---

[1] Will of Robert Meade of Philadelphia, Meade family papers. Robert Meade died between August 13 and 26, 1754—the dates between the last codicil and the proving of the will. American Catholic Historical Society of Philadelphia, *Records*, Vol. III (1888–91), 194.

[2] American Catholic Historical Society of Philadelphia, *Records*, Vol. III, 202.

due time she became as staunch a rebel against the Crown as her husband, who had joined the Friendly Sons of St. Patrick.

The oldest son among ten children, Richard Worsam Meade was born in a farmhouse in Chester County, where the family had fled in September, 1777, as the British invaded Philadelphia. The birth of Richard on June 23, 1778, apparently delayed the return to the city (the British having departed some days earlier) and possibly accounted for the five-shilling fine which George Meade jovially paid for non-attendance at meetings of the Friendly Sons at the City Tavern.[3]

Garrett Meade, the senior partner, is lost from sight in the Barbadoes. The firm now known as George Meade and Company took in brother-in-law Thomas Fitzsimons, who had come from Ireland and married Catherine Meade (George's sister). The partnership was able to subscribe 2,000 pounds sterling to help feed and clothe the Continental Army,[4] but affairs took another turn after the war. Since the colonies lost the trading privileges which they had enjoyed as part of the Empire, the British West Indies had to be abandoned. A more serious blow fell when a number of bills which the firm had purchased on England, Holland, and France were forfeited. Fitzsimons took his leave of the firm, but in bringing its affairs to a close, George Meade managed to settle with the creditors.

He carried on thereafter as an individual, touring cities of England, Holland, and Spain. In England he sat for a portrait by Sir Thomas Lawrence which reveals a marked contrast between the two sides of his face. Of commanding presence, George Meade was known as honest and kindly even if sometimes harsh and irritable and short of temper.

His son, Richard Worsam Meade, was already successful as a seafaring merchant. At age seventeen, after handling some business in the French and Spanish West Indies, Richard took charge of one of his father's vessels bound for England. He toured both that country and France, revisited the West Indies, and entered upon profitable ventures on his own account. Of independent means at twenty-two years of age, he was first among suitors for the hand of Margaret Coates Butler, daughter of merchant Anthony Butler of Perth Amboy, New Jersey,

[3] *Ibid.*, 208.

[4] Bache, *Meade*, 2. A letter from Benjamin Rush to Mrs. Rush, August 12, 1891, mentions contributions by Mr. Fitzsimons, Mr. Anthony (ancestor of Margaret Coates Butler Meade), Mr. Meade, and others to the "African Church," the first Negro church in America. See *Letters of Benjamin Rush* (ed. by L. H. Butterfield), I, 602.

and granddaughter of a wealthy Philadelphian. At the time of his marriage, in January, 1801,[5] young Meade was settling his father's affairs, for his business had been completely wrecked by a venture in unimproved western lands. The collection of debts and satisfaction of creditors proved a dreary business, but in traveling to Spain in 1803, Richard Meade lingered in the city of Cádiz. Thrust out into the sea, with a wide expanse of ocean view, this Venice of Spain contrasted favorably with Philadelphia in its elegance and cleanliness. Whitewashed houses, gleaming in the sun, well-kept parks, and fresh sea breezes attracted the merchant and shipowner, who soon set up his own business there.[6]

His wife, Margaret, who joined him with the two oldest children, brought word that his gout-afflicted father was failing. Notices in Philadelphia newspapers told of the death on November 8, 1808, of George Meade, gentleman, 40 Sansom Street.[7]

To Richard and Margaret Meade were born eight daughters and three sons, of whom the two oldest, Henrietta Constantia and Charlotte Hustler, and the two youngest, Robert Leamy and Mariamne, were natives of Philadelphia. All the others—Elizabeth Mary, Richard Worsam II, Margaret Gordon, María del Carmen, Salvadora, Catherine Hustler (who died young), and George Gordon—were born in Cádiz. Four years after the family's return to Philadelphia in 1817, Henrietta married a navy man, Captain James Dallas, later commodore; and in 1828 Charlotte wed Captain James Duncan Graham of the Army Engineers, who for a time lived in Pensacola, Florida, and later in Washington, D. C. Pensacola curiously recurs several times in the Meade chronicle. Henrietta Meade Dallas died there in 1831, and in the same place Robert, who had married Elizabeth Ricketts of Philadelphia. Robert was only in his twenty-fourth year when he died on October 16, 1841, and little is known of him save that he was associated with his older brother in surveying work in various places.[8]

The Civil War resulted in tragedy for Elizabeth Mary, who in

[5] Meade genealogy in *Pennsylvania Magazine of History and Biography*, Vol. XXIV (1900), 242–43.

[6] *Dictionary of American Biography*, XII, 477.

[7] George Meade's business was carried on at 78 Walnut Street. He was buried in St. Peter's Churchyard, Philadelphia.

[8] Meade to Chief Engineer Gratiot, December 9, 1837, Letters Received, Engineer Corps, 1837, No. 1994, National Archives.

1827 had married Alfred Ingraham of Philadelphia, later moving to Kentucky and then to Mississippi. The Ingrahams lost all of their three sons, two of record in the Confederate cause, and a son-in-law died from exposure in the same service. During Grant's Vicksburg campaign the family was forced to quit its Claiborne County plantation home, a large and handsome house on the road between Port Gibson and Vicksburg. When the place was raided and overrun by Federal troops, the Ingrahams were "completely ruined."[9] Only scattered records remain of Elizabeth Meade Ingraham, "one of the most distinguished women of the South, both in intellect, education, and social position."[10] On October 12, 1872, Elizabeth, an unreconciled Rebel, died at New Orleans.

Unmistakable tragedy marred the career of Richard Worsam Meade II, in his youth a genial, gallant, and generous spirit. The fact that this naval officer was also temperish, wayward, and restless barred normal advancement. Upon entering the navy in 1826, Meade proved himself energetic and active, but thirty-six years went by before he could win a captain's commission. Even then he was retained during the early Civil War years on the receiving ship *North Carolina* in New York harbor. Ceaselessly active, however, he reclaimed a valuable piece of land for the navy and there set up reading rooms for his crews and drill grounds for practice with small arms.[11] Permitted finally to go afloat as captain of the steam frigate *San Jacinto,* he had the bad luck to encounter a fierce gale which disabled his ship, but worse, after refitting, it was storm-wrecked one midnight on a reef in the Bahamas.

Even while high waves continued to toss the vessel against the reef, he worked madly until he had saved everything valuable on board, including guns, ammunition, stores, rigging, and even part of the machinery.[12] Yet to lose one's ship is the worst of navy crimes. Suspended from duty, he was thrice tried for the disaster, but failed to be reinstated, which broke his heart. Meanwhile he suffered a stroke, and from the moment he was retired for physical disability (December 11, 1867), he became "an utterly changed being, soured and disappointed."[13] His temper was menacing and harsh; his Catholicism of the

[9] *Meade,* I, 353; II, 159.

[10] Dorsey, *Recollections of Henry Watkins Allen,* 420.

[11] Rebecca Paulding Meade, *Life of Hiram Paulding,* 259–62.

[12] *Official Records of the Union and Confederate Navies,* Series 1, XVII, 787–89, 793–95.

[13] *Army and Navy Journal* (April 23, 1870), 567.

actively proselyting kind; and relatives began to fear his violence. Too, the lives of several naval officials were threatened.[14]

Captain Meade had spent much time and effort in seeking settlement of the Meade family claim arising from the Florida Treaty. Although advanced by able counsel, the cause was denied on technical grounds by the U. S. Court of Claims and finally by the Supreme Court in Washington. At this latest misfortune, Meade's mind, which had been unstable, obviously gave way. Although confined by his family to an asylum, he somehow obtained a court ruling which released him. When found carrying several loaded pistols as if to carry out threats against his enemies, he was publicly arrested but soon set free.

Meade was often seen in the company of lawyers, who, unless of the worst kind, would not encourage him, and his mere presence was a great embarrassment to peace-loving relatives. On April 16, 1870, finally, he was seized by another stroke, his third, while sitting in a lawyer's office in Brooklyn; and after being taken to a hospital, he expired without regaining consciousness. Descendants more fortunate than he won a place in naval and marine corps annals. The third Richard Worsam Meade advanced to the rank of admiral following Civil War service, his son of the same name also attained the same rank, while Robert Leamy Meade of this fourth generation became a marine corps general. Captain Meade's wife was Clara Forsythe Meigs, daughter of Congressman Henry Meigs of New York and a granddaughter of onetime Secretary of State John Forsythe, who in his day was concerned with the Meade claim. Another son, who served in the navy, and two daughters also survived.

Soon after the war, during his first trip to South Carolina, General Meade came to the assistance of the orphaned family of his sister Mariamne, who in 1845 had married Midshipman Thomas B. Huger of a prominent Charleston family.[15] Mariamne died in 1857, and Captain Huger (of the Confederate Navy) in 1862, at the Battle of New Orleans. (A Meade brother-in-law therefore, as well as several nephews, was lost on the Confederate side, although none were lost among five nephews who served with the North.)[16] The five Huger

[14] Welles, *Diary*, III, 250.

[15] *Meade*, I, 41; II, 278.

[16] Henrietta's son, Captain A. J. Dallas, served in the Twelfth U. S. Infantry; two sons of Captain Richard Worsam Meade served in the Navy and a third in the Marine

children were cared for by a great-uncle, Alfred Huger, formerly the postmaster at Charleston; and some of their descendants now live in the North.

Of Meade's other sisters, Margaret Gordon (1808–87) never married, and María del Carmen (1810–77) was left a widow by the death of Colonel Hartman Bache in October, 1872. Sister Salvadora married Thomas McLaughlin and, after his death, Judge William Patterson of Perth Amboy, where she died in 1886.

The General's own family numbered three sons and four daughters who lived to maturity, although John Sergeant Meade, perhaps the most promising, succumbed to consumption at the age of twenty-three. Colonel George Meade, an aide-de-camp during the war, served in the regular army for several years thereafter, mostly in the West. On December 10, 1874, soon after leaving the service, he married Elizabeth Morris Lewis of Philadelphia, and in the course of time they had ten children, of whom two died young. His business was principally in brokerage and finance.

Son Spencer (born January 19, 1850) became a railroad man and married Fanny C. Florance of Philadelphia; Sarah (born September 26, 1851) married John B. Large. Margaret Butler Meade (born February 26, 1845) never married, nor did Henrietta (born August 3, 1853), nor William, the youngest (born March 18, 1856), who entered the Drexel banking house in Philadelphia but died at thirty-five years of age. Although few of the Meade family were ever long-lived, daughter Henrietta was an interested spectator at the unveiling of the Washington, D. C., statue of her father in 1927, and she survived until 1944, then in her ninety-second year. Recently, in 1957, a bust of the General was unveiled at the lighthouse at Barnegat, New Jersey, which Meade planned and got under way. His name survives today in George Gordon Meade III of Ambler, Pennsylvania, a grandson of Colonel George Meade.

---

Corps; and Major Hartman Bache, Jr., son of Colonel Bache and María del Carmen Meade, was a member of Meade's official staff.

# Bibliography

### 1. MANUSCRIPT COLLECTIONS

James Gordon Bennett Papers, Library of Congress.
Felix Brannigan Papers, Library of Congress.
Zachariah Chandler Papers, Library of Congress.
Cyrus B. Comstock Diary, Library of Congress.
Charles A. Dana Papers, Library of Congress.
William H. Harris Journal, New York Public Library.
Andrew Johnson Papers, Library of Congress.
James Edward Kelly letters in Melvin J. Nichols Collection, Summit, N. J.
Robert T. Lincoln collection of Lincoln Papers, Library of Congress.
Ira J. Lindsley Papers, in a private collection.
George Gordon Meade collection in The Military Order of the Loyal Legion of the United States, Philadelphia.
Meade family collection in possession of George Gordon Meade III, Ambler, Pa.
Meade Papers, Letterbooks, Notebooks, etc., Historical Society of Pennsylvania, Philadelphia.
Miscellaneous Meade letters in MSS Division, Library of Congress; Virginia Historical Society; and New York Historical Society.
Meade letters and reports in Appointment Files, Topographical Bureau Records, and War Records Division, National Archives.
William M. Meredith Papers, Historical Society of Pennsylvania.
Thomas W. Sweeny Papers, New York Public Library.
U. S. Military Academy Records, 1817–37, West Point, N. Y.
Alexander Webb Papers, Yale University Library.

### 2. GOVERNMENT DOCUMENTS

U.S. Congress, Joint Committee on the Conduct of the War, *Reports*. Washington, D. C., 1865. 3 vols.

35, 36, and 37 Cong., *Senate Exec. Docs.*
U.S. State Department, *American State Papers, Foreign Affairs,* Vol. IV.
U.S. War Department, *The War of the Rebellion: A Compilation of the Official Records of the Union and Confederate Armies.* Washington, 1880–1901. 128 vols. Cited in footnotes as *O.R.*

## 3. NEWSPAPERS

Examination of newspaper files indicated that contemporary journals should be regarded as a prime source for Civil War students. Inasmuch as they are somewhat inaccessible, they have been neglected. Principal newspapers consulted were:
*Army and Navy Chronicle* (1835–36); *Army and Navy Journal* (1861–72).
*Daily National Intelligencer,* Washington, D. C.
*Detroit Free Press.*
*Evening Star,* Washington, D. C.
New York newspapers: *Herald, Times, Tribune, World.*
Philadelphia newspapers: *Age, Inquirer, Ledger, North American & U.S. Gazette, Press.*
Wilkes' *Spirit of the Times.*

## 4. MAGAZINES AND HISTORICAL SOCIETY PUBLICATIONS

American Catholic Historical Society of Pennsylvania, *Records,* Vol. III (1888–91).
*American Historical Review,* Vol. XXXIX (January, 1934).
*Blackwood's Magazine,* Vol. XCIV (September, 1863).
*Canadian Magazine,* Vol. X.
Florida Historical Society *Quarterly,* Vol. IX, No. 4 (April, 1931).
*Harper's Magazine,* Vol. CXXX (December, 1914).
*Infantry Journal,* Vols. XXXIV, XLV, XLVI.
*Magazine of American History,* Vol. XVI (October, 1886); Vol. XVII (June, 1887).
Military Historical Society of Massachusetts *Papers,* Vols. I, III, IV–VI, X.
Military Order of the Loyal Legion of the United States, Illinois Commandery, *Military Essays and Recollections,* Vols. I, IV.
*National Geographic Magazine,* Vol. XVII (January, 1906); Vol. XXIV (January, 1913); Vol. LXXX (December, 1941).
*Pennsylvania Magazine of History and Biography,* Vol. XXIV (1900), 242–43.
Southern Historical Society *Papers,* Vols. V, XIV, XXIII.

5. BIOGRAPHIES AND HISTORICAL WORKS

Adams, Charles Francis, Jr. *Studies Military and Diplomatic*. New York, 1911.

Adams, John Quincy. *Memoirs of John Quincy Adams*. Ed. by Charles Francis Adams. Philadelphia, 1874–77. 12 vols.

Alexander, E. P. *Military Memoirs of a Confederate*. New York, 1907.

Andrews, J. Cutler. *The North Reports the Civil War*. Pittsburgh, 1955.

*Antietam to Appomattox: The History of the Corn Exchange Regiment* (118th Pennsylvania Volunteers). Philadelphia, 1905.[1]

Avary, Myrta Lockett. *Dixie after the War*. New York, 1906.

Bache, Richard M. *Life of General George Gordon Meade*. Philadelphia, 1897.

Banes, Charles H. *History of the Philadelphia Brigade*. Philadelphia, 1876.

Bartlett, A. W. *History of the 12th New Hampshire Regiment*. Concord, N. H., 1897.

Bates, S. P. *Battle of Gettysburg*. Philadelphia, 1875.

Bicknell, George W. *History of the Fifth Maine Regiment*. Portland, Me., 1871.

Bigelow, John. *The Campaign of Chancellorsville*. New Haven, Conn., 1910.

Bill, Alfred Hoyt. *Rehearsal for Conflict*. New York, 1947.

Billings, John D. *Hardtack and Coffee*. Boston, 1887.

———. *History of the Tenth Massachusetts Battery*. Boston, 1881.

Bosbyshell, O. C. *The 48th* [Pennsylvania] *in the War*. Philadelphia, 1895.

Bowen, J. L. *History of the 37th Masschusetts Regiment*. Holyoke, Mass., 1884.

Brinton, John H. *Personal Memoirs*. New York, 1914.

Brooks, Noah. *Washington in Lincoln's Time*. New York, 1896.

Browning, Orville Hickman. *Diary of Orville Hickman Browning*. Ed. by T. C. Pease and J. D. Randall. Chicago, 1924.

Bruce, George A. *The 20th Massachusetts Regiment*. Boston, 1906.

Bruce, Robert V. *Lincoln and the Tools of War*. Indianapolis, 1956.

Buell, Augustus. *The Cannoneer*. Washington, D. C., 1890.

Butterfield, Julia L. *Biographical Memoir of General Butterfield*. New York, 1904.

Cadwallader, Sylvanus. *Three Years with Grant*. Ed. by Benjamin P. Thomas. New York, 1955.

Carter, Robert G. *Four Brothers in Blue*. Washington, D. C., 1913.

---

[1] Published anonymously, this book is one of the best regimental histories in print and is highly useful in any study of the Army of the Potomac and its campaigns.

Catton, Bruce. *Glory Road*. Garden City, N. Y., 1952.

———. *Mr. Lincoln's Army*. Garden City, N. Y., 1951.

———. *A Stillness at Appomattox*. Garden City, N. Y., 1953.

———. *This Hallowed Ground*. Garden City, N. Y., 1956.

Chamberlain, Joshua L. *The Passing of the Armies*. New York, 1915.

Claiborne, John F. H. *Life and Correspondence of John A. Quitman*. New York, 1860. 2 vols.

Clark, C. M. *History of the 39th Illinois Regiment*. Chicago, 1889.

Coffin, C. C. *The Boys of '61*. Boston, 1884.

Commager, Henry Steele (ed.) *The Blue and the Gray*. Indianapolis, 1950. 2 vols.

Cortissoz, Royal. *Life of Whitelaw Reid*. New York, 1921. 2 vols.

Coxe, Richard S. *Richard W. Meade*. N.p., 1926. Pamphlet.

Crotty, D. G. *Four Years Campaigning in the Army of the Potomac*. Grand Rapids, Mich., 1874.

Dana, Charles A. *Recollections of the Civil War*. New York, 1899.

Davis, Charles E., Jr. *Three Years in the Army*. Boston, 1894.

Dawson, W. F. (ed.). *A Civil War Artist at the Front*. New York, 1957.

Dennett, Tyler. *Lincoln and the Civil War*. New York, 1939.

Donald, David (ed.). *Inside Lincoln's Cabinet*. New York, 1954.

Dorsey, Sarah A. *Recollections of Henry Watkins Allen*. New York, 1866.

Douglas, Henry Kyd. *I Rode with Stonewall*. Chapel Hill, N. C., 1940.

Dowdey, Clifford. *Experiment in Rebellion*. Garden City, N. Y., 1947.

DuBose, John W. *Alabama's Tragic Decade*. Birmingham, Ala., 1940.

Dunlap, William. *Diary of William Dunlap*. Ed. by Dorothy C. Barck. New York, 1930.

Eisenschiml, Otto, and Ralph Newman. *The American Iliad*. Indianapolis, 1947.

Elliott, Charles Winslow. *Winfield Scott*. New York, 1937.

Emerson, E. W. *Life and Letters of Charles Russell Lowell*. Boston, 1907.

Fiebeger, G. J. *Campaign and Battle of Gettysburg*. West Point, N. Y., 1915.

Fleming, G. T. *Life and Letters of Alexander Hays*. Pittsburgh, 1919.

Floyd, Fred C. *History of the 40th New York* [Mozart] *Regiment*. Boston, 1909.

Ford, A. E. *Story of the 15th Massachusetts Regiment*. Clinton, Mass., 1898.

Ford, W. C. (ed.). *Cycle of Adams Letters*. Boston, 1920. 2 vols.

Freeman, Douglas Southall. *R. E. Lee*. New York, 1947. 4 vols.

———. *Lee's Lieutenants*. New York, 1944. 3 vols.

Fremantle, James Arthur Lyon. *The Fremantle Diary*. Ed. by Walter Lord. Boston, 1954.

Fulkerson, H. S. *A Civilian's Recollection of the War between the States*. Baton Rouge, La., 1939.

Gerrish, Theodore. *Army Life*. Portland, Me., 1882.

Gibbon, John. *Address on the Unveiling of a Statue of George Gordon Meade*. Philadelphia, 1887.

———. *Personal Recollections of the Civil War*. New York, 1928.

Gordon, George H. *A War Diary of Events*. Boston, 1882.

Gordon, John B. *Reminiscences of the Civil War*. New York, 1903.

Gorgas, Josiah. *Civil War Diary of General Josiah Gorgas*. Ed. by Frank A. Vandiver. University, Ala., 1950.

Gorham, G. C. *Life and Public Services of Edwin M. Stanton*. Boston, 1899. 2 vols.

Goss, Warren Lee. *Recollections of a Private*. New York, 1890.

Gould, Joseph. *Story of the 48th Pennsylvania Regiment*. Philadelphia, 1908.

Graham, W. A. *The Custer Myth*. Harrisburg, Pa., 1953.

Grant, Ulysses S. *Personal Memoirs*. New York, 1886. 2 vols.

Gray, J. C., and J. C. Ropes. *War Letters, 1862–65*. Boston, 1927.

Greenslet, Ferris. *The Lowells and Their Seven Worlds*. Boston, 1946.

Hancock, Almira R. *Reminiscences of Winfield Scott Hancock*. New York, 1887.

Hancock, Cornelia. *South after Gettysburg: The Letters of Cornelia Hancock*. Ed. by Henrietta Jaquette. Philadelphia, 1937.

Hardin, M. D. *History of the 12th Pennsylvania Regiment*. New York, 1890.

Haskell, Frank A. *The Battle of Gettysburg*. Madison, Wis., 1908.

Hatcher, Edmund H. *The Last Four Weeks of the War*. Columbus, Ohio, 1891.

Haupt, Herman. *Reminiscences*. Milwaukee, 1901.

Hay, Thomas Robson. *President Lincoln and the Army of the Potomac*. Pamphlet.

Hays, G. A. *Under the Red Patch*. Pittsburgh, 1908.

Headley, J. T. *Grant and Sherman*. New York, 1865.

Hebert, Walter. *Fighting Joe Hooker*. Indianapolis, 1944.

Hein, O. L. *Memories of Long Ago*. New York, 1925.

Henry, Robert Selph. *The Story of Reconstruction*. Indianapolis, 1938.

Henry, W. S. *Campaign Sketches of the War with Mexico*. New York, 1847.

Hesseltine, W. B. *Ulysses S. Grant, Politician.* New York, 1957.

Hicks, John D. *A Short History of American Democracy.* Boston, 1903.

Hill, A. F. *Our Boys.* Philadelphia, 1864.

Hoar, George F. *Autobiography of Seventy Years.* New York, 1905. 2 vols.

Hoke, Jacob. *The Great Invasion.* Dayton, Ohio, 1887.

Hornaday, John R. *Atlanta, Yesterday, Today, and Tomorrow.* N.p., 1922.

Howard, O. O. *Autobiography.* New York, 1907. 2 vols.

Humphreys, A. A. *From Gettysburg to the Rapidan.* New York, 1883.

————. *Virginia Campaign of 1864–65.* New York, 1883.

Humphreys, H. H. *Andrew Atkinson Humphreys.* Philadelphia, 1924.

————. *A Critical Examination of Pennypacker's Life of General George G. Meade.* Tivoli, N. Y., 1901.

Hyde, Thomas W. *Following the Greek Cross.* Boston, 1894.

Johnson, R. U., and C. C. Buel (eds.). *Battles and Leaders of the Civil War.* New York, 1884–88. 4 vols.

Jones, Virgil Carrington. *Eight Hours before Richmond.* New York, 1957.

Kean, Robert G. H. *Inside the Confederate Government: The Diary of Robert G. H. Kean.* Ed. by Edward Younger. New York, 1957.

King, Horatio. *The Army of the Potomac.* N.p., 1898. Pamphlet.

Landon, Fred. *Lake Huron.* Indianapolis, 1944.

Leech, Margaret. *Reveille in Washington.* New York, 1941.

Lewis, Lloyd. *Sherman: Fighting Prophet.* New York, 1932.

*Life and Public Services of Major General Meade (George Gordon Meade), the Hero of Gettysburg and Commander of the Army of the Potomac.* Philadelphia, March, 1864.[2]

Lincoln, Abraham. *Complete Works of Abraham Lincoln.* Ed. by John G. Nicolay and John Hay. New York, 1894. 12 vols.

Livermore, Thomas L. *Days and Events, 1860–1866.* Boston, 1920.

————. *Numbers and Losses in the Civil War in America.* Boston, 1900.

Locke, W. H. *Story of the Regiment.* Philadelphia, 1868.

Lossing, B. J. *A History of the Civil War.* New York, 1912. With Brady photographs.

[2] The author of this volume is unknown. Aside from its ordinary profit possibilities, the book may have arisen from someone's idea that Meade should be better known in his own city, for he had never been able to spend much time there. However, it is hardly worthwhile to consider the work as a political document. Published by T. B. Peterson & Bros., 306 Chestnut Street, Philadelphia, it is a very ordinary printing job. General Meade's comment ran: "I had no idea my services would take up so much printing matter. I must confess I think a little more space might be given to my services prior to the Rebellion. I always thought my services in the construction of lighthouses, and subsequently on the Lake Survey, were of considerable importance."—*Meade,* II, 184.

Lyman, Theodore. *Meade's Headquarters, 1863–65: The Letters of Colonel Theodore Lyman.* Ed. by George R. Agassiz. Boston, 1922.

Marshall, Charles. *An Aide-de-Camp of Lee.* Ed. by Frederick Maurice. Boston, 1927.

M'Bride, R. E. *In the Ranks.* Cincinnati, 1881.

McCall, George A. *Letters from the Frontiers.* Philadelphia, 1868.

McCarthy, Justin. *Reminiscences.* New York, 1899. 2 vols.

McClellan, Carswell. *Notes on the Personal Memoirs of Philip H. Sheridan.* St. Paul, Minn., 1889.

————. *Personal Memoirs and Military History of U. S. Grant.* Boston, 1887.

McClellan, George B. *McClellan's Own Story.* New York, 1887.

McClure, Alexander. *Lincoln and Men of War-Times.* Philadelphia, 1892.

Meade, George. *Life and Letters of George Gordon Meade.* New York, 1913. 2 vols.

Meade, George G. *Report on the Ashburn Murder.* Atlanta, 1868. Pamphlet.

————. *Report of Military Operations . . . in the Third Military District.* Atlanta, 1868.

————. *Survey of the North and Northwest Lakes.* Detroit, 1859.

Meade, George G. II. *With Meade at Gettysburg.* Philadelphia, 1930.

Meade, Rebecca Paulding. *Life of Hiram Paulding.* New York, 1910.

Michie, Peter S. *Life and Letters of Emory Upton.* New York, 1885.

Miers, Earl Schenck, and Richard A. Brown (eds.). *Gettysburg.* New Brunswick, N. J., 1948.

Milton, George Fort. *The Age of Hate.* New York, 1930.

Mitchell, Joseph B. *Decisive Battles of the Civil War.* New York, 1955.

Morgan, John Hill, and Mantle Fielding. *Life Portraits of Washington and Their Replicas.* Lancaster, Pa., 1931.

Mulholland, St. Clair. *Story of the 116th Pennsylvania Regiment.* Philadelphia, 1899.

Nichols, Edward J. *Toward Gettysburg.* State College, Pa., 1958.

Nicolay, John G., and John Hay. *Abraham Lincoln: A History.* New York, 1890. 10 vols.

Oates, W. C. *The War between the Union and the Confederacy.* New York, 1905.

Oberholtzer, Ellis Paxson. *History of the United States since the Civil War.* New York, 1917. 5 vols.

Orwig, J. R. *History of the 131st Pennsylvania Infantry.* Williamsport, Pa., 1902.

Page, Charles A. *Letters of a War Correspondent.* Boston, 1899.

Page, Charles D. *History of the 14th Connecticut Regiment.* Meriden, Conn., 1906.

Palfrey, F. W. *The Antietam and Fredericksburg Campaigns.* New York, 1882.

Pearson, H. G. *James S. Wadsworth of Geneseo.* New York, 1913.

Pennypacker, Isaac R. *General Meade.* New York, 1901.

————. *Meade in Command.* Philadelphia, 1930. Pamphlet.

Phelps, Mary Merwin. *Kate Chase.* New York, 1935.

Philadelphia *Weekly Times. The Annals of the War.* Philadelphia, 1879.

Pinchon, Edgcumb. *Dan Sickles.* New York, 1945.

Poore, Ben: Perley. *Perley's Reminiscences.* Philadelphia, 1886. 2 vols.

Porter, Horace. *Campaigning with Grant.* New York, 1897.

Potter, Woodburne. *The War in Florida.* Baltimore, 1836.

Powell, William H. *The Fifth Army Corps.* New York, 1896.

Prowell, O. R. *History of the 87th Pennsylvania Volunteer Regiment.* York, Pa., 1901.

Pullen, John J. *The Twentieth Maine.* Philadelphia, 1957.

Putnam, George R. *Lighthouses and Lightships.* Boston, 1917.

Randall, J. G. *Civil War and Reconstruction.* Boston, 1937.

————. *Lincoln the President.* New York, 1945–55. 4 vols.

Reed, William H. *Hospital Life in the Army of the Potomac.* Boston, 1866.

Richardson, A. D. *The Secret Service.* Hartford, Conn., 1865.

Roe, Alfred S., and Charles Nutt. *History of the First Regiment of Heavy Artillery, Massachusetts Volunteers.* Worcester, Mass., 1917.

Rosengarten, J. D. *General George G. Meade.* Philadelphia, 1867. Pamphlet.

Rush, Benjamin. *Letters of Benjamin Rush.* Ed. by L. H. Butterfield. Princeton, 1951. 2 vols.

Sandburg, Carl. *Abraham Lincoln* (one-volume edition). New York, 1954.

————. *Abraham Lincoln: The War Years.* New York, 1945. 4 vols.

Sanger, D. B., and Thomas R. Hay. *James Longstreet.* Baton Rouge, La., 1952.

Schaff, Morris. *Battle of the Wilderness.* Boston, 1910.

————. *Sunset of the Confederacy.* Boston, 1912.

Scharf, John T., and Thompson Westcott. *History of Philadelphia.* Philadelphia, 1864. 3 vols.

Schenck, Martin. *Up Came Hill.* Harrisburg, Pa., 1958.

Sedgwick, John. *Correspondence of Major General John Sedgwick.* Ed. by H. D. Sedgwick. New York, 1903. 2 vols.

Shanks, W. F. G. *Personal Recollections of Some Distinguished Generals.* New York, 1866.

Sheridan, Philip H. *Personal Memoirs*. New York, 1888. 2 vols.

Sherman, William T. *The Sherman Letters*. Ed. by R. S. Thorndike. New York, 1894.

Slocum, C. E. *Life and Services of Major General Henry W. Slocum*. Toledo, Ohio, 1913.

Small, Abner R. *The Road to Richmond*. Berkeley, Calif., 1957 (reprint).

————. *The Sixteenth Maine Regiment*. Portland, Me., 1886.

Snow, Edward Rowe. *Famous Lighthouses of America*. Boston, 1933.

Stackpole, E. J. *Chancellorsville*. Harrisburg, Pa., 1958.

Starr, Louis M. *The Bohemian Brigade*. New York, 1954.

Steinman, D. B. *The Builders of the Bridge*. New York, 1945.

Stewart, A. M. *Camp, March, and Battle-Field*. Philadelphia, 1865.

Stewart, R. L. *History of the 140th Pennsylvania Regiment*. Philadelphia, 1912.

Stine, J. H. *History of the Army of the Potomac*. Washington, D. C., 1893.

Storrs, John W. *The 20th Connecticut Regiment*. Ansonia, Conn., 1886.

Strong, George Templeton. *Diary of George Templeton Strong*. Ed. by Allan Nevins. New York, 1952. 4 vols.

Summers, F. P. *The Baltimore & Ohio Railroad in the Civil War*. New York, 1939.

Sweeny, William M. *Biographical Memoir of Thomas William Sweeny*. New York, 1907.

Swinton, William. *Campaigns of the Army of the Potomac*. New York, 1866.

Sypher, J. R. *History of the Pennsylvania Reserves*. Lancaster, Pa., 1865. General Meade gave Sypher access to sundry materials for this work.

Taylor, Emerson G. *Gouverneur Kemble Warren*. Boston, 1932.

Taylor, F. H. *Philadelphia in the Civil War*. Philadelphia, 1913.

Taylor, Walter H. *Fours Years with General Lee*. New York, 1877.

Thomas, Benjamin P. *Abraham Lincoln*. New York, 1952.

Thompson, C. M. *Reconstruction in Georgia*. New York, 1915.

Thomson, O. R. H., and William H. Rauch. *History of the Bucktails*. Philadelphia, 1906.

Toombs, Samuel. *New Jersey Troops in the Gettysburg Campaign*. Orange, N. J., 1888.

Townsend, G. A. *Rustics in Rebellion*. Chapel Hill, N. C., 1950 (reprint).

Trobriand, Régis de. *Four Years with the Army of the Potomac*. Boston, 1899.

Underwood, A. B. *Three Years' Service in the 33rd Massachusetts*. Boston, 1881.

Vautier, John D. *The 88th Pennsylvania Volunteer Regiment*. Philadelphia, 1894.

Walker, Francis A. *General Hancock*. New York, 1897.

―――. *History of the Second Army Corps*. New York, 1886.

Ward, J. R. C. *History of the 106th Pennsylvania Volunteers*. Philadelphia, 1883.

Weld, Stephen M. *War Diary and Letters*. Cambridge, Mass., 1912.

Welles, Gideon. *Diary of Gideon Welles*. Boston, 1911. 3 vols.

Wilkeson, Frank. *Recollections of a Private Soldier*. New York, 1887.

Williams, Kenneth. *Lincoln Finds a General*. New York, 1949. 2 vols.

Williams, T. Harry. *Lincoln and His Generals*. New York, 1952.

―――. *Lincoln and the Radicals*. Madison, Wis., 1941.

Wilson, James H. *Life of Charles A. Dana*. New York, 1914.

―――. *Under the Old Flag*. New York, 1912. 2 vols.

Winston, R. W. *Andrew Johnson*. New York, 1928.

Wise, B. H. *Life of Henry A. Wise*. New York, 1899.

Woodbury, Augustus. *Major General Ambrose E. Burnside and the Ninth Army Corps*. Providence, R. I., 1887.

Woodward, E. M. *History of the Third Regiment of Pennsylvania Reserves*. Trenton, N. J., 1883.

―――. *History of the 198th Pennsylvania Regiment*. Trenton, N. J., 1884.

―――. *Our Campaigns*. Philadelphia, 1865.

*Life of General William Jenkins Worth*. New York, 1856.

# Index

Adams, Charles Francis, Jr., criticizes military strategy: 206
Adams, John Quincy: U. S. secretary of state, 6–8; U. S. president, 8
Agassiz, Louis, of Harvard University: 49
Ambler, Pa., Meade residence at: 358
Amelia Courthouse, Va.: 323, 325
Ampudia, Pedro de, leads Mexican army: 23–24
Anderson, Richard H.: march to Spotsylvania, 241; at Sayler's Creek, 326
Antietam, battle of: 77–80
Appomattox, Va.: Federals approach, 328–30; surrender scene, 334–35, 352
Arista, Mariano, leads Mexican army: 25, 28–29
Ayres, Romeyn B.: at Peeble's Farm, 293; in Appomattox campaign, 310–11, 313

Bache, Hartman: 10, 45–46, 49; weds María del Carmen Meade, 9; employs Meade, 18; death of, 358
Bache, Richard Hartman: 350
Bachelder, John B. ("Historicus"); anti-Meade polemicist: 229–30
Banks, Nathaniel P.: visits Antietam, 82; at Fort Hudson, 215
Barlow, Francis C.: 247; prisoner at Gettysburg, 173; at Cold Harbor, 251; at Petersburg, 262–63, 270–71
Barnegat, N. J., Meade lighthouse at: 358
Beauregard, Pierre G. T.: in Mexico, 42; defends Petersburg, 262, 267; quoted, 265
Beaver Dam Creek, action at: 65
Beckham, Robert F.: in Detroit, 52; joins Confederacy, 53

Beecher, Henry Ward (quoted): 294–95
Berlin (Brunswick), Md.: 187
Bermuda Hundred, army base: 259–60, 264–65
Berry, Hiram, killed at Chancellorsville: 120
Biddle, James C.: at Chancellorsville, 106; quotes John Sedgwick, 134
Birney, David B.: 177, 247; at Fredericksburg, 91–92; at Gettysburg, 156; yields Third Corps to French, 177; at Petersburg, 262; heads Second Corps, 266; at Fort Harrison, 293
Blair, Montgomery, Meade's classmate: 11
Blake, J. E.: 145; in Texas, 23; death of, 37
Boonsboro, Md.: 177, 179
Bowers, Theodore S.: 336
Brady, Mathew B.: at Antietam, 81; seeks Meade sitting, 171
Bragg, Braxton: in Texas, 26; in Tennessee, 193; defeated at Chattanooga, 308
Brandy Station, Va., army base: 205
Bristoe Station, action at: 198–99
Brooks, Noah (quoted): 102, 185
Brown, Jacob, commands Fort Texas: 26
Brown, John: 52
Buena Vista, battle of: 41
Buford, John: advance to Gettysburg, 132; reports on, 134, 137; in action, 135; leaves field, 146; rides to Potomac, 179; scouts upper Rapidan, 194–95; drives enemy cavalry, 195–96
Bull Run: First Battle of, 53; Second Battle of, 73–74
Burgess' Mill, action at: 318
Burkeville, Va.: 287, 324, 335–36, 338
Burnside, Ambrose: 103, 264, 299, 348;

ericksburg; 90–93; made scapegoat, 100; favored by Grant, 285

Frederick, Md., army at: 75, 123 ff., 177

Fredericksburg, Va.: occupied, 88; Federal defeat at, 90–93; Meade's goal, 203, 233; Meade visits, 339

French, William H.: 177, 205, 215; commands at Harpers Ferry, 122; orders to, 122, 130, 158; raids enemy base, 174; commands Third Corps, 177; fails to trap enemy, 189; in action on Rappahannock, 203; in Mine Run campaign, 207 ff.; on way out, 220; leaves army, 232

Front Royal, Va.: 189

Gaines's Mill, Va., action at: 65

Gainesville, Va., action at: 73

Gallagher, Thomas F., at South Mountain: 76

Geary, John W.: occupies Little Round top, 142; Gettysburg movements of, 144, 152, 157

Getty, George: 238, 317

Gettysburg, Pa.: strategic site, 129–30; armies approach, 131 ff.; action at, 135–36, 145 ff.; Meade leaves, 175; honors of battle redistributed, 216–17; political significance, 231

Gibbon, John: meets Meade in Florida, 46; at Antietam, 79; McClellan partisan, 85–86, 294; at Fredericksburg, 90–91; march to Gettysburg, 137–38, 143; on field, 152 ff.; wounded, 164, 173; upholds Meade, 214; considered for corps command, 221; at Cold Harbor, 251; at Petersburg, 262, 271–72; at odds with Hancock, 300; fails of promotion, 302; commands Twenty-fourth Corps, 304

Gillmore, Quincy A., commands in South: 341

Globe Tavern, Warren's victory at: 290–91

Gordon, Jacob: 3

Gordon, John B.: in 1865 campaign, 326; Meade drinks to, 345

Gorgas, Josiah (quoted): 224

Graham, James Duncan: weds Charlotte

Meade, 9, 355; employs Meade in survey work, 15–17; succeeds Meade in Detroit, 54

Grant, Ulysses S.: 127, 194, 255, 294, 307; action and victory at Vicksburg, 11, 171, 178; Meade's comment on, 42; in Chattanooga campaign, 207–208; considered for eastern post, 215; thanked by Congress, 215; promoted to lieutenant general, 224–26; visits Lincoln, 228; visits Meade, 228–29; appearance, 228, 234; retains Meade in command, 231; orders for spring (1864) campaign, 232–33; in Wilderness campaign, 235–41; at Spotsylvania, 243–46; complains of Lee's tactics, 247; dispatch to Stanton, 250; at Cold Harbor, 250–52, 256; upholds Meade in Cropsey affair, 254; plans new strategy, 257; James River movement, 258–64; at Petersburg, 263 ff.; decides on siege operations, 271–72; part in crater affair, 274–83; expels war correspondents, 284; view on army appointments, 285–86; confers with Sheridan, 292; extends army perimeter, 293; lionized, 295; at Hatcher's Run, 296; a nonvoter, 297; position on Sheridan's and Meade's promotion, 298–300; part in Meade-Hancock affair, 300; assists Meade, 303–305; in Appomattox campaign, 308 ff.; visited by Sheridan, 310; part in Warren-Sheridan affair, 314; writes truce notes, 328–30; Lee surrenders to, 332; aids in hunt for Lincoln's assassin, 337; action in Fenian uprising, 342; talks with Meade, 344; elected president, 346; promotes Sheridan over Meade, 347; at officers' reunion, 348; wins 1872 election, 349; at Meade's funeral, 350

Greeley, Horace, New York Tribune editor: criticizes Meade, 206; demands Meade's removal, 229; presidential candidate, 349

Greene, George S., at Gettysburg: 154

Gregg, David McMurtrie: at Gettysburg, 146; in Centreville campaign, 197; in

mattox campaign, 326, 328; visits
Grant, 334
Lookout Mountain, battle of: 225
Loring, C. G., in crater affair: 281
Lyman, Theodore: meets Meade in Flor-
ida, 49; volunteer aide, 194; quoted,
194, 197, 201, 209, 212, 214, 228,
233–34, 240, 245, 247–48, 259, 264–
66, 268, 271, 276, 282, 287, 294, 296,
305, 307, 319, 321, 323–24, 327–28,
330; examines James River crossing,
258; at Petersburg, 264; tributes to
Meade, 299, 351; on leave, 303; feeds
Warren, 314; returns home, 339;
Meade's host, 340
Lyman, Mrs. Theodore: sends cigars to
Meade, 303; visits army, 306
Lyons, Lord, British minister: 58

McCall, George A.: leads Pennsylvania
Reserves, 55 ff.; visits Washington,
60; joins McClellan, 63; praises
Meade, 65; retreat from Gaines's
Mill, 66; failure at Glendale, 67
McCandless, William, at Gettysburg: 168
McCarthy, Justin (quoted): 349
McClellan, George B.: 96, 101–102, 121,
176, 187, 214, 233, 252, 259, 299,
321; in Mexico, 42; commands Union
Army, 54 ff.; Meade's views on, 57;
illness of, 60; strategy of, 62, 65; returns to Army of Potomac, 64–75;
displaced by Halleck, 71; at Washington, 72; at Antietam, 77–84; Lincoln
visits, 81–82; relieved by Burnside,
84; congratulates Meade, 172; criticized, 184; his farewell to army, 185–
86; candidate for president, 294; re-
signs from army, 298; at Society of the
Army of Potomac meeting, 348
McClellan, John: in Mexico, 40, 43; at
odds with brother George, 60
McDowell, Irvin: commands First Corps,
61, 63; characterized, 72; displaced,
75; arranges Meade's funeral, 350
MacKenzie, Ranald S., in closing campaign: 320
McLaughlin, Thomas, marries Salvadora
Meade: 358

Macomb, J. N.: 53
McParlin, Thomas A., army surgeon:
317
Magilton, A. L.: at South Mountain, 76;
at Antietam, 78
Mahone, William: at Petersburg, 271;
at Hatcher's Run, 296, 301
Malvern Hill, Va., action at: 69
Manassas, Va.: 61, 72–73
Mansfield, J. K. F., killed at Antietam:
79
Marin, Mexico, Meade at: 32
Marley, John, Meade's servant: 71
Martindale, John, at Petersburg: 266–67
Matamoros, Mexico, Meade at: 29–30
Mechanicsville, Va., action at: 64
Meade, Catherine, sister of George and
Garrett Meade: 353–54
Meade, Catherine Hustler, sister of Gen-
eral Meade: 4, 355
Meade, Charlotte Hustler, sister of Gen-
eral Meade: 4, 9, 355
Meade, Elizabeth Mary, sister of Gen-
eral Meade: 4, 9, 355; see also In-
graham, Elizabeth
Meade, Garrett: 353
Meade, George, grandfather of General
Meade: 3; marries Henrietta Worsam,
353; career of, 353–54; death of, 355
Meade, George, son of General Meade:
birth, 18; fails at West Point, 60–61,
83; joins Rush's Lancers, 83; progress
cited, 84; letters to mother (quoted),
95, 168, 176, 207, 240, 250, 284, 329,
332; on Meade's staff, 124; in Gettysburg campaign, 138 ff.; in Mine Run
campaign, 212; in Appomattox campaign, 329, 332; with First Artillery,
350; marries Elizabeth Morris, 358
Meade, George Gordon: ancestry and
boyhood, 3, 5, 9–10, 353–55; at West
Point, 11; railroad surveyor, 12, 15;
early army service, 13–15; surveys in
South and in Maine, 15–18; marriage,
17; rejoins army, 18; work on Brandywine lighthouse, 18, 45; with army in
Texas, 19 ff.; at El Palo Alto, 26–27;
at Resaca de la Palma, 27–28; views
of camp life, 29–30; Monterrey, 31–

## MEADE OF GETTYSBURG

By Freeman Cleaves, has been set on the Linotype in eleven and one-half point Caslon Old Face, with one and one-half points of leading, or space, between the lines. Caslon is one of the many classic book faces which were revived for the Linotype to meet the demand for better book types for machine composition.

*University of Oklahoma Press : Norman*